China's growing participation in the institutions of global economic governance in recent years is undeniable, but discussion of them is too often facile. This volume, which brings together an impressive group of scholars, serves as a major contribution to our understanding of the substantial variability of China's behavior over a wide range of economic regimes, and why the details matter.

Margaret M. Pearson, *University of Maryland, USA*

China's emergence as an economic superpower is the defining event of our times. Its smooth integration into the global economy requires adjustments both on its part and on the part of international institutions. This insightful book shows how the adjustment is proceeding in different areas – trade, finance, G20 coordination – and what are remaining challenges. An essential read for understanding China's role in the world.

David Dollar, *John L. Thornton China Center,*
Brookings Institution, USA

A distinguished roster of Chinese and American scholars offer an original and convincing perspective on China's influence over global governance. Issue area by issue area, the authors illuminate both domestic and international drivers of China's orientation toward global economic institutions.

Miles Kahler, *American University and Council on*
Foreign Relations, USA

Global Governance and China

This volume offers systematic analysis of China's growing engagement in global governance institutions over the past three decades. During this period, China has gone from outsider to observer to insider. The volume is based on studies of Chinese involvement in a wide cross-section of regimes, including trade, finance, intellectual property rights, foreign aid, and climate change.

The contributions show that China's participation in global governance reflects the mutually interactive processes of China's own socialization into the global community and the simultaneous adaptation of global institutions and actors to China's growing activism. Both China and the international system are internally complex. Hence, Chinese engagement varies across economic regimes, yielding different results in terms of Chinese compliance, its influence on regimes, and the extent of cooperation and conflict in addressing challenges in international society. The chapters reveal that China is neither purely a savior nor scofflaw of the global economic system, and while China is a defender of the status quo in some areas, it is a reformer in others, and occasionally a revisionist in still other spheres.

A detailed analysis of many areas of global governance, this volume will be essential reading for students and scholars of international relations, Chinese studies, and global governance.

Scott Kennedy is Deputy Director of the Freeman Chair in China Studies and Director of the Project on Chinese Business and Political Economy at the Center for Strategic and International Studies.

Global Institutions

Edited by Thomas G. Weiss
The CUNY Graduate Center, New York, USA
and Rorden Wilkinson
University of Sussex, Brighton, UK

About the series

The "Global Institutions Series" provides cutting-edge books about many aspects of what we know as "global governance." It emerges from our shared frustrations with the state of available knowledge—electronic and print-wise, for research and teaching—in the area. The series is designed as a resource for those interested in exploring issues of international organization and global governance. And since the first volumes appeared in 2005, we have taken significant strides toward filling conceptual gaps.

The series consists of three related "streams" distinguished by their blue, red, and green covers. The blue volumes, comprising the majority of the books in the series, provide user-friendly and short (usually no more than 50,000 words) but authoritative guides to major global and regional organizations, as well as key issues in the global governance of security, the environment, human rights, poverty, and humanitarian action among others. The books with red covers are designed to present original research and serve as extended and more specialized treatments of issues pertinent for advancing understanding about global governance. And the volumes with green covers—the most recent departure in the series—are comprehensive and accessible accounts of the major theoretical approaches to global governance and international organization.

The books in each of the streams are written by experts in the field, ranging from the most senior and respected authors to first-rate scholars at the beginning of their careers. In combination, the three components of the series—blue, red, and green—serve as key resources for faculty, students, and practitioners alike. The works in the blue and green streams have value as core and complementary readings in courses on, among other things, international organization, global governance, international law, international relations, and international political economy; the red volumes allow further reflection and investigation in these and related areas.

The books in the series also provide a segue to the foundation volume that offers the most comprehensive textbook treatment available dealing with all the major issues, approaches, institutions, and actors in contemporary global governance—our edited work *International Organization and Global Governance* (2014)—a volume to which many of the authors in the series have contributed essays.

Understanding global governance—past, present, and future—is far from a finished journey. The books in this series nonetheless represent significant steps toward a better way of conceiving contemporary problems and issues as well as, hopefully, doing something to improve world order. We value the feedback from our readers and their role in helping shape the on-going development of the series.

A complete list of titles can be viewed online here: https://www.routledge.com/Global-Institutions/book-series/GI.

The League of Nations (2018)
by M. Patrick Cottrell

The British Media and the Rwandan Genocide (2018)
by John Nathaniel Clarke

Millennium Development Goals (2018)
by Sakiko Fukuda-Parr

Sustainable Development Goals and UN Goal-setting (2017)
by Stephen Browne

Inside the United Nations (2017)
by Gert Rosenthal

International Institutions of the Middle East (2017)
by James Worrall

The Politics of Expertise in International Organizations (2017)
edited by Annabelle Littoz-Monnet

Global Governance and China
The Dragon's Learning Curve

Edited by
Scott Kennedy

Routledge
Taylor & Francis Group

LONDON AND NEW YORK

First published 2018
by Routledge
2 Park Square, Milton Park, Abingdon, Oxon OX14 4RN

and by Routledge
711 Third Avenue, New York, NY 10017

*Routledge is an imprint of the Taylor & Francis Group, an informa
business*

British Library Cataloguing in Publication Data
A catalogue record for this book is available from the British
Library

Library of Congress Cataloging in Publication Data
A catalog record for this book has been requested

ISBN: 978-0-415-81016-6 (hbk)
ISBN: 978-0-415-81017-3 (pbk)
ISBN: 978-1-315-10052-4 (ebk)

Typeset in Times New Roman
by Taylor & Francis Books

To Mary Beth, Isaac, Brian, Ed, and Cosmo

Contents

List of illustrations   xiii
List of contributors   xiv
Acknowledgments   xix
Abbreviations   xxii

Introduction: Learning to be insiders   1
SCOTT KENNEDY

1 China and the WTO   18
   JAMES SCOTT AND RORDEN WILKINSON

2 Being in the WTO: China's learning and
   growing confidence   42
   WANG YONG

3 Chinese and Japanese FTA strategies and their implications
   for multilateralism   65
   JUNJI NAKAGAWA AND WEI LIANG

4 Organizational factors in China's GPA
   accession negotiations   89
   TU XINQUAN

5 China and the G20: A reform-minded status quo power   110
   REN XIAO

6 China's role in global governance: A comparison of foreign
   exchange and intellectual property   132
   BRUCE REYNOLDS AND SUSAN K. SELL

 7 China's involvement in global health governance: Progress
   and challenges   158
   YANZHONG HUANG

 8 Learning by doing: China's role in the global governance of
   food security   181
   KATHERINE MORTON

 9 China's rise as development financer: Implications for
   international development cooperation   202
   XU JIAJUN

10 China and global labor standards: Making sense of
   factory certification   228
   TIM BARTLEY AND LU ZHANG

11 Domestic politics and Chinese participation in
   transnational climate governance   250
   THOMAS HALE AND CHARLES ROGER

   Index   272

List of illustrations

Figures

6.1   Nominal RMB/US$ exchange rate (1994–2015)   142
8.1   China's per capita production of major non-staple crops   187
8.2   Chinese agricultural development assistance (2000–2010)   191
9.1   Composition of China's foreign aid expenditures
      (cumulative, year-end 2012)   207
9.2   Comparison of China's GDP and net ODA received
      (1982–2011)   208
9.3   Possible scenarios of strategic interaction between China
      and DAC donors   217
11.1 Cumulative number of initiatives in China vs. globally
      (1990–2010)   253
11.2 Initiatives active in China by initiative type   254
11.3 Kinds of initiatives active in China by date first active
      (1990–2010)   255
11.4 Participants targeted by Transnational Climate
      Governance (TCG) schemes in China vs. globally   255
11.5 Locations of projects using voluntary offset standards,
      share of total in 2012   257

Tables

3.1   Comparison of Chinese and Japanese FTA
      negotiations (2017)   67
9.1   China's bilateral and multilateral assistance
      (US$, millions)   207
10.1 Regression analyses of HR and health infrastructure on
      SA8000 certification and other selected variables   242

Contributors

Tim Bartley is Professor of Sociology at Washington University in St Louis. His research focuses on the transnational private regulation of sustainability and fairness in global industries, including the intersection between transnational corporations, social movements, rule-making projects, and domestic governance of land and labor in Indonesia and China. He has published articles in the *American Sociological Review, American Journal of Sociology, Social Forces, Social Problems, Socio-Economic Review,* and other outlets. He is the author of *Rules without Rights: Land, Labor, and Private Authority in the Global Economy* (Oxford University Press, forthcoming), and co-author of *Looking Behind the Label: Global Industries and the Conscientious Consumer* (Indiana University Press, 2015).

Thomas Hale is Associate Professor in the Blavatnik School of Government at the University of Oxford. His research explores how we can manage transnational problems effectively and fairly. His books include *Between Interests and Law: The Politics of Transnational Commercial Disputes* (Cambridge University Press, 2015), *Transnational Climate Change Governance* (Cambridge University Press, 2014), and *Gridlock: Why Global Cooperation is Failing when We Need it Most* (Polity, 2013).

Yanzhong Huang is Senior Fellow for Global Health at the Council on Foreign Relations, and Professor and Director of the Center for Global Health Studies at Seton Hall University's School of Diplomacy and International Relations. He is the founding editor of *Global Health Governance: The Scholarly Journal for the New Health Security Paradigm.* Huang has written extensively on global health governance, health diplomacy and health security, and public health in China and East Asia. He is author of *Governing Health in*

Contemporary China (Routledge, 2012) and numerous reports, journal articles, and book chapters, including articles in *Survival, Foreign Affairs, Public Health, Bioterrorism and Biosecurity,* and the *Journal of Contemporary China.*

Scott Kennedy is Deputy Director of the Freeman Chair in China Studies and Director of the Project on Chinese Business and Political Economy at the Center for Strategic and International Studies. From 2000 to 2014 he was an Associate Professor and Director of the Research Center for Chinese Politics and Business at Indiana University. He is author of *The Business of Lobbying in China* (Harvard University Press, 2005), and editor of *Beyond the Middle Kingdom: Comparative Perspectives on China's Capitalist Transition* (Stanford University Press, 2011). His articles have appeared in *China Quarterly, China Journal, Journal of Contemporary China, Political Science Quarterly, World Policy Journal, Foreign Affairs,* and *Foreign Policy.*

Wei Liang is Professor at the Middlebury Institute of International Studies at Monterey. Liang specializes in international trade and development policy, global economic and environmental governance and international negotiation, and international political economy of East Asia and China. She is co-author of *China and East Asia's Post-Crises Community* (Lexington Books, 2012) and co-editor of *China in Global Trading Governance* (Routledge, 2013).

Katherine Morton is Professor of China's International Relations at the University of Sheffield. Prior to her appointment at the University of Sheffield she was the Associate Dean for Research at the College of Asia and the Pacific, and a Senior Fellow in the Department of International Relations at Australian National University. She is author of *International Aid and China's Environment: Taming the Yellow Dragon* (Routledge, 2006), and has published numerous articles and chapters related to transnational security, global governance, environment and climate change, and international norms.

Junji Nakagawa is Professor of International Economic Law in the Institute of Social Science at the University of Tokyo. He is a leading authority on global and regional trade governance. He is the author or co-author of 12 books, including *WTO: Beyond Trade Liberalization* (Iwanami Shoten, 2013) and *International Harmonization of Economic Regulation* (Oxford University Press, 2011). He is the editor or co-editor of 16 books and the author of over two dozen articles.

Ren Xiao is Professor of International Politics in the Institute of International Studies and Director of the Center for the Study of Chinese Foreign Policy at Fudan University. He is co-editor of *New Frontiers of China's Foreign Relations* (Lexington Books, 2011), as well as numerous articles and reports on various aspects of Chinese foreign policy and international relations theory.

Bruce Reynolds is Professor of Economics (retired) at the University of Virginia. His recent research focuses on China's integration with the international financial system. He is the author of dozens of scholarly books and articles on China's economy, including *Household Credit in China* (Filene Research Institute, 2005), and *Chinese Economic Reform: How Far, How Fast?* (Harcourt, Brace Jovanovitch Academic Press, 1988).

Charles Roger is an SSHRC Postdoctoral Fellow in the Department of Political Science at the University of Toronto. His research focuses on developing our understanding of the dynamics of intergovernmental and transnational governance, particularly in the fields of international political economy and global environmental politics. He is the co-author of *Transnational Climate Change Governance* (Cambridge University Press, 2014), and the co-editor of *Climate Governance in the Developing World* (Polity Press, 2013) and *Global Governance at Risk* (Polity Press, 2013).

James Scott is Lecturer in International Politics in the Department of Political Economy, and the Research Group Leader for International Politics, Philosophy and Economics at King's College London. He works primarily on trade governance, particularly with regard to developing countries in the World Trade Organization (WTO). He is co-editor of *Expert Knowledge in Global Trade* (Routledge, 2015) and *Trade, Poverty, Development: Getting Beyond the WTO's Doha Deadlock* (Routledge, 2013).

Susan K. Sell is Professor Emeritus of Political Science and International Affairs at George Washington University, and Professor, School of Regulation and Global Governance (RegNet) in the College of Asia and the Pacific, Australian National University. Her areas of expertise include international political economy, intellectual property, trade, development, and global governance. She is author of *Private Power, Public Law: The Globalization of Intellectual Property Rights* (Cambridge University Press, 2003), and *Power and Ideas: North-South Politics of Intellectual Property and Antitrust* (SUNY Press, 1997), co-author of *Intellectual Property Rights:*

A Critical History (Lynne Rienner, 2005), and co-editor of *Who Governs the Globe?* (Cambridge University Press, 2010).

Tu Xinquan is Professor and Director of the China Institute for WTO Studies at the University of International Business and Economics in Beijing, China. He is author of *China's Position, Role and Strategy in the WTO* (UIBE Press, 2005). He has been a visiting scholar at the School of Advanced International Studies of Johns Hopkins University, the Korea Institute for International Economic Policy, and Indiana University. His research focuses on Chinese trade policy, the WTO, government procurement, US trade policy, and United States-China trade relations.

Wang Yong is Associate Professor in the School of International Studies and Director of the Research Center on International Political Economy at Peking University. His primary research interests concern international political economy, the politics of the WTO and other international economic institutions, regional integration, and United States–China relations. Among his book publications are *The Political Economy of International Trade* (2008) and *The Political Economy of China-U.S. Trade Relations* (2007). His articles have appeared in *International Affairs*, *Oxford Review of Economic Policy*, *Review of International Political Economy*, and *Global Asia*.

Rorden Wilkinson is Professor of Global Political Economy and Head of the Department of International Relations at the University of Sussex. He is an international political economist specializing in international trade (especially the WTO), global governance, development, "emerging" powers, least developed countries, and small island states. He is co-editor (with Thomas G. Weiss) of *International Organization and Global Governance*. He co-edits, also with Thomas G. Weiss, the Global Institutions series for Routledge. He was awarded the Johan Skytte International Manuscript Workshop Award for his book *What's Wrong with the WTO and How to Fix It* (Wiley, 2014).

Xu Jiajun is Assistant Professor and the Executive Deputy Director of the Center for New Structural Economics at Peking University. She also serves as Secretary-General of the Global Research Consortium on Economic Structural Transformation. She previously was a Junior Research Specialist at the United Nations High Level Panel Secretariat on the Post-2015 Development Agenda. Her research focuses on development finance and global economic governance. She is author of *Beyond US Hegemony in International*

Development: The Contest for Influence at the World Bank (Cambridge University Press, 2017). Her articles have appeared in leading scholarly outlets, including the *Journal of International Development*.

Lu Zhang is Associate Professor of Sociology at Temple University. Her research focus is on globalization, labor and labor movements, development, political economy, and China studies. She is currently researching capital reallocation strategies and labor politics within China and beyond China to new low-cost sites such as Vietnam. She is author of *Inside China's Automobile Factories: The Politics of Labor and Worker Resistance* (Cambridge University Press, 2015), and has contributed to leading academic journals and scholarly books.

Acknowledgments

This book originated with the "Initiative on China and Global Governance" that was launched by Indiana University's Research Center for Chinese Politics & Business (RCCPB) in 2010. The initiative's goal was to attract world-class talent to examine intensively China's growing role in global governance, and what this behavior reveals about both China and the world's global governance regimes. The initiative supported over three dozen scholars from North America, Europe, and Asia, who carried out research, wrote papers, and participated in conferences in the United States, Switzerland, and China. All of the papers for the initiative were originally issued as RCCPB working papers. A subset was edited and issued in the volume, *From Rule Takers to Rule Makers: The Growing Role of Chinese in Global Governance* (2012), edited jointly by myself and Shuaihua Cheng of the International Center for Trade & Sustainable Development (ICTSD). A policy-oriented report, "The United States, China and Global Governance: A New Agenda for a New Era," was written by myself and He Fan of the Chinese Academy of Social Sciences Institute of World Economics and Politics (IWEP) in 2013. A final subset of papers from the initiative, revised multiple times in subsequent years, are the basis of the current volume.

I am deeply grateful to the Henry Luce Foundation and the Asia Program's Director Helena Kolenda and Program Officer Li Ling for their generous and unwavering support for this initiative over the years. Without their commitment, this program of work would not have been possible. I also am thankful for additional funding for the initiative from Indiana University, which also provided support for our Beijing office and a reduced teaching load so I could focus on this initiative and other RCCPB projects.

The RCCPB's staff provided outstanding support for this initiative. Wang Qun, Erica Kendall, and Lily He oversaw the management of

xx   *Acknowledgments*

the relationships with the project's scholars and the organization of conferences in Indiana and Beijing. Zhao Shuang provided critical support to the conference in Geneva in the fall of 2012. The RCCPB was graced with several excellent research assistants who carried out research on several aspects of the initiative's work, including Edwin Way, Zhao Shuang, Yesola Kweon, Gauss Chu, and Dong Lu. The RCCPB's current Director Joyce Man and Assistant Director Roy Hooper have enthusiastically continued to support this initiative in its later stages.

The success of this initiative and the related research projects also depended heavily on the RCCPB's partner in Beijing, the China Institute for WTO Studies at the University of International Business and Economics, led by Director Zhang Hanlin and Deputy Director Tu Xinquan. The institute was the location for extensive research, and it raised funding and co-organized a major conference in October 2011 to commemorate the tenth anniversary of China's accession to the World Trade Organization (WTO), where those papers in the initiative related to trade issues were first presented. I am also grateful to the co-organizers of the initiative's other conferences: Peking University's School of Government (2010), Indiana University's Workshop on Political Theory (2012), ICTSD (2012), and IWEP (2013). Each of these partners has excellent staff who provided professional support from beginning to end. I am particularly indebted to the WTO Institute's Tu Xinquan, ICTSD's Chief Executive Ricardo Melendez-Ortiz, and IWEP's He Fan, each of whom has an abiding enthusiasm for research and international collaboration.

This volume would only be an idea were it not for the participation of a group of first-rate scholars from many parts of the globe, who carried out research, wrote and re-wrote their papers, and engaged in vigorous debate in multiple meetings. Their engagement has created research whose collective product is larger than the sum of its individual parts. All of the contributors to this volume also benefited from other scholars, officials, business people, international organization representatives, and experts who participated in the many gatherings held along the way. I am honored to be a part of this global community.

The Center for Strategic and International Studies (CSIS) provided a warm home for the final stages of this enterprise. I am grateful to Chris Johnson, the Freeman Chair in China Studies, for allowing me the time and space to finish this project, and to Maria Sinclair and Nicole White for their help in preparing the final manuscript.

I am forever indebted to Rorden Wilkinson and Tom Weiss, the co-editors of the series in which this book appears, and to Nicola

Parkin, the acquisition editor at Routledge, for placing their faith in me and not losing hope even as the project extended many moons beyond the original plan.

Finally, I must thank the members of my immediate family, to whom this book is dedicated, for their sacrifices during the years this book was being created and their unwavering love. They each are an inspiration to me.

Scott Kennedy
Washington, DC
July 2017

Abbreviations

ACFTU	All-China Federation of Trade Unions
ACTA	Anti-Counterfeiting Trade Agreement
AIDS	acquired immunodeficiency syndrome
AIIB	Asian Infrastructure Investment Bank
AIPPI	International Association for the Protection of Intellectual Property
AmCham	American Chamber of Commerce in China
AMS	Aggregate Measure of Support
APEC	Asia-Pacific Economic Cooperation
API	active pharmaceutical ingredients
APP	Asian-Pacific Partnership on Clean Development and Climate
ASEAN	Association of Southeast Asian Nations
BIT	bilateral investment treaty
BRI	Belt and Road Initiative
BRICS	Brazil, Russia, India, China, and South Africa
BSCI	Business Social Compliance Initiative
BV	Bureau Versitas
CAB	conformity assessment body
CAFTA	China-ASEAN free trade agreement
CARE	Caring, Awareness, Responsible, Ethical program
CASS	Chinese Academy of Social Sciences
CBO	community-based organization
CCM	country coordinating mechanism
CCP	Chinese Communist Party
CDC	China Center for Disease Control and Prevention/US Centers for Disease Control and Prevention
CDM	Clean Development Mechanism
CDP	Carbon Disclosure Project
CEPEA	Comprehensive Economic Partnership in East Asia

CER	Certified Emissions Reduction
CFDA	China Food & Drug Administration
CFS	Committee on Food Security
CISAR	China International Search and Rescue
CJK	China, Japan, and South Korea
CMA	China Meteorological Administration
CMI	Chiang Mai Initiative
CNCA	Certification and Accreditation Administration of China
CNTAC	Chinese National Apparel and Textile Council
CPC	Centralized Procurement Catalogue
CPPCC	China People's Political Consultative Conference
CSC	China Social Compliance
CSO	civil society organization
CSR	corporate social responsibility
DAC	Development Assistance Committee
DDA	Doha Development Agenda
DRC	Development Research Center
DSM	Dispute Settlement Mechanism
EAC	East Asian Community
EAS	East Asia Summit
EC	European Community
ECA	Export Credit Agency
EPA	economic partnership agreement
ER	exchange rate
ERM	exchange rate mechanism
ETI	Ethical Trading Initiative
EU	European Union
EU-ETS	European Union Emissions Trading System
F	financing-related activities
FAO	United Nations Food and Agriculture Organization
FCTC	Framework Convention on Tobacco Control
FDA	Food & Drug Administration
FDI	foreign direct investment
FLA	Fair Labor Association
FOCAC	Forum on China-Africa Cooperation
FSAP	Financial Sector Assessment Planning
FTA	free trade agreement
G8	Group of 8
G20	Group of 20
GAO	General Accountability Office
GATS	General Agreement on Trade in Services

GATT	General Agreement on Tariffs and Trade
GCC	Gulf Cooperation Council
GDP	gross domestic product
GGO	global governance organization
GHG	global health governance
GOARN	Global Outbreak Alert and Response Network
GONGO	government-organized nongovernmental organization
GPA	Agreement on Government Procurement
GPL	Government Procurement Law
GRI	Global Reporting Initiative
HIV	human immunodeficiency virus
HR	human resources
ICA	Infrastructure Consortium for Africa
ICLEI	Local Governments for Sustainability (formerly International Council for Local Environmental Initiatives)
ICTI	International Council of Toy Industries
IDA	International Development Association
IGO	international governmental organization
IHR	International Health Regulations
ILO	International Labour Organization
IMF	International Monetary Fund
IN	information sharing and networking
INTERFAIS	International Food Aid Information System
IP	intellectual property
IPR	intellectual property rights
IPRCC	International Poverty Reduction Center in China
ISO	International Organization for Standardization
ITO	International Trade Organization
ITU	International Telecommunications Union
JCCT	Joint Committee on Commerce and Trade
LDC	least developed countries
MAI	Multilateral Agreement on Investment
MDG	Millennium Development Goals
METI	Ministry of Economy, Trade and Industry
MFN	most favored nation
MITI	Ministry of International Trade and Industry
MNC	multinational corporation
MOF	Ministry of Finance
MOFA	Ministry of Foreign Affairs
MOFCOM	Ministry of Commerce
MOFTEC	Ministry of Foreign Trade and Economic Cooperation
MOHRSS	Ministry of Human Resources and Social Security

MOST	Ministry of Science and Technology
MoU	memorandum of understanding
NAFTA	North American Free Trade Agreement
NAMA	non-agricultural market access
NATO	North Atlantic Treaty Organization
NBS	National Bureau of Statistics
NDB	New Development Bank
NDRC	National Development and Reform Commission
NGO	nongovernmental organization
NHFPC	National Health and Family Planning Commission
NME	non-market economy
O	operational activities
ODA	official development assistance
OECD	Organisation for Economic Co-operation and Development
OXFAM	Oxford Committee for Famine Relief
PBOC	People's Bank of China
PCF	Prototype Carbon Fund
PCT	Patent Cooperation Treaty
PEPFAR	United States President's Emergency Plan for AIDS Relief
PLA	People's Liberation Army
PPT	Prescribed Procurement Thresholds
PRC	People's Republic of China
R&D	research and development
RAM	recently acceded member
RCEP	Regional Comprehensive Economic Partnership
REACH	Registration, Evaluation, Authorization and Restriction of Chemicals
RMB	renminbi
S&ED	Strategic and Economic Dialogue
SACU	Southern African Customs Union
SAI	Social Accountability International
SARS	Severe Acute Respiratory Syndrome
SASAC	State-Owned Assets Supervision and Administration Commission
SC	standards and commitments
SDR	special drawing rights
SEP	standard essential patent
SEZ	special economic zone
SGS	Société Générale de Surveillance
SIPO	State Intellectual Property Office

SOE	state-owned enterprise
SSIC	Social Survey Institute of China
SSM	Special Safeguard Mechanism
TB	tuberculosis
TBT	Technical Barriers to Trade
TCG	transnational climate governance
TPP	Trans-Pacific Partnership
TRIMs	Trade-Related Investment Measures
TRIPS	Trade-Related Aspects of Intellectual Property Rights
TRM	Transitional Review Mechanism
UK	United Kingdom
UN	United Nations
UNAIDS	Joint United Nations Programme on HIV/AIDS
UNCTAD	United Nations Conference on Trade and Development
UNFCCC	United Nations Framework Convention on Climate Change
UNICEF	United Nations Children's Fund
UNSC	United Nations Security Council
USAID	United States Agency for International Development
USTR	United States Trade Representative
WEF	World Economic Forum
WFP	World Food Programme
WHO	World Health Organization
WIPO	World Intellectual Property Organization
WRAP	Worldwide Responsible Accredited Production
WTO	World Trade Organization

Introduction

Learning to be insiders

Scott Kennedy

- Two pictures of Davos
- Evolving Chinese participation, a stagnating debate
- A normatively ambiguous global governance system
- This volume's contributions
- This volume's contribution

Two pictures of Davos

Each January world leaders gather in the small Swiss hamlet of Davos to share their views about the state of global affairs and discuss how to expand collaboration in addressing the world's many challenges. Although the United Nations (UN) may have more official authority as the venue for multilateral action by sovereign states, the World Economic Forum's (WEF) annual meeting has become the unofficial summit for a wider range of elites from governments, international organizations, industry, finance, academia, and nongovernmental organizations (NGOs). The WEF may be a better barometer than the UN not only for gauging elite opinion on the world's problems, but also on the overall state of global governance.[1]

Global governance is defined here as the rules, procedures, and norms that define appropriate behavior, facilitate cooperation, and manage differences among state and non-state actors from multiple countries. This broad definition is more realistic than narrower ones that focus on specific kinds of institutions or goals. Some observers equate global governance with broad, state-based multilateral institutions such as the World Trade Organization (WTO) or International Monetary Fund (IMF), but global governance comes in all shapes and sizes, including groups like the WEF.[2] Some organizations are sovereign-based, in which states are members; some are composed of both states and non-state actors; and others are purely private, in which members are individuals or non-state groups, such as companies or NGOs. In addition, global economic governance refers both to efforts to set rules, such as summit meetings and other negotiations, as well as to the processes of using and implementing these rules, both globally and within countries, on issues that pertain to cross-border economic activity.

The January 2017 edition of the WEF may be remembered as a watershed moment in international affairs because of the unexpected reversal in roles for China and the United States. Chinese President Xi Jinping was joined by a large retinue of officials and business executives and gave the opening plenary speech. He embraced economic globalization and called for the expansion of rules and institutions to address gaps in the global governance architecture:

> The global economic landscape has changed profoundly in the past few decades. However, the global governance system has not embraced those new changes and is therefore inadequate in terms of representation and inclusiveness. The global industrial landscape is changing and new industrial chains, value chains and supply chains are taking shape. However, trade and investment rules have not kept pace with these developments, resulting in acute problems such as closed mechanisms and fragmentation of rules. The global financial market needs to be more resilient against risks, but the global financial governance mechanism fails to meet the new requirement and is thus unable to effectively resolve problems such as frequent international financial market volatility and the build-up of asset bubbles.[3]

By contrast, the newly elected American president, Donald Trump, not only skipped Davos, but in contrast to President Xi and all previous American presidents since World War II, he made it clear in the months prior to and after Davos that he is highly skeptical of globalization and the multilateral system. He attacked the WTO and regional arrangements such as the Trans-Pacific Partnership (TPP) and instead put forward an agenda to establish a series of bilateral agreements and more assertively use a wide range of domestic fair-trade tools and tax policy, regardless of whether such tactics violate WTO rules.[4]

Observers interpreted this juxtaposition in two competing ways. The first was to highlight the emergent leadership of China as an important champion and ballast of the international system, which was also reflected in its support for the UN Framework Convention on Climate Change (UNFCCC) and its effective hosting of the Group of 20 (G20) process during 2016. The second was a far more skeptical assessment, viewing Xi's claimed allegiance to open markets as superficial, a conclusion made in light of China's highly interventionist state at home and its efforts to promote new initiatives, such as the Asian Infrastructure Investment Bank (AIIB), "One Belt, One Road," the internationalization of the renminbi, and the concept of "Internet sovereignty." From this alternative perspective, China is engaged in a concerted effort to undermine and challenge the liberal post-World War II order established by the United States and Europe, and its posture at the WEF was just convenient theater.[5]

As a matter of fact, China is neither purely a savior nor scofflaw of the global economic system. The purpose of the present volume and its contributing chapters is to demonstrate that the reality is more complex than either of the facile portraits painted above. Rather, China's growing involvement in global governance reflects the mutually interactive processes of China's own gradual socialization into the global community and the simultaneous adaptation of global institutions and actors to China's growing activism. Critically, both China and the international system are internally complex organisms. Hence, Chinese engagement varies across economic regimes, yielding different results in terms of Chinese compliance, its influence over the regime, and the extent of cooperation in addressing problems in international society.

To elaborate on this conclusion, this chapter first provides an overview of the evolution of Chinese engagement in global governance. The main point is that while Chinese participation has changed substantially, the core puzzle framing its participation has remained relatively static. The discussion then turns to considering how the conversation would change by accepting a more complex view of both China and the global governance system. Doing so opens up many more possibilities in terms of explaining Chinese participation and what it means for the regimes and addressing global challenges. We then turn to introducing the chapters of this volume and show how they shed light on underexplored aspects of global governance. The discussion concludes with an effort to synthesize the volume's broader findings, which speak to the challenges of using a compliance approach to judge Chinese behavior, how Chinese behavior is shaped by its domestic environment and the nature of external regimes in which it participates, the extent to which Chinese initiatives support reform or present more fundamental challenges to the current global governance regimes, and the consequences for cooperation and competition between China and other members of the global community.

Evolving Chinese participation, a stagnating debate

Chinese involvement in global governance has expanded dramatically over the past four decades. When the current international economic order was created on the heels of World War II, the Kuomintang-led Republic of China initially joined the United Nations, the General Agreement on Tariffs and Trade (GATT), and other institutions. Given its antipathy to global capitalism, once the People's Republic of China (PRC) was founded in 1949, it turned its back on international economic institutions and instead focused on cooperation with the Soviet Union and other state socialist countries. The PRC replaced Taiwan at the United Nations in 1972, but it was not until China launched the Reform Era in 1978 that it began the gradual journey of integrating itself into established global economic organizations.

In the 1980s China joined the IMF and World Bank, and in 1986 submitted its application to join the GATT. It also acceded to dozens of other more focused international economic organizations such the International Organization for Standardization (ISO), the International Telecommunications Union (ITU), and the World Health Organization (WHO). During its first decade-plus of membership, China adopted a largely passive role, primarily observing and only offering occasional comments and proposals. Chinese participants were hamstrung by their limited English and the short leash given to them by their bureaucratic masters back in Beijing.[6]

The next step in the transition came with China's accession to the WTO in late 2001. At this point, China expanded its effort to become a normal member of international economic organizations. To do so, Chinese leaders studied the written rules and informal norms of various organizations, reading extensively, inviting experts to China, and participating in organizations' training programs. A coterie of experts began to emerge, with better English skills, who could represent China on the international stage. The culmination of this phase was China's inclusion in the WTO's inner circle as part of the Doha Round negotiations in 2008.[7] Though still eyed warily by most of the incumbent dominant members of the system, these meetings in the WTO's infamous Green Room marked China's arrival as a global governance insider. That said, China was still primarily a follower and not a leader that set the agenda or provided public goods at a cost to itself.[8]

The current phase emerged in the wake of the global financial crisis in 2008–2009 and the assumption of power in China by Xi Jinping in 2012. The financial crisis shook the faith of many, including China, in the soundness of existing international institutions' and arrangements' ability adequately to shepherd the global economy. When Xi replaced Hu Jintao in late 2012 as China's preeminent leader, he put aside a long-time Chinese approach to foreign policy, first enunciated under Deng Xiaoping, of being relatively passive and only responding to the initiatives of others, summed up in the principle "hide brightness, nourish obscurity" (*tao guang yang hui*).[9] As a consequence, since then China has become much more active across all aspects of its foreign policy, including global economic governance. At an elementary level, it has tried to obtain a greater "right to speak" (*huayuquan*) in international organizations, both in terms of positions and activity. Former Chinese officials have taken up leadership posts in the IMF, WTO, ISO, ITU, WHO, and elsewhere, and Chinese representatives regularly submit and advocate for proposals at the working level of most organizations. China hosted the Asia-Pacific Economic Cooperation (APEC) Forum in 2014 and the G20 process in 2016. At the same time, it has launched a range of initiatives, both within existing organizations and by establishing new ones. Xi's speech at Davos in early 2017 was the natural outgrowth of an approach that could not be more different from where China began in the 1970s or even in the early days of its WTO membership. This insider is now aspiring to greater leadership and influence.

Although China's role in global governance has changed markedly over the last two decades, the parameters of the conversation about China have remained relatively unchanged. The dominant question motivating experts has been whether China is being effectively integrated into the global system or whether China is undermining the global order to fit its interests.

The most prominent way this question has been addressed has been to discuss the extent to which China has complied with its commitments. Some experts answer in the affirmative, arguing that China has largely lived up to the pledges it has made in the various institutions it has joined. The most often-cited area of successful compliance has concerned trade and the WTO.[10] Experts rarely conclude that China's record has been spotless, but they find it sufficiently robust or at least "acceptable."[11] Observers believe Chinese compliance has grown because either its interests are consistent with regime rules or because Chinese actors have gradually been socialized into the norms of the regimes themselves, initially by simply imitating the behavior of others and then, over time, by gradually absorbing and internalizing the norms themselves and, as a result, reimagining their identity and interests in the process. This socialization has occurred at a broad level in Chinese industry through economic globalization.[12] It has also occurred within individual international institutions including the WTO, IMF, and other organizations.[13]

More pessimistic observers are less sanguine about China's record and find either compliance to be quite spotty or that Chinese behavior has been more corrosive of international regimes than optimists would admit. The Western business community has put the sharpest spotlight on the specific issue of noncompliance with WTO obligations, while others have charged that the inclusion of China and other emerging powers into the Doha Round was responsible for the deadlock in negotiations.[14]

Critics provide three different explanations for why China's compliance record has been weak and why it is unlikely to improve or is, in fact, likely to become more problematic. Some highlight the hindering legacy of traditional Chinese culture and China's distinctive perspective on world affairs.[15] Others focus on China's current authoritarian political system and how that drives a preference for non-liberal institutions, placing it at loggerheads with liberal democracies.[16] Still others stress the simple historical fact that China did not initially contribute to the creation of the post-World War II system and therefore would naturally never be comfortable with an order that was not constructed with its interests in mind.[17]

This final perspective hints at the alternative way the issue of Chinese behavior is framed. As China becomes more powerful, the question is not only one of simple compliance, but how China would use its growing power to shape global governance to its liking. Former US Deputy Secretary of State Robert Zoellick put the issue most clearly when in 2005 he called on China to become a "responsible stakeholder," a country that not only follows the rules but also provides public goods that strengthen the system.[18] The contrary view is that a more powerful China would prefer to undercut the existing order and build an alternative one more consistent with its preferences, what in Chinese is aptly called "to build a separate kitchen" (*ling qi lu zao*).

This framing of the issue is understandable, since China is a new, large member of the global community whose culture, authoritarian political system, and heavy use of industrial policy distinguish it from the incumbents. At the same time, this framing puts *all* of the focus on China and leaves the global governance regimes and other actors entirely unexplored. It implicitly suggests that compliance with the current norms and rules is highly valued and that noncompliance by newcomers is the only source of conflict and obstacle to solving problems.

A normatively ambiguous global governance system

A more balanced approach would not only investigate Chinese views and behavior, but also analyze the norms and actual operating record of the global governance system and its incumbent members.[19] Doing so yields three adjustments to the typical picture. The first is that the rules of the so-called "liberal international order" are not consistently liberal.[20] Although many of the statutes of the WTO and other organizations promote low barriers to trade and investment, most-favored nation status, and national treatment, there are myriad exceptions. The WTO, for instance, permits members to protect domestic industry in the case of challenges to public health, the environment, national security, and sudden external shocks to the domestic economy. The anti-dumping and countervailing duty regimes of the WTO, which are further embodied in the national regulations of members, are inherently protectionist in order to cushion the blow for domestic industry from foreign competition. In many instances, the rules were intentionally written to provide certain protections for everyone; in other cases, the rules promote the interests of some members over those of others, as is the case with intellectual property rights laws which disproportionately favor advanced industrialized economies.[21]

Second, the behavior of incumbent members is also not consistently liberal. Not only do they utilize the loopholes that permit protectionism even when the rules are genuinely liberal, but they also are able to act strategically to promote their particular interests, which may or may not jibe with those of other members of the system. Global governance is often imagined as a dispassionate, rules-based order where parties all pursue cooperation in an open, transparent manner. The reality involves a combination of clear rules and open debate with highly calculated advocacy and gamesmanship.

Third, there are many gaps in the global governance system, with areas where there are rules for only a small subset of actors, where rules are vague and lack enforcement provisions, or where there are no rules at all. In such situations, participants typically justify certain behaviors as appropriate by reference to economic theory, precedent, or common practices. This state of affairs applies to a large portion of international economic activity, among them investment, e-commerce, and currency. Since there are no clear rules, it is more difficult to know precisely what should count as compliant or acceptable behavior.

Recognition that the international economic system is more normatively ambiguous than often recognized leads to two implications for how to interpret China's global governance activities. Illiberal Chinese behavior may not solely be the product of Chinese culture, political institutions, or knee-jerk opposition to a system it did not create. Instead, it may be that the more China becomes an insider, the more its behavior reflects both the liberal *and* illiberal elements of the existing order that it has been taught by the incumbent members and institutions. The literature on learning in international relations focuses on how countries with realist, non-liberal traditions acquire more liberal values through engagement with Western countries,[22] but given what is actually being taught, it is likely that China and other emerging powers are acquiring a complex mix of norms and rules.[23] Even if many Chinese global governance actors began with a realist perspective, the learning process may to some extent reinforce this original prejudice and also have provided them with the language, concepts, strategies, and repertoire of behavior they previously lacked. When China acts to protect domestic industry that appears inconsistent with global norms, it actually may be more fully abiding by the genuine extant system than some would care to admit.

This change in perspective also requires observers to modify how to interpret initiatives to change the status quo. There is an ever-expanding literature that explores the difficulty of the international economic system to address global issues. For some, the source of the problem is the growing role of China and other new entrants, with some focused on China's particular views and others emphasizing the challenge created by having a multiplicity of views and voices, irrespective of their content.[24] Yet others highlight existing institutions' structural weaknesses and the content of the rules themselves, which run deeper than the addition of new members.[25] If one accepts that the status quo may be problematic, then Chinese initiatives cannot simply be pigeonholed as unacceptable and hostile challenges to the status quo, and conversely, Western proposals are not necessarily reformist improvements on a liberal order. Instead, the above discussion suggests that observers need to pay more attention to the content of the proposals than the identity of their authors. If one allows for these possibilities, it is conceivable that new Chinese initiatives could be viewed not as revolutionary but as reformist.[26]

Although to some this shift in perspective may appear to condone Chinese noncompliance or trumpet their new initiatives, in reality, it is simply a call for a balanced analysis in which Chinese behavior and global governance regimes are both proper subjects of critical reflection.

This volume's contributions

The contributions to this volume provide a new window into the evolving and varied relationship between China and global governance regimes. They collectively seek to address three interconnected questions. First, how has China participated in global governance institutions over the past two decades? This requires us to examine its positions and major activities and how they have changed over time. Examining this question will let us determine how China's positions compare to existing norms and rules (where they exist) and allow us to conclude to what extent China is a status quo power, reformer, or revolutionary.

Second, what are the sources of Chinese behavior? It is possible that Chinese views and actions reflect China's domestic political economy as an authoritarian state that intervenes deeply in the economy. It also could reflect lessons China has learned through its studying of existing institutions and the behavior of other participants. If adopted from abroad, we need to better understand not only the content, but also the mechanisms of acquisition.

Third, what explains the pattern of tensions China has with other members of the system? Answering this question will allow us to determine to what extent reducing tensions would be achieved through changes to Chinese behavior, the regimes themselves, or to both.

To answer these questions, the following chapters explore a wide panoply of global economic governance regimes. We examine trade from several angles, including the WTO, regional trade arrangements, and plurilateral agreements. However, trade distinguishes itself from other areas for the extent of detailed and enforceable rules and the composition of the specific participants. Therefore, we also examine Chinese participation in global governance beyond trade, from intellectual property rights and exchange rates to foreign aid and food security. Some attention is placed on summitry and negotiating new rules, but much of the focus is on the application of rules and day-to-day participation in regimes. Moreover, given the explosion of private governance regimes, we do not limit our focus to state-based institutions and actors.[27] Chinese corporate executives and non-profit organizations are also rule makers and participants, and so are included in the analysis.

A great deal of attention has already been paid by others to Chinese involvement in trade governance, but our contributors provide new insights that go beyond earlier research. In their respective discussions of China and the WTO, James Scott and Rorden Wilkinson in Chapter 1 and Wang Yong in Chapter 2 both paint a relatively similar picture of Chinese integration into the world's most important and comprehensive economic global governance institution, though for different reasons. Scott and Wilkinson emphasize the confluence of China's growing export dependence in the 1990s and the high requirements for accession as key factors driving China to fit in. The result was strong pressures to adapt. Even as China has become more successful and shifted from being a quiet member to a more assertive one, it still on many issues has attempted to play a constructive role, including trying to broker a compromise between Western countries and India during the summer 2008 Doha Round negotiations. That said, these analysts are not Pollyannaish and one can deduce from their analysis that tensions will continue to exist between China's effort to address its own developmental challenges and the preferences of the United States and Europe.

Wang Yong highlights the domestic sources of China's effort to learn to be an effective WTO member. Although initially government-led, over time Chinese industry has pushed the government to help it defend itself with WTO-compliant tools, including fair-trade mechanisms. Industry has criticized obstacles to its investment abroad, which partly explains why China has become so interested in negotiating bilateral investment treaties. Similarly, Wang notes Chinese industry's concerns about the WTO's constraints on industrial policy and permission for export controls for sensitive technologies, identifying an area of growing tension between China and its trading partners. He concludes that despite the challenges, most view WTO membership as successful and providing China with the confidence to undertake new initiatives, such as AIIB.

As Junji Nakagawa and Wei Liang demonstrate in Chapter 3, China has followed in the footsteps of advanced industrialized economies in seeking to establish free trade agreements (FTAs), a move which is partly a response to the stalemate in the Doha Round. At the same time, the detailed comparison with Japan shows that China's efforts are distinctive from its wealthier counterparts. China's FTAs typically involve shallower and narrower market-opening commitments and hence serve more as political tools to promote diplomatic ties as opposed to major initiatives to expand China's commercial opportunities.

In Chapter 4 Tu Xinquan finds that China is equally hesitant when it comes to plurilateral arrangements. In his cogent analysis of China's effort to join the WTO's Agreement on Government Procurement (GPA), Tu finds that bureaucratic politics and concerns raised by state-owned enterprises (SOEs) inhibit China's willingness to make major concessions. In his telling, such domestic veto players are difficult for even a determined top leadership to overcome.

When we turn to finance, the options are less between protecting domestic interests and providing greater leadership than they are a question of what type of leader China seeks to be. Ren Xiao argues in Chapter 5 that in the G20 China has played the role of a "reform-minded status quo state," which he defines as a country that "is in general satisfied with the current situation and accepts the existing rules, but it holds that there are shortcomings in the present order and it hopes to make improvements, and do so on the basis of the present rules of the game which it has accepted and endorsed." Ren documents how China's clear national interest has impelled it to promote incremental reform of the international monetary system, to seek greater representation at the World Bank and IMF, to strengthen international financial regulation, and to promote internationalization of the renminbi. Moreover, unlike with the negotiations over joining the WTO's GPA, Ren finds that bureaucratic politics in this case have been less of an obstacle toward China playing a more constructive role in the G20 process, perhaps because China is pursuing a more offensive set of interests in the G20, as opposed to defensive ones in the case of the GPA.

Reynolds and Sell in Chapter 6 also find that Chinese influence is growing in the areas of intellectual property rights (IPR) and foreign exchange, and that China's preferences have been shaped by domestic interest groups and its evolving growth strategy. Although China is still focused on acquiring foreign IPR, growing domestic innovation capabilities are also generating internal demand for greater IPR protection, and China is playing a larger role in international IPR bodies. In currency matters, China has made progress to expand the role of the renminbi regionally and via the IMF's special drawing rights basket. At the same time, the level of tensions with the United States and others has differed in the two areas, with conflict in IPR moderating over time, while those involving exchange rates continue to be highly acrimonious, with Reynolds and Sell suggesting that China's efforts to continue to micromanage the renminbi's value may constitute it seeking an exception to the norm of floating exchange rates maintained by other large economies. This difference in levels of tension appears to be a result of very different regime structures: IPR has clear rules and dispute settlement procedures via the WTO and several international treaties, whereas the rules for foreign exchange are more ambiguous, with no obvious multilateral venue to resolve differences.

China's involvement in global health governance has been a two-way street. In Chapter 7 Yanzhong Huang finds that the global health community has had an enormous effect on China's domestic public health priorities and institutions. At the same time, though China's external role has been "narrow and limited," it has contributed health-related foreign aid, participated in fighting diseases, and helped set global rules via the WHO. China's participation reflects the absorption of global norms and concerns with China's reputation, but at the same time bureaucratic politics and China's emphasis on sovereignty and state authority have weighed heavily on actual policies and their implementation. Public health NGOs, for example, have played only a minor role in China compared to elsewhere.

Katherine Morton's analysis of food governance in Chapter 8 provides an unexpected contrast with Huang's description of public health. Although she finds that China's role has expanded substantially in all three areas—outsourcing production, providing food aid, and global policymaking—China has not adopted the dominant norms of the international community. That is in part because those norms have been in flux for some time. As a result, China has learned primarily through experience, not by studying others. Nevertheless, while there are some tensions between China and Western countries in some ways, for example over conditionality, China is not promoting a radical agenda. Instead, Morton says, it "appears to be pursuing a pragmatic strategy of seeking to bring about substantial reforms from within."

Xu Jiajun in Chapter 9 argues that in the area of foreign aid China's approach presents a larger challenge to existing Western aid norms that privilege grants over loans, advocates against tied aid, and encourages concessional terms to recipients. Xu suggests that not only have Western countries not consistently lived up to their own norms, but the norms themselves have not produced a successful record of aid in the developing world. Hence, China's alternative approach as a "development financer," which she still suggests is a reform and not a radical revision of the existing order, should not be discouraged. She concludes that although convergence in this sphere of global governance is not likely, competition and conflict need not be the only alternatives. Instead, she believes that the proponents of the alternative approaches could adopt a position of mutual recognition and engagement. The emergence of AIIB is the clearest embodiment of this approach and an opportunity for learning by both China and Western countries.

The final two chapters of the book focus on non-state participants in global governance and the challenges they face being effective in China's political environment. In Chapter 10 Bartley and Zhang examine private factory labor certification systems, a practice that has emerged in other countries and has been experimented with in China. They find that there is only a tenuous relationship between receiving certification and a factory's actual working conditions. In some cases, certification papers over serious problems, but even in factories with better conditions, the power of certification is limited.

Similarly, in Chapter 11 Hale and Roger find that China's activism in transnational climate government is state-dominated. NGOs and industry do participate, but they typically follow the lead of state actors and align their goals with the aims of those parts of the Chinese state with which they have a strong relationship, a dynamic that differs dramatically from that found in developed and developing democracies.

This volume's contribution

The contributions to this volume combine to make a multifaceted tapestry that defies simplistic either/or conclusions. Yet important patterns do emerge.

The first is that viewing Chinese behavior strictly through a compliance lens is of limited utility. There are clearer rules in the trade space, and here one can say that China's record is far from perfect, but it is not at all clear that China is "breaking the system." The rules are also relatively clear in IP, and China's compliance record appears to be improving. However, taking a lawyerly measure of Chinese behavior elsewhere is problematic because the rules and norms are either not universal (for example, foreign aid), or are vague (for example, exchange rates).

The chapters in this volume suggest that a somewhat more helpful perspective is to ask to what extent Chinese behavior has been shaped by its domestic environment as opposed to learning from the outside. One certainly sees the effect of China's political system in many areas, including the role of bureaucratic politics (the WTO, GPA negotiations, and IP) and the privileging of a strong state over civil society (public health, labor certification, and transnational climate governance). In addition, the state's commitment to promoting industrial policy goals combined with being open to lobbying by key business interests is visible in many spheres, including in trade, IP, food aid, and development financing. At the same time, Chinese behavior has been heavily shaped by the global governance regimes and to some extent has moved in the direction of other major actors, including in the WTO, IP, public health, and climate governance.

The book's contributions also help observers answer the question of to what extent China is a status quo power. In no single area is China entirely comfortable with every single norm and rule. Nevertheless, in many areas Chinese behavior usually falls roughly within current broad norms. Most Chinese initiatives appear more akin to reforms within the system as opposed to outright opposition, or to use Ren Xiao's term, "revision." In the former category would fit the WTO and trade, the G20 and finance, public health, and food security. The latter arguably would include foreign exchange and foreign aid, although the line between reform and revision can be somewhat ambiguous. It should not be surprising to find that the rules and institutional machinery of the first group of global governance regimes are more developed and disseminated more universally than those in the second group. More complete rules do not remove conflicts or competition, but they create mechanisms for their management.

A final issue that emerges in the discussion is to what extent differences between Chinese behavior and global governance regimes should be seen as a problem that needs to be resolved by either pushing China to converge toward international standards or the international community adopting Chinese reform proposals. Some form of harmonization seems necessary where there are substantial private goods and competing interests at stake, as is the case in trade, finance, and IP. Although there may be reasons for allowing limited degrees of what the WTO terms "policy space" for countries and other actors in these areas, encouraging entirely alternative standards and rules of behavior often would have major distributive consequences that would result in acrimonious accusations of unfairness.

Nevertheless, there may be some regimes that govern purely public goods and where a multiplicity of norms may facilitate experimentation and healthy pursuit of improved approaches to solving problems. Xu's discussion of development financing offers one such potential area where a "live and let live" approach of mutual recognition may be worth trying, particularly when the dominant approach to governance has not produced a stellar track record. In such instances, "responsible stakeholders" might best serve the needs of global governance regimes by welcoming rather than opposing changes to the status quo. In that spirit, the entire international community, including both Chinese and other members, will always have much to learn.

Notes

1 For more on the World Economic Forum, see Geoffrey Allen Pigman, *The World Economic Forum: A Multi-Stakeholder Approach to Global Governance* (New York: Routledge, 2006).
2 Jonathan G. S. Koppell, *World Rule: Accountability, Legitimacy, and the Design of Global Governance* (Chicago, Ill.: University of Chicago Press, 2010).
3 "President Xi's Speech to Davos in Full," *World Economic Forum*, 17 January 2017, www.weforum.org/agenda/2017/01/full-text-of-xi-jinping-keyno te-at-the-world-economic-forum.
4 For an overview of the Trump Administration's approach to international economic affairs, see its "National Trade Policy Agenda for 2017," *International Economic Law and Policy Blog*, 1 March 2017, http://worldtradela w.typepad.com/ielpblog/2017/03/the-us-national-trade-policy-agenda-for-20 17.html.

5 Bessma Momani, "Xi Jinping's Davos Speech Showed the World Has Turned Upside Down," *Newsweek*, 18 January 2017, www.newsweek.com/davos-2017-xi-jinping-economy-globalization-protectionism-donald-trump-543993; Michael J. Mazarr, "China's Opportunity—and Ours," *U.S. News & World Report*, 15 February 2017, www.usnews.com/opinion/world-report/articles/2017-02-15/the-us-should-view-chinas-davos-speech-on-world-order-as-an-opportunity; and Dingding Chen, "Is China Ready for Global Leadership?" *The Diplomat*, 27 February 2017, http://thediplomat.com/2017/02/is-china-ready-for-global-leadership/.

6 Elizabeth Economy and Michel Oksenberg, eds, *China Joins the World: Progress and Prospects* (New York: Council on Foreign Relations Press, 1999).

7 Paul Blustein, *Misadventures of the Most Favored Nations: Clashing Egos, Inflated Ambitions, and the Great Shambles of the World Trade System* (New York: Public Affairs, 2009).

8 For a summary of this phase in which China was less influential than other BRIC members, such as India and Brazil, see Hongying Wang and Erik French, "China's Participation in Global Governance from a Comparative Perspective," *Asia Policy* 15 (January 2013): 89–114.

9 Shaun Breslin, "China and the Global Order: Signalling Threat or Friendship?" *International Affairs* 89, no. 3 (2013): 615–634; Tom Miller, "The Chinese Dream (I): The Empire Strikes Back," *China Economic Quarterly* 19, no. 3–4 (November 2015): 7–12.

10 Nicholas R. Lardy, *Integrating China into the Global Economy* (Washington, DC: Brookings Institution Press, 2002); Deborah Z. Cass, Brett G. Williams, and George Barker, eds, *China and the World Trading System: Entering the New Millennium* (Cambridge: Cambridge University Press, 2003); Supachai Panitchpakdi and Mark L. Clifford, *China and the WTO: Changing China, Changing World Trade* (New York: John Wiley & Sons, 2002); Margaret M. Pearson, "China in Geneva: Lessons from China's Early Years in the World Trade Organization," in *New Directions in the Study of China's Foreign Policy*, ed. Alastair Iain Johnston and Robert S. Ross (Stanford, Calif.: Stanford University Press, 2006), 242–275; Sun Liang and Zhang Xiangchen, "Redefining Development, Reimagining Globalization: The WTO and China's New Economic Vision," *Journal of World Trade* 41, no. 6 (November 2007): 1275–1295.

11 Ka Zeng and Wei Liang, eds, *China and Global Trade Governance: China's First Decade in the World Trade Organization* (New York: Routledge, 2013).

12 Doug Guthrie, *Dragon in a Three-Piece Suit: The Emergence of Capitalism in China* (Princeton, N.J.: Princeton University Press, 1999); and Edward S. Steinfeld, *Playing Our Game: Why China's Rise Doesn't Threaten the West* (Oxford: Oxford University Press, 2010).

13 Ann Kent, *Beyond Compliance: China, International Organizations, and Global Security* (Stanford, Calif.: Stanford University Press, 2007); and Justin S. Hempson-Jones, "The Evolution of China's Engagement with International Governmental Organizations," *Asian Survey* 45, no. 5 (September/October 2005): 702–721. For a sophisticated theoretical discussion of different mechanisms of socialization, see Alastair Iain Johnston, *Social States: China in International Institutions, 1980–2000* (Princeton, N.J.: Princeton University Press, 2008).

14   Chambers of commerce in the United States, Europe, and Japan regularly point to Chinese noncompliance with its WTO obligations and China's continuing barriers to imports and foreign investment. For example, see *American Business in China: 2016 White Paper* (Beijing: American Chamber of Commerce in China, 2016). On the Doha Round, see Blustein, *Misadventures of the Most Favored Nations*; and Kristen Hopewell, *Breaking the WTO: How Emerging Powers Disrupted the Neoliberal Project* (Stanford, Calif.: Stanford University Press, 2016).

15   Ross Terrill, *The New Chinese Empire: And What it Means for the United States* (New York: Basic Books, 2003); Peter Navarro, *The Coming China Wars: Where They Will Be Fought and How They Can Be Won* (Upper Saddle River, N.J.: FT Press, 2008); and Martin Jacques, *When China Rules the World: The End of the Western World and the Birth of a New Global Order* (New York: Penguin 2010).

16   Edward Friedman, "Power Transition Theory: A Challenge to the Peaceful Rise of World Power China," in *China's Rise: Threat or Opportunity?*, ed. Herbert S. Yee (London and New York: Routledge, 2010): 11–32; and Stefan A. Halper, *The Beijing Consensus: How China's Authoritarian Model Will Dominate the 21st Century* (New York: Basic Books, 2010).

17   James Kynge, *China Shakes the World: A Titan's Rise and Troubled Future—and the Challenge for America* (New York: Houghton Mifflin, 2006); Aaron L. Friedberg, *A Contest for Supremacy: China, America, and the Struggle for Mastery in Asia* (New York: Norton, 2011); and Michael Pillsbury, *The Hundred-Year Marathon: China's Secret Strategy to Replace America as the Global Superpower* (New York: St Martin's Griffin, 2015).

18   Robert B. Zoellick, "Whither China: From Membership to Responsibility?" Remarks to National Committee on US-China Relations, New York City, 21 September 2005.

19   Scott Kennedy, "China in Global Governance: What Kind of Status Quo Power?" in *From Rule Takers to Rule Makers: The Growing Role of Chinese in Global Governance*, ed. Scott Kennedy and Shuaihua Cheng (Bloomington, Ind. and Geneva, Switzerland: Research Center for Chinese Politics and Business and the International Centre for Trade and Sustainable Development, 2012), 9–21.

20   G. John Ikenberry, *Liberal Leviathan: The Origins, Crisis, and Transformation of the American World Order* (Princeton, N.J.: Princeton University Press, 2012).

21   Susan K. Sell, *Private Power, Public Law: The Globalization of Intellectual Property Rights* (Cambridge: Cambridge University Press, 2003).

22   Jack S. Levy, "Learning and Foreign Policy: Sweeping a Conceptual Minefield," *International Organization* 48, no. 2 (Spring 1994): 279–312. Also see Jeffrey W. Knopf, "The Importance of International Learning," *Review of International Studies* 29 (2003): 185–207.

23   For a sophisticated discussion of learning that opens up the possibility of states and their representatives learning realist norms, see Adam Liff, *Constructing Power: Norms, International Conflict, and the Military Trajectories of Rising Powers* (book manuscript, 2017).

24   Blustein, *Misadventures of the Most Favored Nations*; Colin I. Bradford, Jr and Johannes F. Linn, eds, *Global Governance Reform: Breaking the Stalemate* (Washington, DC: Brookings Institution Press, 2007); Charles A.

Kupchan, *No One's World: The West, The Rising Rest, and the Coming Global Turn* (Oxford: Oxford University Press, 2012).

25 Koppell, *World Rule*; Alan S. Alexandroff, ed., *Can the World Be Governed? Possibilities for Effective Multilateralism* (Waterloo: Wilfred Laurier University Press, 2008); Kent Jones, *The Doha Blues: Institutional Crisis and Reform in the WTO* (Oxford: Oxford University Press, 2010); Deborah D. Avant, Martha Finnemore, and Susan K. Sell, *Who Governs the Globe?* (Cambridge: Cambridge University Press, 2010); Thomas G. Weiss, *Global Governance: Why? What? Whither?* (Cambridge: Polity, 2013); Thomas Hale, David Held, and Kevin Young, *Gridlock: Why Global Cooperation is Failing When We Need it Most* (Cambridge: Polity, 2013); and Rorden Wilkinson, *What's Wrong with the WTO and How to Fix It* (Cambridge: Polity, 2014).

26 For discussions of potential reforms, see Scott Kennedy and He Fan, "The United States, China and Global Governance: A New Agenda for a New Era," Research Center for Chinese Politics and Business, Indiana University, and Institute of World Economics and Politics, Chinese Academy of Social Sciences, April 2013.

27 Miles Kahler and David A. Lake, eds, *Governance in a Global Economy: Political Authority in Transition* (Princeton, N.J.: Princeton University Press, 2003).

1 China and the WTO

James Scott and Rorden Wilkinson[1]

- **The WTO as an international institution**
- **Reforming China, approaching entry to the WTO**
- **The accession process**
- **China's early WTO diplomacy**
- **Post-2008: a more aggressive China?**
- **Conclusion**

Reflecting the same tensions that are manifest in the wider literature on China's international relations, the literature on China and the World Trade Organization (WTO) is replete with worries about the People's Republic of China's (PRC) intentions. Amrita Narlikar's *New Powers: How to Become One and How to Manage Them* is a good example of a more explicit focus on the intentions debate with specific reference to the WTO.[2] Wei Liang's assessment of China's role in the international political economy similarly seeks to address short-term concerns that China is a system-challenging power while leaving the intentions debate wide open in the longer term.[3] Chin Leng Lim and Jiang Yu Wang set out specifically to challenge recent assertions that "China has 'broken cover' and ... become more 'assertive'" in the Doha Round.[4]

While the tendency to relate in some way to discussions about China's intentions is an understandable response to pressures and tendencies in the literature as well as in international politics more generally, it nonetheless gets in the way of thinking about the factors that shape China's international relations and, in the context of this chapter, its evolving engagement with the multilateral trading system. Our aim in this chapter is to set aside the intentions debate and to explore the impact of WTO membership on China's international relations. We start from the premise that international institutions—by which we mean regularized rules, norms, practices, and decision-making procedures affecting state and non-state behavior, whether manifest formally or informally—are important mediating variables in global politics.[5] They have an impact on the behavior of states and other actors by shaping and constraining what they do in given issue areas in ways that may or may not spill over into wider international politics. In the case of China, the WTO is a key mediating variable for a number of reasons:

1 trade has become a fundamental driver in China's economic growth;
2 trade is a highly institutionalized realm of international relations with myriad bilateral, regional, and global arrangements involved in its governance;
3 these systems of governance are all anchored by the multilateral rules overseen by the WTO; and
4 China is a relatively recent user of these systems, requiring it to undergo a significant learning process and to deal with countries and systems of regulation that were, and are, not favorable to state-managed enterprises and one-party political systems.

It is worth stressing that we are not privileging an institutionalist understanding of China's international relations, or suggesting that it stands out in the myriad factors that shape the PRC's, or, for that matter, any other state's behavior. We acknowledge that China's role in the international system cannot be properly understood without an appreciation of Chinese development that takes in the post-1978 reform period and the remarkable growth that this engendered. Equally, it cannot omit an appreciation of the perceptions that Chinese people have about their past and the political uses to which discourses about the past are put (domestically and internationally). Nor can such an account omit an appreciation of China's current development problematique, political contestations within the Chinese Communist Party (CCP) structure nationally as well as regionally and locally, rapidly rising inequalities (in income, health, and well-being, particularly between urban and rural areas), external perceptions of China and its intentions, the structure of the global political economy and of international politics, and the politics and political economies of those states that to significant degrees have an impact upon China. It is nonetheless also true that without a proper appreciation of the impact that the WTO has had on China (and conversely the effect of China's membership on the WTO and the other member states), aspects of its behavior, and the forces shaping that behavior, cannot be fully understood.

In pursuit of our aims, we begin by setting out some conceptual markers on international institutions generally and the peculiarities of the WTO in particular as a framework for understanding how the institutional features of the multilateral trading system have a bearing on China's trade diplomacy. The chapter then utilizes this framework in pursuit of a more complete understanding of how the institution has shaped China's capacity to act, what effects this has had on the WTO, as well as how China has sought to overcome this mediation over time. Here our purpose is not to establish causal relationships—the outcomes of operating in a given institutional context are more imprecise and multifaceted. Our aim is to set out the parameters that shape a given state's engagement with the WTO and to outline the responses that this interaction has engendered. In this final section, we offer our concluding comments.

The WTO as an international institution

The key to understanding how China's trade diplomacy is affected by its interaction with the WTO requires an appreciation of the "fit" between the organization and the PRC. This, in turn, requires an appreciation of: 1) the institutional features of the WTO, how they have developed over time and shaped the behavior of member states, as well as the institution's relationship with global configurations of power; and 2) the major developments in, and key characteristics of, the political economy of the PRC when China acceded to the WTO. In so doing, we are able to understand how the interaction of the WTO's institutional characteristics combine with the nature of China's political-economic imperatives to shape, but not strictly determine, the PRC's post-accession trade diplomacy.

In this section we piece together insights from the broader literature on historical institutionalism to help better understand the institutional effects the WTO exerts on China's participation therein. We concentrate on the relationship between the production of institutions and prevailing configurations of power, the advantages accrued to institutional innovators, the barriers to membership that new entrants face, and the "price" that is often demanded for accession. Throughout we draw on empirical examples related to the General Agreement on Tariffs and Trade (GATT) and WTO to tie the conceptual and substantive aspects of the argument together. In the following section we explore the major developments in China's political economy to the moment the PRC formally lodged its intention to begin accession negotiations, to better understand the Chinese aspects of this incongruous coming together.

In the sections thereafter we explore the way the accession process shaped Chinese diplomacy as well as the evolution of that diplomacy in the first 10 years of the PRC's WTO membership.

The broad literature on international institutions tells us that they tend to be products of, as well as reflect, the distribution of power at particular historical moments, and that their purpose is inevitably bound up with helping secure, stabilize, and perpetuate dominant orders.[6] International institutions tend to be designed in ways that at a minimum preserve, and more often than not advance, the interests of leading powers. Moreover, because institutions are designed to advance a particular set of interests and because they rely on the support of dominant powers for their survival, even allowing for compromises made along the way, institutions tend to develop in ways that are in keeping with their original aims.

This is clearly the case with the GATT/WTO. The WTO's general purpose, core principles, legal framework, and operating procedures, are all continuations, adaptations, variations, or developments of the GATT. The GATT was originally designed to: 1) kick-start a process of liberalization that would enable the United States to take advantage of the unique economic circumstances in which it found itself at the end of World War II; 2) overcome the problems that had occurred during, and the sub-optimal outcomes promised by the passage of the negotiations for an International Trade Organization (ITO);[7] and 3) assist the European powers with a measure of reconstruction. Importantly, this liberalization was targeted at reducing barriers to trade in those goods in which the United States had a comparative advantage, and that Western Europe needed to assist with reconstruction—largely manufactured, semi-manufactured, industrial, and capital goods. The GATT was not deployed to liberalize trade in agriculture, as this was politically sensitive in both the United States and Europe. Nor was it designed as a vehicle to facilitate trade-led growth for states outside the Western Alliance. What existed among the Allied powers, then, was a shared interest in the creation of an institution designed to liberalize trade in some but not all goods in a manner that spoke to the convergence of their national interests. As obvious as it might seem, the GATT was not designed to serve China's, nor for that matter other developing countries', interests.

Liberalization under the GATT was conducted through a process of exchange between the most significant trading nations in rounds of negotiations. This, in turn, ensured that the largest trading states dominated negotiations and secured disproportionate advantages for themselves while offering relatively few commercial advantages for smaller, less able, and newer acceding parties. Moreover, because liberalization occurred through a process of negotiating, areas that had not been liberalized but in which commercial advantage could be accrued could only be liberalized in exchange for new market openings. This requirement for exchange when added to the way power relations were embedded in the institution ensured that consecutive trade rounds produced ever greater asymmetries in economic opportunity.[8]

In seeking at a minimum to preserve, and more often than not to advance, the interests of dominant powers, institutions often comprise rules and procedures that establish and preserve institutional—or what Robert Keohane terms "first mover"[9]—advantages vis-à-vis later entrants. As Keohane puts it, "[s]ignificant advantages must accrue to institutional innovators, such as conferring on them control over future rules or creating barriers to entry to potential competitors. Otherwise, latecomers could free ride on the accomplishments of their predecessors."[10] Moreover, one might add, the incentives to continue to participate in an institution would erode if the advantages of institutional innovators were not somehow preserved.

In the GATT/WTO, these first mover advantages have been manifest in two ways: first, in the pursuit of a form of trade liberalization that has resulted in consecutive trade deals that disproportionately favor the leading industrial states, in terms of protecting sunset and uncompetitive industries as well as in securing market openings in emerging sectors; and second, in the embodiment of a set of procedures that put acceding states at a relative disadvantage and which have become more, rather than less, demanding as threats to core institutional advantages have increased (and perceived trade advantages eroded).

With regard to the second of these two manifestations, accession under the GATT was not, of course, uniformly less complex and demanding than accession under the WTO has been. Japan, for instance, was kept out of the GATT for nearly 10 years despite strong US sponsorship. Even when it did accede, 40 percent (then 14 states) of the contracting parties invoked Article XXXV (non-application) of the GATT allowing the withholding of trade benefits.[11] That said, in most cases former colonies were simply "grandfathered" into the GATT— that is, acceding to the General Agreement with almost no, or very few, conditions—albeit without any real say in future agenda-setting.

The absence of what Sylvia Ostry calls "detailed legalisms" in the early years of the GATT ensured that many of the institution's vague rules attained substance only through practice and were open to manipulation by the dominant contracting parties.[12] This was particularly the case with regard to accession. Initially this was seen as a "strength" of the GATT. Not only did it require acceding states to learn a host of behavioral norms that were not formally codified in the GATT, but it also enabled the dominant contracting parties to make adjustments to the interpretation of GATT rules to suit changed conditions and to maintain institutional benefits. However, as the GATT developed over time, and specifically from the Tokyo Round (1973 to 1979), pressure grew for greater transparency in GATT rules and procedures, and the contracting parties became increasingly preoccupied with codifying existing ways of operating.[13] Although this codification brought with it a greater transparency in GATT practices, it also entrenched a bias for the interests of the leading states.

The Uruguay Round continued this process of codification, but it also exacerbated the capacity of existing members to extract greater and farther-reaching concessions—including in areas formally outside the WTO's purview (so-called "WTO-plus")—from acceding states. As Simon Evenett and Carlos Primo Braga have shown, WTO-plus commitments have increasingly become a feature of accession protocols, and the specific needs of developing countries have often been dealt with insufficiently.[14] Moreover, as Lei Wang has illustrated, under WTO auspices the non-application clause has also been strengthened so that the capacity of acceding states to reciprocate non-application has been removed. As Wang explains, one consequence of this is that "the acceding party is likely to [be] blackmailed by the threat of non-application ... Therefore, it could be said that ... non-application is reinforced by the WTO provisions ... [putting the] acceding party in a particularly disadvantageous position."[15]

Surveying 61 "postcolonial" states that attained independence in the post-war era and that joined the GATT/WTO between 1951 and 2004, Mark Copelovitch and David Ohls show that the timing of accession to the GATT/WTO is dependent on the interplay of three factors: 1) the extent of trade relations with existing contracting parties/member states; 2) the existence of preferential trade agreement arrangements involving the acceding state; and 3) a state's political institutions.[16] They argue that those states with more extensive trade ties with existing contracting parties/member states were more likely to accede earlier—that is, under the less stringent GATT rules—if they were also engaged with key trading partners in bilateral or regional trade agreements and if they were governed by more democratic regimes. Thus, those states less likely to threaten core GATT interests tended to accede earlier and more expeditiously, whereas those that presented more of a challenge to the trade regime experienced slower, more complex, and more demanding accession processes. On the basis of their analysis, the relative political and economic isolation of China from the Western states that dominated the GATT, its lack of binding trade agreements with existing contracting parties, and its political institutions would have militated against early Chinese accession to the GATT had it shown an interest in becoming a contracting party.

Taken together the various facets of what we know about international institutions help us understand why things happen in the way that they do in the WTO and offer insights into the way China's diplomacy is shaped by the manner of its accession to and involvement in the institution. We know that institutional development matters. It matters who created an institution, why it was created, how it was created, what rules and practices were put in place, and the particular kinds of behavior and outcomes they give rise to, what accommodations were reached with non-dominant actors to ensure their participation, and how the institution has developed through time. Each of these factors matters because they play a role in shaping the kinds of politics, diplomacy, and governance that an institution produces. We also know that China was not involved in the creation of the GATT/ WTO (though the Kuomintang government was an original signatory to the GATT), and as such it had no influence on why and how the institution was created, what rules and practices were put in place, what accommodations were reached, and how the GATT developed over time. China sought access to the trade regime at a time, in the mid-1980s, when the membership was already well established and the shape and form of the governing institution well developed. China's economy was still in the throes of reform away from the collectivization of the Maoist period, and it was still relatively isolated, politically and economically. Moreover, China had little experience in dealing with Western institutions and had quite a different diplomatic culture. What inevitably occurred then was an incongruous coming together in which China's continued economic development would take place shaped in part by its encounter with the WTO. Thus, to better understand this coming together we need now to turn to the principal developments in China's recent political economy.

Reforming China, approaching entry to the WTO

The nature of the reforms undertaken in China since 1978 shaped the manner of its accession to the WTO, and China's accession, in turn, has had a dramatic impact on the onward process of reform in the PRC.[17] Four distinct phases can be identified in China's move toward a more open, market-driven economy.[18] Initially, the process involved large-scale industrial expansion driven by the production of mass consumer products for the domestic market facilitated by a balanced pattern of growth that encouraged rising demand.[19] Yasheng Huang identifies the origins of this broad-based growth in the gradual releasing by the CCP of controls over private activity in rural areas, creating a burgeoning entrepreneurial non-farm rural sector that resulted in fast-rising incomes for some of the poorest sectors of the population.[20] This was accompanied by state policies to raise agricultural prices, though these appear to have been of lesser importance. Whatever the combination of causes, the result was double-digit annual growth in net real income for sections of the rural population from 1979 to 1984. Poverty was reduced on a massive scale (though it was far from eradicated), inequality fell, and rising domestic demand facilitated high rates of industrialization and associated improvements in productivity.

In the wake of the 1989 Tiananmen Square demonstrations China entered a second phase of reform. Many of the earlier rural reforms were reversed as the state clamped down on the private sector. Investment fell but rising exports following the depreciation of the renminbi helped to compensate for the fall in gross domestic product (GDP).

The third period begins with Deng Xiaoping's 1992 "Southern Tour" and runs to WTO entry in 2001.[21] It saw the partial reversal of the clampdown on the private sector and increasing attention diverted toward urban areas. Growth was still high over the 1990s, but it was increasingly driven by the expansion of the urban sector and rising urban wages coupled with high rates of investment.[22] With the refocusing on the urban sector, inequalities between rural and urban populations began to expand rapidly.

The fourth phase of China's reform process dates from the immediate post-accession (that is, post-2001) period. This has been characterized by export- and investment-led growth, with household consumption (as a percentage of GDP) falling sharply, savings and investment rates increasing, and rapidly growing inequalities. The relative decline of household consumption has made China's growth highly dependent on state investment and exports to the West, creating an unsustainable imbalance and placing long-term growth in jeopardy. Two principal reasons are identified for low rates of domestic consumption (which are around half those of the United States[23]) and associated high savings rates. First, Chinese workers face an increasing burden of privatized healthcare, education, and housing as state provision has declined, increasing the need to save for future social costs. Coupled with this is the slowing down of job creation in this phase of China's development.[24]

Second, growing inequalities, particularly between rural and urban areas, mean that an increasing amount of China's wealth is concentrated among the relatively rich, who tend to have higher savings rates.[25] China's Gini coefficient has risen at a staggering rate over the last 30 years, from a relatively egalitarian 0.2 to a highly unequal 0.5— a rate of change that is unprecedented anywhere else in history.[26] China has surpassed the levels of inequality in most Latin American countries except Brazil, traditionally the regional leader in global inequality.[27] Sensitivity to this problem led to the government's refusal to publish an official estimate of China's Gini coefficient in the early 2000s[28] until 2013 when the National Bureau of Statistics at the State Council Information Office press conference disclosed the Gini coefficient from 2003 to 2012, noting that the Gini coefficient had risen to an all-time high of 0.491 in 2008 and gradually began to fall.[29] World Bank calculations differ from China's official estimates—for example, the World Bank estimates inequality was 0.49 in 2012 and China estimates 0.474.[30] The National Bureau of Statistics did publish an official estimate for the Gini coefficient in 2015 of 0.462.[31]

What we see then is that China has undertaken a period of transformation from a state-planned to a more market-led economy that has been almost four decades in the making. However, this transition has orientated the economy toward an over-reliance on export markets and has resulted in increasing inequalities between urban and rural areas. The imperative to join the WTO was in part generated by the need to stabilize market access, particularly through achieving permanent "normalized" trade relations with the United States, as well as securing further foreign market openings for Chinese exports. With this structure in mind the PRC approached WTO accession. The problem, however, was that as the accession process unfolded, and the country's economy developed over the first decade of WTO membership, its development priorities changed. Principal among its current concerns is the need to tackle inequalities and labor market inflexibilities as well as to shift toward a growth model based more on domestic consumption and less on export markets and investment. Yet, China's accession to the WTO reflected earlier prerogatives that sit awkwardly with its current needs. We examine how this has been the case in the next section.

The accession process

China had been one of the original contracting parties to the GATT, but the Taiwan-based Kuomintang government withdrew in 1949 following the Communist revolution. In 1986, the PRC sought to rejoin the GATT by taking up its original seat rather than going through a formal accession process. However, this proved unacceptable to the United States and European powers, among others, and China was forced to go through a full-blown accession process during which it was required to make new and significant concessions to existing members, many of which resulted in dramatic changes to China's existing political economy.

Until Russia's accession in December 2011, China's accession process had proven to be the most protracted in GATT/WTO history, taking 15 years to complete.[32] It was complicated by the transition in 1995 from GATT to WTO and the need to negotiate bilateral concessions on a new range of areas, notably services, non-tariff measures, and intellectual property rights, with the United States and the European Union, among others. By the time the process was complete some 60 percent of goods entered China duty-free, mostly as components to be assembled and re-exported as finished goods.[33]

Over the course of this 15-year period, the accession process waxed and waned with a notable period of intensification in negotiations from 1999 as the Chinese government sought to conclude discussions. A number of external and internal reasons underpinned the shift in intensity.[34] China's leadership was divided between those seeking greater liberalization and more conservative forces opposing further global economic integration, and the step-change in accession negotiations from 1999 onwards is best explained by the political dynamics between these factions. For the liberalizing elements, it was hoped that accession would help reform state-owned enterprises (SOEs) and raise confidence in China, thereby increasing foreign direct investment (FDI) in the wake of the Asian financial crisis. For others, liberalization threatened to hand increasing influence in China's affairs to outside parties. In the end, it was the liberalizing forces that held sway. Zhu Rongji's restructuring of the central government saw internal blockages to trade liberalization reduced and his powerbase strengthened.[35] Moreover, Zhu and his supporters sought to use WTO accession as a means of securing further reform. As Shaun Breslin argues, WTO accession was seen as "an external tool to *enforce* marketization and reform [at home], brought about by international globalizing elites wishing to lock China into multilateral trade norms and aiming to promote domestic political and economic change within China."[36]

For all the euphoria that accompanied China's entry into the WTO, the final accession protocol was highly onerous. Though in principle entitled to accede as a developing country, China's attempts to do so were blocked by the major trading powers. Instead, China was required to give concessions that far exceeded the obligations of developing countries that had previously acceded. Indeed, in some areas, China's obligations went beyond those of *developed* countries, for example in being required to eliminate all agricultural export subsidies.[37] China bound all of its tariff lines and did so at a lower average level than comparable developing countries. Tariffs on non-agricultural goods were reduced to an average of 9.2 percent (from a pre-accession level of 42.9 percent) and those on agricultural products to 15.7 percent (from 54 percent).[38] This compares to India's 34.4 percent (non-agricultural) and 113.1 percent (agricultural), and Brazil's 30.7 percent (non-agricultural) and 35.4 percent (agricultural).[39] Tariff peaks were also eliminated. Key areas that had been heavily restricted were opened up, such as banking and insurance, and policies that had previously been applied to FDI to encourage the creation of domestic productive capacity, such as domestic content requirements, were banned through the requirement to apply the Agreement on Trade-Related Investment Measures (TRIMs) without exceptions.[40] Moreover, existing WTO members were allowed to discriminate against Chinese exports for a transition period following its accession.[41]

Inevitably, the institutional design of the GATT/WTO shaped China's accession process. The lack of clear rules governing accession, particularly with regard to the concessions that can be extracted from acceding states, coupled with the asymmetries built into the rules that serve to enhance the power of the existing members (particularly the most powerful) at the expense of countries wishing to join, ensured that the dominant states were able to extract their "pound of flesh."[42] A different institutional design incorporating a more formalized process, for example one in which the concessions expected of acceding states were specified in the rules rather than it being left to existing members to extract whatever they could, would have led to a different outcome. As it was, China's entry into the WTO occurred under a highly burdensome agreement. As President Clinton said of the accession protocols, China "makes one-way concessions to open its markets to American goods, services, and farm products ... [while] the United States makes no new market access commitments."[43]

There have been a number of legacies of this process for China's trade diplomacy. First, the burdensome requirements of accession were highly unpopular domestically, being seen by some (as well as manipulated by others) as reminiscent of the "unequal treaties" forced on China by Britain in the nineteenth century,[44] or the "Twenty-One Demands" imposed by Japan in 1915.[45] As a result, it has been important for the government to be seen to be protecting the interests of the people and not caving into Western pressure, protecting agricultural producers and industrial employment.[46] This has, in turn, reduced the negotiating room the Chinese delegation has had in the Doha Development Agenda (DDA). Second, the large reductions in tariffs that were made at accession have also restricted China's current negotiating space. China's bound rates (averaging 10 percent) and applied rates (averaging 9.6 percent) are very close, ensuring that any deal made in the subsequent trade round, under the DDA, would "bite" immediately into applied tariffs. This is unlike most other developing countries, the majority of which have a large amount of "water" (that is, the gap between the rate at which it is applied and the ceiling at which it is bound, the maximum rate that could be applied) in their tariff schedules. For these two reasons China has been left with little negotiation room. Unsurprisingly, it sought, in the early stages of the DDA, to carve out a new category of "recently acceded members" (RAMs) in an effort to resist taking on further liberalization.

The picture that emerges is that the barriers to new entrants in the GATT/WTO rules shaped China's accession process, which in turn has had an impact on Chinese diplomacy within the DDA.[47] This, in turn, has been refracted back into the PRC's domestic political economy. It has also had serious international consequences, to which China has had to respond. China's stance on the issue of RAMs, for instance, has generated much negative commentary and has been deemed tantamount to a refusal to participate in the DDA.[48] This has ensured that the PRC has had to respond to such accusations (and the negative images upon which they feed).[49] So, in addition to being better understood within the context of the institutional framework embodied by the WTO and the way in which this shapes the interaction among members, China's stance on new trade concessions also needs to be understood as encouraging a particular kind of diplomatic behavior engendered by a complex of global political and institutional factors. Nonetheless, what is clear is that the way the WTO and the PRC came together, and the experience of and outcomes generated by the accession process, had a marked impact on China's trade diplomacy. The next two sections explore how, from this basis, China's diplomacy has evolved over the course of its first decade of WTO membership.

China's early WTO diplomacy

China's participation in the WTO post-accession can be split into two periods. In the early years (2001 to 2008) China generally kept what looked from the outside to have been a "low profile"—though this relative quiet belies much activity, including the building of the largest trade mission to the WTO, and a steep learning process. What looks like a low profile comes from China's reticence to take the lead on any issue or attempt to rewrite the rules in any way.[50] The only areas in which China stood out were over Taiwan and the Transitional Review Mechanism (TRM). With regard to the first, the PRC put pressure on the WTO Secretariat to downgrade Taiwan's membership status to an "office of permanent representative" rather than "permanent mission." This pressure resulted in the then WTO Director-General Supachai Panitchpakdi approaching the Taiwanese delegation with a request to change its membership status, which was inevitably refused.[51] This, in turn, resulted in the PRC's refusal to negotiate with Taiwan, though in subsequent years this stance has softened and a number of official consultations between the two delegations have taken place, with the delegations associating freely in Geneva.[52] That said, tensions continue to emerge at times. For instance, in 2007 Taiwan briefly blocked the appointment of China's Zhang Yuejiao to the Appellate Body, claiming that this would compromise its impartiality.

The second issue on which China has taken a particular stance was over the review mechanism put in place to monitor the implementation of its accession agreements. The TRM was highly unpopular within China and caused considerable resentment, invoking "images of foreigners, especially the United States, snooping into China's affairs."[53] The TRM also served as a nagging reminder of the high price China paid for accession.[54] The Chinese government resented the singling-out for special treatment embodied in the TRM process and other areas of the accession protocol and resisted its requirements, complying with the letter of the law on the TRM issue but no more. As a senior Chinese delegate put it to us, China's delegation used the ambiguities of the text to exercise a form of passive resistance. Since the TRM articles were unclear about whether China needed to make a formal written response to questions raised, the Chinese delegation chose only to respond orally and not to provide a text.

Inevitably, the TRM process was at times acrimonious. As Margaret Pearson notes, "[i]n one meeting, a senior member of the PRC delegation … reportedly 'made a pounding-the-table type of speech,' directed at the United States that linked the TRM process to 'neo-imperialism'".[55] Though China resented greatly the TRM and considered it unnecessary, the United States and the European Union invested considerable resources in the process. By 2002, the United States had 53 full-time staff serving in China, Geneva, and Washington working exclusively on

China's WTO compliance.[56] It was with considerable relief on the Chinese side that the final TRM review was undertaken in 2010, after which China became part of the normal WTO Trade Policy Review Mechanism. The experience nonetheless generated "bad feelings" among China's trade delegation and the resentments generated have certainly not been forgotten.[57]

Beyond these issues, China maintained a relatively low profile compared with other large developing countries (particularly India and Brazil) during the immediate post-accession years. It would be a mistake, however, to assume that China was not actively engaged. In 2003 China made the third largest number of written submissions to the WTO. China joined the G20 coalition that was created around the Cancún Ministerial Conference—though it has offered only support, rather than leadership, to the coalition. China was initially conciliatory as a defendant and reluctant as a complainant in the Dispute Settlement Mechanism, choosing to settle cases bilaterally rather than proceed to a panel,[58] though this has since changed with China becoming more active.[59]

China's initial period of relative "quietude" was perhaps to be expected of an initial period and a process of institutional learning and adaptation. It was perhaps also to be expected that as China became more familiar with WTO practices, it would take on a more active role. It is this move to a more active phase that has prompted suggestions in the literature that China has become more aggressive and begun to show more obviously its real "intentions." It is to this more "active" period that we now turn.

Post-2008: a more aggressive China?

The current preoccupation with China's "intentions" has inevitably led to perceptions that the PRC is no longer a passive and conciliatory player but a disruptive one. Indeed, perceptions of this change in Chinese diplomacy are seen by some as a significant element in the inability of members to reach an all-encompassing deal in the DDA. As Fred Bergsten, a key proponent of this view, argues:

> China's refusal to contribute positively to the Doha Round ... has all but ensured the talks' failure. Beijing has declared that it should have no liberalization obligations whatsoever and has invented a new category of WTO membership ("recently acceded members") to justify its recalcitrance. Such a stance by a major trading power is akin to abstention and has practically guaranteed that the Doha negotiations will go nowhere.[60]

Bergsten's view is close to recent rhetoric from the Office of the United States Trade Representative (USTR), the Department of State, and, to a lesser extent, the European Union trade missions. For the United States, not only is greater liberalization by China required to secure its agreement to any deal negotiated under the DDA, but also further Chinese concessions form a core part of what the US perceives as the "development" content of the round.[61] Here, the institutional aspects of the WTO loom large for China. Its position as a RAM is the consequence of its accession process, but the dynamics of a trade negotiation, particularly one that is at the kind of critical juncture at which the Doha Round finds itself, are such that China is being pressured to concede. This, in turn, shapes China's diplomacy. Two examples are used below to explore how the WTO has shaped Chinese diplomacy and given rise to the perception of China becoming more assertive: 1) the WTO's negotiation process and the July 2008 mini-ministerial; and 2) the issue of RAMs.

The negotiation process and the 2008 mini-ministerial

To understand China's role in the negotiation process it is worth restating how WTO negotiations are conducted. The WTO carried forward the GATT practice of trade negotiations being undertaken within small groups comprising the most significant trading nations. Agreements reached within these groups are then expanded out to less significant members in a series of "concentric circles,"[62] or via what Gilbert Winham terms a "pyramidal" system.[63] This institutional practice places certain key states at the epicenter of negotiations and ensures they are able to have a direct influence on agendas while those on the sidelines are less able to influence the process.

Negotiations in the Doha Round are generally held to have peaked in the post-Hong Kong Ministerial Conference (2005) period. From 2006 through 2007 the core negotiating group was the G6, comprising the United States, the European Union, Japan, India, Brazil, and Australia.[64] When this group failed to find a compromise, the core was reduced further in 2007 to the G4 when Japan and Australia were sidelined. However, the DDA came closest to a major agreement at a mini-ministerial meeting held between 21 and 29 July 2008, at which point the round collapsed. The mini-ministerial involved the G7—the United States, European Union, Japan, Australia, India, Brazil, and China. Crucially, this was the first time China had been involved in the core negotiating group. Before this, China had participated in the standard negotiating group meetings but not in the elite small group, so-called "Green

Room" sessions. It is unsurprising, then, that upon entry into a core negotiating group, China should adopt a more active and assertive role. Yet, this more assertive stance—the product of WTO negotiation practices—did not translate into the disruptive role Bergsten and others have argued, nor did it result in the collapse of the DDA. Indeed, a more detailed examination of the role played by China in the negotiations suggests that claims of a move to greater assertiveness are unfounded.

The July 2008 mini-ministerial collapsed over the issue of the Special Safeguard Mechanism (SSM)—an element of the agriculture agreement that would, if agreed, provide developing countries with the capacity to raise tariffs if they were faced with a surge in imports that threatened the livelihoods of rural producers. The principal division was between the United States (which wanted higher thresholds before the SSM could be used and lower permitted tariff increases) and India (which wanted a more generous mechanism). China was blamed for intransigence and standing with India against a deal, both by the US delegates and by the media.[65]

However, our interviews with delegates from all of the trade missions involved, as well as with senior figures in the WTO Secretariat, suggest that China did not simply support India's position. Rather, China attempted to broker a deal between the positions of India and the United States. When these two would not make concessions, China made it known that it would accept any compromise that the United States and India came to, and left them to it. Yet, India and the United States failed to reach an agreement, and the talks broke down in acrimony. As such, the collapse is less attributable to China and rather more attributable to India and the United States. Indeed, Kamal Nath (India's then Minister of Commerce and Industry) is reputed to have been highly pleased about India being blamed for the collapse as it would assist him in what were up-and-coming domestic elections.[66] Meanwhile, senior WTO officials have suggested that the United States may have actually sought to engineer a collapse over the SSM to prevent the discussions moving to cotton,[67] an area in which the United States would find it impossible to offer the kind of concessions being demanded by the Cotton Four (Benin, Burkina Faso, Chad, and Mali), and which are strongly supported among WTO members.[68] China's role was, by contrast, more compromising over the SSM issue.

This is not to say that China's position was not, and does not remain, an obstacle to finding a comprehensive agreement. Like the United States, there were other issues, such as non-agricultural market access (NAMA), that it was more concerned with and may have proven unwilling to compromise over had the negotiations not collapsed over the SSM first. The industrial countries blame the impasse on the emerging countries not offering enough (particularly in NAMA); the emerging countries blame the impasse on the industrial countries demanding too much and not offering enough (particularly in agriculture). There is little to be gained here debating which interpretation is correct, and we do not intend to comment either way. Rather, the point here is to elucidate the role played by institutional factors, notably the informal practices and procedures surrounding the process of negotiating within the WTO, in forming a perception of China as becoming more assertive in 2008.

The RAMs

Linked to the perception of China being overly assertive and intransigent is the issue of RAMs. In the quote above, Bergsten explicitly identifies this issue as signifying a destructive role being played by China in the round. However, our focus on the institutional aspects of China's involvement in the WTO sheds a different light on the matter. As noted above, the concessions extracted from China during accession were highly onerous. Furthermore, accession was formally completed at the Doha Ministerial Conference itself—that is, simultaneously with the launch of the DDA. The DDA was given a completion date of "no later than 1 January 2005."[69] Had the DDA proceeded to this timeline, China would have found itself required to implement DDA liberalization while still implementing the later stages of its accession protocols. Reflecting this, my interviews with senior members of the Chinese delegation shared that China's early position emphasized the importance of granting RAMs lesser commitments characterized by "four Ls": that the cuts expected of them should be "lesser," "longer," "lower," and "later" than other members. This position flowed from the unprecedented scale and scope of commitments China undertook at accession and the fact that new concessions within the DDA would bite immediately into China's applied tariffs.

China received little support for its position on RAMs, and the issue became less important as the negotiations repeatedly missed deadlines. Yet, rather than insisting on "abstaining" from the negotiations, China showed flexibility in its position, in effect dropping "lesser" and "lower" from its position. This entailed accepting that China would have to implement the full extent of agreed tariff cuts, albeit with a longer implementation period.[70] Though some RAMs have been permitted to abstain from making reductions beyond their accession commitments in NAMA, China was excluded from this list. While the texts—that is, the documents that represent progress so far in the round and which are based on the status of the negotiations in July 2008—are "Chair's texts" and do not necessarily have the support of all members, China has indicated that it accepts them and is willing to proceed on that basis. As such, China's position is that it will contribute tariff cuts to the round in line with all other developing countries, from bound tariff rates that are substantially lower than other developing countries, with only a three-year extended implementation period. This cannot be characterized as "abstention" from the round, to use Bergsten's phrase. Moreover, it is an area in which China has become *more amenable* to compromise in recent years rather than more aggressive.

These two examples—the willingness of China to make concessions on the issue of RAMs and China's role in the July 2008 mini-ministerial—illustrate the impact institutional factors have played in shaping China's diplomacy in the WTO. They show that China has played an active and broadly constructive role while being unwilling to meet the demands made by the United States and the European Union. The early years of China's membership in the WTO were characterized by a period of learning institutional practices and procedures. As the PRC became involved in the small group meetings, it inevitably became more assertive. There is little to suggest, however, that this represented a turn toward greater intransigence and belligerence, or that China has been uniquely unwilling to compromise among those core countries. China has, nonetheless, suffered at the hands of analysts who have been quick, as Breslin argues, to "filter ... actual experiences of how China acts" through the sieve of the intentions debate and project them as proof of a more assertive turn.[71] Such interpretations can be avoided by a greater appreciation of how the WTO shapes its members' behavior.

Conclusion

What we see, then, is that the WTO's institutional practices, procedures, and culture have influenced China's diplomatic style. The WTO grew out of the GATT and adopted all the GATT's practices and procedures. When China acceded in 2001, the WTO, though only six years old, had more than 50 years of institutional history structuring how its diplomacy takes place. China's ability to influence these practices and procedures was, and is, highly circumscribed. The early years following accession constituted a period in which China sought to learn the rules of the game and integrate itself into WTO processes.

During this period of "learning the WTO ropes" China was understandably relatively quiet, though there were a few issues on which it was more forthright. The first was the issue of Taiwan and ensuring that it was not referred to as an independent country within official WTO literature. This, of course, is a standard feature of China's foreign policy. Second, China initially resisted the demands for further liberalization in the DDA, using the concept of the RAM, though it subsequently changed this position. We also see that China's diplomacy has been affected by the broader global political economy setting, and its own economic rise therein. China's spectacular economic growth has propelled it rapidly to a more prominent position within global politics, and has led to a nervous and at times hostile reaction from other nations, particularly elements in the United States; however, it has also reinforced adherence to a path of economic reform and development that is now approaching its limits.

China's negotiation position within the DDA has also been affected by a number of domestic factors. First, the accession process itself has had an effect on attitudes toward the WTO. Though the WTO is popular among significant sections of the Chinese people, particularly those who have benefited from the process of reform and who associate the reform process with requirements for WTO accession, for others the onerous conditions attached to accession and the discriminatory elements they contained were inequitable and humiliating. This dual, dichotomized reaction to accession perhaps reflects the dichotomized effect of reform in which some segments of society have benefited enormously while others have seen little gain or are indeed left worse off. The CCP is responding to this, cognizant of the implications for social order, for example through the introduction of a greater social safety net. Nonetheless, with the reform process linked in many people's minds to WTO accession and increasing levels of inequality and "losers" from opening, the Chinese government must be mindful of the domestic audience and needs to be seen as protecting China's interests strongly against the demands of the West.

The accession also placed China in an almost unique position among developing countries in having almost no water in its tariffs. Any likely DDA package will bring about little new market access into India or Brazil, for instance, because of the large disparity between bound and applied rates[72]—to which the outcome of the December 2013 Bali Ministerial Conference amply testifies.[73] For China, by contrast, any deal will immediately bite into applied rates. This has played a role in China's initial reluctance to accept any further liberalization on top of that already brought about by accession. Somewhat paradoxically, the high degree of liberalization demanded by the European Union and United States as payment for entering the WTO may have helped to prevent further market-opening agreements and led the DDA to an impasse.

The oft-used phrase that "all trade politics is domestic politics" is clearly at work with regard to China's relationship with the WTO. Yet this phrase portrays an overly one-directional interaction in which domestic politics constrains and shapes behavior and diplomacy within the WTO.

This chapter has highlighted the complex, reciprocal relationship between domestic factors affecting the WTO, and the WTO as an institution in turn affecting its member states. China's current economic path, its domestic politics, and national diplomacy have all been affected by WTO accession and subsequent membership. Moreover, this has occurred as a product of the peculiarities and unique characteristics of the WTO. This is not to privilege, or exaggerate, the impact of the WTO—ultimately China's political economy is driven by its domestic political and economic circumstances, US politics, and the exigencies of global capitalism, among other factors. However, to understand China's behavior—for example, the perceived shift around 2008 in its diplomacy from passive to more assertive—an appreciation of how the institutional character of the WTO impacts its member states is necessary. China's continued economic development and the politics surrounding its trade relations, particularly with the United States, will have a strong impact on global economic fortunes over the coming decades. It is therefore critical that the role played by the WTO in mediating these processes continues to be explored.

Notes

1 We are grateful to the Research Center for Chinese Politics and Business at Indiana University and the Henry Luce Foundation for their help in financing the research for this chapter. The analysis draws from a program of targeted interviews conducted with key individuals working in diplomatic missions and international organizations based in Geneva, Switzerland. These interviews were set up, and preliminary conversations conducted, between January and April 2011, with the interviews themselves taking place during May and June 2011. Follow-up meetings designed to fill in any gaps and try out some of the ideas contained herein were held in September 2011. The results of this research were then compared against a critical examination of the extant literature. We are particularly grateful to Bernard Kuiten, Patrick Low, Victor do Prado, Faizel Ismail, Sun Zhenyu, Zhang Xiangchen, Zhang Wei, Rashid Kaukab, and Yonov Fredrick Agah for their kind assistance, time, and effort, as well as to the many other people we spoke with while researching but who wish not to be identified for reasons of anonymity. Responsibility for what follows nonetheless lies with us.

2 Amrita Narlikar, *New Powers: How to Become One and How to Manage Them* (London: Hurst and Company, 2010).

3 Wei Liang, "China: Globalization and the Emergence of a New Status Quo Power?" *Asian Perspective* 31, no. 4 (2007): 125–149.

4 Chin Leng Lim and Jiang Yu Wang, "China and the Doha Development Agenda," *Journal of World Trade* 44, no. 6 (2010): 1309–1331.

5 We prefer the term "mediating" rather than the more common "intervening." For benchmark works on international institutions see Robert O. Keohane, "International Institutions: Two Approaches," *International Studies Quarterly* 32, no. 4 (1988): 379–396; and Barbara Koremenos, Charles Lipson, and Duncan Snidal, "The Rational Design of International Institutions," *International Organization* 55, no. 4 (2001): 761–799.

6 Robert O. Keohane, *International Institutions and State Power* (Boulder, Col.: Westview Press, 1989); Hans J. Morgenthau, *Politics Among Nations: The Struggle for Power and Peace* (New York: McGraw-Hill, 1993), Revised by Kenneth Thompson, 299–307; Craig Murphy, *International Organization and Industrial Change: Global Governance Since 1850* (Cambridge: Polity, 1994), 2; John Gerard Ruggie, "Third Try at World Order: America and Multilateralism after the Cold War," *Political Science Quarterly* 109, no. 4 (1994): 553–570; and Robert W. Cox, *Approaches to World Order* (Cambridge: Cambridge University Press, 1996), 99.

7 Herbert Feis, "The Geneva Proposal for an International Trade Charter," *International Organization* 2, no. 1 (1948): 51; Clair Wilcox, *A Charter for World Trade* (London: Macmillan, 1949), 47–49.

8 Sylvia Ostry, *The Post-Cold War Trading System* (London: University of Chicago Press, 1997); Rorden Wilkinson, *The WTO: Crisis and the Governance of Global Trade* (London and New York: Routledge, 2006).

9 Robert O. Keohane, *Power and Governance in a Partially Globalized World* (London and New York: Routledge, 2002), 253.

10 Keohane, *Power and Governance*, 253.

11 Gardner Patterson, *Discrimination in International Trade: The Policy Issues 1945–1965* (Princeton, N.J.: Princeton University Press, 1966), 276.

12 Ostry, *The Post-Cold War Trading System*, 89.

13 L. Alan Winters, "The Road to Uruguay," *The Economic Journal* 100, no. 403 (1990): 1288–1303.

14 Simon J. Evenett and Carlos A. Primo Braga, "WTO Accession: Moving the Goalposts," in *Trade, Doha, and Development: A Window into the Issues*, ed. Richard Newfarmer (Washington, DC: World Bank, 2006), 231–245.

15 Lei Wang, "Non-Application Issues in the GATT and WTO," *Journal of World Trade* 28, no. 2 (1994): 71–72.

16 Mark S. Copelovitch and David Ohls, "Trade, Institutions, and the Timing of GATT/WTO Accession in Post-Colonial States,"*Review of International Organizations* 7, no. 1 (2012): 81–107.

17 On China's reforms, see among many others, Nicholas R. Lardy, *Foreign Trade and Economic Reform in China 1978–1990* (Cambridge and New York: Cambridge University Press, 1992); and Lowell Dittmer and Guoli Liu, *China's Deep Reform: Domestic Politics in Transition* (Lanham, Md.: Rowman & Littlefield Publishers, 2006).

18 Andong Zhu and David M. Kotz, "The Dependence of China's Economic Growth on Exports and Investment," *Review of Radical Political Economics* 43, no. 1 (2011): 9–32.

19 Zhu and Kotz, "The Dependence," 14; Dic Lo and Yu Zhang, "Making Sense of China's Economic Transformation," *Review of Radical Political Economics* 43, no. 1 (2011): 35–55.

20 Yasheng Huang, *Capitalism with Chinese Characteristics: Entrepreneurship and the State* (Cambridge: Cambridge University Press, 2008), 55–56.
21 Zhu and Kotz, "The Dependence of China's Economic Growth on Exports and Investment," 20–22.
22 Zhu and Kotz, "The Dependence of China's Economic Growth on Exports and Investment," 17–20.
23 Zhu and Kotz, "The Dependence of China's Economic Growth on Exports and Investment," 22.
24 Dorothy J. Solinger, "Chinese Urban Jobs and the WTO," *The China Journal* 49 (2003): 61–87.
25 Peilin Li, "China's New Stage of Development," *China: An International Journal* 9, no. 1 (2011): 137–138.
26 Li, "China's New Stage of Development," 137.
27 Gabriel Wildau and Tom Mitchell, "China Income Inequality Among World's Worst," *Financial Times*, 14 January 2016, www.ft.com/content/3c521faa-baa6-11e5-a7cc-280dfe875e28.
28 *Caixin Online*, "Government Refuses to Release Gini Coefficient" (2012), www.marketwatch.com/story/china-refuses-to-release-gini-coefficient-2012-01-18.
29 "National Bureau of Statistics for the First Time Published Ten Years of Gini Coefficients Data," State Council Information Office of the People's Republic of China, 19 February 2013, www.scio.gov.cn/zhzc/2/32764/Document/1421797/1421797.htm.
30 "National Bureau of Statistics for the First Time Published Ten Years of Gini Coefficients Data," State Council Information Office of the People's Republic of China, 19 February 2013, www.scio.gov.cn/zhzc/2/32764/Document/1421797/1421797.htm; Gabriel Wildau and Tom Mitchell, "China Income Inequality Among World's Worst," *Financial Times*, 14 January 2016, www.ft.com/content/3c521faa-baa6-11e5-a7cc-280dfe875e28.
31 "The National Economy is Running Steady, Stable, and Good," National Bureau of Statistics, 19 January 2016, www.stats.gov.cn/tjsj/zxfb/201601/t20160119_1306083.html.
32 See Heike Holbig and Robert Ash, eds, *China's Accession to the World Trade Organization: National and International Perspectives* (New York: RoutledgeCurzon, 2002).
33 Shaun Breslin, "Reforming China's Embedded Socialist Compromise: China and the WTO," *Global Change, Peace and Security* 15, no. 3 (2003): 213–230, 214.
34 See Wang Yong, "China's Stakes in WTO Accession: The Internal Decision-making Process," in *China's Accession to the World Trade Organization: National and International Perspectives*, ed. Heike Holbig and Robert Ash (New York: RoutledgeCurzon, 2002), 20–40; Hui Feng, *The Politics of China's Accession to the World Trade Organization: The Dragon Goes Global* (London and New York: Routledge, 2006).
35 Yong, "China's Stakes in WTO Accession," 27.
36 Breslin, "Reforming China's Embedded Socialist Compromise," 214.
37 C. Fred Bergsten, Bates Gill, Nicholas R. Lardy, and Derek Mitchell, *China: The Balance Sheet: What the World Needs to Know about the Emerging Superpower* (New York: Public Affairs, 2006), 36.
38 WTO, "Statement by HE Mr Bo Xilai, Minister of Commerce: Hong Kong Ministerial Conference," WT/MIN(05)/ST/59, 14 December 2005;

WTO Tariff Profiles, available for each member country from www.wto.org/english/thewto_e/whatis_e/tif_e/org6_e.htm.

39 WTO Tariff Profiles available at http://stat.wto.org/TariffProfile/WSDBTariffPFHome.aspx?Language=E.

40 Robert Z. Lawrence, "China and the Multilateral Trading System," in *China and the New World Economy*, ed. Barry Eichengreen, Yung Chul Park, and Charles Wyplosz (Oxford: Oxford University Press, 2008), 145–167, 148.

41 WTO, "Accession of the People's Republic of China: Decision of 10 November 2001," 23 November 2001, WT/L/432.

42 This is the term used by one of our interviewees, an ambassador from a large developing country.

43 William Clinton, "Expanding Trade, Projecting Values: Why I'll Fight to Make China's Trade Status Permanent," *The New Democrat*, 1 January 2000.

44 Laura J. Loppacher and William A. Kerr, "Integrating China's Biotechnology Industry into Global Knowledge Creation," *Journal of World Intellectual Property* 7, no. 4 (2005): 549–562, 550.

45 Yong, "China's Stakes in WTO Accession," 33.

46 Lim and Wang, "China and the Doha Development Agenda," 1320; Narlikar, *New Powers*, 96.

47 Lim and Wang, "China and the Doha Development Agenda," 1321.

48 See, for example, Fred C. Bergsten, "A Partnership of Equals: How Washington Should Respond to China's Economic Challenge," *Foreign Affairs* 87, no. 4 (2008): 57–69, 60.

49 See Zhenyu Sun, "The Doha Round and the Future of the WTO," in *Trade, Poverty, Development: Getting Beyond the WTO's Doha Deadlock*, ed. Rorden Wilkinson and James Scott (Abingdon and New York: Routledge, 2012), 141–154.

50 Lim and Wang, "China and the Doha Development Agenda," 1309; authors' interviews.

51 See Margaret M. Pearson, "China in Geneva: Lessons from China's Early Years in the World Trade Organization," in *New Directions in the Study of China's Foreign Policy*, ed. Alastair I. Johnston and Robert S. Ross (Stanford, Calif.: Stanford University Press, 2006), 242–275, 249; Lawrence, "China and the Multilateral Trading System," 152.

52 Pearson, "China in Geneva," 248; and authors' interviews.

53 Pearson, "China in Geneva," 250.

54 Lawrence, "China and the Multilateral Trading System," 153.

55 Pearson, "China in Geneva," 251.

56 Paulo D. Farah, "Five Years of China's WTO Membership: EU and US Perspectives on China's Compliance with Transparency Commitments and the Transitional Review Mechanism," *Legal Issues of Economic Integration* 33, no. 3 (2006): 263–304, 289.

57 Pearson, "China in Geneva," 251; and authors' interviews.

58 Marcia Don Harpaz, "Sense and Sensibilities of China and WTO Dispute Settlement," *Journal of World Trade* 44, no. 6 (2010): 1155–1186.

59 Lim and Wang, "China and the Doha Development Agenda," 1324; and Wenhua Ji and Cui Huang, "China's Experience in Dealing with WTO Dispute Settlement: A Chinese Perspective," *Journal of World Trade* 45, no. 1 (2011): 1–37.

60 Bergsten, "A Partnership of Equals," 60.
61 See Jonathan Lynn, "US Accuses China of Blocking Talks on Doha Round," *Reuters*, 24 June 2010; and "Deputy USTR: US Making Little Real Headway on its Key Doha Demands," *Inside US Trade*, 30 March 2011.
62 Aileen Kwa, *Power Politics in the WTO: Updated 2nd Edition* (Bangkok, Thailand: Focus on the Global South, 2003), 36.
63 Gilbert Winham, *International Trade and the Tokyo Round Negotiation* (Princeton, N.J.: Princeton University Press, 1986), 174–175.
64 For a history of the DDA negotiation process see *Bridges Weekly Trade News Digest*, available at www.ictsd.org. For the detail that follows, see particularly volume 10 issue 27, volume 11 issues 18 and 20, and volume 12 issue 27. For detail on the July 2008 Ministerial see also South Centre, "The WTO's Mini-Ministerial of July 2008: Agriculture, NAMA, Process Issues and the Road Ahead," Analytical Note, SC/TDP/AN/MA/AG (2008); and Paul Blustein, "The Nine-Day Misadventure of the Most Favored Nations: How the WTO's Doha Round Negotiations Went Awry in July 2008," Brookings Institution, 2008, www.brookings.edu/research/a rticles/2008/12/05-trade-blustein.
65 "US: China, India Threaten Doha Round of WTO Talks," *Associated Press*, 28 July 2008; "WTO: China Throws Up Barrier to Doha Agreement," *The Guardian*, 28 July 2008: 21.
66 Authors' interviews.
67 Authors' interviews; see also Blustein, "The Nine-Day Misadventure."
68 See Donna Lee, "Poverty and Cotton in the DDA," in *Trade, Poverty, Development: Getting Beyond the WTO's Doha Deadlock*, ed. Rorden Wilkinson and James Scott (Abingdon and New York: Routledge, 2012), 72–90.
69 WTO, "Doha Ministerial Declaration," WT/MIN(01)/DEC/1, 20 November 2001, paragraph 45.
70 See WTO, "Textual Report By the Chairman, Ambassador Luzius Wasescha, On the State of Play of the NAMA Negotiations," 21 April, TN/MA/W/103/Rev.3/Add.1 (2011), paragraphs 18–20. The RAM measures in the agricultural texts do not apply to China, as they merely reduce the extent of cuts expected in Aggregate Measure of Support (AMS), while China has no AMS binding. See WTO, "Negotiating Group on Agriculture, Report by the Chairman, H.E. Mr. David Walker, to the Trade Negotiations Committee," 21 April 2011, TN/AG/26. China's current AMS is listed as zero—see WTO, "Committee on Agriculture: Notification: China," 24 March 2010, G/AG/N/CHN/17.
71 Shaun Breslin, "The Soft Notion of China's 'Soft Power'," *Asia Programme Paper*, ASP PP 2011/03 (London: Chatham House, 2011).
72 See James Scott, "South-South Trade and North-South Politics: Emerging Powers and the Reconfiguration of Global Governance," BWPI Working Paper 131/2010 (Manchester: University of Manchester, 2010).
73 Rorden Wilkinson, Erin Hannah, and James Scott, "The WTO in Bali: What MC9 Means for the Doha Development Agenda and Why it Matters," *Third World Quarterly* 35, no. 6 (2014): 1032–1050.

2 Being in the WTO

China's learning and growing confidence

Wang Yong

- **Early capacity building: China as a learner of WTO rules**
- **Government-led defense of Chinese interests**
- **Increasing the proactiveness of industry in defense of their interests**
- **Puzzled learning: growing concerns about WTO rules**
- **Learning to lead in the WTO**
- **Conclusion**

China's accession to the World Trade Organization (WTO) has brought forth tremendous changes to the country in the 15 years since it joined. Emerging as the "workshop of the world," China has become a vital part of the global economy. In addition, China has become an important player in the WTO and the Doha Round, and is exercising growing influence on the multilateral trading system. Whereas the previous chapter focused on how the WTO as an institution shaped Chinese trade policy and participation in the global trading system, this chapter will examine how the nature of state–society relations in China affects its ability to learn the WTO's rules and be more effective in utilizing those rules to safeguard its trade interests.

There are several forms of learning. One involves the physical effort of capacity building so that China is better able to comply with its commitments. Learning is also part of a process for China to be able to defend its interests more effectively, first in terms of defense against trade protectionism by other trading partners, and second in terms of seeking legal protection of domestic industry based on WTO rules. In the time since joining the WTO, China, with relatively weak industry associations, has depended on government-led initiatives to carry forward the above-mentioned objectives of learning. At the same time, membership in the WTO itself has forced an adjustment of this situation, and Chinese industry is gradually becoming more proactive.

China's WTO-related learning has evolved from a government-led defense of Chinese interests to a proactive industry-led defense of their interests. This has involved both capacity building and ultimately increasing identification with the WTO rules themselves. After reviewing the different dimensions of China's learning process, we will discuss the implications of this case for China's role in global governance more generally.

Early capacity building: China as a learner of WTO rules

The constraining power of WTO commitments is significant, and during the early years of its membership, the Chinese government made a great effort to comply with those WTO rules that are regarded as a yardstick to judge if policy proposals are compatible with international norms.

Modifying old laws and regulations to ensure their compatibility with WTO rules was perceived as part of learning new rules and capability building. First, harmonizing Chinese laws and regulations with WTO rules and the accession protocol was regarded as a great success by government officials insofar as it demonstrated China's commitment to meeting the obligations of a responsible member of the WTO. In order to adapt to the accession commitments, the Chinese government modified components of various laws and regulations incompatible with WTO rules, and accelerated the pace of legislation to make new laws and regulations in the fields of trade and market disciplines. By abolishing, revising, and promulgating over 300 laws and regulations at the national level and 190,000 regulations at the local level, China showed its commitment to integrating itself with the global economy and embracing the WTO principles of non-discrimination, transparency, and rule of law.[1]

Promoting the knowledge of WTO rules among government officials and the general public also became an important part of learning. China's Ministry of Foreign Trade and Economic Cooperation (MOFTEC), which in 2008 was renamed the Ministry of Commerce (MOFCOM), played a major role in offering training and education to officials and the public on WTO rules. In order to promote the awareness of China's accession commitments and WTO rules, MOFTEC published a series of explanatory volumes titled *The Knowledge of China's WTO Accession Reader*, to introduce WTO rules to the general public. However, the leaders recognized that only if the government officials understood the WTO rules adequately could the country ensure that its commitments would be realized in practice. Therefore, the Chinese government provided systematic training to cadres of different levels, from those in charge of economic affairs to the senior leaders. From 2001 to 2006, 38 training programs were held and were attended by more than 6,400 officials. After joining the WTO, the Chinese central government organized a large number of training classes for senior provincial and municipal leaders to help them understand WTO rules and their implications for Chinese policy and practices.[2]

The Chinese government also promoted knowledge about WTO rules among businesses and industry. The negotiation of China's accession to the WTO had attracted a great deal of attention from Chinese businesses, and for understandable reasons, some of them expressed their concerns about the impact of the WTO commitment. To address these concerns, the Chinese government offered the business community training programs to show them how they could take advantage of the WTO fair-trade rules to defend themselves from the impact of opening the Chinese market. The Chinese government carefully designed training programs tailored to the specific conditions and interests of different industries. All in all, the central and local governments provided more than 400 WTO rules training courses and seminars to local businesses and organization leaders. After providing general overviews, the government-led training programs shifted their focus to the needs of specific industries and local professionals by offering special seminars and training sessions to support research institutes and experts, and sponsored them to carry out special research projects.[3]

International assistance played a very important role in the first stage of WTO-related capacity building in China's public education campaign. This included bilateral aid projects and technical support programs from the WTO Secretariat, all geared toward helping China adapt to the challenges of WTO accession and be in a better position to engage in WTO multilateral negotiations. By 2006, at least three important bilateral aid projects had been carried forward: 1) the Canadian Agricultural Project (2003–2008) was designed to improve the quality of China's agricultural products and help build a food safety and standard system in line with WTO agricultural rules; 2) the European Union (EU) Capacity-Building Project (2004–2010) offered training and technical support to trade-related government departments, social organizations, enterprises, and research institutions to help them enhance their understanding of WTO rules; and 3) the US Long-Distance Education and Training Project (2003–2004) provided highly interactive WTO training courses to Chinese government agencies.[4]

To carry forward such a huge education and capacity-building movement, the Chinese leadership kept two objectives in mind. The first was to meet the country's WTO accession commitments and demonstrate that China was a "responsible member" of the international community. The other, more important goal was to serve the strategy of implementing market reforms and recover the momentum lost in the pre-WTO accession period.

Government-led defense of Chinese interests

The most important change since China joined the WTO has taken place in the relationship among state, market, and society. WTO accession ushered in a brand-new era of China's reform and opening-up strategy. As some analysts predicted accurately at the moment of the accession, joining the WTO would produce a mechanism of reversing the causal direction of policies and reset the pace and agenda of China's reform.[5] Before WTO accession, the government had the final say on setting the agenda of reform and opening-up, which was based on the consideration of its own policy objectives and understanding of China's situation and the global economy. After WTO accession, however, the Chinese government had to follow its commitments in the accession protocol and WTO rules when making decisions. Generally, the new context of WTO membership has pushed the Chinese government to make greater efforts to meet externally imposed demands and standards, which has ushered in more comprehensive reforms than ever before. As a result, WTO accession has helped restructure the relationship between state, market, and society. This "reversed direction" of setting the reform agenda has been a development that has concerned those critics of the decision to join the WTO, with them making accusations of "losing sovereignty" to Western developed countries.[6]

As part of the more comprehensive reforms brought forth by WTO accession, the state has restructured its role from a manager of enterprises and a monopolizer of information toward a provider of public service to market players (enterprises) and the entire society. For example, the central and local governments set up a public service system to help Chinese enterprises deal with the problem of the harm caused by imports and trade remedy measures targeting Chinese exports abroad, reflected in the cases of Datong and Shenzhen, which will be discussed below. On the other hand, the government, especially the WTO affairs team within MOFCOM, in order to conduct successful commercial diplomacy, needs Chinese enterprises to report their complaints about other countries' trade and investment environments. The government officials truly hope the enterprises can play an active role in this regard.

In a previous study I conducted about the institutional politics of China's WTO accession, I found a state-centered policymaking process that involved complicated and sometimes frustrating coordination among different government agencies which needed top leadership intervention in order to push forward the pace of negotiations.[7] Only in the years just before accession were the public and companies consulted in the final negotiations in response to rising complaints and skepticism about the lack of policy transparency and possibly excessive concessions made to foreign countries.

The public has paid great attention to how WTO accession has potentially changed Chinese government behavior and has urged the government to be more open and transparent in decision-making. By setting up the WTO Affairs Division (first within MOFTEC and later within MOFCOM) and local WTO affairs centers, the Chinese government promised to take the role of public service provider, extend assistance to Chinese companies to deal with overseas trade remedy cases, and resist the negative impact of imports.

While emphasizing that Chinese enterprises should become the subject of dealing with trade friction, Chinese officials tend to think a strong government is still needed. However, in contrast to seeing themselves as needing to intervene in the economy, they believe the government should be a strong public service provider to serve the interests of enterprises. As Director-General of MOFTEC's WTO Affairs Division Zhang Xiangchen stated in 2007, Chinese enterprises were facing extremely complicated trade friction and a complicated trading environment which they were not familiar with and were not able to handle effectively.[8] He cited Europe's Registration, Evaluation, Authorization and Restriction of Chemicals (REACH) as an example, which involved thousands of products companies had to register. In his view, the government had to extend assistance and service to Chinese companies by setting up service centers equipped with databases. While putting pressure on the EU, the Chinese government had to help Chinese companies adapt to the changing regulatory environment.[9]

We can identify some reasons for the need for a strong role in dealing with trade frictions. The most important is the underdevelopment of professional trade and industry associations in China and the extremely weak ability of the companies to handle these challenges on their own.

As a provider of public services, the WTO affairs centers sponsored by local governments have played a very important role. The municipal governments of Datong and Shenzhen are good examples of cities that have provided good services which have benefited their firms and other localities. Under the coordination of the WTO Affairs Center of Shenzhen, six Shenzhen multimeter producers joined hands to deal with the US "Section 337" investigation. In the end, they succeeded in keeping their share of the US multimeter market while also enhancing the cohesion of the whole industry. Shenzhen has upheld its position as an example of how to effectively handle trade frictions in China. Its success is attributed to the establishment of "a practical and efficient public service system for WTO affairs." In 2002 Shenzhen set up a special system coordinated by the WTO Affairs Leading Small Group which interfaced with membership-based institutions and was supported by different WTO affairs offices. This system is guided by the mission "to serve industry and enterprises."[10]

Shenzhen has also set up an "early-warning system" regarding potential export frictions. For example, in 2005 they developed the antidumping and industry-injury warning system, conducting the first comprehensive research of foreign antidumping regulations and cases, including the US "Section 337" investigations (related to intellectual property rights disputes), as well as the use of "alternative-country" methodology in EU antidumping investigations. A database including imports, exports, and trade disputes was also established.[11]

The Shenzhen WTO Affairs Center has remained actively involved in the WTO's trade policy review process and bilateral policy consultation process, providing to central officials the views and complaints about foreign trade and investment barriers faced by local enterprises abroad. In this regard, the Shenzhen WTO Affairs Center has been a bridge between the government and business community.[12]

Shenzhen is a good example of how a government-sponsored WTO affairs center in a developed coastal area can be organized to help local enterprises and exporters defend their legitimate interests. In the interior province of Shanxi, there have been some successful cases of defending domestic industrial interests by applying trade remedies. The successful antidumping case brought by the Oak Hill Group (now known as Bluestar), located in the city of Datong, reflects the transformation of the local government to a role as public service provider and demonstrates its ability to forge cooperative relationships with domestic enterprises.[13]

Starting in 2003 the Oak Hill Group, which submitted its application with a firm from Chongqing, applied to MOFTEC/MOFCOM on three occasions seeking relief from the dumping of chloroprene rubber from Japan, the United States, and the EU. Its accusations were confirmed by the government based on China's antidumping statutes, and it succeeded in having antidumping import tariffs placed on these imports. In the initial case the original antidumping levy was set at 2 to 151 percent. At a midterm review, Oak Hill won again, with the tariffs being adjusted to a range of 9.9 to 43.9 percent. In the "sunset" review investigation, MOFCOM decided to continue the imposition of the antidumping tariffs.

In a report released by the Datong Business Bureau, several points are perceived as important in ensuring the legitimacy and success of this case, including an in-depth study of antidumping rules, a strict examination of the key facts, and adherence to the detailed rules related to antidumping prosecution.[14] For example, meeting the requirements related to the qualifications of being an applicant and providing the necessary content and evidence in the petition occurred before presenting to MOFCOM and receiving its final decision.

The Datong Municipal WTO Affairs Center, in their own reports, summarize their practices encouraging Chinese enterprises to learn WTO rules to safeguard their legitimate interests. The report argues that the legal awareness of the city's foreign trade enterprises was generally low, and in the case of international trade frictions, they were passive and ultimately subject to sanctions that could deeply damage their interests. The report cites the example of the city's activated carbon companies, who though accused of dumping in other markets, did not stand up in these cases and lost their markets in the end. The report emphasizes the significance of promoting foreign trade law and WTO rules within the Chinese business community, and the role of helping them to organize lawsuits collectively.

As the Datong report argues, though the petitioners in antidumping cases should be companies, the local government trade agency should play a coordinating role with MOFCOM, municipal foreign law societies, municipal associations representing trade enterprises, the China Association of Foreign-Invested Enterprises, and other organizations in order to set up a smooth working environment ensuring the effective processing of cases. The report concludes by identifying future areas of work, including establishing a complete industry injury early-warning system and training more qualified trade prosecution lawyers to support corporate litigation.[15]

The Shenzhen and Datong cases are important in showcasing the deep transformation of the relationship between players of the state and market, increasingly characterized by the government's self-definition of public service provider and the will to work with enterprises to defend domestic interests. It is particularly noteworthy that we recognize the "central" role of the local government-sponsored WTO centers in assisting the corporate sector fight for their own interests within the WTO legal framework.

Increasing the proactiveness of industry in defense of their interests

In terms of the public education related to WTO rules, officials and experts highlight that Chinese enterprises could benefit from relying on WTO rules against discriminatory treatment on Chinese exports imposed by foreign partners or taking advantage of trade remedy measures to protect China's domestic industry. In particular, Chinese officials and researchers argue that the multilateral WTO rules can help China deter abuse of the domestic rules by other countries such as the United States.[16] In the post-accession period, the value of WTO rules has become more evident in checking the rise of trade protectionism in an era of growing Chinese exports, which would necessarily generate more trade friction.

From the beginning, Chinese trade officials were urged to study how to mobilize WTO norms to protect domestic industry and trade interests. For example, MOFTEC Minister Shi Guangsheng urged that WTO rules be internalized in Chinese laws and regulations and be compatible with the aim to "protect industry and market order." As Shi stated, WTO accession means other countries are committed to opening their markets to Chinese exports as well, and hence China has the right to demand that they abide by WTO rules. He emphasized that China could mobilize the WTO rules to resist new types of trade protection measures, such as misusing quarantine standards, safeguards, antidumping, and other tactics.[17]

In the first stage after China joined the WTO, China was frequently involved in WTO cases under the Dispute Settlement Mechanism (DSM) in Geneva as a third party. MOFCOM has tried to attend as many of the WTO cases as a third party as possible in order to get first-hand experience in handling cases, understanding how to interpret WTO laws, and accumulating experience for future cases. As of March 2017, China had been a third party in 139 of the WTO's 524 cases. As a sign of the efforts early on to learn from others, the staff of MOFTEC's Treaty and Law Division were actively and "substantially" involved in 15 WTO DSM cases in 2005, including cases regarding the zeroing calculation method in antidumping investigations, Japanese seaweed trade, and the US–European dispute pitting Boeing and Airbus over aircraft subsidies. Based on first-hand experience as a third party, they collected rich information and reported what they had learned to the relevant ministries of the State Council, industry associations, and enterprises.[18] According to Harsha V. Singh, the former Deputy Director-General of the WTO, "with the transformation of world economic power landscape, China has been evolved from a reticent player to a more active one by being the most frequent third party in WTO disputes."[19] Participation as a third party has proven to be an effective way for China to become familiar with WTO rules and DSM practices, and thereby an effective way to learn how to defend its interests.

Just as China has become the world's largest exporter, it has also become the world's second largest importer. With increasing confidence after getting more familiar with WTO rules, and driven by a rapid surge of imports and great impact to domestic interests, Chinese industries and enterprises have filed a growing number of trade remedy cases with the central government. As former WTO Director-General Pascal Lamy noticed:

> China refrained from using trade remedies in the first few years of its WTO accession. In recent years, however, we have seen the frequency increase. China is among those countries that initiated the most antidumping investigations. In 2009, China ranked fifth among WTO members in the initiation of antidumping actions. In 2010, China ranked sixth, but the number of initiations in 2010 (8 cases) was much lower than in 2009 (17 cases). Of course, there is a distinction between cases initiated and final measures applied. It is clear that China has become a frequent user of trade remedy instruments.[20]

On the other hand, Lamy points out the surge in cases against Chinese exports. As he states, "[i]t is also clear that in 2009 and 2010 China was by far the biggest target of antidumping investigations (77 investigations in 2009 and 43 in 2010) and countervailing measures (13 measures in 2009 and 6 in 2010) applied to allegedly subsidized Chinese exports."[21] According to the WTO's own database, between 1995 and mid-2016, China was the target for 22.8 percent of all the world's antidumping cases (1,170 out of 5,132 in total).[22]

One could account for the growing number of trade remedy cases involving China as due to the increasing confidence originating from the country's newly gained power and influence, pressure for protection from domestic industries, and the tactical consideration to provide a counterweight against those countries targeting China's exports. Scott Kennedy emphasizes the growing activity of China's domestic industry as an important reason for the rising number of trade remedy cases initiated by Chinese companies, though it does not mean they necessarily win all the cases.[23] In addition, the Chinese government clearly faces complaints and criticism from the public and business about its weak will and limited ability to use WTO rules to defend the legitimate interests of Chinese business and industry. Some commentators contend that it is necessary to launch Chinese cases based on WTO rules, and only by using tough countermeasures can China constrain the surge of protectionism against its exports.

Despite the growing proactive approach of Chinese industry, they are perceived to be still far from effectively utilizing all the chances to put pressure on foreign business and the government practices of their trading partners. For example, the WTO trade policy review process could be another chance for Chinese industry to address their concerns about the policies and behavior of other trading partners. With the changed relationship between state and market, the government also expects Chinese enterprises to feed "shells into the cannon," by providing complaints and opinions to Chinese government agencies in charge of trade policy and listening to industry complains. Whether involved in bilateral or multilateral negotiations, open-minded trade officials clearly tend to think that it is necessary and useful for Chinese enterprises to submit their complaints about the trade and investment barriers they face.

For instance, former Vice Minister of MOFTEC Gu Yongjiang encouraged this approach as a response to US trade pressure. More recent officials in charge of WTO affairs, such as Zhang Xiangchen, have made similar appeals to Chinese companies on different occasions. In preparing for the US trade policy review conducted by the WTO in 2006, MOFTEC called for the public to submit complaints and comments about the US commercial environment. Though most Chinese enterprises moved too slowly to take advantage of such an opportunity, trade officials received a long list of approximately 400 submissions complaining about US export controls on high-technology products, discriminatory treatment about investment from China, and foreign exchange rate manipulation, among other topics.[24] Obviously, Chinese industry interests have been more active in initiating domestic trade remedy cases than in addressing the unfair or discriminatory policies of other countries. The main reason is that Chinese industry is just beginning to engage in international operations outside China, particularly in the investment arena. However, with more companies "going global," Chinese industry will probably have more practical incentives to use the WTO's Trade Policy Review of other countries as a way to address their own concerns.

Puzzled learning: growing concerns about WTO rules

As expected, WTO accession has not only brought growth and prosperity to China, but also has created an increasingly pluralistic and
diversified society. Generally speaking, the public has maintained its
confidence in the multilateral trading system and believes WTO
accession has helped the Chinese economy and propelled social and
political reforms.

As we know, WTO accession caused debate in China. One of the
biggest concerns was the worry about the competitiveness of Chinese
industries in face of the competition from multinational corporations
(MNCs). Skeptics used the metaphor of a "wolf coming" to describe
the impact of WTO accession. However, the Chinese leadership, led by
President Jiang Zemin and Premier Zhu Rongji, had developed an
obviously optimistic perspective on this issue. Since the mid-1990s, they
promoted the new concept of "integrating with international norms," a
strategy designed to take advantage of WTO accession negotiation to
push forward reform of state-owned enterprises (SOEs) by meeting the
obligations of WTO membership.

The optimism of the leaders has been consistent with the mood of
the general public. According to one poll conducted by the Social
Survey Institute of China (SSIC), on 15 November 1999, 98.9 percent
of those interviewed shared Premier Zhu Rongji's view that "China
joining the WTO is in the interests of Chinese people." Some 80 percent of those polled believed that after WTO accession, tariff rates
would be reduced, raising the standard of living.[25] In the years following China's WTO accession, SSIC conducted the survey again in
2004 and 2007. The December 2004 poll shows that 74 percent of
people surveyed confirmed that WTO accession had brought about
"positive" change for China, reflected in more market-oriented reforms,
increasing exports, and improvement of government services.[26] In the
2007 survey, the majority of interviewees talked about the benefits of
the WTO membership such as cheaper goods (91 percent), more job
creation (69 percent), setting a more solid foundation for China's
position in the global economy (79 percent), and the strengthened
international status of China (72 percent).[27]

In 2011, when the country celebrated the tenth anniversary of
China's WTO accession, Chinese government officials presented a
positive view of the economic and social benefits resulting since China
became a WTO member. For instance, they argued that over its first
decade of membership, China's gross domestic product (GDP) grew at
an average rate of 10.5 percent, household income increased from

about $800 to $3,300, and China rose from being the sixth to the second largest trading nation in the world.[28]

At the same time, we also have heard complaints about China's export-driven growth model over this period and reflections about the costs and benefits of China's WTO membership relative to the objective of promoting China's development. The 2008 financial crisis and subsequent challenges render this debate more complicated and relevant. Different from the pre-WTO accession years, Internet-based new media have begun to play a major role in helping to disseminate the different (and sometimes critical) opinions about China's economic strategies and development model. Partly beyond government control, the new media have created a different policy environment and provided interest groups with a new way to influence policymaking.

Since joining, we have witnessed increasing criticism of the policy to promote processing exports because it is too costly in terms of the environment and labor rights, as well as critiques that the policy of opening the domestic market in the hope of acquiring foreign technology from multinational corporations is naïve. Critics have called for greater attention to cultivating the "indigenous innovation" capabilities of Chinese companies. Assisted by the old veterans of the state-owned economy and the emerging private sector, these voices obviously succeeded in placing pressure on decision-makers of different government agencies. Sany Heavy Industry, a domestic private construction equipment company, for instance, played a big role in resisting the US Carlyle Group's attempted acquisition of the Xuzhou Construction Machinery Company (Xugong). In addition, the cases of failed Chinese efforts to invest in and purchase overseas properties, American resource and technology companies in particular, astonished a public which now pays more attention to the rise of foreign investment protectionism. These failed acquisitions include CNOOC-Unocal, Haier-Maytag, Huawei-3Com, and Huawei-3Leaf. Since the global financial crisis of 2008, the Chinese media and elite also have become more skeptical and critical of the US-led global economic order, which is widely perceived as "unfair" and sacrifices the interests of weak and disadvantaged nations. Such perceptions, combined with the increasing sense of economic insecurity, create the broad context of policymaking that emphasizes self-strengthening and enhancing domestic innovation and competitiveness, and urges the government to provide more subsidies and support to China-based companies.

When the media sympathized with Sany's opposition to the Carlyle Group's attempted acquisition of Xugong and criticized US protectionism in the case of CNOOC-Unocal, they seemed to forget the basic fact that, generally speaking, WTO rules do not cover most aspects of foreign investment unless they are related to specific trade measures, the so-called TRIMs (Trade-Related Investment Measures). However, these cases do show an overall growth in Chinese industry activism and the growing need for a multilateral investment regime to regulate investment administration systems in separate countries. Though China's official policy currently does not support such a multilateral investment regime because it has a foreign investment governance system that is connected to its industrial policy (such as the foreign investment catalogue), it has the potential to change current policy given the fact that the country is emerging as a big investor in international markets.

The debate also has addressed the question of how to strike a balance between abiding by WTO rules and self-innovation with the aim of defending China's economic and cultural security. The latter concern has arisen as a result of the WTO rulings on market access for culture-related imports. The need to promote innovation and restructure Chinese industry to generate more value-added comes from the fact that the country has entered a new stage of development and is no longer limited to labor-intensive processing trade. At the same time, though, China has faced greater international pressure to contribute to global economic rebalancing, and only innovation can turn this goal into reality.[29] Given these factors, an increasing number of people inside and outside the government tend to perceive WTO obligations as a barrier to China's innovation. They contend that the current body of WTO rules actually blocks industrial upgrading and inhibits the transformation of China's growth model. Current WTO rules resulting from negotiations in the Uruguay Round were deliberately designed to shrink the "policy space" of developing nations and intended to open Third World markets.[30] Bloggers point to Chinese losses in recent WTO cases, such as the rulings constraining China's right to limit the access of imported audio-video products and the nullification of China's quota-licensing systems for imported minerals and commodities to exemplify the repercussions of the Uruguay Round. They argue that the WTO "has finally shown its ugly face," and "even without WTO membership China could develop well," because China could open other markets just by reaching bilateral and regional trade arrangements.[31]

The strict export controls on high-technology transfers imposed on China by developed countries is another source to account for growing domestic skepticism about the role of the WTO. The critics frequently refer to the automobile industry as a case to show the negative impact of the WTO. Xu Binjin, former deputy minister of MOFTEC and a veteran of China's state-owned automobile industry, pleads that China has paid too much attention to becoming a "model" student of the WTO and that WTO accession has not yet helped China develop its own technology, all while China has become a big car maker and a big market for others in the world.[32] When we look at the reforms of almost four decades, Xu insists that Chinese SOEs have not yet absorbed imported technologies or strengthened their own innovation capabilities. In Xu's view, part of the reason for this failure lies in the poorly designed evaluation system of the performance of SOEs and local government, which is tilted toward higher GDP and tax revenue numbers and ignores technological progress. As for the specific case of China's automobile industry, he argues that the WTO obligations restrain China's innovation growth because the accession to the WTO has stimulated Chinese automobile companies to set up joint ventures with foreign car companies. He complains that in the WTO accession negotiations over the automobile sector, the Chinese government conceded too much to the demands from the West regarding the terms and length of the transition period. Initially, China demanded a 15-year transition, but later reduced its demand to 10, eight, and finally just five years. Xu reaches the conclusion that it is now the right time for China to go its own way and promote indigenous innovation based on a better utilization of imported technology. Unlike in the past, the Chinese government nowadays should be able to give more support and the booming automobile market could be another source of support for a domestic innovation program.[33] Though this school of thought is in the minority and official policy disagrees, the Chinese public may tend to agree with Xu.

In the context of rising skepticism about WTO rules, we can see that there is less support for the organization when compared with 2001 when WTO membership was a driving force behind economic reforms. Liberal-minded economists often refer to the rapid expansion of the SOEs or the phenomenon of "state-advance, private recede" (*guojin mintui*) as a sign of the government's weakened political will to enact reforms. Relatedly, some of China's trade officials attribute recent losses by China at the WTO to conflicting policy objectives and poor interagency coordination. Clearly, there is a tense relationship among different agencies over how to ensure China's domestic policies are compatible with WTO rules. On one hand, central government agencies have strengthened intervention in promoting growth and high-technology sectors to boost the competitiveness of SOEs and private companies—what some studies call "state capitalism." On the other hand, MOFCOM represents the central government as a whole in international affairs and takes seriously its responsibility to polish China's image as a "responsible power." Obviously, MOFCOM should respond to protectionism abroad, but it also must push back on the policies and practices of other central government agencies that may be incompatible with WTO rules. This complicated and sensitive dynamic is not limited to the central government, but is common in local governments as well. The Shenzhen WTO Affairs Center's report gives empirical evidence of the difficulties in interagency policy coordination.[34]

Sun Zhenyu, China's first ambassador to the WTO, believes that China's increasing record of losses in WTO cases in Geneva is related to the government's stimulus packages and greater intervention in the economy, which may be in tension with WTO rules. Sun is pessimistic about China's influence at the WTO because of the comparative disadvantages of new entrants to the WTO because they are less aware of the WTO rules than their predecessors. As a result, he expects China to continue to lose in WTO DSM cases as long as inadequate interagency policy coordination continues to be the reality.[35]

Learning to lead in the WTO

Though a small group of people talk about the great costs of joining the WTO and being victimized by a US-led international system, mainstream thinking seems to dominate the debate. The mainstream view holds that the Chinese economy's strong performance during the global financial crisis has greatly strengthened China's power; the existence of the WTO has effectively blunted a rising tide of trade protectionism; and China can rely on the multilateral trading system to defend its newly gained economic interests better than ever. Despite some differences of opinion, the deepest lesson learned from this crisis is that it is in China's best interest to support the multilateral trading system. These lessons about the importance of the multilateral system have been reinforced by growing concerns about globalization and the rise of protectionism, including in the United States.

When international commentators emphasize the growing power and influence of China in the wake of the global financial crisis, Chinese leaders and the public tend to focus on the challenges the crisis presented to the country and the institutional advantages of having a state-centered governance system. For example, former Deputy Director-General of the WTO Harsha V. Singh believes we have entered a new era with "the emergence of a new globally significant China after the financial and economic crisis in 2009."[36] Chinese leaders obviously disagree with such external analysis, which some Chinese media have re-packaged as the "theory of Chinese responsibility" (for the financial crisis) or the "China threat theory." However, in recent years some have begun to echo that sort of international analysis and urge the leadership and the public to recognize the new reality that China has already become a major power.[37]

To some extent, the views and concerns of the Chinese leadership and public about the country's fragile and vulnerable situation are justified. China's per capita GDP still ranks very low (though rising from around 100th in 2010 to 80th in 2016), and China will remain in a long period of transition because of the problems it needs to overcome. The deepening interdependence between the Chinese economy and the global economy has become another source of China's fragility and vulnerability, evidenced by the great impact of the global financial crisis on China's exports and overall economy.

Faced with a more challenging environment in the aftermath of the global financial crisis, the Chinese leadership and the public have rediscovered the value of WTO norms and rules in resisting trade protectionism. With more reliance on exports and an open international market, China has now placed more confidence in the multilateral trading system, believing that the WTO rules are an effective weapon China can use to defend its own economic interests. Since the global financial crisis, China has become a major target of trade protection measures, not only from developed countries like the United States, but also from emerging economies like India.

In a speech celebrating the tenth anniversary of China's WTO accession, Xu Kuangdi, vice chairman of the Tenth China People's Political Consultative Conference (CPPCC) National Committee and honorary president of the China World Trade Organization Society, argues that China's accession to the WTO has sped up the process of opening up the country, and as a result, has actively promoted the deepening of the reform of the country's governance system and economic development.[38] In contrast to the initial concerns about competition from big international businesses, Wan Jifei, president of the China International Chamber of Commerce, pointed out that through WTO membership China's economy has become integrated with the global economy, cultivating Chinese companies to join the ranks of the Fortune 500, thereby "dancing with wolves" instead of being attacked by them. As Wan argues, Chinese enterprises have deepened their understanding of the international rules, which has helped them to protect their own interests and serve the objective of resisting trade protectionism.[39]

China's leadership highly values the principle of free trade and the role of the multilateral trading system in promoting the growth and welfare of the world. During the financial crisis in 2009 Minister of Commerce Chen Deming published a commentary giving a comprehensive explanation for China's trade policies. He argued, "[f]ree trade promotes the well-being of the people of the world. Free trade can expand markets, deepen the division of labor and stimulate competition, thereby stimulating economic growth and improving the people's living standards. In the history, those which had efficient economic activity were often the countries advocating free trade."[40]

Chen positively evaluated the critical role of the multilateral trading system in the past 60 years, and states that through the years the GATT/WTO has become a more universal organization and formed a set of international trade rules that effectively safeguard the free trade order. A majority of countries have achieved rapid development in an era of free trade and economic globalization. He emphasizes that China is a good case that demonstrates the positive role of foreign trade in stimulating China's development in the last three decades. The WTO rules, he stresses, help countries avoid going down the road of global trade protectionism reminiscent of the 1930s.[41] Former trade officials such as Long Yongtu share this positive perception of the role of the WTO in helping to prevent the global economy from slipping into the protectionism that led to the Great Depression in the early 1930s. He argues that the WTO has set up a strict dispute settlement mechanism that makes the spreading of trade protection measures impossible.[42]

Such voices can be heard from the public as well. For example, Chu Zhaogen, a grassroots commentator on current affairs, contends that China should not always blame the WTO for losing cases at the WTO, but instead the Chinese should reflect on the sources of this frustrating record. Chu notes that in 2009 China's exports accounted for 9.6 percent of global exports, but for 40 percent of the total antidumping cases and 75 percent of all countervailing duty cases. He attributes the disproportionate number of cases to China's experience of violating trade rules and its "twin surplus" policy. With exports creating costs in labor and the environment, he suggests China slow down the growth of its exports and emphasize outward investment. Chu concludes by citing Pascal Lamy, who has said that the WTO needs China to be a responsible leader and that if China deliberately violates WTO rules, the injury to the organization will be substantial.[43]

Official media such as *International Business News* (*gouji shangbao*) also positively assess the role of WTO accession in boosting the country's position in global governance more broadly. A recent commentary hails the WTO accession as an important platform for China to take part in making international economic and trade rules. As one of three pillars of the world economic system, it argues that the WTO is the single international organization regulating global trade with over 150 members accounting for over 97 percent of world trade. Since its WTO accession, China has attended all the ministerial and senior official-level negotiations and consultations of the WTO, G20, and G33, submitting more than 100 proposals alone to the Doha Round negotiations. Gradually, China has increased its leading role in the WTO, reflected in the WTO Mini-ministerial Conference in Dalian in 2005 and the WTO Ministerial Conference in Hong Kong later that year. In July 2008, China participated in the most important core meetings for WTO negotiations.[44]

In the years since, China has taken a growing role in the WTO's governance. Former Chinese official Zhang Yuejiao served on the Appellate Body from 2008 to 2016; soon after she stepped down, another former Chinese official, Zhao Hong, joined the body. Equally significant, Yi Xiaozhun, China's former ambassador to the WTO, became a deputy director-general in late 2013. More broadly, the number of Chinese staff at the WTO reached 14 in 2016, placing it tied with the largest number of staff from an Asian country.[45]

The official Chinese media's celebration of the strengthened role of China in WTO negotiations is consistent with the reality that China moved from being a peripheral to a central participant in Doha Round negotiations. China made concessions during the talks, though not major sacrifices to Chinese interests, but it cannot be seen as the sole cause of the Doha Round's collapse, with some Western commentators laying the blame at the feet of emerging economies such as India and China. The reasons for the Doha Development Agenda's (DDA) failure are complex but certainly are related to the reluctance of interest groups in developed and developing countries to make adequate concessions to strike a major deal. Specifically, the changing nature of Chinese state–society relations and the growing influence of China's business interests have put government negotiators in a more difficult position to make concessions. This is true despite the limited agreement reached in Bali in December 2013. As a result, we can conclude that China's changing state–society relations have had both a positive and negative effect on Chinese learning and their effectiveness in global governance.

During the period when the Chinese government and the public celebrated the tenth anniversary of China's accession to the WTO, the Chinese Communist Party (CCP) held the Sixth Plenary Session of the Seventeenth Party Congress. This meeting emphasized the need for more policies promoting China's relations with the global economy.

Although culture is perceived as a highly "sensitive" industry given the CCP-centered political system, China's failure in the WTO case concerning the distribution of audio-visual products taught China's leadership that the country needs to compete fiercely in the international market to be stronger. In order to realize this objective, the key is to let the market play a larger role, as opposed to shying away from competition. As a commentary in the official *People's Daily* argues, "to marketize culture is to promote market competition to force the growth and strengthening of China-based cultural enterprises in the broad context of international competition. In the context of stronger Western culture, only by winning the market can the socialist value system win the right to speak and win the initiative. This is exactly the challenge a socialist culture must face."[46] Obviously, China's official policy is not to steer clear of cultural markets but to grow and compete with Western cultural enterprises under the same rules of the WTO. The coincidence of the celebration of China's WTO accession anniversary and the CCP resolution on reform of the cultural products industry should send a very positive signal for relations between China and the global economy. This positive mindset can be seen in other fields, with many recognizing that China needs to be a quick learner and that moving up the learning curve is the only way to prosper in the face of fierce international competition.

Conclusion

The 15 years since China joined the WTO have brought forth tremendous changes to the country. Most significant is the restructuring of relations between state, market, and society. The state is still powerful, but it has largely reshaped its role toward being a public service provider to the market and society. Chinese society has become much more open and diversified, and as a result, the rising industry and business interests will continue to project their influence on government policy related to the WTO, in some cases indirectly generating more cases about Chinese trade policies under the WTO's dispute settlement system.

In the context of this great transformation, the Chinese have developed a contradictory image of themselves and the outside world: China is a strong power *and* a vulnerable country, a beneficiary *and* a victim of the multilateral trading system, and a defender *and* critic of the international system. As a newer member of the WTO, China is still undergoing a learning process, as it is still not as familiar with the system and the rules as older members. China's elites and general public have developed mixed feelings about the WTO, characterized by a sense of achievement and a sense of frustration.

Though the size of China's economy and the amount of overall trade have become quite impressive, as the discussion above demonstrates, the costs and benefits of being part of the WTO are hotly debated. The biggest concerns appear to be that China may be trading too much to the detriment of its environment and the interests of labor, and that it may face more challenges than other countries in pushing forward industrial upgrading because of the increasingly strict measures on technology transfer imposed by foreign governments and MNCs on China. However, the most important lesson China took away from the impact of the global financial crisis is that the Chinese economy has become an inseparable part of the global economy. As a result, China has no choice but to continue accepting and supporting the WTO, as well as relying on WTO rules to protect itself from protectionism.

China's experience in the 15 years since WTO accession has profound implications on the future role of China in participating in global governance and the future of global governance itself. Clearly, the growing practical interests in the multilateral trading system will help ensure that Chinese decision-makers and the public continue to be enthusiastic about following the WTO rules and making greater efforts to strengthen the multilateral trading system. This commitment is obviously important to the WTO as an institution. Furthermore, based on the WTO learning experience, China's political leaders and the public now have formed a more positive attitude about enlarging China's participation in other global governance bodies, both older organizations such as the International Monetary Fund (IMF) and the World Bank, and newer ones such as the G20. Subsequently, China has started to play a more active leading role in building new regional institutions such as the Asian Infrastructure Investment Bank (AIIB) and the Belt and Road Initiative (BRI). The Chinese want both to strive for a more powerful position in these bodies and to take on more obligations to support the expansion of these organizations' influence in world affairs. Both China and the world will benefit from this proactive approach and policy of engagement.

Notes

1 Xiaozhun Yi, "A Decade in the WTO, a Decade of Shared Development," in *A Decade in the WTO: Implications for China and Global Trade Governance*, ed. Ricardo Meléndez-Ortiz, Christophe Bellmann, and Shuaihua

62   *Wang Yong*

Cheng (Geneva: International Centre for Trade and Sustainable Development, 2011), 1–2.

2   WTO Affairs Department, Ministry of Commerce, "WTO-related Technical Assistance Work after China Joined WTO" [Zhongguo rushi hou kaizhan de yu WTO youguan de jishu yuanzhu gongzuo baokuo naxie fangmian de neirong], 2 May 2006, http://chinawto.mofcom.gov.cn/column/print. shtml?/k/am/200605/20060502256945.

3   WTO Affairs Department, Ministry of Commerce, "WTO-related Technical Assistance Work after China Joined WTO."

4   WTO Affairs Department, Ministry of Commerce, "WTO-related Technical Assistance Work after China Joined WTO."

5   Yong Wang, "China in the WTO: A Chinese View," *China Business Review* 33, no. 9–10 (2006): 42–48.

6   For example, Deqiang Han, *Collision: Pitfall of Globalization and China's Realistic Choice* [Pengzhuang-quanqiuhua xianjing yu zhongguo xianshi xuanze] (Beijing, China: Economic and Management Press, 2000).

7   Yong Wang, "Why China Went for the WTO," *China Business Review* 26, no. 7–8 (July–August 1999): 42–45; Yong Wang, "China's Domestic WTO Debates," *China Business Review* 27, no. 1–2 (January–February 2000): 54–62.

8   Xiangchen Zhang, *The Summary of the Statement in the 2007 Annual Conference of the Shenzhen WTO Affairs Advisory Board*, 5 December 2007, http://guangdong.mofcom.gov.cn/aarticle/sjdixiansw/200712/2007120530 4383.html.

9   Zhang, *The Summary of the Statement in the 2007 Annual Conference of the Shenzhen WTO Affairs Advisory Board.*

10 Jinsheng Zhang, "Use WTO Rules to Respond to Trade Friction" [Yunyong Shimao Guize Yingdui Maoyi Moca], *Seeking Truth (Qiushi)*, no. 22 (2009): 41.

11 Zhang, "Use WTO Rules to Respond to Trade Friction."

12 Zhang, "Use WTO Rules to Respond to Trade Friction."

13 Zhongzhou Li, "Look Back at the Ten Years Since China's WTO Accession" [Rushi shinian huimou], *Journal of WTO Economic Guide* [*WTO jingji daokan*] no. 8 (2009): 84–87 (September 2011), www.wtoguide.net/htm l/2011-09/977.html.

14 Li, "Look Back at the Ten Years Since China's WTO Accession."

15 Li, "Look Back at the Ten Years Since China's WTO Accession."

16 Wang, "China in the WTO: A Chinese View."

17 "To Protect the Interests of Domestic Industry, Shi Guangshang says Make Full Use of WTO Rules and Regulations; and Clean-up of China's Foreign Trade Laws by June" [Baohu guonei chanye liyi, Shi Guangsheng shuo yao chongfeng yunyonghao shimaozuzhi guize zhongguo waijingmao falvfagui qingli 6 yue wancheng], *China Business Times*, 1 April 2002, http://finance. sina.com.cn/roll/20020401/187794.html.

18 Treaty and Legal Affairs Department, Ministry of Commerce, *Major Work of Treaty and Legal Affairs Department in 2005* [Tiaoyue falusi 2005 nian zhuyao gongzuo], 2 May 2006, http://tfs.mofcom.gov.cn/aarticle/az/200605/ 20060502123175.html.

19 Harsha V. Singh, "WTO Membership: Impact on China and Global Trade," in *A Decade in the WTO Implications for China and Global Trade Governance*, ed. Ricardo Meléndez-Ortiz, Christophe Bellman, and

Shuaihua Cheng (Geneva: International Centre for Trade and Sustainable Development, 2001), 3–5.

20 Paula M. Miller, "Interview: China's WTO Anniversary: China's Role in the WTO, Interview with WTO Director-General Pascal Lamy," *China Business Review* 38, no. 4 (October–December 2011): 24–27.

21 Miller, "Interview: China's WTO Anniversary."

22 "Statistics on Antidumping," World Trade Organization, www.wto.org/eng lish/tratop_e/adp_e/adp_e.htm.

23 Scott Kennedy, "China's Porous Protectionism: The Changing Political Economy of Trade Policy," *Political Science Quarterly* 120, no. 3 (Fall 2005): 407–432.

24 Treaty and Legal Affairs Department, Ministry of Commerce, *Major Work of Treaty and Legal Affairs Department in 2005*; Xiangchen Zhang, "The Summary of the Statement in the 2007 Annual Conference of the Shenzhen WTO Affairs Advisory Board," 5 December 2007, http://guangdong. mofcom.gov.cn/aarticle/sjdixiansw/200712/20071205304383.html.

25 Haosheng Bao, "Survey Shows 99% of People Agree with China Joining WTO" [Diaocha xianshi zhongguo 99% minzhong zantong rushi], *Zhonghua caishuiwang*, 18 November 1999, www.zgtax.net/plus/view.php?aid=7009.

26 "Survey Shows Majority of Public Satisfied with the Changes Three Years after China's Accession to the WTO" [Diaocha xianshi duoshu gongzhong dui zhongguo rushihou sannian de bianhua gandao manyi], *China Net (Zhongguowang)*, 8 December 2004, www.china.com.cn/zhuanti2005/txt/ 2004-12/08/content_5724065.htm.

27 Social Survey Institute of China, *Public Opinion on China's WTO Accession: Five Year's Report* [Youguan Zhongguo Rushi Wunian de Mingyi Diaocha Baogao], 26 March 2007, www.jxstj.gov.cn.mydc3/news_view.asp? newsid=231.

28 Yi, "A Decade in the WTO."

29 On the debate on China's role in global economic rebalancing, see Yong Wang, "Seeking a Balanced Approach on the Global Economic Rebalancing: China's Answers to International Policy Cooperation," *Oxford Review of Economic Policy* 28, no. 3 (2012): 569–586.

30 Samir Amin, "Fifty Years is Enough," *Monthly Review* 46, no. 11 (1995): 8–50; Robert Wade, "What Strategies are Viable for Developing Countries Today? The World Trade Organization and the Shrinking of Development Space," *Review of International Economy* 10, no. 4 (2003): 621–644.

31 Jianming Shao, "WTO Finally Shows its Overbearing and Despicable Face" [WTO Zhongyu luchule badao beilie de zuilian], *Home of Utopia*, July 2011, www.wyzxsx.com/Article/view/201107/246685.html.

32 Bangning Ge and Liyue Zhang, "After Ten Years Since WTO Accession, Has China's Automobile Industry Entered a Stage of Life and Death?" [Rushi shinian hou, Zhongguo qiche zhi shengsi cunwang jieduan], *Sohu Qiche*, 8 September 2011, http://auto.sohu.com/20110908/n318812064_4.shtml.

33 Bangning Ge and Liyue Zhang, "After Ten Years Since WTO Accession, Has China's Automobile Industry Entered a Stage of Life and Death?"

34 "Strengthen Local WTO Affair Functions to Maintain Industrial Security" [Qianhua difang WTO qianghua difang WTO zhineng weihu chanye anquan], *Shenzhen Special Zone Daily*, 15 December 2010, www.chinawto. mofcom.gov.cn/aarticle/j/al/201012/20101207309041.html.

64   *Wang Yong*

35 Chinese Academy of Social Sciences, "US and China-US Relations in the Eyes of Chinese" [Zhongguoren yanzhong de meiguo yu zhongmei guanxi], *Outlook Oriental Weekly* [*Liaowang dongfang zhoukan*], 13 September 2011, http://news.sina.com.cn/c/sd/2011-09-13/115323147530_3.shtml.
36 Singh, "WTO Membership: Impact on China and Global Trade," 3.
37 Qiren Zhou and Xiao Qin, "Collective Rule with Multi-polarity: To Seek China's International Positioning in 2020" [Yiyuan duoji gongzhi: xuqiu Zhongguo], Peking University National Development and Research Institute, 20 October 2011, www.nsd.edu.cn/cn/article.asp?articleid=15145.
38 "The Symposium to Commemorate the Tenth Anniversary of China's Accession to the WTO Held in Beijing," *Xinhua News Agency*, 7 September 2011, http://cwto.mofcom.gov.cn/aarticle/p/201109/20110907745917.html?1251893037=3639458075.
39 Others critically assessed the international competitiveness of big Chinese companies in the same celebration chaired by Wan Jiefei. For example, former vice trade minister and WTO accession negotiator Yu Xiaosong contended that none of China's top 500 companies meet the standards of global MNCs. Yu Xiaosong, "Among China's Top 500 There is No True Multinational Corporation" [Zhongguo wubaiqiangli meiyou zhenzheng de kuaguogongsi], *Xinlang Caijing*, 1 March 2011, http://finance.sina.com.cn/hy/20110301/10539449975.shtml.
40 See commentary in Chinese on foreign trade by Chinese Minister of Commerce Chen Deming in *Seeking Truth (Qiushi)*, 26 June 2009.
41 Deming Chen, "How to Understand Several Questions Regarding Domestic Commerce and Foreign Trade" [Guanyu guoneiwai maoyi de jige renshi wenti], *Seeking Truth (Qiushi)*, no. 6 (June 2009): 21–24, www.qstheory.cn/zxdk/2009/200907/200906/t20090609_1786.htm.
42 Yongtu Long, "Trade Protectionism Doesn't Change Trade and Investment Liberalization Trend Worldwide" [Maoyi baohu zhuyi meiyou gaibian quanqiu maoyi he touzi ziyouhua de qushi], *Changgan Forum* video, 3 September 2010, http://video.sina.com.cn/p/finance/economist/jingjixueren/20100903/111861133241.html.
43 Zhaogen Chu, "China's Integration into the World Firmly Strengthened by Winning WTO Cases" [WTO shengsu jianding Zhongguo rongru shijie], *China Youth Daily*, 30 March 2011, http://zqb.cyol.com/html/2011–03/30/nw.D110000zgqnb_20110330_6–02.htm.
44 "To Commemorate the 10th Anniversary of China's Accession to the WTO Special Report" [Jinian zhongguo jiaru shimaozuzhi 10 zhounian tebie baodao], *Guoji Shangbao*, 7 September 2011, http://cwto.mofcom.gov.cn/article/n/201109/20110907745892.shtml.
45 The largest number of full-time staff are French, 171 of 647. There are 33 Americans who work at the WTO. *WTO Annual Report 2016*, www.wto.org/english/res_e/booksp_e/anrep_e/anrep16_chap9_e.pdf.
46 Ren Zhongping, "Cultural Power of the Chinese Way—on Promoting the Development and Prosperity of Socialist Culture" [Wenhua qiangguo de zhongguo:lun tuidong shehuizhuyi wenhua dafazhan dafanrong], *People's Daily*, 15 October 2011: 1, http://paper.people.com.cn/rmrb/html/2011-10/15/nw.D110000renmrb_20111015_7-01.htm.

3 Chinese and Japanese FTA strategies and their implications for multilateralism

Junji Nakagawa and Wei Liang

- China's FTA strategy
- China's policy shift from multilateralism to FTAs
- China's FTA strategy
- Japan's FTA (EPA) strategy
- Japan's policy shift to EPAs and BITs
- Japan's EPA/BIT strategy
- Comparing China's and Japan's approaches to FTAs
- Implications for wider regional arrangements
- Conclusion

China and Japan are the two largest economies and the two most important political powers in Asia. In the past decade, along with the bottom-up efforts to build trade and investment links, there has been an effort to consolidate and facilitate these developments through formal agreements. Although many governments have been involved in these efforts, China and Japan have acted differently in the way they have negotiated free trade agreements (FTAs). Whilst Japan has sought to negotiate comprehensive FTAs with selective countries bilaterally, China has adopted a more pragmatic and flexible approach to negotiate relatively shallow FTAs. As a consequence, Asia is creating a system of overlapping trade regimes, or a noodle bowl. By early 2014, East Asia had concluded 77 FTAs, with another 51 in various stages of completion.[1]

This chapter examines the process of China's and Japan's FTA negotiations, the domestic and external factors that have contributed to the formation of their distinctive FTA strategies, and the terms of the FTAs, as well as the implications for regional integration and the multilateral trading order. This chapter attempts to determine whether Asia's emerging noodle bowl, created largely by the parallel FTA negotiations by China and Japan, is likely to induce harmful trade diversion and fragmentation or promote the integration of the region's economy. The next two sections briefly review the FTA negotiations of China and Japan, the domestic factors that can explain the policy shift from multilateralism to FTAs, their FTA partner selection criteria, the content of their FTAs and the characteristics of their negotiation strategies, respectively. We then more directly compare the FTA strategies of China and Japan and deliberate on the future directions of their FTA strategies.

China's FTA strategy

China's economic reform strategy has arguably followed the Japanese development model in terms of protection and controls as well as heavy dependence on the US market for its exports. Japan and China have greatly profited from an open world economy, and hence, both have been strong believers in multilateralism. This explains why East Asia is an FTA latecomer compared to the Americas, Europe, and Africa. By the end of 2002, of the 30 leading economies in the world, only five were not members of any such FTAs: Japan, China, South Korea, Taiwan and Hong Kong.

The policy shift took place in 2000, when China witnessed the Asian financial crisis and its prolonged World Trade Organization (WTO) accession negotiation in the final phases. China officially proposed its first FTA negotiation with Association of Southeast Asian Nations (ASEAN) members in November 2000. China has entered into a number of regional and bilateral trade agreements since, or is in the process of doing so. China signed its first FTA agreement (trade in goods) with ASEAN in 2004, and by March 2017 it had concluded 14 FTA negotiations, including agreements with Hong Kong (2004), Macao (2004), ASEAN (2005), Chile (2006), Pakistan (2007), New Zealand (2008), Singapore (2008), Peru (2009), Costa Rica (2010), Taiwan (2010), Iceland (2013), Switzerland (2013), Australia (2015), and South Korea (2015). China is also in the process of negotiating FTAs with the Gulf Cooperation Council (GCC), Norway, Japan and South Korea (CJK), the Southern African Customs Union (SACU) (which includes Botswana, Lesotho, Namibia, and Swaziland), the Regional Comprehensive Economic Partnership (RCEP), Sri Lanka, Maldives, Georgia, and Israel (see Table 3.1).[2]

Table 3.1 Comparison of Chinese and Japanese FTA negotiations (2017)

Country	Signed agreement	FTA under negotiation	FTA joint study
China	Hong Kong (2004) Macao (2004) ASEAN (2005) Chile (2006) Pakistan (2007) New Zealand (2008) Singapore (2008) Peru (2009) Costa Rica (2010) Taiwan (2010) Iceland (2013) Switzerland (2013) Australia (2015) South Korea (2015)	SACU (2004) GCC (2005) Norway (2007) CJK (2012) RCEP (2013) Sri Lanka (2014) Maldives (2015) Georgia (2015) Israel (2016)	China-India (2003) China-Colombia (2012) China-Moldova (2014) China-Fiji (2015) China-Nepal (2016) China-Mauritius (2016)
Japan	Singapore (2002) Mexico (2005) Malaysia (2006) Philippines (2006) Chile (2007) Thailand (2007) Indonesia (2008) ASEAN (2008) Vietnam (2008) Switzerland (2009) Brunei (2010) Peru (2011) India (2011) Australia (2014) Mongolia (2015)	South Korea (2003) GCC (2006) Canada (2012) Colombia (2012) CJK (2013) European Union (2013) RCEP (2013) Trans-Pacific Partnership (2013)	Turkey (2012)

Note: Dates in parentheses signify the date the FTA study group started, the negotiations began, or the FTA came into effect, depending on the column.
Sources: PRC Ministry of Commerce, *China FTA Network*, http://fta.mofcom.gov.cn/english/; Ministry of Foreign Affairs of Japan, *FTA and EPA*, www.mofa.go.jp/policy/economy/fta/.

China's policy shift from multilateralism to FTAs

China's extensive and growing trade interest left it with little option but to participate fully in the multilateral trading system with WTO as its focal point. It did so at the end of 2001, accepting terms that have been imposed on no other nation before or since.[3] Among a number of motives behind China's decision to join the WTO and its willingness to bind itself by the global trade regime, its commitment to multilateralism is an important one. No matter how prolonged and frustrating the negotiation process, joining the WTO was always the policy priority of the Chinese leadership. Furthermore, joining the WTO was seen as a strong political commitment made by the Chinese government to Western countries that its open-door policy was irreversible.[4]

Why did the policy shift take place in the early 2000s? The initial policy consideration was more political than economic. First, since China's rapid economic growth in the 1990s, there have been great concerns about the "China threat" raised by the Southeast Asian countries. Politically, Southeast Asian countries were not sure of China's true intentions as it became more powerful. Economically, China has become a competitor in their exports to the United States and European Union (EU) and in their efforts to attract foreign direct investment (FDI). China joining the WTO would inevitably intensify this economic competition, as they all exported similar labor-intensive products and all relied on the markets of developed countries. Furthermore, the outbreak of the Asian financial crisis in the late 1990s reminded China of the importance of developing a regional policy; it would be difficult for China to avoid the contagion of such a crisis, even though it had a low level of intra-regional trade with other Asian neighbors and tight capital controls in the late 1990s. Within this context, in the Ninth Five-Year Plan, published in 1996, the Chinese government for the first time stated that, "China shall actively participate and develop regional economic cooperation," as well as "strengthen South-South Cooperation," and "promote and develop the economic and trade cooperation with developing countries." The same plan, however, also called for China to "actively participate and defend the global multilateral trading system, develop both bilateral and multilateral trade, so that they can promote each other and the market can be diversified."[5] A well-thought-out FTA strategy would help reassure China's Asian neighbors of the cooperative aspects of China's "peaceful development" strategy.[6]

Second, as China deeply integrated itself into global production networks, its unique trade patterns and heavy dependence on processing trade turned it into a major trading country. The scope of China's processing trade and related demand on raw materials, energy products, and intermediate inputs turned China's attention to securing its import markets from developing countries in Africa, Latin America, and Asia. Hence, an important motive for China's decision to pursue FTAs with Australia, ASEAN, Chile, Peru, and the Gulf countries was to secure essential primary materials in order to hedge against potential supply shortages, including those created by increases in commodity prices. The pursuit of FTAs in this perspective again reflects the Chinese leadership's desire to ensure the achievement of its key national security goals, particularly the long-term sustainability of its economic development strategy.[7]

China's FTA strategy

What are the main characteristics of China's FTA strategy? As we have seen above, two concerns seem to have dictated the choice of the target countries, namely, enhancing China's political relations with its Asia neighbors and securing its ever-increasing need for energy and raw materials by building closer business ties with resource-abundant developing countries. Among the 10 FTA agreements China has signed, the agreements with Taiwan, Hong Kong, Macao, ASEAN, Pakistan, and Singapore were primarily driven by geopolitical concerns (Taiwan, Hong Kong, and Macao as part of greater China, to be good neighbors with ASEAN, and Pakistan as its political ally). In contrast, its agreements with Peru, New Zealand, Chile, and Costa Rica were primarily resources-driven. Given that China has signed most of its FTA agreements with small and medium-sized economies, the negotiation process has been very flexible, pragmatic, and gradual, and the scope of agreements tends to be shallow and non-controversial for its partners. The agreements contain three characteristics.

1 Moderate trade liberalization

General Agreement on Tariffs and Trade (GATT) Article XXIV.8 provides that the duties and other restrictive regulations of commerce are eliminated on "substantially all the trade" between the constituent members of free trade areas and customs unions. China's FTA strategy has been criticized by many scholars as "low quality" and "economically less meaningful."[8] Why has China preferred these "shallow" agreements over comprehensive ones?

It is easy for China domestically to agree on these less demanding and less painful trade concessions, especially after it made considerable concessions over its WTO accession. Given that many view China as still in the process of adjusting to its WTO concessions, Beijing is not willing to make deeper cuts on trade liberalization. Therefore, China prefers not to make many WTO-plus concessions in most of the FTA agreements it signs (the FTAs with Hong Kong, Macao, and Taiwan are exceptions). As noted by Antkeiwicz and Whalley, China's FTAs are featured by "diversity in terms of both form and coverage," brevity and "hence the inevitable vagueness of the texts involved," and "the absence of explicit and clear dispute resolution procedures with conciliation between the parties being relied upon."[9] The recently concluded China-South Korea FTA was considered the "most comprehensive" one negotiated by China so far,[10] but its liberalization rate is still as low as 90 percent and only covers 70 percent of agricultural products.[11]

Many of the FTA agreements China has negotiated have excluded sensitive sectors and issues that may be difficult to deal with in the short term, such as intellectual property protection, dispute settlement mechanisms, special sectoral liberalization, the environment, and labor standards. For instance, China and ASEAN placed a wide range of important manufacturing goods and agricultural products on the sensitive track. In the China-South Korea FTA, it excluded sensitive products such as rice, steel, and automobiles.

2 Politicized FTA agreements

China has negotiated more than half of its FTAs by placing geopolitical and strategic goals over economic considerations. China's efforts with the China-ASEAN FTA (CAFTA) are widely seen as an example of the primacy of geopolitical considerations in its engagement with Southeast Asia. A troublesome and uneasy neighborhood can only be a distraction from a focus on economic development. In fact, Chinese officials admitted to us that geopolitical considerations trump economic benefits when China negotiates economic issues with neighboring countries.[12] Before the negotiations were launched, China already expressed its willingness to make more economic concessions. China's Deputy Economic Minister and chief WTO negotiator Long Yongtu promised that ASEAN would be among the first to benefit from China's further opening-up.[13] At a meeting of senior ASEAN and Chinese economic officials in Brunei in August 2001, Chinese Premier Zhu Rongji made a strong push, proposing tariff reduction and other measures to be phased in over seven years, from 2003 to 2009. China offered to open its own market in some key sectors to ASEAN countries five years before they were required to reciprocate. It would also grant special preferential tariff treatment for certain goods, as well as special and differential treatment of ASEAN's Indochina members.[14] China also allowed ASEAN countries to determine at what pace their trade would be liberalized and what should be included in the trade liberalization scheme. Consequently, the initial CAFTA agreement is far from comprehensive, with only 40 percent of goods subject to a reduction in tariffs to 5 percent or less. The accord seeks to broaden the range of goods to 60 percent of imports within two years, but the agreement has also incorporated many exceptions for sensitive products.[15]

China has also accepted flexible plans from trading partners in order to reach FTAs. Just as with China's FTA negotiation with Pakistan (a trade in goods agreement signed in 2005 and a trade in services agreement signed in 2009), China agreed to negotiate a trade in goods agreement (signed in 2004) separately from a trade in services agreement (signed in 2007) with ASEAN members to ease the political tensions for some of the ASEAN countries. The greater unilateral flexibility China demonstrated also shows that reaching agreements with these countries is primarily a means to meet political and foreign policy objectives.

Furthermore, the recognition of China's market economy status has become a prerequisite for China to negotiate FTAs. Upon China's WTO accession, China agreed to be labeled a non-market economy (NME) for 15 years (until December 2016). The adoption of NME status for antidumping investigations has meant the imposition of much higher antidumping duties than would otherwise have been the case.[16] The Chinese leadership has sought to use FTA negotiations to foster recognition of China as a "market economy" in trade negotiations.[17] China believed this could help to set precedents and pressure for other WTO members, particularly the United States, the EU, and Japan, to consider granting China "market economy" status before the 2016 deadline. By June 2011, 97 countries already recognized China's market economy status, but the largest economies such as the United States, the EU, Canada, and Japan, have still not done so. However, even if this prerequisite of recognizing market economy status was not a barrier to China's FTA negotiations, its ability to help China finally gain its market economy status in the WTO has still been limited. Many countries would see this effort as unnecessarily politicizing China's FTA negotiations.

3 Resources-driven FTAs

Given its increasing energy needs, Beijing has adopted a global strategy of securing energy and natural resources. A categorically different kind of case is presented by China's FTA with Chile, signed in 2005, which serves as an example of using an FTA as an instrument to ensure supplies of inputs essential for China's continued development. Copper, a critical industrial input, accounted for 30 percent of China's imports from Chile, and this may significantly increase under the new FTA agreement, which underlines the assurance of uninterrupted supplies. China's FTA with Chile also ensures continuity of energy supplies. Similarly, China has great interest in securing a deal with GCC countries to improve its access to oil, and with Australia to have better access to iron ore and other minerals. In addition to these, China has also completed FTA negotiations with other resource-rich countries such as Costa Rica, Peru, and New Zealand.

Policy implications

The tendency for China to negotiate moderate trade deals has made it difficult for China to negotiate FTAs with developed countries, which tend to prefer comprehensive arrangements for trade in goods and services and other issues beyond the existing WTO rules, such as competition policy, environmental and labor standards, intellectual property rights (IPR), and investment policy, issues focused on in the Trans-Pacific Partnership (TPP) negotiations. China has largely chosen not to include these issues in the main agreement of its FTAs and instead prefers to address them in stand-alone side agreements or memoranda of understanding (MoUs). This can partially explain why China so far has negotiated most FTAs with developing countries, why the three developed countries that China has reached agreements with are all small economies, including New Zealand, Iceland, and Switzerland, and also explains the long stall in the China-Australia FTA negotiations.[18]

China can continue to evade the above-mentioned WTO-plus rules on substantial trade liberalization by claiming its developing country status (and the special and differential treatment granted to developing countries). However, as the second largest economy and the largest exporter in the world, it is hard to justify the negative impact of China's FTA negotiations on the global trade system. In response to a warning by WTO Director-General Pascal Lamy that China's pursuit of separate bilateral and regional FTAs may negatively affect its long-term economic interests, the spokesman of China's Ministry of Commerce (MOFCOM) responded that "bilateral free trade agreements and the multilateral World Trade Organization are both important channels to facilitate global trade and liberalize investment," and that the two mechanisms should be combined because FTAs can be considered as "important supplements" to the WTO.[19]

Japan's FTA (EPA) strategy

Japan has long preferred multilateral trade liberalization to preferential trade arrangements. It has criticized FTAs as discriminatory against non-parties and detrimental to the GATT/WTO-based multilateral trading system from which it has substantially benefited during its post-war growth. However, it finally made a policy shift toward preferential trade arrangement in the early 2000s. It signed its first FTA, what it prefers to call "economic partnership agreements" (EPA), with Singapore in January 2002, and it has since concluded EPAs with Mexico (2004), Malaysia (2005), the Philippines (2006), Chile (2007), Thailand (2007), Indonesia (2008), ASEAN (2008), Vietnam (2008), Switzerland (2009), Brunei (2010), Peru (2011), India (2011), Australia (2014), and Mongolia (2015). Additionally, Japan joined the negotiation of the TPP in July 2013, and signed it in February 2016. It is also negotiating EPAs with Colombia, Turkey, and the EU, trilateral FTAs with China and South Korea (CJK), and the 16-member East Asian RCEP.

Japan also accelerated negotiation of bilateral investment treaties (BIT) in the early 2000s. Before 2000 it had concluded eight BITs, beginning with the first with Egypt in 1977. However, since 2000, it has concluded 19 BITs. These recent BITs provide for not only investment protection but also investment liberalization.[20]

Japan's policy shift to EPAs and BITs

Competitive dynamics best explain Japan's policy shift toward EPAs and BITs.[21] Japan has used them to respond to economic, political, and legal competitive challenges.

First, Japan had to restore the competitiveness of its businesses abroad, which had suffered due to the trade and investment diversion caused by other FTAs. This was most salient in the case of Mexico after the North American Free Trade Agreement (NAFTA) and later the Mexico-European Union FTA.[22] Also, Japanese companies became interested in using EPAs to revamp their production networks in East Asia and to forestall the advances of rival foreign companies in the region, which in the aftermath of the Asian financial crisis had aggressively courted FDI and foreign export production.[23] Finally, the failure of the Multilateral Agreement on Investment (MAI), sponsored by the Organisation for Economic Co-operation and Development (OECD) in 1998, and the failure of the 1999 WTO Seattle Ministerial Conference to incorporate "trade and investment" into the agenda of the first negotiating round of the WTO, led Japanese companies to lobby for investment rule-making at the bilateral and regional levels. The 1999 policy statement of Keidanren (Japan Business Federation), while expressing expectations for the upcoming WTO negotiations, emphasized the importance of strengthening Japan's efforts to develop a network of EPAs with investment chapters and BITs because they were "extremely important in terms of the foreign business activities of Japanese companies."[24] In sum, Japan's policy shift was influenced by the economic interests of its businesses facing competitive challenges abroad, a shift supported by the Ministry of International Trade and Industry (MITI), renamed the Ministry of Economy, Trade and Industry (METI) in 2001.[25]

On the other hand, the agricultural lobby opposed the substantive liberalization of agricultural trade through bilateral negotiations. This was the major reason for Japan not to start negotiation of its first EPA with Mexico, which had approached Japan to explore a bilateral trade deal as early as the summer of 1998, but with Singapore because the latter offered to exclude agriculture from the negotiations.[26] Japan had to deal with the opposition of its agricultural lobby when it negotiated its second EPA with Mexico, which exports a substantial number of agricultural products to Japan. However, a compromise was reached by excluding several agricultural products from the commitments and by applying tariff rate quotas on pork and oranges.[27] This became a precedent for Japan's negotiations with other agricultural exporters, such as Thailand, Chile, and the TPP.

Japan's policy shift was also influenced by its two central foreign policy concerns in the early 2000s: the maintenance of the security alliance with the United States and the need to respond to China's rise in the region. As Japan shaped its EPA policy, it had to aim for a delicate political compromise in which Japan maintained its key security alliance with the United States, displayed a commitment to the construction of an Asian regional integration, and struck a balance between competition and cooperation with China. These considerations influenced Japanese EPA policy in three important aspects: 1) the selection of EPA partners, notably the Koizumi government bypassing China in the negotiation of bilateral EPAs (2001–2006); 2) the competitive courting of Southeast Asian nations, for example the Japan–Singapore EPA, China's November 2001 announcement to establish an FTA with ASEAN, and Japan's response in January 2002 with the proposal for a Japan-ASEAN Comprehensive Economic Partnership; and 3) the attempt to define the contours of an East Asian Community (EAC), with China insisting on "ASEAN plus three" and Japan calling for "ASEAN plus six," adding in Australia, New Zealand, and India.[28]

Finally, Japan's policy shift to bilateral agreements was influenced by its determination to achieve a high level of legalization through bilateral/regional channels.[29] The aforementioned failures of multilateral investment rule-making through the MAI and the WTO motivated

Japanese businesses to lobby the government to shift the forum for investment rule-making to EPAs/BITs. Japanese FDI in East Asia rapidly increased in the 1990s, a trend that continued after the Asian financial crisis. For Japanese companies investing in the region, protection of investment through clear and transparent rules and their enforcement through investor-state arbitration are of critical importance. As these were not provided through multilateral fora, they lobbied the government to secure them through investment chapters of EPAs and BITs.[30]

The rivalry between multilateral and bilateral rule-making raises the possibility that a new rule adopted and disseminated by FTAs/BITs will later be incorporated at the multilateral level. Such bottom-up standard setting by bilateral channels is particularly prominent in the areas of trade rules currently under negotiation in the Doha Round. The most salient example is the rules on intellectual property protection, known as TRIPS-plus.[31]

Japan's EPA/BIT strategy

Two concerns seem to have dictated the main characteristics of Japan's regional agreement strategy, enhancing business interest and minimizing the negative impact on agriculture. On the one hand, Japan's businesses, notably big businesses, have been lobbying to secure their competitive edge in global trade and investment by concluding EPAs/BITs with their major counterparts. On the other hand, the agricultural lobby has been opposing the substantive liberalization of agricultural trade. Therefore, Japan chose the target countries primarily because they were major trade/investment targets and were not major exporters of agricultural products. This is the major reason why Japan did not negotiate an EPA with China and the United States until recently, both being major exporters of agricultural products. This is also the reason for the comparatively low ratio of Japan's EPAs of its global trade.[32]

As for the content of Japan's EPAs and BITs, they have three major characteristics: moderate trade liberalization; relatively aggressive investment liberalization and investment protection; and moderate legalization on rules covered by the WTO.

1 Moderate trade liberalization

Japan has taken advantage of the flexibility in GATT/WTO rules and the precedents set by the EU and others to keep certain goods out of its FTAs.[33] It has made no liberalization commitments on many agricultural products (such as rice, wheat, and starch) in its EPAs. Even in its EPA with Singapore, whose agricultural exports to Japan are negligible, the few products in the agricultural sector, principally cut flowers and goldfish, were excluded. Consequently, the liberalization ratio of Japan's EPAs is relatively low, with 84.4 percent (Japan-Singapore EPA) to 88.4 percent (Japan-Philippines EPA), while those of US FTAs are higher than 95 percent.[34] Although Japan has made some commitments on imported agricultural products (such as tropical fruit and fish),[35] it has made limited commitments on some products that are produced domestically (pork, beef, sugar, cheese, etc.), mainly through import quotas.[36]

In comparison with the low level of agricultural liberalization, Japan's liberalization commitments on manufactured products have been substantial. First, it abolished tariffs on a wide range of industrial products whose rates were already low.[37] Second, on sensitive manufactured products of its counterparts, Japan has adopted a conciliatory approach. For instance, the Japan-Thailand EPA adopted a phasing out of Thai tariffs on steel products and auto parts. It also provided for the renegotiation of tariff reduction on autos with engines of less than 3000cc. All these were sensitive manufactured products of Thailand. On the other hand, Japan maintained high tariff rates on a small number of sensitive manufactured products such as leather products, petroleum, and petrochemical products.

Japan's liberalization commitments in services trade have also been moderate. Acceptance of nurses and care workers as movement of natural persons (known as Mode 4) has been the major area of Japan's liberalization commitments through its EPAs. Japan made such commitments with the Philippines, Indonesia, and Vietnam. However, Japan only opened the market for these service providers to a limited extent, due mainly to the strong opposition from its domestic service providers, by setting quotas and imposing strict language and other requirements.

2 Relatively aggressive investment liberalization and investment protection

In contrast to the BITs that Japan concluded before the early 2000s, Japan's BITs and the investment chapters of its EPAs after the early 2000s adopt a relatively aggressive stance toward investment liberalization and investment protection. First, Japan's new-generation BITs provide for national treatment at the pre-investment stage. For instance, Article 2.1 of the Japan-South Korea BIT provides that each party shall accord national treatment with respect to the establishment, acquisition, and expansion of investments. Investors are, thus, secured access to the market of the host country insofar as access is secured to the nationals of the latter, except in the sectors specified in the annex to the agreement.[38]

Second, Japan's new-generation BITs provide for the prohibition of performance requirements with respect to a broader range of investment activities than is covered by the WTO Agreement on Trade-Related Investment Measures (TRIMs). For instance, the Japan–South Korea BIT prohibits the parties from imposing requirements related to export levels, domestic content, sourcing domestic inputs, and other measures that help domestic industry.

Third, Japan's new-generation BITs provide enhanced protection to foreign investors at the post-investment stage through both an umbrella clause and institutional arrangements for the improvement of the business environment. An umbrella clause is a provision of a BIT whereby a host country commits itself to perform the obligations it has assumed for individual investments based on the contracts with foreign investors. Such contracts are often concluded with respect to massive investment projects such as infrastructure building and natural resource development. As a result of an umbrella clause, the host government's breach of an obligation in an investment contract automatically establishes a breach of obligation under the BIT, and the dispute settlement mechanism under the treaty, including investor-state arbitration, becomes available to the complainant.

Japan's new-generation BITs also establish institutional arrangements for business environment improvement. Many of them establish a sub-committee on improvement of the business environment under the bilateral joint committee for the implementation and operation of the BIT. Such sub-committees comprise representatives of government officials and investors of both parties. They meet regularly, discuss a wide range of issues to improve the business environment, and make recommendations and provide advisory opinions for the solution of issues. Some of them establish liaison offices or contact points on improvement of the business environment within the government, which receive complaints from foreign investors, transmit them to the relevant authorities, and provide investors with necessary information and advice in collaboration with the relevant authorities. These institutional arrangements enable foreign investors to consult with host governments through low-profile, informal channels, with the support from their home governments. They cover a wide range of issues with respect to the improvement of the business environment, such as public safety, improvement of infrastructure, labor relations, and IPR protection.[39]

3 Moderate legalization on rules covered by the WTO

Japan's EPAs contain provisions that secure a higher level of legal protection than provided under the WTO agreements. These WTO-plus elements are most salient with respect to technical barriers to trade, protection of IPR, and competition policy. On technical barriers to trade, many of Japan's EPAs provide for reaffirmation of the rights and obligations under the WTO Agreement on Technical Barriers to Trade (TBT). However, some provide for mutual recognition, whereby the parties accept the accreditation of the conformity assessment body (CAB) of the exporting country, based on the criteria and procedure provided by the importing country.[40] This enables exporters to acquire an accreditation on their export products *ex ante* in the exporting country, and thus to save on costs and time. Some of Japan's EPAs provide for a higher level of IPR protection than the WTO TRIPS Agreement. For instance, the Japan-Malaysia EPA buttresses IPR protection through simplified procedures, strengthened legal rights, and strengthened enforcement. Trade and competition policy were among the Singapore issues, which were proposed but later dropped as among the new agenda items of the Doha Round. Some of Japan's EPAs resuscitate them by incorporating commitments to implement each party's competition law domestically, cooperation on notification and information sharing with respect to the application and enforcement of competition law and policy, and, occasionally, positive comity.[41]

Japan has also sought WTO-plus commitments from its EPA counterparts in trade facilitation and government procurement. With respect to trade facilitation, some of Japan's EPAs contain provisions for cooperation for the promotion of paperless trading,[42] the simplification and harmonization of customs procedures,[43] and cooperation and information exchange between customs authorities of contracting parties.[44] EPA negotiations with countries not partaking in the WTO's plurilateral Agreement on Government Procurement (GPA) are frequently the only way in which Japanese companies can gain access to their government procurement markets, which was the case in the Japan-Mexico EPA.

Japan's legalization strategy through WTO-plus provisions of its EPAs places its approach in between those of the United States and China. Compared to the United States, Japan's FTAs have not made binding obligations in financial services or labor and environmental standards. On the other hand, Japan's EPAs are more comprehensive in terms of issue coverage and more legalistic in terms of defining precise obligations and establishing formal dispute settlement mechanisms than Chinese FTAs. Mireya Solís of the Brookings Institution thus argues that the spread of a distinct Japanese approach to preferential trading is a central concern in Japan's competitive EPA/BIT strategy, especially toward China.[45]

Policy implications

Domestically, Japan's EPA strategy was shaped as a compromise between two conflicting sectors, export- and investment-oriented businesses, and the highly protective agricultural sector. This dictated the choice of targets and the relatively moderate liberalization ratio of Japan's EPAs. However, Japan seems to have changed this policy stance in March 2013 by declaring its intention to join the TPP negotiation, given that the TPP negotiation was allegedly premised on an overall trade liberalization including sensitive agricultural products. For Japan to conclude the TPP negotiation successfully, it had to strike a new balance between its industrial and agricultural interests, so that the latter may accept an overall trade liberalization in exchange for a substantive amount of compensation or support for structural adjustment.

Given that an EPA is a comprehensive agreement, with many subject matters to be negotiated, Japan may opt for a lighter agreement such as a BIT, double taxation treaty,[46] and/or a social security agreement[47] with its major trade/investment counterparts. Japan's Ministry of Foreign Affairs (MOFA) announced a policy on the strategic utilization of BITs in June 2008. It enumerated several criteria for selecting counterparts of its BITs, including countries where it has made a substantial amount of investment or where it is likely to make such investment, countries whose business environments need improvement, and countries that are important to Japan as providers of energy resources and other mineral resources.[48]

Comparing China's and Japan's approaches to FTAs

A comparison of the Chinese and Japanese FTA strategies is revealing. Japan tends to use EPAs as a tool to build production networks that benefit its largest industries, while China uses them as a foreign policy tool to promote economic and political partnerships.[49] Japan focuses more on trade in services and investment, while trying to protect its agriculture sector. Therefore, Japan's EPAs are more robust than China's, though they are still viewed as "selectively comprehensive" compared with the gold-standard arrangements of the United States and the EU. Japan also has negotiated EPAs with more developed countries than China; the only developed countries with which China has agreements are Singapore, New Zealand, Switzerland, Australia, and South Korea. China focuses more on trade in goods and tariff reduction of manufacturing products, making its FTAs narrower in scope. Its incremental approach is uniquely open to continuous negotiation to further trade liberalization after early harvest programs. For example, the initial CAFTA was far from comprehensive, with only 40 percent of goods subject to tariff reduction, but the negotiation continued after the signing of the goods trade agreement. The subsequent negotiations deepen and broaden the extent of liberalization. The average tariff on ASEAN exports to China was slashed to 0.1 percent in 2010, while that on Chinese exports to the older original six ASEAN members was slashed to 0.6 percent. Currently, around 7,000 items traded between China and ASEAN are zero-rated.[50] A trade in services agreement was also added to the package later in 2007, and an investment agreement was completed in 2009. Over the last few years China has seemed more willing to negotiate more comprehensive FTA agreements. For instance, China agreed to provide free duty to approximately 84.2 percent of Swiss exports to China, and to include trade in services, investment, and competition in the China-Switzerland FTA concluded in 2013.[51] China has begun the bilateral negotiation to upgrade/expand its FTA agreement with ASEAN (again), Pakistan, New Zealand, and Switzerland.

Both China and Japan have signed many "low-risk, low-return" FTAs. To Japan, its ability to promote its economic interests through an aggressive EPA program has been constrained by the need to protect its agricultural sector and rigid immigration policy.[52] To protect its agricultural sector, it has chosen FTA partners either with little agriculture trade (Singapore), or those that are willing to exempt a lot of agricultural products from tariff cuts (Mexico and Malaysia). To China, its geopolitical or resources-driven FTA strategy determines its soft approach in the negotiations by not pushing hard for trade liberalization. Hence, the two countries have ended up with differently composed, yet both watered-down FTAs that neither harm nor energize their economies.

Like Japan, most of China's FTA partners are not with its top trading partners. Among its top 10 trading partners, only Singapore and South Korea are among its FTA partners. Hence, China's trade with all its FTA partners in 2012 only accounted for 22 percent of China's global trade.[53] For instance, Georgia only accounted for 0.004 percent of China's total exports and Sri Lanka just accounted for 0.1 percent. While Japan's partner selection criteria are based on the potential business opportunities in the target countries without seriously damaging its domestic agriculture, China tends to negotiate with countries that depend more on the Chinese market. Not only does China hold a trade deficit with most of its FTA partners, but it is also their number one or two export destination. With this asymmetric trade relationship, China has more bargaining power in FTA negotiations.[54] However, one principle that has guided China's FTA negotiations is "give more and receive less, be equal partners to achieve a win–win outcome."[55] In terms of policy implications, this principle results in FTA negotiations that are more political than economic. Consequently, China has failed to reach more economically meaningful (and more demanding) FTAs with its important trading partners by taking advantage of its ever-increasing influence and market leverage.

Implications for wider regional arrangements

Will Japan and China be able to take the initiative in establishing regional integration in the Asia-Pacific? We can only speculate on a few possible scenarios due to various policy options and uncertainties. One possible scenario is the formation of an EAC. Another possible scenario is the formation of broader regional integration in the Asia-Pacific. Yet another possible scenario is the formation of a trilateral FTA among China, Japan, and South Korea. Each scenario has different options, which will lead to different results.

The idea of an EAC was first proposed by the then Japanese Prime Minister Koizumi in January 2002. It originally meant the formation of a comprehensive EPA between Japan and the ASEAN.[56] It was intended that the formation of a formal community in East Asia would strengthen the deeply interdependent business relationship in the region. Japan has since been advocating for the idea of an EAC. As we saw above, China also started to promote the idea of an EAC around the same time, soon after its accession to the WTO. However, the two countries have taken different approaches as to the geographical and subject matter coverage. China has been promoting the idea of an EAC consisting of the ASEAN plus three (China, Japan, and South Korea). The coalition government after Prime Minister Koizumi, while endorsing the ASEAN plus three concept, advocated the idea of a Comprehensive Economic Partnership in East Asia (CEPEA), where ASEAN plus six (China, Japan, South Korea, Australia, New Zealand, and India) would be involved. With respect to the subject matter coverage, Japan opted for a full-set negotiation, consisting of financial and monetary cooperation, liberalization of trade in goods and services, investment liberalization and protection, IPR, competition, and government procurement. On the other hand, China prioritized liberalization of trade in goods, putting off negotiations on the liberalization of trade in services and investment.

The rivalry between the two countries seemed to have been watered down in November 2012, when the leaders of the 16 participating countries in the East Asia Summit (EAS) announced the launch of the RCEP negotiation. They approved the Guiding Principles and Objectives for negotiating the RCEP, which stated a broad range of subject matter coverage including trade in services and investment.[57] Although this may look like the triumph of Japan's idea, it should rather be taken as a policy response by China in light of the advancement of the TPP negotiation. The negotiation of RCEP started in May 2013, with the stated goal of its conclusion by the end of 2015. By March 2017 RCEP countries had concluded 17 rounds of negotiation but it was still too early to tell if an agreement would be reached by the end of 2017. The Chinese government openly promoted ASEAN's leadership role in East Asia, particularly through the EAS. However, given the different levels of economic development and political systems among ASEAN's 10 members and the relatively smaller size of their economies compared with China, Japan, and South Korea, ASEAN has not become the effective leader in the region. Now RCEP seems to have evolved as a de facto China-dominated negotiation.

An absence of internal leadership in East Asia has motivated the United States to try to lead regional economic integration. The TPP negotiations among 12 countries in the region was the main vehicle for such an initiative. Although the original TPP looked like a minor trade agreement to Japan, the United States' decision to join it dramatically increased the economic and political significance of the TPP.

Japan joined the negotiations in July 2013. As the 11 countries had long since started the negotiations of the enlarged TPP, Japan had to make substantive commitments on the wide range of subject matter such as comprehensive tariff eliminations including agricultural products and liberalization of trade in financial services, both of which have posed political challenges to the government of Japan. From a Chinese perspective, Japan's proposal of ASEAN plus six is a policy compromise to the US proposal. More importantly, it displays the reluctance on the part of Japan to form any kind of FTA with China at this stage, even though an ASEAN plus three may make good economic sense.[58] By proposing an "Asia only" arrangement, China seeks to secure its trade ties with East Asian countries and push for China-led regional integration. Because Beijing believes that the TPP has the potential to become the substitute for Asia-Pacific Economic Cooperation (APEC) and reflects US interests to maintain its economic dominance in the region, China has felt a sense of discomfort. Given the scope, depth, and sensitivity of the negotiations and issues covered, there is no plan for China to participate in TPP in the short term. Clearly, China is not ready to commit to the high level of trade liberalization required by the TPP. Additionally, the TPP goes against China's longstanding FTA strategy of flexibility and pragmatism.

To many in China, the TPP could potentially serve as an instrument to contain China. First, it could fundamentally undermine Beijing's efforts over the past decade to integrate regional economies through consolidating the supply chain in East Asia. China built the concept for the framework centered on ASEAN plus three, but it would be difficult for this framework to grow concurrently with the TPP. Second, other Asian countries are economically benefiting from China's ascent through expanding their trade with China, but they are also concerned about China's growing clout. Bringing the United States into the region would help ease this "China threat" by strengthening security ties with the United States. In addition to Vietnam and Malaysia, Thailand, Indonesia, and other countries are leaning toward the TPP to secure a competitive edge in the US market when it is liberalized. Third, after Japan opted for the TPP, an FTA among China, Japan, and South Korea lost momentum. When the three countries got together in Beijing in October 2010 to discuss a trilateral FTA, they identified five major hurdles that needed to be addressed: agriculture, differences among the three countries over their stance on regional security issues, the US presence, the history issue between Japan and South Korea, and the jockeying for leadership between Japan and China.[59] In May 2012, the leaders of the three countries declared their decision to start the trilateral FTA negotiation[60] and the negotiation started in March 2013. Although negotiations seemed to pick up pace in 2015, apparently political tension among the three countries has impeded and stalled the negotiations and little progress has been made so far. To China, Japan's decision to join the TPP negotiation was indicative of Japan's foreign policy priorities, namely, to reconnect with the United States economically and to strengthen the US–Japan military alliance politically. Consequently, shaping the future of Asia's regionalism (to be Asia only or Asia-Pacific) depends much on whether the TPP or the RCEP prevails.

As the new Trump Administration has decided to abandon the TPP, it has created uncertainties for the other 11 TPP parties. Article 30.5 of the agreement requires that it be ratified by at least six countries which represent 85 percent of the TPP's combined gross domestic product (GDP). It means that the TPP will not be able to enter into force unless the United States ratifies it. Furthermore, the biggest driver for most TPP participants was access to the US market. Although Japan's Abe administration is still trying to persuade the United States to come back to the TPP, there seems to be little chance for success in this attempt, at least for the time being. Japan and other TPP parties may consider a plan B, such as TPP 11 without the United States.

Finally, there may be a third possible scenario for establishing regional integration in the Asia-Pacific, namely, a trilateral FTA among Japan, China, and South Korea. A trilateral EPA would be an important first step for further integration in the region and an integral part of the ongoing RCEP negotiations. In light of the fact that Japan and the EU started negotiating an EPA in April 2013, and also given that Japan joined the TPP negotiations in July 2013, the year 2013 became a watershed moment for China and Japan in their FTA/EPA strategies. The political tensions between China and Japan, and between South Korea and Japan, have facilitated the bilateral China-South Korea FTA negotiation, which was concluded in 2015. The conclusion and now the failure of the TPP negotiation also incentivized China to modify its FTA strategy and to be more willing to make market access and trade liberalization concessions in the parallel RCEP and China-Japan-South Korea trilateral FTA negotiations.

Conclusion

Though Japan and China had traditionally exhibited preference for multilateral approaches to trade liberalization, the option of FTAs has acquired new significance and urgency since the beginning of the twenty-first century. The factors that seem to be influencing the recent trade policies of Japan and China include geopolitical considerations as well as the risk of being excluded from the global FTA race, and the desire to ensure steady supplies of critical raw materials. The two countries are increasingly pursuing FTAs with their neighbors in South and Southeast Asia, as well as with the world at large. Though they have developed distinctive FTA strategies in the process, both countries have insisted that FTAs are complementary to multilateralism. Given the difficulties of negotiating a region-wide FTA in East Asia, both countries will continue their approach to embrace both multilateralism and open regionalism.

As the two largest economies in Asia (and the second and third largest economies in the world), the actions and interactions of China and Japan have a direct impact on global trade norms. Their FTA strategies may not be as robust as those of the United States and the EU, but their FTAs have also resulted in freer, if not complete free trade. On the other hand, the WTO has many advantages that neither FTAs nor BITs can provide. The result of liberalization negotiations will be applied to all 164 members of the WTO on a most favored nation (MFN) basis. Also, the dispute settlement mechanism of the WTO secures the implementation of the legal obligations of each member, which is very hard to secure in practice via a dispute settlement procedure of an FTA or a BIT. Neither FTAs nor BITs can replace the WTO as a mainstream forum for trade liberalization and rule-making. As two major beneficiaries of the multilateral trading system, Japan and China are likely to continue to place a great emphasis on reinvigorating that system.

Notes

1 Masahiro Kawai and Ganeshan Wignaraja, "Trade Policy and Growth in Asia," Paper Prepared for the ADBI Invited Session "Can Asia Sustain Growth?," 8 June 2014.
2 Chinese Ministry of Commerce, *China FTA Network*, available at http://fta.mofcom.gov.cn/english/. Accessed 3 March 2017.
3 Nicholas Lardy, *Integrating China into the Global Economy* (Washington, DC: Brookings Institution Press, 2002).
4 Interview with Chinese trade officials, Summer 1999.
5 Shuchao Henry Gao, "China's Strategy for Free Trade Agreements: Political Battle in the Name of Trade," *Research Collection School of Law.* Paper 966 (2011).
6 Saori N. Katada and Mireya Solís, "Cross-Regional Trade Agreement in East Asia: Findings and Implications," in *Cross Regional Trade Agreements: Understanding Permeated Regionalism in East Asia*, ed. Saori N. Katada and Mireya Solís (Berlin, Germany: Springer, 2008), 147–159.
7 Saori N. Katada and Mireya Solís, "Under Pressure: Japan's Institutional Response to Regional Uncertainty," in *Northeast Asian Regionalism: Ripe for Integration?*, ed. Vinod Aggarwal, Min Gyo Koo, Seungjoo Lee, and Chung-in Moon (Berlin: Springer, 2008), 109–147.
8 C. Fred Bergsten, Charles Freeman, Nicholas R. Lardy, and Derek J. Mitchell, "China's Challenge to the Global Economic Order," in *China's Rise: Challenges and Opportunities* (Washington, DC: Peterson Institute of International Economics, 2008), 9–32.

9   Agata Antkiewicz and John Whalley, "China's New Regional Trade Agreements," *The World Economy* 28, no. 10 (2005): 1539–1557.
10 Interview with Chinese trade officials, Spring 2017.
11 CSIS, "What is the Road Ahead for the New China Korea FTA?" Korea Chair Snapshot, 14 November 2014.
12 Interview with Chinese trade officials, Summer 2008.
13 Jason Leow, "Asean-China FTA Talks Get Under Way," *Straits Times* (Singapore), 15 May 2002.
14 Lijun Shen, "China-ASEAN Free Trade Area: Origins, Developments and Strategic Motivations," *ISEAS Working Paper: International Politics & Security Issues Series*, no. 1 (2003).
15 "Japan Needs Trade Pact with ASEAN," *The Yomiuri Shimbun*, 19 July 2005.
16 China accession terms permit other WTO members to use NME methodology in their AD investigation against China until 2016. See detailed discussion in Ka Zeng and Wei Liang, "U.S. Antidumping Investigations Against China: Does China's WTO Membership Restrain the U.S.' Use of Discriminatory Antidumping Practices?" *Review of International Political Economy* 17, no. 3 (August 2010): 562–588.
17 Saori N. Katada and Mireya Solís, "Cross-Regional Trade Agreements in East Asia: Findings and Implications."
18 Interview with PRC Ministry of Commerce officials, Summer 2010.
19 "China to Advance Bilateral and Regional Free Trade Negotiation," *Xinhua News Service*, 15 September 2006.
20 See METI, "Outlines of BITs and Japan's BIT Policy" [Tōshi kyōtei no gaiyō to Nihon no torikumi], 10 (in Japanese), March 2016, www.meti.go.jp/policy/trade_policy/epa/pdf/BITrsrc/bitoverview.pdf.
21 Mireya Solís, "Japan's Competitive FTA Strategy: Commercial Opportunity Versus Political Rivalry," in *Competitive Regionalism: FTA Diffusion in the Pacific Rim*, ed. Mireya Solís, Barbara Stallings, and Saori N. Katada (Basingstoke and New York: Palgrave Macmillan, 2009), 198–215.
22 See Japanese Ministry of Foreign Affairs, *Japan-Mexico Joint Study Group on the Strengthening of Bilateral Economic Relationship Final Report* 14, no. 1 (2002), www.mofa.go.jp/region/latin/mexico/relation0207/part2.pdf.
23 Mark S. Manger, *Investing in Protection: The Politics of Preferential Trade Agreements between North and South* (Cambridge: Cambridge University Press, 2009), 189.
24 Keidanren (Japan Federation of Economic Organizations), "Challenges for the Upcoming WTO Negotiations and Agenda for Future Japanese Trade Policy," Section 3 no. 1 (18 May 1999), www.keidanren.or.jp/english/policy/pol102/index.html.
25 Solís et al., *Competitive Regionalism*, 201–204; Mireya Solís and Saori Katada, "The Japan-Mexico FTA: Cross-Regional Step in the Path Towards Asian Regionalism," *Pacific Affairs* 80, no. 2 (2007): 290–291.
26 Takashi Terada, "The Making of Asian's First Bilateral FTA: Origins and Regional Implications of the Japan-Singapore Economic Partnership Agreement," Australia-Japan Research Centre, *Pacific Economic Paper* no. 354 (2006): 10–12.
27 Sekizawa notes that by this compromise "the taboo was broken" that Japan would not negotiate EPAs involving agricultural products. Yōichi Sekizawa,

"Japan's FTA Policy: An Analysis of its Political Process" [Nihon no FTA seisaku: Sono seiji katei no bunseki], Institute of Social Science, University of Tokyo, *ISS Research Series* no. 26 (2007): 48.

28 Solís et al., *Competitive Regionalism*, 207–211.

29 By "legalization" we mean obligation, precision, and delegation. See F. M. Abbott, R. O. Keohane, A. Moravcsik, A.-M. Slaughter, and D. Snydal, "The Concept of Legalization," in *Legalization and World Politics*, ed. J. Goldstein, M. Kahler, R. O. Keohane, and A.-M. Slaughter (Cambridge, Mass.: The MIT Press, 2001), 17–18.

30 Junji Nakagawa, "Competitive Regionalism through Bilateral and Regional Rule-Making: Standard Setting and Locking-in," in *Competitive Regionalism*, ed. Mireya Solís, Barbara Stallings, and Saori N. Katada (Basingstoke and New York: Plagrave MacMillan, 2009), 74–96.

31 TRIPS are Trade-Related Aspects of Intellectual Property Rights. Nakagawa, "Competitive Regionalism through Bilateral and Regional Rule-Making," 82–83.

32 An EPA (FTA) ratio is the ratio of the amount of trade (export and import) covered by EPAs that a country has concluded to its global trade. As of June 2015, Japan's EPA ratio was 23 percent, while that of South Korea, the US, and the EU is 67 percent, 40 percent, and 29 percent (excluding intra-EU trade), respectively. JETRO, *JETRO World Trade and Investment Report 2016* [JETRO Sekai boeki toshi hokoku 2016] (Tokyo: JETRO, 2016), 45.

33 John Ravenhill, "The New Bilateralism in the Asia Pacific," *Third World Quarterly* 24, no. 2 (2003): 308.

34 See Japan's Cabinet Office, "Analysis on a Comprehensive Economic Partnership" [Hōkatsuteki keizai renkei ni kansuru kentō jōkyō], 19 October 2010, www.mofa.go.jp/mofaj/gaiko/fta/pdfs/siryou20101106.pdf.

35 See Japan's commitments in its EPAs with Malaysia, Philippines, Brunei, Indonesia, ASEAN, and Vietnam.

36 See Japan's commitments in its EPAs with Mexico, Chile, Thailand, and Switzerland.

37 The simple average MFN concessional rate of Japan's tariffs on non-agricultural products was 2.5 percent in 2008, and its trade weighted average rate was 1.2 percent in 2007. See, *World Tariff Profiles 2009* (WTO/UNCTAD/ITC), 98.

38 Annex I to the Japan-Korea BIT enumerates sectors excluded from the application of national treatment under Article 2 for each party. This includes defense, broadcasting, fisheries, the tobacco industry, and others for Korea, and nuclear energy, space, the broadcasting industry, and others for Japan.

39 Trade Policy Bureau, METI, *2015 Report on Compliance by Major Trading Partners with Trade Agreements* (WTO, FTA/EPA, BIT), 1201–1211, www.meti.go.jp/english/report/downloadfiles/2013WTO/03_08.pdf.

40 See, for instance, Chapter 6 of the Japan-Singapore EPA on "Mutual Recognition," in particular Article 46, www.mofa.go.jp/policy/economy/fta/singapore.html.

41 See, for instance, Articles 103 and 104 of the Japan-Switzerland EPA and Articles 9 to 21 of the Implementing Agreement of the Japan-Switzerland EPA, www.mofa.go.jp/policy/economy/fta/switzerland.html.

42 See, for instance, Articles 57 to 61 of the Japan-Thailand EPA and Article 8 of the Implementing Agreement of the Japan-Thailand EPA.
43 See, for instance, Article 53 of the Japan-Thailand EPA, www.mofa.go.jp/p olicy/economy/fta/thailand.html.
44 See, for instance, Articles 55 and 56 of the Japan-Thailand EPA and Articles 1 to 7 of the Implementing Agreement of the Japan-Thailand EPA, www.mofa.go.jp/policy/economy/fta/thailand.html.
45 See Solís et al., *Competitive Regionalism*, 207.
46 As of October 2014, Japan had concluded 62 double taxation treaties. Japan Ministry of Finance (MOF), *The Tax Treaty Network of Japan* [Wagakuni no sozeijōyaku nettowāku], www.mof.go.jp/tax_policy/summa ry/international/182.htm.
47 As of January 2014, Japan has signed social security agreements with 17 countries. Ministry of Health, Labour and Welfare, *International Social Security Agreement* [Shakai Hoshō Kyōtei], www.mhlw.go.jp/topics/ bukyoku/nenkin/nenkin/shakaihoshou.html.
48 Japan Ministry of Foreign Affairs, *On the Strategic Utilization of BITs* [Nikokukan tōshikyōtei no senryakuteki katsuyō nitsuite], June 2008, www. mofa.go.jp/mofaj/gaiko/investment/pdfs/bit_katsuyo.pdf.
49 Arthur Lord, "Demystifying FTAs: A Comparative Analysis of American, Japanese and Chinese Efforts to Shape the Future of Free Trade," Johns Hopkins University, *The Asia-Pacific Policy Paper Series*, no. 11 (2011).
50 Mu Yang and Siam-Heng Heng, "Promoting China-ASEAN Economic Cooperation under CAFTA Framework," *International Journal of China Studies* 1, no. 3 (2010): 667–684.
51 Marc Lanteigne, "The Sino-Swiss Free Trade Agreement," *CSS Analyses in Security Policy*, no. 147 (February 2014).
52 Raymond J. Ahearn, "Japan's Free Trade Agreement Program," *CRS Report for Congress*, 22 August 2005.
53 Xiaoming Pan, "China's FTA Strategy," *The Diplomat*, 1 June 2014, www. thediplomat.com/2014/06/chinas-fta-strategy/.
54 Shuchao Henry Gao, "China's Strategy for Free Trade Agreements: Political Battle in the Name of Trade."
55 Interview with negotiators from Ministry of Commerce, PRC. Summer 2010.
56 Prime Minister Koizumi Mail Magazine, 17 January 2002, www.kantei.go. jp/jp/m-magazine/backnumber/2002/0117.html.
57 Japan Ministry of Economy, Trade and Industry (METI), "Guiding Principles and Objectives for Negotiating the Regional Comprehensive Economic Partnership," www.meti.go.jp/press/2012/11/20121120003/201211200 03-4.pdf.
58 Interview with Chinese Ministry of Commerce (MOFCOM) officials, July 2010.
59 Keiko Yoshioka, "Joining TPP Could have China Fallout," *Asahi Shimbun*, 14 January 2011, www.asahi.com/english/TKY201101130323.html.
60 Aaron Back, Toko Sekiguchi, and Yuka Hayashi, "China, Japan, South Korea Agree to Trade Talks," *Wall Street Journal*, 13 May 2012.

4 Organizational factors in China's GPA accession negotiations

Tu Xinquan

- **Background of China's GPA negotiations**
- **The lack of political momentum in negotiations**
- **Institutional and organizational constraints in the negotiations**
- **Academic and public involvement in GPA negotiations**
- **Conclusion**

On 28 December 2007, China delivered its application and initial offer for acceding to the Agreement on Government Procurement (GPA) to the World Trade Organization (WTO) Secretariat.[1] The negotiations, which have yet to be completed, will define China's openness in an economically and politically significant market: government purchasing for its own consumption and investment. The GPA contains general principles and rules over government procurement, as well as specific commitments of individual parties. As a plurilateral agreement under the WTO, the GPA accession negotiation is similar to the negotiations for WTO accession. The negotiations take place bilaterally between the acceding member and interested parties, then shifts into a multilateral phase. With the 15-year experience of tough WTO membership talks, China should be comfortable with this process. In addition, the WTO accession has proven to be successful, which is why the Chinese government launched a series of events to commemorate the achievements of the tenth anniversary of China's WTO membership and regularly praises the multilateral institution.

However, in its first four years, China's GPA negotiations showed features different from those related to their original WTO accession. Specifically, China is taking a very different approach in terms of its political leadership, organizational arrangements, and the involvement of academics and the public. Without a formal political process based on interest groups as in democracies, these institutional features represent a Chinese style of trade politics. They have heavily influenced the negotiations so far and will assuredly shape the future results as well.

This chapter will describe the organizational features of China's GPA accession negotiations and compare them with the original WTO accession negotiations from multiple perspectives. The side-by-side portrait reveals why their unfolding has been so different and will impact the coming negotiation and the eventual outcome.

Background of China's GPA negotiations

China's commitments related to government procurement

It is hard to say that China had a government procurement regime prior to its WTO accession. The first relevant regulation was the *Interim Regulations on Government Procurement*, promulgated by the Chinese Ministry of Finance in April 1998. One year later the Committee on Financial and Economic Affairs of the National People's Congress established a drafting group for a Government Procurement Law (GPL). Another piece of procurement-related legislation is the Tendering Law, first adopted in August 1999. Designed to deter corruption through public tendering rather than to promote value for money in procurement or give preference to domestic-sourced goods and services, this law applies to both government and private tendering in construction projects.

After three years of preparation, the GPL was enacted in June 2002. However, the implementing regulations for the GPL are still under discussion, meaning that there are only abstract principles rather than concrete and applicable provisions. For example, Article 10 of the GPL provides that "[g]overnment procurements should target domestic commodities, engineering works, or services," but there is no benchmark of what constitutes domestic, nor further regulations on what will happen if a government procuring entity does not obtain domestic products.[2] This is more of a slogan rather than a legal article without compulsory requirements. However, due to this empty clause, China has a formal buy-national policy, which is subject to the GPA.

The key goal of the WTO's GPA is to eliminate discriminatory laws and practices against foreign supplies and suppliers in sales to the government.[3] In this sense, while China had no discriminative legislation, it was unnecessary to demand China to join the GPA. However, negotiating partners would not lose this opportunity to get from China as much as possible, since China was eager to enter the WTO.[4] Finally, although members are supposed to opt into joining the GPA, China was required to take some obligations relating to government procurement.[5] At the very beginning, China was not willing to accede to the

GPA. China made these commitments purely because of foreign pressure and coercion because it was considered a part of necessary costs to ensure WTO membership. In comparison, China believed from the beginning that joining the WTO was fundamental to its own interests. China's reluctance to join the GPA has resulted in a lack of political momentum in negotiations.

In the Working Party Report for China's WTO accession, China committed to initiating negotiations for membership in the GPA by tabling an "Appendix 1 offer" "as soon as possible."[6] This commitment makes it clear that China must accede to the GPA; however, the timing is ambiguous. Taking advantage of this lack of clarity, China did not submit its first application until the end of 2007, six years after joining the WTO, which hardly counts as "soon." Despite that, China has already undertaken obligations relevant to the GPA through its commitments in the Working Party Report (paragraph 339), to "providing all foreign suppliers with equal opportunity to participate in that procurement pursuant to the principle of most favored nation (MFN) treatment." Such a commitment goes beyond the requirements of the GPA since the GPA only demands non-discrimination among the GPA parties rather than the entire WTO membership.

Concerning the procurement of state-owned enterprises (SOEs), China asserted that:

> all laws, regulations and measures relating to the procurement by state-owned and state-invested enterprises of goods and services for commercial sale, production of goods or supply of services for commercial sale, or for non-governmental purposes would not be considered to be laws, regulations and measures relating to government procurement. Thus, such purchases or sales would be subject to the provisions of Articles II, XVI, and XVII of the General Agreement on Trade in Services (GATS) and Article III of the General Agreement on Tariffs and Trade (GATT) 1994.[7]

This means that from China's perspective it is not necessary to cover SOEs in the GPA since they have already undertaken the obligation of national treatment. However, the incumbent GPA parties have not been convinced by the commitment. They are afraid that SOEs submit to government directives in some cases to secretly give preference to domestic products. If SOEs are covered by the GPA, foreign suppliers believe they could challenge such actions via the GPA through the WTO's dispute settlement mechanism to deter hidden preferences for SOEs.

Nonetheless, covering SOEs in the GPA would cause serious challenges for the negotiations.[8] First, Chinese SOEs vary widely in terms of the extent of their market orientation. Even if covered by the GPA, it would be very difficult in practice to distinguish between governmental and commercial procurement by SOEs. Second, the total size of Chinese SOEs' investment and consumption is much larger than that of any other country. Since GPA negotiations are based on strict reciprocity, it is almost impossible to find a comparable SOE sector in incumbent parties. The negotiations on government procurement are not actually concerned about the scope or definition of it, but the reciprocity between members' offers. Third, the purchases of Chinese SOEs fall outside the narrow definition of "government procurement" provided by the GPL. No state enterprises that have escaped direct governmental control would like to be administered by the government again because China joined the GPA, which could be a logical expectation based on how government procurement is defined. Therefore, China's powerful state sector would be a natural opponent of GPA accession if the other WTO parties insisted on putting them under the GPA's coverage.

The United States and European Union (EU) have already requested that China list a bunch of specific SOEs in their offer. However, the Chinese negotiators have been unprepared to do this. Even with SOEs not being directly involved in the negotiation, it is still difficult for the Chinese government to make such a dramatic turn. In the context of decades of market reform, SOEs are supposed to be treated as independent market actors, not government procuring entities. Therefore, it would be very hard for the government to admit this and for SOEs to accept it.

Disputes over government procurement with other members since WTO entry

Since the GPL entered into force in 2002, all levels of the Chinese government have endeavored to develop their own regulations and practices on procurement. While the Tendering Law is focused on the procedural fairness and has no particular policy implications, the GPL clearly states that government procurement should help achieve social and economic objectives, including protecting the environment, supporting ethnic minorities and underdeveloped regions, and promoting small and medium-sized enterprises (Article 9). Further, Article 10 requires government procurers to purchase domestic products. In this sense, the GPL creates a new policy tool that government agencies welcome.

In 2004, the National Development and Reform Commission (NDRC) and the Ministry of Finance (MOF) jointly promulgated *Opinions on Implementation of Government Procurement of Energy-efficient Products*, in which government procurement was taken as a formal policy tool towards specific goals for the first time. Given the overwhelming legitimacy of lower emissions, the policy did not attract much attention from foreign companies and countries. In February 2006 the State Council issued the *National Guideline on the Medium- and Long-Term Program for Science and Technology Development (2006–2020)*, which clearly claimed to implement government procurement policy with the intention of promoting indigenous technology innovation.[9] At the end of 2006, the Ministry of Science and Technology (MOST), the MOF, and the NDRC jointly issued a document entitled *Trial Measures for the Administration of the Accreditation of National Indigenous Innovation Products*, which defines the products that are eligible for the status of "indigenous innovation" and then for the preferable considerations in government procurement.[10] These measures resulted in a series of complaints from foreign companies in China because they essentially excluded products made by foreign-invested companies because of a requirement that the manufacturer of the product should have ownership of the trademark. Since then, the element of China's indigenous innovation policies related to government procurement have been under continuous attack from foreign companies in China.

While the word "procurement" was not visible in the American Chamber of Commerce in China's (AmCham) 2005 White Paper, AmCham began to list government procurement as a particularly important part of leveling the playing field for technology competition in its 2006 edition.[11] The criticism became much fiercer after Notice No. 618 was jointly issued by MOST, the NDRC, and the MOF in November 2009, which aimed to establish an Indigenous Innovation Product Accreditation System.[12] American and European companies in China kept pressing the Chinese government to clarify the relevant regulations and make sure there would be no discrimination against them as a result.

In the early years after China's WTO entry, European and American attention on China's GPA commitment was relatively low. The top priority at that time was making sure China implemented its broader WTO commitments. At the same time, the Chinese government did not use government procurement as a policy tool to support domestic industries, and foreign companies were treated positively as opposed to discriminated against, in Chinese government procurement.[13] As the

Chinese government began to realize the value of government procurement in pursuing some industrial policy goals and to make some movements in this direction, foreign companies and governments subsequently and promptly focused on China's commitment in its WTO package and pressed China to give up the initiative. Of course, it would be best to integrate China into the GPA, which is why at the April 2006 meeting of the US-China Joint Committee on Commerce and Trade (JCCT), Vice Premier Wu Yi agreed to commence China's GPA accession negotiations before the end of 2007.[14] It is hard to say that the Chinese government was truly prepared to launch the negotiations, not to mention willing to join the GPA as soon as possible. With a procurement regime established only three years earlier, the government had just begun to understand what it was and how it should be regulated and used. However, because of increased foreign pressure and China's actual WTO commitments, the Chinese government had to show respect for its international obligations. This lack of internal motivation placed the GPA negotiations in a totally different starting point from those for China's overall WTO accession.

The long years of GPA negotiations

China delivered its initial offer along with its application at the end of 2007.[15] The responses from negotiating parties were largely critical. Although they praised the submissions as a good start, they were very dissatisfied with China's offer. To be fair, China's offer was narrow. First, the coverage of entities was limited to a portion of central government agencies, not to mention sub-national or nongovernmental entities. Second, the coverage of goods and services was also very small and only included general products. Third, the thresholds were much higher than the average level of the incumbent parties. Fourth, China introduced several exemptions in the general notes. It is obvious that China knew that this offer would not meet foreign expectations. In other words, China deliberately delivered a weak proposal to meet the bare minimum requirements in its WTO commitments and simultaneously show its passive attitude toward the negotiations. The underlying message might be "do not hold too high expectations of us."

In the face of continuous pressure from the United States and EU, China came up with a revised offer on 9 July 2010. This new version contained modest progress in terms of the central entities covered, agreeing to raise the thresholds over time, and included a new offer on the procurement of services. However, the improvement was far less than expected. In January 2011, China announced that it would submit a third "offer to the WTO Government Procurement Committee before the Committee's final meeting in 2011, which will include sub-central entities."[16] In previous GPA accession negotiations for Taiwan and South Korea, the third offer was usually the final one or at least close to the final one. Some Chinese officials expressed this goal. For example, then Chinese Ambassador to the WTO Sun Zhenyu admonished parties not to be "too demanding" of the Chinese offer.[17]

Commerce Minister Chen Deming also implied that this coming new offer might be the last one. On 30 November 2011, the Chinese government fulfilled its commitment to come up with the third offer. The largest improvement was that local governments were covered for the first time in Annex 2, including five of the richest provinces: Beijing, Tianjin, Shanghai, Zhejiang, and Jiangsu. Their joint gross domestic product (GDP) accounts for about one-quarter of the national total.

Nonetheless, the incumbent GPA parties were not fully satisfied with the results. For them, this was the best time to open the Chinese government procurement market. Once China became a signatory, it would be much more difficult to press the Chinese government to make further concessions. This is a lesson they had learned from China's WTO accession. The Chinese government was willing to implement its commitments, but reluctant to make new ones. More importantly, the Chinese state plays a much more significant role in the economy than in other countries, despite 30 years of market-oriented reforms. In the wake of the global financial crisis, the Chinese government seemed more confident in its economic management approach. For example, Premier Wen Jiabao stated in his work report that, "[w]e must be guided by realities in deciding when market forces are to play the greater role and when government control is to play the greater role."[18] This actually means that the government still prevails over the market since the power of choice rests in the hands of the government. Therefore, one should expect that the share of the Chinese government procurement market on the whole market would continue to expand. This is certainly a very attractive prospect for foreign suppliers.

As a result of continuous pressure and negotiations, the Chinese government made other offers in November 2012, January 2014, and most recently in December 2014.[19] China was to submit a revised offer in early 2017.[20] However, the Chinese negotiators added new concessions in a manner akin to squeezing toothpaste out of a tube. The changes were still marginal, with nine more provincial governments included, lowering the thresholds gradually, and listing some more services sectors. All these improvements are far from what the other parties expect from China. The negotiations of China's accession have gone on for a long time and created a new historical record, with no end yet in sight.

Key elements of China's GPA accession negotiations

Agreeing on what constitutes government procurement is the problem most central to China's GPA accession. Neither the 1994 GATT documents nor the GPA itself has a clear-cut definition of government procurement. The GATT defines it as procurement for governmental purposes, but leaves unanswered what governmental purposes are. The GPA adopted as part of the Uruguay Round in 1994 only specifies the contractual means of procurement. The GPA revised in 2011 combines the above two approaches and develops a more comprehensive definition of government procurement, which refers to any kind of procurement by covered entities for non-commercial purposes. The scope of coverage of government procurement is subject to negotiation for each party. This ambiguity was feasible because the current parties are mostly developed market economies. Government procurement is an exception to the whole market, which is mostly for the consumption of government. However, in the case of China, the role of government is too large to be separated from the market. In fact, the government is a major investment and market entity in China. The state sector, including SOEs as well as central and local government agencies, accounts for one-third of the total fixed asset investment, meaning that it is the single largest investor in China.[21] For example, the Chinese Railway Ministry is almost the only constructor of railways, investing trillions of dollars in recent years on the high-speed railway system. The Beijing–Shanghai High-Speed Railway alone cost 220 billion Renminbi (RMB). Interestingly, in March 2011, the National Audit Office found that more than RMB 4 billion in contracts were awarded without proper tendering.[22]

Therefore, the role various levels of the Chinese government play as an investor poses a serious challenge to the current GPA system. As arguably the weakest part of the world trading system, the GPA has no ability to accommodate China's massive state sector. It is also hard for the Chinese government to put its investment under the scrutiny of an international organization.

Moreover, China's own government procurement regime is far from consistent or coherent. According to the national GPL:

> Government procurement refers to all the purchasing activities with fiscal funds conducted by state organs at all levels, public

institutions, and social organizations where the intended goods, construction, and services are those listed in the *Centralized Procurement Catalogue (CPC)* published by the procuring authority or those whose value exceeds the respective *Prescribed Procurement Thresholds (PPT)* for goods, construction, or services.

This is a very narrow definition. It excludes all state enterprises, but the fact is most governmental investments are conducted by SOEs. For example, the China Three Gorges Corporation, an SOE, was the nominal constructor and investor of the huge Three Gorges project. Although the State Council established the company, its procurement is not regulated by the GPL. As for procured items, it only covers those listed in the central procurement catalogue or those with values above a certain threshold. In addition, the GPL only considers purchases as procurement when budgetary fiscal funds are used. This means that even the purchases of covered procuring entities are not subject to the GPL as long as they are not financed by fiscal funds. This limitation is quite problematic and unviable.

In fact, almost all public entities, including many governmental agencies, have financial earnings beyond fiscal grants. For example, a majority of the earnings of China's public hospitals are dependent on their semi-commercial activities such as drug sales and medical services. Fiscal funds from the Ministry of Health or local governments only cover the salaries of faculty and staff, and construction projects. The same holds true in many public universities and schools. In reality, these public institutions are required by their supervising governmental agencies to follow government procurement regulations. Their procurement is also subject to public tendering by themselves or other designated centralized procuring entities. Usually these institutions follow specific tendering regulations stipulated by their supervising agencies based on the Tendering Law. However, they do not take this kind of procurement as *government* procurement but rather *centralized* procurement because their procuring funds are not from fiscal allocations. Therefore, they do not have to obey the buy-domestic rule provided for in the GPL. As such, most of their procurement is not subject to the GPA.

The fragmented Chinese government procurement system poses a great challenge to its accession to the GPA. As previously mentioned, the GPA has no clear definition of government procurement. Therefore the scope of government procurement of individual parties largely rests on their own legal definition. While China's current government procurement regime does not clearly specify its coverage, it is difficult for

both Chinese and foreign negotiators to ascertain what they are negotiating about. For example, even though a public university is listed in
China's offer, it is still debatable whether all its procurement is subject
to GPA rules because its purchases, using its own funds, instead of
those out of the government budget, do not have to abide by China's
government procurement regime, and hence, do not have to follow the
WTO's GPA rules. The GPA accession negotiations will certainly help
clarify and integrate China's government procurement regime, but if
China accedes to the GPA before these inconsistencies are resolved,
implementation will be quite troublesome.

The lack of political momentum in negotiations

It is commonly recognized that the success of China's accession to the
WTO largely depended on the political determination and support of
the Chinese leadership.[23] There was strong opposition from a lot of
industries and the ministries behind them. Also, some academic
research questioned the motives of the United States and questioned
the economic benefits of entry. However, the top leaders were firmly
supportive of WTO accession because they believed that overall it was
beneficial to China both politically and economically. Importantly,
China's leaders did not consider WTO accession as a purely economic
issue, but also a critical step in the broader process of reform and
opening. Such political momentum significantly facilitated the technical level of the negotiations. President Jiang Zemin and Premier Zhu
Rongji repeatedly emphasized the correctness and necessity of WTO
accession in domestic events and affirmed China's willingness to accede
to the WTO.[24] They also gave high priority to this issue in various
international meetings with WTO members. In the most difficult
period, when negotiations almost collapsed in 1999, President Jiang
and Premier Zhu stepped in personally to keep the negotiations going.
In April 1999, Premier Zhu met with US negotiators in person and
resolved the last issues in question. Their contributions were vital to
the final conclusion of the negotiations. As Chinese top leaders were
convinced of the significance and necessity of the WTO, their power
and determination were critical to accession.

While the WTO accession negotiations attracted the attention of top
leaders, the GPA negotiations have been largely neglected. President
Hu Jintao never mentioned the negotiations in public, nor talked about
this issue with his counterparts. Premier Wen Jiabao at several points
did mention the ongoing negotiations and claimed foreign companies
would be accorded national treatment in China in government

procurement, but he did not indicate his own attitude toward the accession to the GPA.[25] The new Chinese leadership that came into office in late 2012 showed they were strongly in favor of further reform and opening. *The Decision on Major Issues Concerning Comprehensively Deepening Reforms* adopted by the Third Plenary Session of the Eighteenth Chinese Communist Party (CCP) Central Committee in November 2013 commits to accelerate the negotiations on government procurement.[26] As a part of the comprehensive governmental reforms, Premier Li Keqiang has aggressively promoted government procurement of public services. However, at present it is still unclear whether China's leadership is positively or negatively disposed toward the GPA, which suggests they are unsure of the consequences of joining. So they have shied away from expressing a strong opinion on the issue.

Of course, the GPA accession is by no means comparable to the WTO accession in economic or political terms. However, its significance should not be underestimated either, especially its effect on the government and SOEs. WTO rules are designed to restrict government intervention in market activities, while the GPA directly regulates the government's own activities. Once it has joined the GPA, the government's autonomy on consumption and investment are greatly reduced. In China, government-sponsored investment has long been considered a useful tool to induce and stimulate social investment. In response to the 2008 global financial crisis, the Chinese government launched an RMB 4 trillion stimulus package. If SOEs were covered by the GPA, they would have to follow the government procurement rules. According to Geneva sources quoted by *Inside US Trade*, China's sixth revised offer is expected to cover more SOEs and more provinces than previous offers.[27] WTO accession has demonstrated that greater market access and openness is not harmful to the Chinese economy, but the GPA accession is largely not an issue of market access but a major reform of the government and state sector.

For the Chinese government, it would make sense to use the opportunity of GPA accession to streamline its government procurement regime. Since the state sector will remain very large in the foreseeable future, its procurement should be put under a stricter and more transparent regulatory system to ensure good value for money and reduce corruption. In recent years, corruption related to tendering has expanded. This is no good for the legitimacy of the Chinese government and is worth more attention. Although the direct benefits of GPA accession might not be very visible, the negotiating process could at least again be an opportunity for the government to use foreign pressure to reform the current system.

It is a bit puzzling that there has been no systematic analysis on the costs and benefits of China's accession to the GPA.[28] This may be the case partially because it is difficult to estimate the economic impact of joining the GPA. Government procurement is a domestic system so it is almost impossible to grasp the trade implications of opening up the government procurement market. Previous GPA negotiations, such as the US-EU negotiations, calculated the covered market size rather than conducting a traditional analysis of the change in trade policy. In qualitative terms, the benefits of GPA entry are not so visible. Even the most direct gains of access to other parties' government procurement markets are uncertain because of the possible poor implementation of the agreement as well as because of the discrimination against Chinese SOEs in some members' investment and procurement policies. Major parties such as the United States and the EU cannot show solid statistical evidence that their procurement markets are large, open, and attractive for Chinese supplies and suppliers. In fact, there is some research showing that the market access effect of GPA entry is highly questionable. A study conducted by the European Commission finds that only 3.5 percent of EU government procurement expenditures went to non-EU entities between 2007 and 2009.[29] Interestingly, the study also shows that the import penetration rate of China's public sector is 6.1 percent, higher than that of the United States (4.6 percent) and Japan (4.7 percent), and a little lower than that of the EU (7.5 percent) and Canada (6.9 percent).[30] Anirudh Shingal finds that despite the GPA, the proportion of services contracts awarded to foreigners has declined over time for Japan and Switzerland.[31] Therefore, the space of expanding foreign market access through GPA accession for China seems limited and far from guaranteed.

Another big problem is that no one can give an accurate accounting of China's government procurement market. This is partly due to the vague definition of government procurement in the GPL. Currently, the MOF publishes annual procurement statistics, but this only covers the procurement of central and local governments as defined by the GPL. Total procurement in 2011 was RMB 1.13 trillion, accounting for only 2.4 percent of GDP.[32] The narrow coverage surely dissatisfies the partners who are eager to occupy China's huge government market. The EU Chamber of Commerce in China gave an alternative estimate, of RMB 7 trillion in 2009, ten times the official figure.[33] In comparison, EU procurement under the coverage of the GPA in 2007 was €293 billion (or RMB 2.5 trillion).[34] China has to calculate its offer based on the principle of reciprocity and is unlikely to accept the US and EU calculations of the market size.

At the same time, the costs of GPA entry are clearer: the government will lose its discretion in choosing between government control and market forces. While government control over investment and consumption is considered a vital tool to facilitate economic and social development, surrendering these powers seems to be too large a cost to join the GPA. In fact, the supporters of GPA accession in China believe the most significant benefit is the promotion of reform and the improvement of China's government procurement system. Following the approach of the WTO accession negotiations, foreign pressure and international rules are seen as a tool to fight against domestic resistance and help establish a more market-oriented and open system. This argument made sense in the case of WTO accession. At present, though, the Chinese economy is much stronger and the Chinese government is more confident in its policies. It is harder to prove the necessity and feasibility of adopting new norms. Although the Chinese leadership is clearly aware of serious problems in its procurement system, they do not think it necessary to depend on foreign pressure to tackle this issue.

Since China was keen to enter the WTO in the late 1990s, its negotiating counterparts had sufficient leverage to compel China to accept some unreasonable conditions. In contrast, China has no serious interest in joining the GPA. Therefore, China is likely to stick to its negotiating positions based on its own preferences. Conversely, while China could have lost big had it not become a WTO member (for example, the United States might have revoked China's MFN status), in the case of GPA accession China has much less to lose if it does not join the GPA since the other GPA parties have not allowed China into their government procurement markets and still may not do so once China joins.[35] Therefore, China is waiting to be offered better conditions from the current GPA parties. It has been difficult to energize China's top leaders to feel a sense of urgency to join the agreement.

Institutional and organizational constraints in the negotiations

Unlike the WTO accession negotiations, the Chinese government did not establish an inter-ministerial coordination body on GPA negotiations. This partly reflects the government's lack of emphasis on the issue. Therefore, the government chose a single ministry as the coordinating agency. Although the Ministry of Commerce (MOFCOM) is the lead agency for trade, including negotiating China's WTO accession, the GPA covers both government procurement and trade policy. As a result, the MOF was designated as the primary domestic regulatory authority for government procurement, and hence, became the lead agency for China's GPA accession negotiation.

If there were a consensus among the Chinese leadership about the significance of the GPA, it would not be important who was in charge of the negotiations. There would be a common target for all the relevant ministries, and they would not take their own interests into account. In the case of WTO accession, MOFCOM (then the Ministry of Foreign Trade and Economic Cooperation—MOFTEC) was not superior to other ministries, but due to top leadership support, MOFTEC could coordinate with other ministries to shape consistent negotiation proposals. Sometimes, it even ignored the opposition of some ministries. An inter-ministerial working group headed by State Councilor Wu Yi, who was a former commerce minister, also played the essential role of resolving conflicts among different ministries.[36]

The choice of lead agency seems to have had a great effect on the process and results of the GPA negotiation. First, compared with MOFCOM, the MOF has less experience and expertise in international negotiations. The actual agency responsible within the ministry is its Treasury Department, which is also charged with regulating government procurement. Their expertise largely focuses on domestic regulation rather than the trade policy implications of government procurement. They have no experience in hosting international negotiations in terms of coordinating with other ministries or bargaining with other countries. Second, the MOF is not a proponent of trade liberalization as MOFCOM has been. Although it basically favors GPA accession, its primary motive is to use this opportunity to enhance its jurisdiction and power in government procurement and promote consistency in procurement regulations. The MOF does not see GPA accession as a step toward further trade liberalization. Therefore, it is difficult for the MOF to mobilize traditional supporters of free trade and to confront protectionists. Third, the MOF has not had sufficient coordination authority to establish a consistent negotiation strategy. The MOF is the legitimate regulatory agency for government procurement, but the powerful NDRC, which drafted and oversees the Tendering Law, also has an interest in government procurement management, creating an overlap in authority between the two agencies. However, the NDRC is in charge of making and implementing Chinese industrial policy and has close connections with most manufacturing and service sectors. Hence, the NDRC is often considered a representative of Chinese industrial interests, especially those of large SOEs.

Without a superior inter-ministerial coordination body, the MOF has taken full charge of coordinating and negotiating China's positions.

However, whereas MOFTEC tended to confine the negotiations to a small circle and make decisions using their own professional negotiators in order to avoid open debate, the MOF has actively solicited participation across many ministries and agencies. The MOF has established a GPA research working group, which is led by the MOF and comprises a wide range of agencies. This actually parallels the function of the State Council WTO Leading Work Group during the WTO accession negotiations. This group is of a much lower rank than its WTO counterpart, however. While the WTO group was led by a vice premier, the head of the GPA group is a vice minister. Its members from ministries are mainly division-level directors-general, whereas the WTO coordinating group was composed of higher-ranking vice ministers and ministers.

The working group is divided into a number of sub-groups, namely for general issues, services procurement, goods procurement, construction procurement, SOE procurement, military procurement, and local government procurement. Each sub-group conducts research on the scope and size of government procurement and the effect of GPA accession on industry competitiveness, and then puts forward possible proposals under the GPA's Appendix 1 based on their analysis. The advantage of this approach is that it could increase enthusiasm and participation of the relevant ministries and gather valuable information and inputs from them. The disadvantage is that it makes coordination more complicated since it generates a wider diversity of ideas among the negotiating team. Another problem is that research results and conclusions are offered sporadically and are hard to integrate into a single proposal.

A significant change occurred after the new leadership stepped into office. In November 2013, the Chinese government established a leading group on GPA negotiations headed by Vice Premier Zhang Gaoli, with more than 20 ministries and agencies as members. The group significantly enhances the level of inter-ministerial coordination and shows the importance the government attaches to the negotiations. Nonetheless, it is a little perplexing that the leading group has reportedly never convened a meeting. The reason is allegedly that the MOF has not yet submitted a reasonable and feasible solution to the negotiations. If this were true, it would mean a continuing lack of consensus in the Chinese leadership regarding GPA accession.

Academic and public involvement in GPA negotiations

China is often viewed as an authoritarian state in which public opinion has little influence on the central policymaking process. However, if policymakers want to achieve a specific policy goal, they have to take into account public opinion and get public support.

During China's WTO accession process, there were two or three waves of public GATT-WTO fever. Not only were all levels of government mobilized to study the WTO rules, but the Chinese public and academia actively participated in the discussions. Over 3,000 WTO-related books were published during the years surrounding WTO accession. These discussions were generally supportive of China's further opening-up and WTO accession. These publications and opinions were also used as an argument for Chinese leaders and MOFTEC to counter opponents from industrial ministries.

Chinese scholars, especially economists, took a supportive attitude toward WTO accession. Since the mid-1990s Chinese economists have adopted Western economic theories and approaches. Their research on the national economic impact of WTO accession was based on general equilibrium models, which inevitably present a positive overall effect of trade liberalization. Influential think tanks in China such as the Chinese Academy of Social Sciences (CASS) and the Development Research Center (DRC) conducted comprehensive studies on the effects of WTO accession for the economy and specific sectors. While they found some industries would possibly suffer losses, they concluded that the overall economic effects were positive. This kind of conclusion was a useful retort to industrial protectionism in the name of the national interest. These studies reached the same conclusion as those carried out by famous foreign economists from international organizations such as the World Bank and overseas academic institutions.[37] Their neutrality and professionalism made their studies even more influential than those of their counterparts in China. Many professors and researchers in this area were frequently invited to give lectures and interviews with government agencies, companies, universities, and the media, creating a national atmosphere in favor of WTO accession. For the Chinese negotiators, academic research and involvement provided considerable support in domestic bargaining. They also actively organized scholars to conduct more research and propaganda activities. For example, chief negotiator Long Yongtu personally edited a set of books with contributions from scholars from universities and research institutions.[38]

Public opinion was also in favor of WTO accession. The Chinese government managed to persuade the public that joining the WTO was beneficial to them, as it would lead to less expensive imports and domestic products, and to more choice for consumers. The government also convinced the public that the overall growth of the economy would diffuse benefits broadly to the public. As a result, although there was increasing nationalism in the late 1990s in China, the public was positively disposed to China's decision to join the WTO. Close academic and public involvement played a positive role in negotiators securing national support and facilitating domestic coordination.

As for the GPA accession negotiations, similar public support and involvement could be helpful. However, academia and the public are hardly aware of the issue, not to mention actively participating. There are only a small number of scholars based at various universities who have taken part in research on GPA accession, including the Central University of Finance and Economics, Tsinghua University, Zhongnan University of Economics and Law, the University of International Relations, and the University of International Business and Economics. Some of them were invited by the MOF and other ministries to be consultants in the negotiations. However, this is still a very small circle. Most of these scholars are experts who focus on the legal and technical aspects of government procurement rather than economics and trade policy. Hence, there are few studies that involve a cost–benefit analysis of GPA accession. Their studies could help explain the current Chinese government procurement system and how it would be affected by joining the GPA, but they might be unable to answer why joining GPA is beneficial for China.

It is understandable that government procurement and the GPA have not gained much attention from academia. China's own government procurement system was only created in the last decade. Scholars need more time to accumulate their knowledge on this topic. Since a lot of problems have arisen in the operation of this system, most attention by scholars has focused on addressing technical issues. It may be too early for them to care about the GPA. For those who focus on the WTO, trade policy, and economics, the GPA is much less important than other issues such as the Doha Round, trade remedies, and free trade agreements (FTAs). Most books on the WTO ignore or only touch superficially on this plurilateral agreement. However, for Chinese negotiators, it is necessary to pay more attention to support, stimulate, and foster academic research. The MOF has a huge annual research budget available for GPA research. These funds are assigned to relevant agencies which in turn organize their own teams. Most funds go to institutions directly supervised by these agencies. Although some outside scholars are also invited into these teams, the overall research circle is still very limited.

By contrast, the public has paid close attention to government procurement because of so many corruption cases related to big public works projects. It is widely reported that many officials manipulate tendering procedures to award contracts to those who bribe them. Almost all malfeasance occurs in backroom transactions relating to project tendering.[39] A more recent example is Liu Zhijun, the former Minister of Railways. The public also cares about government procurement because they are directly affected by its inefficiencies and deficiencies, especially those who work in government agencies and public institutions. Therefore, the public would be happy to see a more transparent and efficient system in place. However, they are unaware of the GPA accession negotiations and its potentially positive effects in improving the government procurement regime because the media do not cover this issue.

Compared to WTO accession, Chinese academia and the public have not been mobilized to support GPA accession. Their support might not be indispensable for the negotiators, but it would undoubtedly be very helpful. The negotiators should try their best to activate academic and public participation in the negotiations and seize this kind of legitimacy to counter domestic resistance.

Conclusion

Joining the GPA is an important part of China's further integration into the world trading system following WTO accession. Though its economic and political significance is not comparable to that of WTO accession, it would still be very helpful for China to construct a transparent, open, and efficient government procurement regime.

The accomplishment of China's WTO accession negotiations partly depended on the organization of the process. In particular, the negotiators successfully managed to mobilize supportive actors ranging from top leaders to the public to overwhelm strong domestic opposition.

However, in the case of the GPA, the negotiators have not expended enough effort trying to form a wide and strong constituency in favor of accession. The greatest constraint on GPA accession is the lack of attention and support from the Chinese leadership. This is largely due to the nature of GPA accession itself, but another reason is that its significance is underestimated. China has created a different coordination mechanism and appointed a new chief negotiator for the GPA negotiations. This change has had a negative effect on the process and results. A lower-ranked coordination body is not powerful enough to eliminate wide divergences among the relevant ministries and other actors. Also, without sufficient expertise and authority, it is difficult for the MOF to play the role smoothly as the chief negotiator and coordinator. The failure to activate public and academic involvement is another reason why the negotiators cannot dominate the floor with greater legitimacy.

There are many internal and external factors that could influence the process and results of an international economic negotiation, but the organizational aspects are arguably most critical in some sense. In the case of the WTO accession negotiation, the 1998 government restructuring and subsequent new coordination regime instantly enhanced the momentum and efficiency behind entry.[40] Similarly, it might be time to restructure China's negotiating team for GPA accession and to take full advantage of the negotiations as an opportunity to set up a transparent, open, and efficient government procurement regime.

Notes

1 The background and process of China's GPA accession has been discussed in Robert Anderson, "China's Accession to the WTO Agreement on Government Procurement: Procedural Considerations, Potential Benefits and Challenges, and Implications of the Ongoing Re-negotiation of the Agreement," *Public Procurement Law Review* 16, no. 4 (2008): 161–175.

2 There are several different English translations of this clause, demonstrating that even Chinese people cannot understand its actual meaning.

3 Peter Trepte states that the original goal of negotiation on government procurement was the achievement of reciprocal trade advantages. Peter Trepte, "The Agreement on Government Procurement," in *The World Trade Organization: Legal, Economic and Political Analysis*, ed. Patrick F.J. Macrory, Arthur E. Appleton, and Michael G. Plummer (New York: Springer, 2005), 1123–1164.

4 According to a US official involved in the negotiations, US companies operating in China were not very interested in demanding China enter the GPA upon WTO accession since they enjoyed some advantages over competitors from other countries for Chinese government contracts due to the importance of the US–China relationship to China.

5 Several WTO members, including Croatia, Saudi Arabia, Mongolia, Ukraine, the former Yugoslav republics of Macedonia, and Chinese Taipei all committed to accede to the GPA in their WTO accession protocols.

6 *Report of the Working Party on the Accession of China* (WT/ACC/CHN/49), paragraph 341, 1 October 2001.

7 *Report of the Working Party on the Accession of China* (WT/ACC/CHN/49), paragraph 47.

8 Wang Ping has done a comprehensive analysis on the topic. See Wang Ping, "Coverage of WTO's Agreement on Government Procurement: Challenges of Integrating China and Other Countries with Large State Sectors into the Global Trading System," *Journal of International Economic Law* 10, no. 4 (September 2007): 887–920.

9 State Council of the People's Republic of China, *National Guideline on the Medium- and Long-Term Program for Science and Technology Development (2006–2020)*, www.gov.cn/jrzg/2006-02/09/content_183787.htm.
10 See Jingxia Shi, "China's Indigenous Innovation and Government Procurement," *ICTSD Bridges Review* 14, no. 3 (2010), www.ictsd.org/i/news/bridges/84883/.
11 American Chamber of Commerce in China, *White Paper* (2005, 2006), www.amchamchina.org.
12 The European Chamber of Commerce in China claimed that the "Notice 618 greatly alarmed the foreign business community" in their *European Business in China Position Paper* (2010/11): 111, www.europeanchamber.com.cn/images/documents/marketing_department/beijing/publications/2010/public_procurement.pdf.
13 Although there is no systematic evidence showing that governments prefer products made by foreign companies, in 2009 55 percent of the government's procurement contracts for mechanical and electronic products were given to foreign companies. See Li Ruogu, "West Should Embrace Competition," *China Daily*, 11 January 2011, www.chinadaily.com.cn/opinion/2011-01/11/content_11829673.htm.
14 US Department of Commerce, "US-China Trade Talks Achieve 'Clear Progress'," April 2006, www.trade.gov/press/publications/newsletters/ita_0406/jcct_0406.asp.
15 The Chinese text is available at www.gov.cn/gzdt/2008-05/13/content_971032.htm.
16 White House, "US-China Joint Statement," 19 January 2011, www.whitehouse.gov/the-press-office/2011/01/19/us-china-joint-statement.
17 "'Don't be Too Demanding' on GPA Offer," *China Daily*, 6 August 2010.
18 Wen Jiabao, *Report on the Work of the Government, Delivered at the Fourth Session of the Eleventh National People's Congress*, 5 March 2011.
19 World Trade Organization, *Committee on Government Procurement Moves Ahead on Multiple Accessions*, 11 February 2015, www.wto.org/english/news_e/news15_e/gpro_11feb15_e.htm.
20 "China to Submit Revised Offer to Join Procurement Agreement at WTO," *Inside US Trade*, 27 February 2017, https://insidetrade.com/daily-news/china-submit-revised-offer-join-procurement-agreement-wto.
21 From January to August 2011, state-owned enterprises contribute RMB 6.24 trillion of a total of RMB 18.1 trillion in fixed asset investment. National Bureau of Statistics, *China Statistical Yearbook 2012*, www.stats.gov.cn/tjsj/ndsj/2012/indexeh.htm.
22 "Some Beijing-Shanghai High-Speed Railway Projects Were Started Without Bidding: Chief Auditor," *Xinhua News Agency*, 27 June 2011, http://news.xinhuanet.com/english2010/china/2011-06/27/c_13952500.htm.
23 Joseph Fewsmith, "The Political and Social Implications of China's Accession to the WTO," *China Quarterly* 167 (September 2001): 573–591.
24 Wei Liang, "Regime Type and International Negotiation: A Case Study of US/China Bilateral Negotiations for China's Accession to the WTO," PhD Dissertation, University of Southern California (2003): 294–301.
25 "Chinese Premier Reassures Foreign Firms on Business Environment, Government Procurement," *Xinhua News Agency*, 29 April 2010, www.news.xinhuanet.com/english2010/china/2010-04/29/c_13272937.htm.

26 Translated text is available at: www.chinadaily.com.cn/language_tips/news/2013-11/20/content_17118489.htm.

27 "China to Submit Revised Offer to Join Procurement Agreement at WTO," *Inside US Trade.*

28 Wang Ping believes that the lack of such analysis has resulted in the lack of political momentum paid to GPA accession. Wang Ping, "China's Accession to the WTO Government Procurement Agreement: Challenges and the Way Forward," *Journal of International Economic Law* 12, no. 3 (September 2009): 663–706.

29 European Commission, *Cross-Border Procurement above EU Thresholds: Final Report* (2011): 10.

30 European Commission, *Cross-Border Procurement above EU Thresholds: Final Report*, 24.

31 Anirudh Shingal, "Services Procurement under the WTO's Agreement on Government Procurement: Whither Market Access?" *World Trade Review* 10, no. 4 (October 2011): 527–549.

32 "Scope and Scale Continuously Expand in Ten Years Since Issuance of Government Procurement Law," 29 June 2012, www.politics.people.com.cn/n/2012/0629/c70731-18413380.html.

33 European Chamber of Commerce in China, *Public Procurement in China: European Business Experiences Competing for Public Contracts in China* (2011): 15, www.europeanchamber.com.cn.

34 Robert D. Anderson, Philippe Pelletier, Kodjo Osei-Lah, and Anna Caroline Muller, "Assessing the Value of Future Accessions to the WTO Agreement on Government Procurement (GPA): Some New Data, Sources, Provisional Estimates, and an Evaluative Framework for Individual WTO Members Considering Accession," *WTO Working Paper*, ERSD-2011-15 (6 October 2011).

35 Although only the United States has explicit limitations on imports in government procurement, other GPA members have their own ways to restrict foreign supplies and suppliers in their procurement practices.

36 Liang, "Regime Type and International Negotiation," 301–304.

37 World Bank, *WTO Accession, Policy Reform and Poverty for China* (Washington, DC: World Bank, 2002).

38 The book series, "Globalization, WTO, China," was published by Chinese Foreign Economic and Trade Press.

39 It is reported that from September 2009 to March 2011, 15,010 government officials were found to be involved in corruption crimes related to construction project tendering. See "Hidden Rules in Governmental Projects," *Southern Weekend*, 4 August 2011.

40 Hui Feng, *The Politics of China's Accession to the World Trade Organization: The Dragon Goes Global* (New York: Routledge, 2006).

5   China and the G20

A reform-minded status quo power

Ren Xiao

- Creating theoretical space for a reform-minded status quo power
- China becomes a member of the international monetary leadership
- The G20's ascent and China's participation
- Five key issues
- The G20 and global economic governance
- Conclusion

Creating theoretical space for a reform-minded status quo power

Is China a revisionist power in world politics? What kind of world is today's China pursuing? What kind of power will China be in the future? These are profound and controversial questions that have attracted much attention. Some realist international relations theorists predict that the basic pressures of the international system will force the United States and China into conflict. They argue that a rising China is revisionist at both the regional and global levels and is thus challenging the existing world order.[1] According to John Mearsheimer, all major powers inevitably seek global hegemony, and China is no different. On that basis, he predicts an inevitable clash between the United States, the established power and global hegemon, and China, the rising global power and aspirant hegemon.[2] Mearsheimer's assessment of China is more a deduction from his theory of "offensive realism" rather than solidly based on empirical research, and is seen by scholars such as David Shambaugh as being "disconnected from reality and history."[3]

However, realists are not unified. Those who place more attention on the potential variation in intentions and strategy of both the rising and incumbent powers see conflict as less than inevitable. For Robert Art, although China will try to shape its environment, "[g]reat-power status does not doom a state to be aggressively expansionist and warlike, especially in the modern era, when the generation of wealth has been severed from territorial conquest and when nuclear weapons make great-power war problematic. China's growing power will not inevitably bring a hot or even a cold war with the United States. After all, power is not destiny."[4] Conversely, realist observer Christopher Layne places as much weight on the United States as China, arguing "a Sino-American war is not inevitable. Whether such a conflict occurs will hinge more on Washington's strategic choices than on Beijing's."[5]

Studies based more on empirical analysis have also raised doubts and find that evidence points to a different assessment.[6] Alastair Iain Johnston's exploration of a wide range of policies finds that it is hard to conclude that China is a clearly revisionist state operating outside, or barely inside, the boundaries of a so-called international community. In 40-odd years China moved from being a revolutionary revisionist state to a more status quo-oriented one.[7] Feng Huiyun's statistical analysis of the public statements of China's top leaders challenges claims that Chinese leaders share revisionist beliefs, finding that, aside from Mao, none of the others has been an offensive realist.[8]

Finally, those who focus on the domestic and international constraints of China's actions argue against seeing China as revisionist. Evan Medeiros argues that China "is not trying to tear down or radically revise the current constellation of global rules, norms, and institutions on economic and security affairs."[9] He argues that even as China's capabilities grow, "the internal constraint and external restraints on a revisionist turn in China's foreign and defense policies remain substantial, and some of them will increase."[10] In his seminal study, *Social States*, which analyzes China's membership in various security institutions, Johnston argues that China has been socialized in those institutions to become more cooperative. His findings point in the direction of China as a status quo power.[11] China's compliance with and observation of the rules of the game in the World Trade Organization (WTO), discussed in this volume by James Scott and Rorden Wilkinson in Chapter 1, and Wang Yong in Chapter 2, provide reassuring examples.

However, the debate between status quo and anti-status quo posits a false dichotomy and requires more nuance. Johnston helpfully offers five indicators to assess whether an actor is a status quo seeker. They move from the least to the most challenging of the status quo and are further grouped into two sets.[12] The first set, which includes the degree of participation, acceptance of the norms of the community, and desire for change when possible, is especially illuminating for the case of China in the Group of 20 (G20). This multi-tiered sliding scale is theoretically helpful, but we need more than a linear spectrum with two end-points.

To be a status quo power does not mean only accepting the existing international rules and structures. As Barry Buzan notes, a peaceful rise requires both the rising power to accommodate itself to the rules and structures of international society, while at the same time other powers accommodate some changes in those rules and structures by way of adjusting to the new disposition of power and status.[13] A peaceful rise does not exclude involvement in rule changes, so long as this is made not through force or coercion, but rather through mutual accommodation. It is too narrow to define a status quo power as one that wholeheartedly accepts the existing rules without any aspirations for rule change. History may stand on the side that all rising powers seek rule change one way or another. The real question is in what way a rising power seeks rule change. Fundamentally different from Germany and Japan between World Wars I and II, during which they attempted to overthrow the status quo by way of annexation and invasion, and eventually by waging an all-out war, China's behavior in recent decades suggests that today's China first learns the rules of the game, then applies them, and then at the same time seeks to change those rules through accommodation, negotiation, and consensus building where it finds the rules unfair or unreasonable.

To summarize, a status quo state wishes to maintain the existing order, and a rigid status quo state even uses its resources to oppose any changes to current rules. An anti-status quo state is not only strongly dissatisfied with the existing rules, but also seeks to overthrow them as the guiding norms for state behavior. A reform-minded status quo state sits in between. Such a state is in general satisfied with the current situation and accepts the existing rules, but it holds that there are shortcomings in the present order and it hopes to make improvements, and do so on the basis of the present rules of the game which it has accepted and endorsed. A reform-minded status quo state wants to make the desirable changes in an incremental rather than a radical or revolutionary way, likely over a long time span. This often requires it to work with other actors to build consensus in terms of approach. In this sense, it is often much more multilaterally oriented rather than tending toward unilateral action.

This chapter explores China's approaches to the international system from the lens of the relationship between China and the G20, and its relationship to reform of the international monetary system. The evidence from this area of global governance leads me to conclude that China is basically a status quo power but at the same time is reform minded, wishing for constructive changes. In general, China is satisfied with its status in the international system, while hoping for improved world political and economic governance through more proactive participation in international institutions such as the G20.

China becomes a member of the international monetary leadership

China originally faced the question of whether it should pursue membership or accept an invitation to join the Group of 8 (G8). Given China's economic and political rise, this possibility was repeatedly raised around the turn of the century. Some discussed whether the G8 should be turned into a G9 in order to include China, or a G10 to also include India.[14] Internal meetings were held within the Chinese government, and the conclusion was reached that China should not seek or accept membership in the G8 for three reasons.[15] First, China identified itself as a developing country, and joining the G8 would not be perceived positively in the developing world, since this would likely be seen as a major move to join the group of Western powers and change its longstanding position and policies. China's key foreign policy principle that "developing countries are the basis" would be affected, and for Beijing this would be too high a price to pay. Second, no matter whether it was a G8 or G9, such a grouping would be dominated by the Western powers. Beijing could not accept being a junior partner. Third, China did not want to undermine the authority of the United Nations (UN) "as the legitimate engine of global governance."[16]

From the G8's perspective, it saw non-Western powers as emerging and believed the world was changing profoundly, leading them to worry that the G8 would lose momentum and risk losing its significance. Hence, bringing in major developing powers and making them dialogue partners gradually became a necessity. Starting from the June 2003 Evian Summit hosted by France, the G8 regularly held dialogues with five major developing countries: China; India; Brazil; South Africa; and Mexico.[17] This formula made the +5 appear collectively as a group of which China was a part. In this case, China did not have to worry about being singled out and it could also take advantage of this opportunity to conduct its emerging power diplomacy. However, for Beijing, particularly the Ministry of Foreign Affairs (MOFA), there was an awareness that since the dialogues always occurred in places where the G8 summits were held, the meeting arrangements, agenda, and outcome design were all controlled by the G8, and the developing powers largely had to accept them. In this sense, the two groups were not equal.

When the global financial crisis broke out in the fall of 2008, triggered by the sub-prime mortgage crisis in the United States and then spread to the rest of the world, the West encountered the most serious crisis since the Great Depression of the 1930s. It was clear the G8 was unable to cope with a crisis of such magnitude. With dramatic shifts in the global power distribution and pressing global challenges, international institutions established after World War II seemed fragile and lacked legitimacy in responding to said challenges. Far-reaching reforms appeared necessary for creating an architecture of legitimate global institutions that would be representative, relevant, and effective. Against this backdrop, the elevated G20, of which China is a core member, stepped onto center stage of global economics and politics.

Below I first outline China's broad approach to the G20, which has remained consistent in the years since. The discussion then turns to five core issues that have been raised in the G20 process to measure how China has behaved and what policies it has adopted. The five issues are: reform of the international monetary system in general; reform of international financial institutions, particularly the International Monetary Fund (IMF) and World Bank; international financial regulation; the future of the dollar; and the internationalization of the renminbi. A review of China's overall posture and its position on these issues is a good indicator to allow us to judge whether China is a status quo power, a modest reformer, or a radical anti-status quo power.

The G20's ascent and China's participation

The G20 mechanism initially came into being after the 1997–1998 Asian financial crisis, primarily as a gathering of finance ministers and central bank governors to discuss and, if possible, coordinate their international economic policies. As such, by including major developing countries as well as developed ones, the G20 forum created a venue for the future shape of global governance. Since the G20's inauguration in 1999, China has sent its finance minister and governor of its central bank, the People's Bank of China (PBOC), and they have actively participated in all of the G20 meetings.[18]

By 2008, when Lehman Brothers collapsed and the crisis was deepening and spreading, the G20 became a readily available vehicle for taking collective action. Initiated by the United States, the first ever G20 summit took place in Washington in November 2008. Chinese President Hu Jintao attended the summit and gave a speech that comprehensively laid out China's fundamental position and proposals with regards to fighting the massive crisis and reforming the international financial system. The speech is an important document for understanding Chinese policies. It proposes reform of the international financial system aimed at establishing a new international financial order that is fair, just, inclusive and orderly, and fostering an institutional environment conducive to sound global economic development. Hu also put forward four major proposals regarding reform in line with the principles of comprehensiveness, balance, gradualism, and pragmatism.

First, reform needs to be comprehensive. A general design should not only focus on improving the international financial system, monetary system, and international financial rules and procedures, but also take into account the development stages and characteristics of different economies. Second, reforms need to achieve balance among the interests of all parties and build a decision-making and management mechanism with wider and more effective participation. Third, reform should be incremental and proceed in a phased manner and achieve the final objectives of reform through sustained efforts under the precondition of maintaining stability of the international financial market. Fourth, reforms need to be pragmatic, with measures contributing to international financial stability, global economic growth, and the welfare of people in all countries.[19]

Moreover, China proposed four reform measures: advancing reform of international financial organizations; increasing the representation and voice of developing countries; improving the international currency system; and promoting the diversity of the international monetary system. From the first G20 summit, China underscored that the international community should pay particular attention to the damage the crisis has brought to developing countries. Hence, China proposed helping developing countries maintain financial stability and economic growth, sustaining and increasing assistance to them, and maintaining economic and financial stability in those countries.[20]

Between the Washington and London summits, stabilizing the world economy and preventing it from slipping further into chaos were inevitably the G20's top priorities, while reforming the international monetary system and strengthening the financial surveillance system were put high on the agenda, an approach toward which China was positive. Two explorative essays by Vice Premier Wang Qishan and the central bank Governor Zhou Xiaochuan right before the London Summit were suggestive. Wang called for the G20 to "look beyond the needs of the top 20," believing the developing world should have a stronger say in how the international financial system is run. He suggested that the G20 focus on readjusting the governance structure of international financial institutions and increasing the representation and voice of developing countries, with clear goals and a timetable set at the London Summit.[21]

Through its participation in the G20, China emphasized three ways to help developing countries via the international financial system.[22] The first was to help developing countries cope with the crisis by increasing and improving development financing and poverty reduction programs. This would include strengthening the capacity building of the development institutions, ensuring development resources, and implementing the Millennium Development Goals (MDGs). China called on developed countries to realize sooner rather than later their committed goals: provide official development assistance reaching 0.7 percent of their national income; write off debts developing countries owe them, open up their markets; and transfer technology to jointly promote global poverty reduction and development.

The second component was to build the capacity of multilateral development banks such as the World Bank to better help the developing countries to deal with the crisis. This included improving their ability to reduce poverty, promote sustainable development, enhance countries' capital adequacy standards, increase anti-cyclical interventions, and, through simplifying loan conditionality and developing highly practical aid tools, help countries meet the challenges of capital outflow and impediments to trade financing. The third was to deepen international economic and trade cooperation and oppose trade protectionism. The rise of protectionism, China argued, would seriously weaken the global economic recovery and obstruct the process of poverty reduction and sustainable development.

China's role in the G20 took a major step forward when it hosted the process for the year 2016, including the long series of ministerial meetings and the summit of leaders in Hangzhou in September of that year. In the months leading up to the summit, China put forth a broad initiative to make the global economy more "innovative," "invigorated," "interconnected," and "inclusive."[23] The day after the conclusion of the summit, the *People's Daily* published a "G20 Blueprint on Innovative Growth," emphasizing that "[i]nnovation is one of the key driving forces for global sustainable development, playing a fundamental role in promoting economic growth, supporting job creation, entrepreneurship and structural reform, enhancing productivity and competitiveness, providing better services for our citizens and addressing global challenges."[24] The energy, time, and resources China devoted to hosting the G20 summit and articulating policy proposals are another strong indication of China's desire to play a leadership role in global economic governance.

Five key issues

An understanding of China's broad approach to the G20 and the global economy, which it has maintained consistently since G20 summits began, is a good foundation for examining more specific aspects of China's promotion of reform in international monetary governance.

Reform of the international monetary system

The issue of the international monetary system reform is not new. As early as February 1965, French President Charles de Gaulle opened the attack by arguing that the "dollar system" provided the United States with an "exorbitant privilege." The time had come, de Gaulle said, to establish the international system "on an unquestionable basis that does not bear the stamp of any one country in particular."[25] Following the collapse of the Bretton Woods system in 1973, as former Federal Reserve Chairman Paul Volcker put it, "[a]gain and again the question was posed: Can we have a stable system without a dominant country that is itself extraordinarily stable? And was the United States any longer stable to play that role?"[26] There have been a number of proposals in this regard that did not materialize. The outbreak of the global crisis in 2008 simply provided fresh momentum to the long-standing issue of reforming the global monetary system. Questions raised include: is the current system unstable? Is it inefficient? What role did the US dollar-dominated system play in the crisis?

China stayed outside the system for many years until it joined the IMF and World Bank in 1980, and during the next two decades, China's task was to get used to the rules of the game and to utilize the resources available, particularly from the World Bank, to serve its modernization drive. The World Bank's story in China was an exceptionally successful one. Since then crises have served as watersheds. The 1997–1998 Asian financial crisis exposed the deficiencies of the Western-dominated rescue system. The IMF proved incapable of effectively helping countries hit by the crisis, and in some cases, such as Indonesia, worsened the situation. Despite this fact, reform of the system did not appear in Beijing's mind until the start of the twenty-first century, articulated clearly by PBOC Governor Zhou Xiaochuan's famous March 2009 paper.

For Zhou, the crisis called for creative reform of the existing international monetary system toward an international reserve currency with a stable value, rule-based issuance, and manageable supply, so as to achieve the objective of safeguarding global economic and financial stability. He suggested that the international reserve currency be disconnected from any individual nation and be able to remain stable in the long run, thus removing the inherent deficiencies caused by using credit-based national currencies. He suggested broadening the scope of the IMF's special drawing rights (SDR), setting up a settlement system between the SDR and other currencies, and promoting the use of the SDR in international trade, commodities pricing, investment, and corporate book-keeping.[27]

Zhou's paper aroused enormous attention and quickly became influential largely because of the combination of the background of the crisis and China's rising status. However, there was not a consensus in China on these views. The paper first appeared on the central bank's website, not in the *People's Daily*, often the outlet of more formal policy statements or resolutions. It was likely a trial balloon, as it could be understood as an expression of personal views. The MOFA did not want China to be seen as a revisionist state aspiring to radically change the current system. Around the 2009 G8+5 dialogue in Italy, Russia echoed Zhou's proposal and reiterated its suggestion to discuss the issue of inventing a supra-sovereignty international reserve currency. In response to media questions, Vice Foreign Minister He Yafei emphasized that creating a supra-sovereignty international reserve currency was an ongoing issue under discussion in academic circles and not the position of the Chinese government.[28] His clarifications highlighted the ever-present question of viability and revealed that China's foreign affairs authorities carefully wanted to soothe the outside anxiety and to attempt to lower the temperature.

Reform of international financial institutions

"A half century after its founding, it is clear that the IMF has failed in its mission," declared Nobel Prize-winning economist Joseph Stiglitz just after the Asian financial crisis.[29] For many years the IMF and the World Bank have had governance structures severely skewed toward the interests of developed countries. Since the G20 started holding summits, calls have been made for a more representative group of 20 leading economies to take ultimate authority over the IMF to give the organization greater political clout in resolving global crises.[30] Hence, reform of international financial institutions has become a regular G20 theme.

Around the same time as Governor Zhou's paper, Chinese Vice Premier Wang Qishan published an essay in *The Times* of London calling for a range of reforms in the IMF. These included: 1) increase the IMF's resources through the quota-based system and voluntary contributions, striking a balance between the rights and obligations of the contributing countries; 2) determine contributions based on countries' vastly different stages of development, the composition and amount of foreign exchange reserves, and a country's level of dependency on foreign exchange reserves; 3) in increasing the IMF's resources, give top priority to increasing quotas—if quota-based contributions fall short of immediate needs, the IMF can issue bonds, which China could buy, as such bilateral borrowing arrangements should be discussed separately outside the IMF; and 4) enhance IMF capacity building, reform its governance structure, and ensure that the resources play a significant role in easing the international financial crisis and countering the global economic downturn. To this end, resources should be subject to scientific assessment, proper planning, and rigorous oversight to ensure that they are fair, just, transparent, and effective.[31]

In the eyes of Beijing, the United States and the West for many years dominated decision-making at the core of the Bretton Woods institutions, with others having little influence. For better and fairer world economic governance, there must be changes in line with the changes in the world distribution of power. During its finance ministerial meeting prior to the London Summit, the G20 agreed to speed up IMF governance structural reform to reflect the shifting global economic power balance. It was also agreed upon to finish the next share review soon, to increase the speaking and representation rights of the emerging economies and developing countries, a move favorable to China in terms of increasing its institutional power because of its emerging economic power status.

During the 2009 annual meetings of the IMF and World Bank, Finance Minister Xie Xuren put forward more concrete proposals. First, the selection of the heads of the IMF and the World Bank should be based on the principles of openness, transparency, and merit. Second, the two major institutions should increase the percentage of employees, especially among upper management, from developing countries. Third, the IMF should continuously improve its governance structure to ensure its legitimacy and representation. In the mid-to-long term it should establish a share adjustment mechanism to reflect on an ongoing basis changes in countries' relative status in the world economy. Fourth, the IMF should explore schemes for reforming and improving the entire international monetary system. Efforts should be made to fundamentally overcome its inherent flaws and provide a stable monetary environment for global economic growth and financial stability.[32]

To China's satisfaction, some reform measures have been taken and the international efforts have born fruit. In 2010, the World Bank changed its voting structure to give nations such as China (now its third-largest shareholder), Brazil, India, Indonesia, and Vietnam greater say in running the institution. That same year, China's voting share rose to 4.42 percent from 2.77 percent, above that of the United Kingdom, France, and Germany. It was a long overdue measure that went toward recognizing the Asian giant's status as the world's third- or second-largest economy. It is considering other ways to shift the balance of power further.

Similar adjustment took place at the IMF. During the fourteenth quota review in December 2010, the IMF's board of governors agreed to make China the third-largest member. European countries gave up two of their eight seats on the 24-member board. More than 6 percent of IMF voting power was transferred to under-represented countries, after which China became the third-largest member of the 187-member institution.[33] In addition, China committed resources beyond the quota contributions to the IMF in case of a liquidity shortage. Reflective of these changes, China has become an important voice in the IMF decision-making process, as well as on surveillance discussions of its member countries' economies.[34] In July 2011, Zhu Min, a Chinese national and special advisor to the IMF managing director, was appointed the IMF's deputy managing director, a breakthrough for China. Although it took several years longer than expected, quotas were finally reapportioned in January 2016, with China's increasing from 3.8 percent to 6.0 percent.[35] This reform elevates China to the third-largest IMF quota and voting share after the United States and Japan. What is more, for the first time, four emerging market economies (China, Brazil, India, and Russia) are among the 10 largest members of the IMF.[36]

International financial regulation

The global financial crisis strikingly revealed problems with the current international financial regulation system that enabled the crisis and financial malpractice. Starting from Wall Street, the heart of the US financial capital, the crisis exposed the terrible repercussions of mismanagement of the financial sector and that unconstrained greed could undermine and erode financial health. There was consensus in the G20 that they should immediately focus attention on strengthening financial regulation. The real question was how that should be done, and China came up with its own answers.

Right before the G20 London Summit, PBOC Vice Governor Hu Xiaolian laid out China's proposals.[37] First, include all the financial market actors in the scope of regulation, but especially strengthen regulation over institutions of systemic influence. Consistent rules are needed to prevent "regulation arbitrage." Second, use policy tools that ameliorate pro-cyclical risks. This includes encouraging financial institutions to raise internal rating capabilities and maximize utilization of externally provided ratings. The use of fair-value accounting rules needs to be adjusted in time. Third, further promote the accuracy and forward-looking nature of the Financial Sector Assessment Planning (FSAP). Evaluation systems that are suitable for the particular development situation of emerging economies should be created since directly copying the models of the developed countries may not be appropriate. Fourth, speed up the integration of the international settlement system and bankruptcy laws, as well as establish global norms and best practices for large-scale cross-border financial institution bankruptcy settlements.[38]

In the run-up to the June 2010 Toronto Summit, China supported decisions to: strengthen financial institutions' capital adequacy and liquidity requirements; decrease the moral hazard of the financial institutions that have systemic influence; tighten up the regulation of hedge funds, credit rating agencies, CEO salaries, and over-the-counter derivatives; and set up globally consistent accounting standards. The G20 ministers also agreed, under the premise of respecting concrete national situations and policy options, to make rules regarding the financial sector's shouldering of government rescue costs in order to reduce financial systemic risks.[39] At the Toronto Summit, China echoed the concerns about credit ratings. China underscored the need to develop an objective, fair, reasonable, and uniform method and standard for sovereign credit ratings so that ratings accurately reflect a country's credit risk in a given situation. The supervision of credit rating agencies should be enforced and the regulations and accountability system on credit rating agencies should be strengthened.[40] Although not stated openly at the Toronto Summit, China's position implied that the three largest global rating agencies—Moody's, Standard & Poor's, and Fitch—had betrayed international investors and were faithful servants of the biggest debtor nations, a situation that needed to change in the years ahead.[41]

The future of the dollar

As noted above, the crisis cast doubt on the future role of the US dollar as the most dominant key currency. According to Evan Medeiros, Zhou Xiaochuan's famous proposal "reflected China's anxiety over its deep vulnerability to the dollar's value and to the overall health of the US economy. It also reflected the impotence of the renminbi (because of China's closed capital account) to present any kind of alternative."[42] Not surprisingly, China has a desire for reform of this system, but is realistic about potential change. For Zhou, issuing countries of reserve currencies face the dilemma between achieving their domestic monetary policy goals and meeting other countries' demand for reserve currencies. The frequency and increasing intensity of financial crises following the collapse of the Bretton Woods system suggests the costs of such a system may have exceeded the benefits. There are inherent vulnerabilities and systemic risks in the existing dollar-based international monetary system.[43]

In his written answers to questions submitted by *The Washington Post* prior to his state visit to Washington in January 2011, President Hu Jintao responded to the question on the US dollar's future role by pointing out:

> The current international currency system is the product of the past. As a major reserve currency, the US dollar is used in a considerable amount of global trade in commodities as well as in most investment and financial transactions. The monetary policy of the United States has a major impact on global liquidity and capital flows and therefore, the liquidity of the US dollar should be kept at a reasonable and stable level.[44]

His careful phrasing suggested that it is not desirable for China to let its destiny be determined by a foreign country and its policies, which can likely be conducted at the expense of other countries' interests.

What is the right and viable approach? There is a consensus that gradual reform is needed to allow greater participation and representation, to allow more currencies to prop up the system, and to establish more effective operating mechanisms. However, progress will depend on the shifting balance of power, competing interests, and interactions among the world's economic and political powers.

Beijing is determined to participate in reform proactively, to be better informed, and have a bigger say in the international monetary system. In the short run, under the current dollar-based system, China has played an active role in G20 efforts to promote global economic growth, international cooperation, and concrete institutional reforms. Looking ahead, things are bound to change even more. As Chinese scholar Yu Yongding wrote, "[t]he lack of alternatives to the dollar as a reserve currency has bred a false sense of security in the United States.

Yet when China reduces its current surplus (and diversifies from dollar assets) the effects would be felt in the US Treasury markets." Hence, he concluded, "China's development is putting to an end the period of unquestioned western supremacy."[45] Because Chinese policymakers do not want China to appear to be challenging the United States, taking actions to purposefully weaken the dollar, or attempting to replace the current system with a fundamentally different one, China has spearheaded the establishment of initiatives that enhance or complement the existing system rather than replace or challenge it.

Internationalization of the renminbi

Theoretically, given China's prominence in world trade, in manufacturing, and increasingly in financing as well, it would be logical for the renminbi to become one of the global economy's three or four major currencies. Unsurprisingly, its internationalization has become one of China's policy objectives. The benefits of doing so include less need for China to hold US dollar assets, the elimination of exchange rate risks for Chinese firms, greater funding efficiency for Chinese financial institutions, and the promotion of Shanghai as an international financial center. In the intermediate term, having trade settlement in renminbi would help mitigate exchange risk and reduce transaction costs for enterprises trading with China.[46]

However, in some quarters, "the debate over the role of the US dollar and the emergence of the renminbi is seen as threatening to the status quo."[47] By contrast, Fred Bergsten believes China's rise will naturally be followed by global currency status for the renminbi. He believes the international monetary system is becoming bipolar and may soon be tripolar, led by the US dollar, euro, and renminbi. He believes that the United States should accept this and even promote its acceleration.[48]

The outbreak of the financial crisis provided the backdrop against which China embarked on an initiative in July 2009 to promote trade settlement in the renminbi. This was done in reaction not only to the US dollar liquidity crunch following the global financial crisis, but also given China's growing economic stature and the need to rebalance its own currency composition of huge external reserves. The aim was essentially to reduce the overdependence on the US dollar as the major settlement currency. It was widely believed in China's research and policy circles that the United States was taking advantage of the dollar's special status and was pursuing an irresponsible policy by creating the flooding of liquidity in the name of "quantitative easing," in essence creating a money-printing machine, inflating asset bubbles, and pushing up exchange rates to the detriment of developing economies.[49]

China's pilot renminbi Trade Settlement Scheme marked an important step toward the goal of internationalizing its currency. This program allowed trade in the renminbi between Mainland China, Hong Kong, Macao, and Association of Southeast Asian Nations (ASEAN) countries. In the early phase the initiative was restricted to just five mainland cities and 370 designated Chinese enterprises, but was soon expanded.

Within two years, cross-border renminbi settlement increased explosively, renminbi settlement in cross-border trade rose from RMB 500 billion in 2010, or 2 percent of the total, to RMB 530 billion in just the first four months of 2011. China also began to initiate experiments in cross-border renminbi investments. Non-mainland enterprises were permitted to invest in the Chinese mainland using the renminbi.[50] By the end of 2011, cross-border renminbi settlement expanded to the whole country, and 181 countries have begun using the renminbi in trade.[51] Furthermore, while Hong Kong is an offshore trading center for the renminbi, Britain and Hong Kong teamed up to develop London into a new hub for the renminbi market, by strengthening the ties between Hong Kong and London in terms of their settlement systems, market liquidity and the development of renminbi-denominated financial products.[52] Singapore, Taipei, and other financial centers are also vying for a share of the growing offshore renminbi business.

During the G20 Cannes Summit in November 2011 attendees agreed to review the basket of currencies that compose the IMF's SDR. At that time, the SDR was made up of the US dollar, the euro, the Japanese yen, and the British pound. French President Nicolas Sarkozy proposed including the renminbi, arguing that it would better reflect the new realities of the global economy. According to the summit declaration, the basket should "reflect the role of currencies in the global trading and financial system and be adjusted over time to reflect currencies' changing role and characteristics."[53] Approved by the Executive Board of the IMF in November 2015, and effective since October 2016, the renminbi was finally included in the SDR basket.[54]

The G20 and global economic governance

There are different assessments of the G20, including its usefulness and impact. It is easy to brand the G20 a failure. For example, after the Seoul Summit in 2010, a *Financial Times* editorial said it did not embody "collective leadership, but joint abdication of power."[55]

However, the G20 has taken some important actions. The London G20 Summit in 2009 produced a US$1.1 trillion global recovery plan, featuring national stimulus efforts, calls for increased IMF resources, and greater trade financing. The London Summit also transformed the Financial Stability Forum—a loose grouping founded by the G7—into a more influential Financial Stability Board open to all G20 nations, and tasked it with guiding new financial regulatory policies. The G20 summits in Pittsburgh, Toronto, and Seoul, as well as the preparations for the Cannes Summit under France's chairmanship, achieved agreements on exempting emergency food supplies from export bans and on agricultural assistance for Africa. France used the G20 to spark debate on what a future international monetary system might look like.[56] During the IMF spring 2012 and the G20 ministerial meetings, a consensus was reached to add $430 billion to existing funds in order to empower the IMF. China announced during the June 2012 G20 summit held in Los Cabos, Mexico, that it would contribute $43 billion.

For China, the G20 is an important platform. It emerged from the backdrop when Western countries were widely held responsible for the outbreak of the financial crisis and the G8 was incapable of coping with it. The ability for developing countries to host G20 summits enabled major developing countries to engage in global economic governance on a more equal footing than ever before. This has provided a rare opportunity for major emerging countries and China actively participated in the process when it hosted the Hangzhou Summit in 2016.

Second, given China's comprehensive national power, no matter what form global economic governance takes in the future, it would not be realistic without China's participation. Since the United States and Europe enlist China's cooperation, Beijing puts itself in a positive and advantageous position by choosing to participate in the G20 and global economic governance on an equal footing and helping emerging economies obtain greater representation.

Third, it is beneficial to make the G20 an effective mechanism over the long term. After the 2009 Pittsburgh Summit, the G20 started a process of establishing regulations and building institutions, and began a transition from crisis fighting to long-term effective global economic governance. This development had far-reaching implications as it has fundamentally changed the situation in which for many years the developed countries monopolized international economic affairs, and has helped upgrade developing countries' right to have a voice. It is beneficial for China to participate in global governance in a wider platform and defend the legitimate interests of China and other developing countries.[57] More recently, China was actively involved in creating the New Development Bank, a BRICS (Brazil, Russia, India, China, and South Africa) development bank headquartered in Shanghai, and initiating the Asian Infrastructure Investment Bank (AIIB).

Fourth, there are three outstanding questions that need to be resolved about the G20. The first is its legitimacy. The concerns of non-G20 nations need to be addressed and their interests taken into consideration. Second is the G20's effectiveness. The G20 is geared toward combating emergencies. When the global financial crisis subsided, clashes of different interests and aspirations emerged, thus posing challenges for the G20 states to continue coordinating their actions or policies to improve global governance. The third is about the distribution of power. Schemes have to be worked out for proper and improved arrangements regarding financial regulation, share management, and voting power in international financial institutions. Beijing is aware that this will take time and will be a long, complex, and even tortuous process.

In short, China wants the status of the G20 as the premier global economic governance platform to be consolidated, turning China's growing influence into institutional power, a goal it made some headway on in 2016. By adequately and reasonably taking advantage of its newly increased institutional power in the international governing organizations such as the IMF and World Bank, Beijing hopes to effectively safeguard and expand its development interests and shape a favorable institutional environment for its participation in international economic cooperation and competition at a higher level.

Conclusion

China has become an increasingly pluralistic society. More actors are now involved in the foreign policy decision-making process. In the case of the G20, while local governments are not involved, several bureaucratic organizations play a role, including the MOFA, MOF, and the PBOC. They coordinate policy amongst themselves, and although there was some difference of opinion about creating a "supra-sovereign currency," our research does not find major policy differences among them regarding China's involvement in the G20 process. This is likely due to relatively clear-cut portfolios and policy terrains. Also, the finance minister and the central bank governor often attend many international meetings together, such as the joint IMF and World Bank meetings. With respect to the research community, quite often there are different views, but there does not appear to be much argument on the issue of the G20.

As defined earlier, a reform-minded status quo power sits somewhere between a rigid and anti-status quo power. A status quo state accepts the existing rules of the game and does not seek to change them because generally it is satisfied with the current situation. China has bene- fited from the existing international system and has become the world's second-largest economy. Logically, it does not aspire to overthrow this system within which it is doing well. In this sense, China is indeed a status quo power.

At the same time, China does not want to rigidly stick to this exist- ing system without any adaptations. Rather, China has argued that the current international order is flawed and contains a number of unjust and unreasonable elements that have needed to be changed for a long time.[58] In this sense, China is not a stubborn but rather a reform-minded status quo power.

This chapter has analyzed the case of China in the G20 process and has examined China's position and policies on relevant issues, includ- ing reform of the international monetary system, international finan- cial institutions regulation, the future of the dollar, and the internationalization of the renminbi. The evidence demonstrates that China has actively participated in the G20's deliberations, put forward suggestions, sought expanded share and voting power corresponding with its rising status, and promoted the internationalization of the renminbi. In other words, while having accepted and observed the current international rules of the game, China seeks changes for greater institutional power and better global governance. This aspiration became stronger when it appeared that China had fallen into the "dollar pitfall" where China could be "abducted" by the large reservoir of the US Treasury bonds it had purchased and accumulated, whose value is determined by US domestic policy decisions. When the dollar devalues, China's dollar assets shrink. Despite MOFA equi- vocations, this real risk prompted Beijing's desire for a new interna- tional reserve currency that is independent from a particular nation's policies.

There are two features to China's actions that make it reformist and not revolutionary. The first is incrementalism, meaning being patient and attempting to bring about changes gradually over a fairly long period. The other is seeking consensus in multilateral settings and working with other actors in global economic governance. After all, governance is a collective endeavor. Crisis usually drives changes. The G20's elevation to summit status and its rise to prominence were a product of the global financial crisis when the G8 was unable to fight the crisis alone. Against this backdrop, countries had to join hands to combat the crisis collectively and further explore reform. With the rise of developing powers, the G20 process inevitably bears the color of reform.

Nevertheless, on the issue of UN Security Council (UNSC) reform, as one of the five permanent members that possess veto power and thus have a vested interest, China is more rigid and reluctant to extend veto power to other nations. This is not very different from two other permanent members, the United States and Russia, who share the same position. If one looks at this case of the UNSC reform alone, one could easily come to the conclusion that China is a rigid status quo seeker. However, on the particular issue of UNSC reform, China's position has more to do with Japan's ambition for a permanent seat and with the Sino-Japanese relationship than China's overall international governance principles.

Let us not lose sight of the forest for the trees. China has been espousing necessary changes for a "new international political and economic order." When that sounded too revisionist given that China has benefited from the existing order, Beijing opted for the more moderate rhetoric of "pushing the international order to change in the direction of becoming more just and reasonable."[59] China wants to avoid being seen as anti-status quo. In the meantime, China does have aspirations and ideals for a better world. For example, it wishes for more even distribution of power between established and emerging powers, better treatment of less developed countries, and fairer representation of countries of different levels of development in international organizations. In general, China espouses constructive reforms but accepts the existing international rules and wants to integrate further into the global system. China's behavior in the G20 proves this conclusion.

Notes

1 Richard Bernstein and Ross H. Munro, *The Coming Conflict with China* (New York: Alfred A. Knopf, 1997); Aaron Friedberg, "Ripe for Rivalry: Prospects for Peace in a Multilateral Asia," *International Security* 18, no. 3 (1993): 5–33.
2 John J. Mearsheimer, *The Tragedy of Great Power Politics* (New York: W.W. Norton, 2001).
3 David Shambaugh, "Asia in Transition: The Evolving Regional Order," *Current History* 105, no. 690 (April 2006): 153–159.
4 Robert J. Art, "The United States and the Rise of China: Implications for the Long Haul," *Political Science Quarterly* 125, no. 3 (Fall 2010): 259–291, 390.
5 Christopher Layne, "China's Challenge to US Hegemony," *Current History* 107, no. 705 (January 2008): 13–18. For another analysis that emphasizes

the US response to China, see Charles Glaser, "Will China's Rise Lead to War?" *Foreign Affairs* 90, no. 2 (March/April 2011): 80–91, 89.

6 Elizabeth Economy and Michel Oksenberg, eds, *China Joins the World: Progress and Prospects* (New York: Council on Foreign Relations, 1999); Alastair Iain Johnston, "Is China a Status Quo Power?" *International Security* 27, no. 4 (Spring 2003): 5–56; Feng Huiyun, "Is China a Revisionist Power?" *The Chinese Journal of International Politics* 2, no. 3 (Summer 2009): 313–334; Alastair Iain Johnston and Robert S. Ross, eds, *Engaging China: The Management of an Emerging Power* (London and New York: Routledge, 1999).

7 Johnston, "Is China a Status Quo Power?," 49.

8 Feng, "Is China a Revisionist Power?," 334.

9 Evan S. Medeiros, "Is Beijing Ready for Global Leadership?" *Current History* 108, no. 719 (September 2009): 250–256, 254.

10 Evan S. Medeiros, "Is Beijing Ready for Global Leadership?," 255–256.

11 Alastair Iain Johnston, *Social States: China in International Institutions, 1980–2000* (Princeton, N.J.: Princeton University Press, 2008).

12 Johnston, "Is China a Status Quo Power?"

13 Barry Buzan, "China in International Society: Is 'Peaceful Rise' Possible?" *The Chinese Journal of International Politics* 3 (2010): 5–36. For a view that sees any change in the existing rules as being anti-status quo, see A. F. K. Organski and Jacek Kugler, *The War Ledger* (Chicago, Ill.: The University of Chicago Press, 1980), 19–20.

14 See, for example, J. J. Kirton, "The G7/8 and China: Toward a Closer Relationship," in *Guiding Global Governance: G8 Governance in the Twenty-First Century*, ed. J. J. Kirton, J. P. Daniels and A. Freytag (Aldershot: Ashgate, 2001), 189–222.

15 Interview with a Chinese government official, 2 March 2011.

16 Hugo Dobson, "Leadership in Global Governance: Japan and China in the G8 and the United Nations," in *China, Japan and Regional Leadership in East Asia*, ed. Christopher M. Dent (Cheltenham and Northampton, Mass.: Edward Elgar, 2008), 181–202, 197.

17 Amazingly, in his address at Evian on 1 June 2003, well before the global financial crisis, President Hu Jintao of China stated: "At present, it is particularly necessary to underscore the need for reform and improvement of the international financial system, with a view to enhancing its capacity to prevent and manage financial crisis." See "Promote All-Round Cooperation for Common Development," Address by President Hu Jintao of the People's Republic of China at Informal Summit at Evian, in Ministry of Foreign Affairs, *China's Foreign Affairs 2004* (Beijing: World Affairs Press, 2004), 477–479.

18 Dobson, "Leadership in Global Governance," 197–198.

19 "Tide Over Difficulties Through Concerted Efforts," Remarks by President Hu Jintao, President of the People's Republic of China, at the Summit on Financial Markets and the World Economy, Ministry of Foreign Affairs, *China's Foreign Affairs 2009* (Beijing: World Affairs Press, 2009), 545–549.

20 "Tide Over Difficulties Through Concerted Efforts," Remarks by President Hu Jintao, President of the People's Republic of China.

21 Wang Qishan, "G20 Must Look Beyond the Needs of the Top 20," *The Times*, 27 March 2009.

22 "The Ministry of Foreign Affairs Held Briefing to Introduce President Hu Jintao's Forthcoming Participation in the Second G20 Summit," *People's Daily* [*Renmin ribao*], 24 March 2009.

23 "Talking about G20: Innovative, Invigorated, Interconnected, Inclusive," The State Council of the People's Republic of China, 30 August 2016, http://english.gov.cn/news/video/2016/08/30/content_281475429230537.htm; David Dollar, "New Considerations for China's 2016 G20 Presidency," *G20 Monitor*, The Lowy Institute for International Policy, May 2016, www.lowyinstitute.org/publications/g20-monitor-chinese-2016-g20-host-year. Also see Wang Yi, "Strive to Achieve Ten Results from G20 Hangzhou Summit," Chinese Ministry of Foreign Affairs, 26 May 2016, www.fmprc.gov.cn/mfa_eng/zxxx_662805/t1367533.shtml.

24 "G20 Blueprint on Innovation," *People's Daily* [*Renmin ribao*], 6 September 2016, http://en.people.cn/n3/2016/0906/c90000-9111019.html; Yves Tiberghien, "Assessing the G20: Great Impetus Amid Frictions," *Australian Institute of International Affairs*, 8 September 2016.

25 Quoted in Paul Volcker and Toyoo Gyohten, *Changing Fortunes: The World's Money and the Threat to American Leadership* (New York: Times Books, 1992), 42.

26 Volcker and Gyohten, *Changing Fortunes*, 125–126.

27 Zhou Xiaochuan, "Reform the International Monetary System," People's Bank of China, 23 March 2009, www.bis.org/review/r090402c.pdf.

28 Xinhua News Agency interview with Vice Foreign Minister He Yafei, Rome, Italy, 5 July 2009.

29 Joseph E. Stiglitz, *Globalization and Its Discontents* (New York and London: W. W. Norton, 2002), 15.

30 "Reform Blueprint Gives G20 Authority over IMF," *Financial Times*, 9 February 2011.

31 Wang Qishan, "G20 Must Look Beyond the Needs of the Top 20."

32 Interview with Finance Minister Xie Xueren, *Xinhua News Agency*, 6 October 2009.

33 Coverage of the December 2010 IMF Board of Governors meeting, *Financial Times*, 13–14 November 2010.

34 Lee Il Houng, "What IMF Wants China to Do," *China Daily* (*Asia Weekly*), 15–21 July 2011. (Lee Il Houng is a senior resident representative of the IMF in China.)

35 "IMF Reforms: China, India, Brazil, Russia Get Greater Say," *The BRICS Post*, 28 January 2016, http://thebricspost.com/imf-reforms-china-india-brazil-russia-get-greater-say/#.WL7ncVXytQI.

36 International Monetary Fund, *Press Release: Historic Quota and Governance Reforms Become Effective*, 27 January 2016, www.imf.org/en/News/Articles/2015/09/14/01/49/pr1625a.

37 People's Bank of China Vice Governor Hu Xiaolian's proposals for the G20 London Summit, see *People's Daily* [*Renmin ribao*], 24 March 2009.

38 "The Ministry of Foreign Affairs Held Briefing to Introduce President Hu Jintao's Forthcoming Participation in the Second G20 Summit," *People's Daily*.

39 Agreements from the G20 ministers meetings, see *People's Daily* [*Renmin ribao*], 19 June 2010.

40 Hu Jintao's speech at the G20 Toronto Summit, see *People's Daily*, 28 June 2010.

41 Guan Jianzhong, "Search for New International Credit System," *China Daily Asia Weekly*, 8–14 July 2011.

42 Evan S. Medeiros, "Is Beijing Ready for Global Leadership?" 255.

43 Zhou Xiaochuan, "Reform the International Monetary System."

44 A full transcript of *The Washington Post* interview with Chinese President Hu Jintao is available at www.washingtonpost.com/wp-dyn/content/article/2011/01/16/AR2011011601921.html.

45 Yu Yongding, "China's Best Way Forward,"*Financial Times*, 19 January 2011.

46 Karl Wilson, "Gaining Currency," *China Daily (Asia Weekly)*, 18–24 November 2011.

47 Andrew Sheng, "International Monetary System Needs Overhaul," *The Daily Yomiuri*, 5 November 2011.

48 Fred Bergsten, "Why the World Needs Three Global Currencies," *Financial Times*, 16 February 2011.

49 Economy Minister of Germany Rainer Bruderle said quantitative easing by the US Federal Reserve was tantamount to manipulating the dollar's exchange rate. See Alan Wheatley, "Covering up the Big Divide on Currencies," *International Herald Tribune*, 26 October 2010.

50 "RMB Internationalization is Steadily Progressing" [Renminbi guojihua wenjian tuijin], *People's Daily* (overseas edition), 15 July 2011.

51 "Cross-border Renminbi Business has Gained a Breakthrough" [Kuajing renminbi yewu huo tupo], *People's Daily* (overseas edition), 12 January 2012.

52 "London Gets a Push as Renminbi Trading Site," *International Herald Tribune*, 17 January 2012.

53 "Communiqué: G20 Leaders Summit," Cannes France, 3–4 November 2011, www.oecd.org/g20/summits/cannes/Cannes%20Leaders%20Communiqu%C3%A9%204%20%20November%202011.pdf.

54 Scott Kennedy, "Let China Join the Global Monetary Elite," *Foreign Policy Magazine*, 20 August 2015, http://foreignpolicy.com/2015/08/20/china-currency-imf-special-drawing-rights-renminbi/.

55 "G20 Show How Not to Run the World," *Financial Times*, 13 November 2010.

56 Robert B. Zoellick, "Five Myths about the G20," *The Washington Post*, 30 October 2011.

57 Interview with a Chinese government official, April 2011.

58 The Director-general of the Policy Planning Department of China's Ministry of Foreign Affairs said: "We can clearly see from the 2008 financial crisis that the current international system is not entirely functional." See Le Yucheng, "Different Kind of Exceptionalism," *China Daily (Asia Weekly)*, 1–7 July 2011.

59 Ren Xiao, "China in the G20: Between Status Quo and Reform," in Scott Kennedy and Shuaihua Cheng, eds, *From Rule Takers to Rule Makers: The Growing Role of Chinese in Global Governance* (Bloomington and Geneva: Indiana University Research Center for Chinese Politics and Business and the International Centre for Trade and Sustainable Development, 2012), p. 56.

6 China's role in global governance
A comparison of foreign exchange and intellectual property[1]

Bruce Reynolds and Susan K. Sell

- **Intellectual property and exchange rate policies**
- **Chinese behavior: intellectual property**
- **Chinese behavior: exchange rate policy**
- **China's assertiveness and effectiveness**
- **Conclusion**

On the eve of Chinese Vice President Xi Jinping's 2012 Valentine's Day visit to Washington, the US Business and Industry Council took out a full-page advertisement in *The Washington Post*. The caption read: "From China, With Love." Above it were pictures of Valentine's Day candy hearts reading "IP Theft" and "Currency Manipulation." Two of the most fraught issues in US–China economic relations are intellectual property (IP) protection and exchange rate (ER) policy. This chapter describes how China's pursuit of its preferred IP and ER regimes has become more assertive and more effective over time.

We also seek to explain that change. We assume that China's overarching goals—economic growth and political stability—have been constant. Instead, we hypothesize that changed behavior within these two governance regimes flows potentially from four causal factors: 1) growing governance expertise and capacity as China has trained lawyers and economists and vastly expanded the range of its participation in global governance organizations (GGOs); 2) growing relative economic power—China's export market share was 14.2 percent in 2015 compared to the United States' 9.4 percent; 3) changes within China's domestic political economy, as interest groups emerge and organize; and 4) shifts in China's growth strategy—low-wage to high-tech, export-led to consumption demand-led, an "industry-first" focus to a consumer/household focus.

Comparing the IP and ER areas, two conclusions hold for both. First, China's behavior within each has demonstrated a recursive dynamic between growing domestic interest articulation, experience/ capacity, relative power, and foreign pressure. The first three have caused foreign pressure to be less effective in inducing Chinese policy change. Second, China's behavior has become more assertive and effective in promoting its preferred regimes within GGOs. Recent successes in ER (an advantageous use of pegging in 2008 to 2010), the renminbi's inclusion in the International Monetary Fund's (IMF) special drawing rights (SDR) basket of currencies in 2015, and in the World Trade Organization (WTO) (prevailing in key elements of a landmark IP enforcement dispute) are just three examples. We expect China to continue to press for reformist, but not radical, rule adjustments in its favor.

We also find notable differences between the two governance areas. In particular, in IP one would have to applaud the success of the WTO framework in mediating conflict. However, when it comes to disputes over what exchange rate mechanism (ERM) China should adopt, the IMF, despite its deep expertise and authority, has played a peripheral role, and other fora—the Organisation for Economic Co-operation and Development (OECD), G20, etc.—are even less important. This may flow from the striking differences in the nature of the two governance regimes, which we highlight in the next section.

Our qualitative analysis is based on archival research, primary documents, secondary literature, and field research. We conducted interviews in Beijing and Washington, DC, with officials, academics, representatives of US firms in China, DC-based nongovernmental organizations (NGOs), and American private sector analysts.

The first section puts the issues into context. The second section chronicles the central conflicts in IP and ER over three time periods. Section three traces changes over this period in China's assertiveness and effectiveness within IP and ER global governance, and relates those changes to our four causal stories. The final section discusses our conclusions and the implications of our analysis for the future.

Intellectual property and exchange rate policies

Global governance in IP and ER differs in multiple dimensions: the formality of the international regime, the existence of explicit rules; the strength of the regime; and the extent of membership. In general, the more explicit the rules and the more binding they are, as in IP, the more states are expected to comply with them. When rules are vague and commitments are ambiguous, as in ER, states retain more policy space and more powerful states have more autonomy.

The term IP covers patents, copyright, trademarks, trade secrets, geographical indications, plant variety protection, and *sui generis* forms of property protection. IP policy is subject to explicit, formal, extensive, binding, and enforceable regulation through the WTO Agreement on Trade-Related Aspects of Intellectual Property Rights (TRIPS). TRIPS is the most important multilateral IP agreement because it mandates broad coverage and high standards for IP protection. As of 2017, 164 member states belonged to the WTO. WTO rules exert a strong effect on member states, as violators are vulnerable to economic sanctions. IP rules target firms' actions, whether private or state-owned, and member states must implement them in their national laws.

Regulating the ERM differs dramatically. IP rules apply across myriad markets; here the sole issue is arrangements for currency exchange. No explicit rules, no legislation, only Article IV of the IMF agreement, a scant 800 words, written with a distinctly "gentlemen's agreement" flavor. Article IV speaks of avoiding "manipulating exchange rates ... to gain an unfair competitive advantage," but also explicitly permits a pegged ERM. There is no enforcement, only jawboning in annual IMF Article IV "consultations," or in bilateral or plurilateral venues. Almost all OECD states allow their exchange rate to float on the market. Many small and developing states peg their rate to the US dollar.

Each governance system will ideally provide a public good. IP protection is supposed to provide incentives for producers to innovate and for authors to create cultural products. By offering exclusive, limited rights innovators and creators may get rewarded for their contributions. Many argue that without the incentives that property rights provide, inventions and culture would be under-produced. Yet such rights also impede diffusion of the innovations—diffusion that benefits consumers and follow-on innovators. Policymakers must strike the right balance between producers' and consumers' interests. IP rights create scarcity in goods that are not formally scarce, which can increase the cost of goods. These rights can be abused to kill competition, secure monopoly power, and promote rent-seeking behavior. Many analysts argue that the scope and scale of IP protection that works for OECD countries is not appropriate for countries at earlier stages of development or net importers of IP-protected goods and services, such as China.

Regulation of ERMs through the IMF is intended to provide stability and predictability about future exchange rates. These features promote long-range commitments, growth, and price stability. Current economic wisdom holds that a flexible exchange rate, with minimal government intervention, best meets the needs of large countries.

However, support also exists for a pegged ERM. *The Economist* observes: "Tellingly, the official international financial architects … have steered clear of the subject."[2]

Chinese behavior: intellectual property

The United States and China have long battled over IP protection. Over time China has become more assertive, reflecting a dynamic nested within a broader relative international power shift. China's intellectual property policies over the past 40 years are a product of domestic choices, international pressures, and a dynamic economic development model. This section examines three periods: market opening in 1978 through 1991; the 1992 US–China Memorandum of Understanding (MoU) and China's route to WTO accession in 2001; and post-WTO accession policies through 2015.

Beginning in the 1970s, US business leaders pressed their government to combat inadequate protection of their IP abroad. Through unilateral pressure, bilateral negotiations, and regional and multilateral agreements, the United States prompted much of the rest of the world to adopt its preferred high standards of IP protection. China entered this vortex in 1979 when the United States and China established diplomatic relations. After China joined the WTO in December 2001, US influence over China's IP policies weakened. Subsequently China has implemented some innovative domestic IP and anti-monopoly policies that preserve policy space for China to pursue its own development path.

1978–1991: domestic priorities and international pressure

China's evolving development model has altered its approach to GGOs. Deng Xiaoping's 1978 "Reform and Opening" blueprint began China's engagement in the rapidly globalizing economy. China began to replace structures of a command economy with a regulatory state.[3] One of China's first economic reforms was its 1979 "Law of Joint Ventures Using Chinese and Foreign Investment."[4]

Determined to attract foreign investment without destabilizing the overall economy, in 1980 Deng Xiaoping established special economic zones (SEZs) as enclaves for foreign investment, first in Shenzhen and then in Zhuhai, Shantou, and Xiamen. China established the SEZs to assemble finished goods for export.[5] Foreigners invested in turnkey factories and set up production facilities for low-value-added assembly work.

Under US pressure China launched IP reform in 1979. The two governments signed a bilateral trade agreement offering reciprocal IP protection (national treatment). The United States accused China of failing to apply IP laws, while China protested that the United States was asking for too much.[6] In 1980 China set up its first patent office and joined the World Intellectual Property Organization (WIPO). In 1984 it adopted a patent statute and acceded to WIPO's Paris Convention for the Protection of Industrial Property.

Chinese leaders identified science and technology as key to China's economic future. Moving to upgrade its technological and scientific capabilities, China realized the importance of protecting IP in a market-based system, but at the same time sought technology transfer and diffusion of IP-protected technology. Its 1984 patent law was designed to promote both local innovation and diffusion by offering invention, industrial design, and utility model patents (so-called "petty patents"). China's law specified that invention patent specifications would be publicly disclosed after 18 months. State-owned enterprises (SOEs) could not license their technology without administrative approval, and pharmaceutical products, chemicals, and process inventions were excluded from patent protection.[7] These provisions were weaker than OECD patent laws, creating friction between OECD trading partners. Most of the patenting activity in this period was domestic, with petty patents being both popular and easy to obtain.

While much of this activity responded to foreign pressure, domestic policy priorities drove it as well. The Central Committee of the Chinese Communist Party (CCP) issued the Decision on the Reform of the Economic System in 1984, followed by the 1985 Central Committee's and State Council's Decision on the Reform of the Science and Technology System.[8] China established a National Science Foundation and rolled out three government research and development (R&D) programs that offered financial incentives for science and technology personnel to become entrepreneurs. Under a 1984 incentive program 11 technicians from the Chinese Academy of Sciences formed the firm Legend, now Lenovo, a major global PC supplier.[9]

During this period the Chinese decided that they needed to master IP protection to acquire enhanced R&D capabilities. Foreign firms were reluctant to transfer valuable technology without confidence that the Chinese would protect it. While state-owned enterprises could produce items such as television sets, they had not acquired capabilities for capturing more value in the production chain.[10]

This first era began with bold domestic economic change and a commitment to engaging in global markets. Now open to foreign investment, foreign pressure certainly played a role in China's early reform and opening-era IP policies. However, China also adopted important domestic policy changes to spur further indigenous development and encourage local incremental innovation through its utility model and design patents.

1992–2001: shifting gears in response to foreign pressure and domestic change

Relations over IP remained tense throughout the late 1980s and 1990s. The United States decried China's failure to protect US-held IP. Threats of trade wars, counter-threats, and official reports of egregious violations of US-held IP rights ensued. In January 1992 the United States and China concluded an MoU on IP.

In 1992 China amended its patent law to conform to OECD standards. It extended the invention patent term from 15 to 20 years, and the utility model and design protection from five to 10 years. It allowed for patenting of chemicals, pharmaceutical products, food and beverages, and chemical products.

The proximate cause of the 1992 amendment was US pressure, but the deeper domestic shift to reignite economic reforms put on hold by the 1989 Tiananmen crisis was captured by Deng Xiaoping's famous Southern Tour (*nanxun*). Domestically, China doubled down on its efforts to improve its scientific and technological capacity. It sought to deepen market reforms and to promote commercialization of its scientific achievements. New laws in 1993 offered royalty-sharing opportunities for domestic inventors and designers, qualified ownership possibilities, and increased autonomy for SOEs. In 1995 the government committed to providing further investment in and incentives for basic research, high technology, and commercializing technology.[11] These changes led to both a surge in domestic patenting and a large spike in foreigners filing invention patents in China.

Despite the 1992 reforms, the US Trade Representative (USTR) continued to pressure China. Tempers flared again in 1995. China rebuffed US demands that China shut down 29 factories that allegedly produced millions of copies of American software and movies.[12] The United States threatened to block Chinese accession to the WTO and to levy US$2.8 billion worth of trade sanctions. China claimed that it would hold up applications of American companies seeking to establish businesses in China and suspend joint venture negotiations with American automobile manufacturers.[13] In 1995 and 1996, in the shadow of US pressure and China's efforts to join the WTO, China and the United States reached multiple IP agreements.[14]

China's quest to join the WTO gave its trading partners leverage in the accession process. The United States and the European Community

(EC) opposed its accession for many years and only relented after China made major concessions that the United States and EC demanded, such as waiving the developing countries' grace period for implementing TRIPS. China would enjoy no transition period.[15]

This second era began with foreign-induced policy change in which China aligned its patent laws with stricter OECD standards. Its desire to join the WTO kept foreign pressure on pre-accession policy change steady and effective. China adopted domestic policies to further invigorate and incentivize domestic technology production and innovative activity.

2001–2015: post-accession and the push for indigenous innovation

Since China joined the WTO in 2001, US influence over China's IP policy has weakened. China has implemented some innovative domestic IP policies and strategies for developing technological capabilities. Four important trends in this period have been capacity-building initiatives, a sharp rise in Chinese patenting and IP litigation, China's commitment to indigenous innovation, and its anti-monopoly policies.

Despite extensive foreign direct investment (FDI) and robust exporting, China captures very little of the value of the goods it assembles and sends abroad. Concerned about technology leakage, foreign firms tend to keep their core technologies to themselves. For each Chinese-made Apple iPad that sells for $499, China retains only about $25, mainly from labor costs.[16] Chinese leaders are eager to spur indigenous innovation to capture more value in licensing fees and royalties.

China has introduced new incentives. In 2003 the government began to use invention patent filings as criteria for promotion and tenure in universities and provided patent subsidies to encourage domestic filing. China designated funds to attract accomplished Chinese scientists and scholars, "sea turtles," who studied or worked abroad to return to China.[17] (In Chinese, "sea turtle" is a homophone for "return from overseas.") In 2005 about 35,000 "sea turtles" returned.[18] Gross domestic spending on R&D as a percentage of gross domestic product (GDP) surged from 1.13 percent in 2003 to 2.08 percent in 2013.[19]

China adopted a number of important initiatives to promote more IP-intensive development. Its Medium- to Long-Term Plan for Scientific and Technological Development (2006–2020) established priorities for industrial development in sectors such as pharmaceutical and agricultural biotechnology, civilian aircraft, clean energy, and new materials.[20] The 2008 National Intellectual Property Strategy highlighted the importance of IP as a strategic resource.[21] Its 2010 National Patent Development Strategy underscored China's commitment to promote innovation, and its Twelfth Five-Year Plan (2011–2015) emphasized core technology development. In 2014 the General Office of the State Council circulated an Action Plan on Further Implementing National Intellectual Property Strategy (2014–2020).

China has invested in improving its IP management and capacity. China increased the number of IP courts, trained judges in IP, and introduced a university IP curriculum. To manage the huge increase in patenting activity it has expanded its State Intellectual Property Office (SIPO) from 2,700 patent examiners in 2007 to 11,306 in 2013.[22] SIPO is now the largest patent office in the world.

Most benchmarks of success for China's various IP initiatives are quantitative. While quantity does not necessarily indicate quality, quantitative progress has been remarkable. Between 2005 and 2015 patent applications to SIPO jumped from 476,264 to 2,799,000;[23] of these, in 2014 Chinese filed 2,210,616 applications whereas foreigners filed 150,627.[24] Of the 1,102,000 invention patent applications in 2015, Chinese filed 968,000 applications whereas foreigners filed 134,000.[25] During 2002 and 2003 China filed more trademark applications than any other country.[26] China's copyright applications for computer software went from 21,500 in 2006 to 82,000 in 2010.[27] In 2014 China became the third largest user of the Patent Cooperation Treaty (PCT) behind the United States and Japan. WIPO administers the PCT, collecting fees from firms that seek patent protection in multiple countries with a single international application. Between 2009 and 2010 alone Chinese PCT applications surged by 55.6 percent.[28] In 2014 the Chinese firm Huawei became the top PCT applicant, with 3,442 applications; another Chinese firm, ZTE, was third (just behind Qualcomm) with 2,179 PCT applications.[29]

China has learned lessons the hard way, but has been a quick student. Getting burned by foreigners' strategic patenting and being sued taught China important lessons. While the patent system can be a tool to spur innovation, firms can also deploy it as a market weapon. Strategic patenting is not about stimulating innovation, but rather extracting maximum value from global value chains of production.[30] Foreigners often have charged very high licensing fees for mature, trivial, and even off-patent technology.[31] The Chinese have learned that foreign firms used patenting strategies including "litigation threatening, alliance, and overcharging synchronously, to earn excess benefits."[32] Until 2008 China had no anti-monopoly legislation to protect itself against these abuses.[33]

Litigation has educated Chinese firms. In 2004 the Chinese firm Zhejiang Dongzheng Electrical Co. prevailed against a North

American electronics firm, Leviton Manufacturing Co. Inc., in a patent infringement case. The Chinese firm's president promoted its victory as a model and urged other Chinese firms to fight back.[34] A French electronics firm, Schneider Electronics, had competed with the Chinese firm, Chint, for European markets since the mid-1990s. Schneider sued Chint for IP infringement in 19 cases in Europe and six in China, winning injunctions against Chint. In 2006 Chint used its utility model portfolio to counterattack, suing Schneider for infringement. SIPO ruled in Chint's favor[35] and in 2009 Schneider paid Chint $23 million to settle the lawsuit.[36] Chinese firms now routinely sue foreigners for Chinese-held utility model infringement. Foreign firms claim that these cases are difficult to fight and refer to utility model patents as "junk patents."[37] Chinese firms' strategic patenting suggests that they are learning to game the system to extract rents just as OECD-based firms have been doing for decades.

China has emerged as the world's most litigious country over IP.[38] Domestic litigation has surged, with most cases involving Chinese litigants suing other Chinese firms. Between 2003 and 2010, IP lawsuits in China rose from 9,000 to 42,902.[39] In 2015, China's Supreme People's Court adjudicated 130,200 IP cases, up 11.73 percent from 2014.[40] The Chinese firms Huawei and ZTE, competitors inside China, now sue each other for infringement in European markets. Between 2008 and 2015, the number of intellectual property cases (criminal, administrative, and civil) in Chinese local courts rose from 28,833 to 109,386.[41]

This complex of policies and practices represents a more comprehensive strategy to promote indigenous innovation, strategic sectors, and technology transfer. National champions,[42] patenting incentives, government procurement policies, standard setting, R&D investment, and IP management are all elements of China's indigenous innovation incorporated in its 2006 National Science and Technology plan. US firms doing business in China have claimed that indigenous innovation is "a blueprint for technology theft on a scale the world has never seen before."[43]

China has stepped up its implementation of its 2008 Anti-Monopoly Law. The US government and private firms have expressed concern that China is using it to target foreign companies and promote Chinese industrial policy.[44] For example, *Huawei v. InterDigital* addressed the licensing of foreign intellectual property for 2G and 3G mobile phone standards. The Chinese companies Huawei and ZTE failed to obtain a license from the US company InterDigital for its standard essential patent (SEP) portfolio. InterDigital took actions to assert its intellectual property rights and block importation of Huawei's allegedly infringing product into the United States.[45] Huawei retaliated in 2012 by suing

InterDigital at the Shenzen Intermediate People's Court for abuse of its dominant market position and for the court to determine the maximum royalty rate for a license for the InterDigital SEP portfolio. The Chinese court ruled in Huawei's favor on both issues and set the royalty rate very low. US observers concluded that the court was motivated by industrial policy rather than competition. Indeed, the official website of the Guangdong Courts posted this conclusion about the case:

> Huawei's success in the anti-monopoly lawsuit is quite meaningful. Qiu Yongqing, the Chief Judge [of the Guangdong Higher People's Court], believes that Huawei's strategy of using anti-monopoly laws as a counter-measure is worth learning by other Chinese enterprises. Qiu suggests that Chinese enterprises should bravely employ anti-monopoly lawsuits to break technology barriers and win space for development.[46]

China has been pursuing anti-monopoly policies that target foreign intellectual property.

US pressure on China to enforce IP protection remains strong. The US International Trade Commission reported that IP infringement in China and China's indigenous innovation policies cost US firms $48 billion in 2009.[47] In the wind energy sector, foreign firms' market share has gone from 75 percent in 2004 to 14 percent in 2009, a result that the US Chamber of Commerce attributes to technology transfer requirements for joint venture partners, local content requirements, and preferential treatment for Chinese wind energy firms.[48]

China still depends on foreign technologies. Even its leading firm, Huawei, admitted in an internal document that "all of its core technologies were obtained through mergers and acquisitions or patent licensing."[49] Some analysts expect China to make little progress in crossing over to a truly innovation-based economy. Yet with China's increasingly educated population, its phenomenal economic growth, its engagement with international institutions such as the WTO that expand its market access, and its shift to promoting economic growth through domestic consumption by the rising middle class, the combination of supply and demand factors will most likely drive future innovation.

Chinese behavior: exchange rate policy[50]

Figure 6.1 traces the nominal exchange rate (price of the dollar in renminbi) from 1994 to 2015. In two periods (1995 to 2005 and mid-2008 to mid-2010) the rate is pegged to the dollar (and also for five months in 2015). Policy shifts between pegging and managed move-ment and trends toward a market-based ERM as China has built the necessary institutions and expertise.

1978–1994: absorbing and accepting international norms

From 1949 to the late 1970s, China maintained a pegged, overvalued exchange rate.[51] The government retained all foreign exchange, and monopolized all trade. The GDP share of trade was low and declining.

Then came rapid change. By the mid-1980s, firms could sell foreign exchange on swap markets in dozens of cities. By 1988, China had a dual-track ERM: the swap market and a higher official rate. Over the next six years, the official rate moved ever closer to the swap rate. By 1994, 80 percent of all foreign exchange transactions occurred on the swap market. Then a further reform unified the two rates at 8.28 renminbi/dollar, probably close to an equilibrium rate.

Just as Deng's Southern Tour had an effect on IP policy, it also led to changes in currency policy. By 1994, China's target ERM approxi-mated Western economists' conventional wisdom at that time: free purchase and sale of the renminbi for both trade and finance, coupled with a managed float.[52]

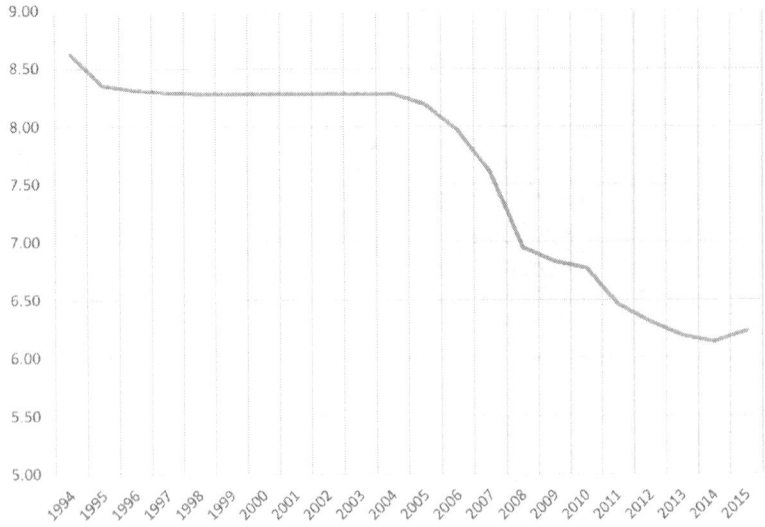

Figure 6.1 Nominal RMB/US$ exchange rate (1994–2015)

Source: *China Statistical Yearbook 2016* (Beijing: National Bureau of Statistics), 602.

We see no sign of domestic pressures from differentially affected interest groups. China moved toward the institutions of the industrialized world it proposed to join. This is a case of what Edward Steinfeld calls "institutional outsourcing." He argues: "China rescued itself [after 1978] from an existential crisis by linking itself to a particular kind of global economic order ... by internalizing the rules of the advanced industrial West ... by playing our game."[53]

1995–2005: *China backs into a peg; then, under fire, abandons it*

From 1995 to 2005, China's peg required strict capital controls. Why did China choose to peg, given the 1994 commitment to a managed float and full convertibility? At the end of the period, China de-pegged, in the face of intense foreign pressure. What explains this second decision, and its timing? Unlike 1980 to 1994, politics—external and domestic—are central.

In 1994, the renminbi was appreciating. China chose to grab a peg: intervening to first slow and then stop the rise. Steinfeld argues convincingly that this initial shift in the ERM emerged from central government rivalries and interest group pressure.[54] Chinese President Jiang Zemin's power was not yet secure. Export manufacturers in coastal provinces, hurt by a strengthening renminbi, played Jiang and other leaders against each other.

The East Asian financial crisis solidified China's decision to peg. In mid-1997, Southeast Asian currencies were attacked by speculators and fell chaotically. GDP dropped by up to 13 percent. Political unrest followed. Economists who had endorsed a managed-float ERM the year prior belatedly recognized that this middle path between a free float and a hard peg was not viable without capital controls.

China faced a stark choice: continue integrating with the world financial system and risk a willy-nilly devaluation, or maintain and tighten capital controls and continue to peg its exchange rate. By October 1997, China's decision was clear. The ERM hardened into a dollar peg and capital controls tightened. Exchange rate movement ceased.

By pegging, China emerged as a reliable regional leader, upstaging Japan. In February 1998 Japan had devalued by 20 percent. By June, US Treasury Secretary Robert Rubin called China "an island of stability in Asia," while Rubin's aides derided the Japanese finance minister as the "Minister for the Destruction of the World Economy."

Domestic interests pushed the other way. State enterprises were shutting down. In December 1997, what *The Economist* called an "articulate group of manufacturers and academics" inside China argued forcefully for devaluation.[55] However, in March 1998, resisting pressure to devalue, the government instead launched a large public works project that successfully offset the shock of falling exports.

Interviews with Chinese who were involved reveal that the foreign policy payoff was a welcome side effect but that the main motivation was domestic stability. An intensely conservative central government bureaucracy was alarmed by the sudden exchange rate shifts in China's neighbors and the social unrest that followed.[56] This event also taught policymakers that IMF orthodoxy could change overnight.

From 1997 to 2000, the pegged rate fortuitously tracked an equilibrium.[57] Then the current account surplus grew steadily, crossing the red line of 3 percent of GDP in 2003–2004. Although appreciation was needed, by 2003 policymakers had grown comfortable with the predictability of a pegged rate and increasingly powerful domestic interests defended it. Meanwhile, recession had US politicians searching for scapegoats abroad and demonizing China even though the trade imbalance flowed more from US policies than a pegged renminbi.[58]

By August 2002 the finance ministers of Canada, Britain, and several European countries had joined the "currency manipulation" chorus. Through 2003 the US Congress turned up the heat, but it was not until late 2004 that the first inter-ministerial debates over exchange rate policy occurred. De-pegging was probably approved at the December Economic Work Conference. In May and June 2005, the Central Economic and Finance Leading Group hammered out a draft decision, which was taken through the State Council and then to the Politburo and announced on 21 July 2005.

The IMF and US Treasury wanted China to float the renminbi but the US Congress and the US Chamber of Commerce simply wanted renminbi appreciation. China grudgingly acceded to the appreciation, but via a managed float. Had they moved to a free market float, appreciation would have been faster. Still, the nominal ER, which had remained unchanged for eight years, appreciated by 2.1 percent on the spot. Then appreciation slowed to a crawl. By June 2008 the renminbi had risen only 18 percent in nominal terms and only 9 percent in real terms. Speculators still enjoyed a one-way bet: the renminbi would only move up. Hence, capital controls had to remain in place.

It would have been in the interests of both China and the world had the adjustment come two years earlier. Three factors contributed to the delay:

1   Unlike 1997, the external shock was inflationary—higher export demand from the United States. The appropriate exchange rate response was appreciation rather than devaluation. Exporters

naturally lined up against releasing the nominal peg. One informant said: "China bore a lot of costs from not devaluing [in 1997]. After the crisis, what was originally a temporary solution became comfortable, and the lobbying force of the exporters was strong. In 2003, even a 1 or 2 percent rise in the exchange rate will create real problems for us. I argued before the premier (for ER movement), but failed."[59]

2   Domestic politics worked against an early resolution. The shock emerged during the 2003 political transition when risk-averse Chinese central government politicians tended to freeze up. "In Chinese politics," we were told, "the middle is always right." Also, Chinese politics had become increasingly consensual. Just as Zhu Rongji was less powerful than Deng, so Zhu's successors were less able than Zhu to enact change.[60]

3   Foreign pressure stoked nationalism. A senior Ministry of Finance official commented angrily: "This is a sovereignty issue. No other country has a say in this."[61] Logan Wright argues that the issue rose to the Politburo only because of punitive threats from Senators Charles Schumer and Lindsey Graham and that the decision was delayed by perhaps two months until they agreed to withdraw their amendment.[62] Interviewees agreed that the shift would have come a year earlier had it not been necessary visibly to resist foreign demands.[63]

To summarize, in the 1995 to 2005 period, China's ERM shifted twice. In 1997, the East Asian crisis derailed a managed float and a temporary dollar peg then evolved into a fixed policy. Between 2000 and 2005, global trade imbalances originating in the United States led to pressure on China to de-peg. Although this pressure caused China to dig in its heels, in the end the ERM shifted to a moving peg. We see interaction between foreign pressure, lobbying interests within China, and an increasingly consensual and conservative Chinese leadership.

2005–2010: China charts her own course

Figure 6.1 shows a steady nominal appreciation after July 2005: 17 percent over 36 months. In July 2008, China again froze at 6.83. This rate persisted through 2009 and the first half of 2010, provoking renewed strident calls from the US Congress for appreciation. The 2005 "reform" brought precisely 36 months of modest flexibility and gradual appreciation, then a renewed peg for precisely 24 months to July 2010 when China again de-pegged.

Some explain the 2008 re-peg as political, or a way China could assert itself against the West. One government official who took this view said: "We're saying that we will make these changes whenever we want to, on our timetable, not yours."[64] In July 2008, China was preparing for the fall party meetings where the Hu-Wen administration expected to win a second five-year term, which would be an opportune time to flex muscles. One can also argue that US pressure broke the Chinese peg after two years. At the time of the Chinese decision (21 June 2010), Congressional action was looming and a G20 meeting was just a week away.

Additional insight can be found by considering the role of China's trade with Europe.[65] When the dollar is depreciating against the euro, yuan–dollar appreciation is tolerable for Chinese exporters to Europe. Beginning in January 2006, the dollar depreciated steadily against the euro and by July 2008 had lost more than 20 percent of its value. The yuan appreciated against the dollar by less than 20 percent. The net result was that Chinese exports to the United States were disadvantaged, but exports to Europe actually received a boost. However, after 2008, this reversed in that if the yuan had continued to appreciate against the dollar, it would have appreciated twice over for eurozone trade. It is not hard to imagine Chinese ministries, local governments, and exporters crying for a peg after June 2008 and getting it.[66] In this period, Chinese currency management became more confident and sophisticated. A senior, knowledgeable informant summarized the difference: "In 1997, and even in 2003, we barely understood the difference between real and nominal exchange rates. Any volatility in the yuan was viewed as threatening. Now, at a technical level, we're much more sophisticated. We've also created swap mechanisms that enable our producers to hedge against currency and interest rate movements, which reduces their concerns somewhat."[67]

2010–2015: dueling institution-building, internationalizing the renminbi

In the second decade of the twenty-first century, a weakened IMF acceded to power sharing, but it is modest, and China, with $4 trillion in reserves and growing dominance in world trade, began to build competing international lending mechanisms and plurilateral trade pacts. By 2016, China's currency joined the SDR club of official IMF currencies alongside the dollar, euro, yen, and pound. However, domestic turbulence and stalled reforms suggest that this internationalization of the renminbi may have been premature.

The 2008 IMF voted to redistribute voting power but redistribution was miniscule. China's share rose by less than 1 percent, to 3.81. At the

September 2009 Pittsburgh Summit, Brazil, Russia, India, China, and South Africa (the BRICS) balked at joining a new IMF lending authority to cope with the global financial crisis and extracted the promise of a further eventual shift of 5 percent in voting power.[68] The US Congress then dragged its heels until acceding, in December 2015, to a token 0.2 percent reduction in US voting share. With a US-sized GDP and four times the population, China within the IMF still had one-quarter the US vote and no real power.

Predictably, China began to build competing institutions. In 2010, China adapted a pre-existing Southeast Asian currency swap arrangement, multilateralizing it as the Chiang Mai Initiative (CMI). In June 2012, CMI resources were doubled to $240 billion, with an implementing agency in Singapore. The CMI was still not an Asian IMF.[69] Its surveillance and conditionality mechanism would still come from the IMF, but like a sapling growing up in the shadow of an aging oak, the CMI could quickly supplant a collapsed IMF.

Two other stout saplings grew up to provide long-term development funding: the so-called "BRICS Bank" (or New Development Bank—NDB) and the Asian Infrastructure Investment Bank (AIIB). The NDB has a $50 billion capitalization, subscribed equally from the five BRICS countries, and a headquarters in Shanghai. The 2015 AIIB launch resembled a birthday party where one invitee (the United States) refused to attend. In March, as Australia, South Korea, and Britain signed up, a US official complained, "[w]e are wary about a trend." France and Germany were similarly rebuked by the United States. However, by the opening ceremony in January 2016, only four of the world's 20 largest economies were absent: the United States, Canada, Mexico, and Japan, with Japan likely to join soon.

As we note below, China was also active in world trade governance, creating the Regional Comprehensive Economic Partnership (RCEP) in response to the Trans-Pacific Partnership (TPP). Selling TPP domestically, then-US President Barack Obama argued: "We can't let countries like China write the rules of the global economy. We should write those rules."[70] RCEP, covering 3 billion people and 40 percent of world trade, may be an effective countermove.

Amid these dramatic developments—China as rule maker and institution-builder in world trade and finance—2015 promised to be a turning point for the renminbi as well. Its use as a settlement currency had grown rapidly: from ninth (behind the Mexican peso) in 2013 to fifth in January 2015. More than 20 renminbi trading hubs, from Singapore to London to Toronto, had integrated China with global financial markets. Controls on capital flows were being progressively loosened.

All this positioned the renminbi to claim inclusion in the IMF's SDR market basket of currencies, along with the dollar, euro, yen, and pound.

The IMF SDR vote came in December—but with consummation delayed to 1 October 2016. Meanwhile, flies were circling the wedding cake. The US Federal Reserve sent ever-stronger signals of an interest rate hike, as the US economy continued to be strong. Chinese growth slowed. China's commitment to reform was questioned in the wake of ham-handed interventions in a falling Chinese stock market. The SDR imprimatur from the IMF should have spiked confidence in the currency, but now market pessimism overwhelmed it. Throughout 2016, Chinese leaders stoutly asserted that the renminbi should not devalue as hedge fund managers worldwide staked out bets against them.

As in 2005 and 2008, speculators sensed a one-way bet, but this time, proving them wrong involved buying renminbi rather than selling. Foreign reserves shrank for the first time since 1992. Capital outflows accelerated, reaching $100 billion a month in January. The People's Bank of China (PBOC) was in the awkward position of a much-applauded student, the chosen valedictorian, who arrives at the graduation platform just as the market awards him an F in a critical spring term course. Markets can be as misguided as governments. However, as China's foreign exchange fell below $3 trillion, the country had at most two years, perhaps much less, to seek a revised grade on the exam.

China's assertiveness and effectiveness

To the extent that China has been effective in achieving its goals by working within the global governance system, it will presumably favor the status quo. China's core goal is rapid economic growth via industrialization, and its industrialization strategy is rapid integration into the world economy. Over the last 25 years, China's strategy and goal have succeeded beyond anyone's wildest imagination.

As the current rules have benefited China, we expect China to favor reformist, not radical, change. Not every rule works to China's advantage. China will push to reform the rules, in part by asserting its own power as a rule maker. Looking at IP and ER, China has been effective in pursuing its goal of growing influence. Has China successfully asserted itself by remaking rules?[71]

Intellectual property

China has gained impressive competence in IP policy and GGOs in a short time and is a skilled participant in the WTO. Highlights of China's participation include its effective performance in a landmark WTO copyright case, and its more assertive participation in the TRIPS Council and WIPO.

Since joining the WTO China has been an observer in almost every Dispute Settlement case to learn first-hand how the system works. China has been a quick student and defended itself ably in the WTO Copyright enforcement case. It has affirmed a considerable amount of policy discretion under the Agreement on TRIPS.

In April 2007 the United States brought its first IP enforcement case against China to the WTO. The case claimed that China had violated TRIPS in three ways: 1) by denying copyright protection for censored works; 2) by donating and/or auctioning off goods seized in counterfeit raids rather than destroying them; and 3) by lacking criminal sanctions for counterfeiting and piracy below certain thresholds.

The WTO panel's report upheld most of China's practices.[72] The WTO ruled that China's denial of copyright protection for censored works was in violation and in 2010 China amended its copyright law in response to the panel's rulings.[73]

China prevailed on the matter of disposing of pirated and counterfeit goods seized in raids. China has an agreement with the Red Cross to donate these goods and sometimes China removes infringing trademarks and auctions off seized goods.[74] The panel ruled that China's practices did not violate TRIPS, but ruled that simply removing the infringing trademark before auction was insufficient.[75]

The United States argued that China violated Article 61 covering criminal penalties for infringements. This third claim addressed the "commercial scale" issue—how much infringement constitutes "commercial scale"? TRIPS negotiators had never agreed. China argued that in TRIPS the term "'commercial scale' was intentionally vague ... because a large bloc of Members would never have accepted a more specific and intrusive obligation."[76] China pointed out that the United States' bilateral agreements define "commercial scale" to cover *any* activity for financial gain, underscoring that "the United States failed to secure in the TRIPS ... negotiations the obligation that it nonetheless seeks to impose here."[77] The United States submitted industry-generated reports of losses to infringement in China, press articles, and anecdotal evidence for its case. Both China and the WTO panel criticized the evidence for being "insufficient" and "uncorroborated," and maintained that the accuser "failed to satisfy its burden of proof."[78]

This ruling highlighted ample discretion in implementing TRIPS and did little to assuage US rights-holders' concerns about inadequate enforcement. Dissatisfied with WTO mechanisms, US rights-holders pushed the USTR to pursue a plurilateral agreement to secure more effective IP enforcement. The United States negotiated the Anti-Counterfeiting Trade Agreement (ACTA) with select trading partners (mainly OECD countries and countries already bound by TRIPS-Plus agreements with the United States). The ACTA is TRIPS-Plus, incorporating features and provisions that the United States could not secure at the multilateral level. China raised its concerns about ACTA in the WTO TRIPS Council. At the June 2010 TRIPS Council meeting China, along with India, Argentina, Venezuela, and Mauritius, expressed concern over TRIPS-Plus enforcement trends and ACTA. At the October 2010 TRIPS Council meeting, China suggested that ACTA might be incompatible with TRIPS.[79]

China has also supported a "development agenda" in WIPO that would incorporate developing countries' concerns about IP. China supports a number of pro-development provisions that were never incorporated into TRIPS. The development agenda drove the United States to the plurilateral level (e.g., ACTA) for IP rule-making as countries like China asserted their interests against the United States in the WTO and WIPO.

China has stepped up to provide more leadership in intellectual property. In June 2012 Beijing hosted the Diplomatic Conference on the Protection of Audiovisual Performances. The Conference adopted the Beijing Treaty on Audiovisual Performances, a new IP treaty that WIPO will administer. In July 2014 WIPO established a China Office in Beijing. Private sector IP practitioners recognized China's efforts in this area by electing the first Chinese member, Ma Hao, to the vice presidency of the International Association for the Protection of Intellectual Property (AIPPI) in September 2015. China also won the bid to host the AIPPI's 2020 World Congress.[80] These examples suggest that China is eager to earn recognition as a respectable player in intellectual property governance.

Exchange rate mechanism

China's IP policy has had many disparate goals. ER policy, by contrast, has been part of broad macroeconomic policy with one overriding goal: rapid economic growth through sustained industrialization.

During 1980 through 1994, China passively accepted the misguided global norm of a flexible ERM that left it vulnerable to speculative attack and financial disruption. The opportunity for regional leadership amid the 1997 crisis, coupled with concern over stability, led to a dollar peg. Domestic interest groups solidified that peg; the 2005 break was tardy and fraught. After 2008, China pegged, then broke the peg, based on perceived national interest.

Increasingly through this period, China challenged US positions in other areas of international financial governance. At an October 2008 Asia–Europe international financial system conference, China supported the European view that weak financial regulation led to the world crisis, and thus financial regulation must be strengthened. In March 2009, PBOC Governor Zhou Xiaochuan called for an international reserve currency "disconnected from individual nations," and suggested SDRs as an option. In June 2009, Liu Mingkang, the head of the Chinese Bank Regulatory Commission, outlined lessons for the West in prudential bank management. After 2010, China asserted its role within the existing IMF/WTO system, as well as building new institutions (CMI, AIIB, RCEP) outside it.

Moving from a pegged or managed exchange rate to a free float has always been in China's perceived long-term interest, but here, too, we see assertiveness. The norm of a market-set renminbi was reiterated yearly or biennially in IMF Consultations and in United States–China Strategic and Economic Dialogue (S&ED) closing statements. However, even at the risk of some embarrassment (after receiving the SDR designation), China has continued to manage its exchange rate in response to domestic political and economic needs. It pegs when pegging suits. Effectively, a "China exception" now exists within that global norm.

Conclusion

We began this chapter proposing to link the Chinese policy choices over time to four causal stories: growing capacity and expertise, growing economic power; domestic politics; and an evolving growth strategy. The first two of these clearly shaped both the IP and ER experience. Compared with the situation 25 years ago, China can now confidently chart its own course in these waters and carry other countries in its wake. Domestic interest groups' roles are harder to define, measure, and analyze, even though they did shape ER policy choices. In both ER and IP, the central government must heed many voices— local governments, firms, and bureaucratic forces at every level—to an extent that would have been unthinkable in the early 1990s. In the IP arena, but not ER, firms themselves are increasingly actors.

Our conclusions about China's evolving development strategy are more complex. China is moving from low-wage assembly processes to higher-skill, higher-technology processes, due to rising educational levels and heavy investment. OECD countries may come to regret the aggressive approach they deployed to get China to embrace the IP regime. If China successfully crosses the bridge from imitation to innovation, then hefty royalty and licensing fees will be flowing from West to East.

The remaining components of a development strategy story are more ambiguous. Primary reliance upon export-led growth must end. China's share of world exports might rise from 13 percent to 15 percent, or even 20 percent, but in the long run, China's exports can grow only as fast as world trade grows. At that point, where will households get the income needed to substitute for exports as China's growth engine? An appreciated currency, raising their real incomes? Higher interest on their deposits? Higher wages? Lower prices? China has always put producers first, and all of these options would sap the power of China's industrial sector.

The third section documented China's increasingly assertive role in global governance. China is beginning to enjoy a voice at the table commensurate with its rising economic power. In the WTO copyright enforcement case, China effectively retained policy space tailored to its needs. It is likely China will increasingly pursue WTO dispute settlement channels to push back against aggressive US and European challenges. China's renewed use of a dollar peg in 2008 and strong government ER intervention since then blazes a trail for smaller countries such as Malaysia which might otherwise have trouble standing up to the IMF, the United States, and Wall Street on this issue.

All of this means no more cakewalk for the United States and Europe in multilateral forums. China has built up significant goodwill throughout the developing world using its soft power, investment, and non-onerous treaty provisions. Gridlock between developed and developing countries across a number of multilateral fora, such as the WTO and WIPO, has chased the United States and Europe out of multilateral fora to pursue plurilateral, regional, and bilateral routes to achieve their goals.

China's multilateral engagement has been more supportive than leading, and its preferences have been more reformist than radical. Competition between the BRICS will increase over time, but for now some of these countries have been effective champions for some developing countries' IP and ER concerns. China and India have supported access and benefit-sharing agreements and prior informed consent for those seeking to exploit their biological diversity. China also has pushed back against US plurilateral IP efforts. The TPP negotiations, with their TRIPS-Plus IP provisions and uncertain consequences for the balance of economic power in Asia, have raised China's hackles even as it weighs the pros and cons of one day joining the TPP or another organization that eventually adopts the TPP's approach to IP.

However, in both IP and ER, we concur with Ren Xiao and others in this volume. As China's power and participation grow, it will seek greater institutional power, both for its own purposes and to advance a broader global governance agenda. It will be a status quo power, promoting reform as opposed to radical change.

Notes

1 We gratefully acknowledge the support of Indiana University's Research Center for Chinese Politics & Business, and Scott Kennedy for his leadership and assistance both in Bloomington and Beijing.
2 "Fix or Float? It All Depends," *The Economist*, 28 January 1999.
3 Margaret Pearson, "The Business of Governing Business in China," *World Politics* 57 (2005): 296–332.
4 Lan Xue and Zheng Liang, "Relationships between IPR and Technology Catch-up," in *Intellectual Property Rights, Development and Catch-up*, ed. Hiroyuki Odagiri, Akira Goto, Atsushi Sunami, and Richard Nelson (New York: Oxford University Press, 2010), 317–360.
5 Xue and Liang, "Relationships between IPR and Technology Catch-up," 338.
6 Chengfei Ding, "The Protection of New Plant Varieties of American Businesses in China After China Enters the WTO," *Drake Journal of Agricultural Law* 6 (2001): 333–349, 339.
7 Xue and Liang, "Relationships between IPR and Technology Catch-up," 325–326.
8 Xue and Liang, "Relationships between IPR and Technology Catch-up," 324.
9 Xue and Liang, "Relationships between IPR and Technology Catch-up," 325.
10 Xue and Liang, "Relationships between IPR and Technology Catch-up," 335.
11 Xue and Liang, "Relationships between IPR and Technology Catch-up," 336.
12 David Sanger, "US Threatens $2.8 billion of Tariffs on China Exports," *New York Times*, 1 January 1995.
13 Sanger, "US Threatens $2.8 billion of Tariffs on China Exports."
14 Agreement Regarding Intellectual Property Rights, People's Republic of China-United States, 26 February 1995, 34I.L.M. 881; Implementation of the 1995 Intellectual Property Rights Agreement—1996, June 1996, People's Republic of China-United States, http://tcc.export.gov/Trade_Agreem ents/All_Trade_Agreements/exp_005361.asp.
15 Jung Yang, "Bringing the Question of Chinese IPR Enforcement to the WTO under TRIPS," *University of Pittsburgh Journal of Technology Law & Policy* 10 (2010): 1–27, 6.
16 Peter Drahos, "The US, China and the G-77 in the Era of Responsive Patentability," Queen Mary University of London, School of Law, Legal Studies Research Paper No. 105/2012, https://papers.ssrn.com/sol3/papers. cfm?abstract_id=2022874.

17 Maximilian Mayer, "China's Rise and the Politics of Knowledge," paper prepared for the International Studies Association Annual Convention, 1–4 April 2012, San Diego, Calif.: 11.

18 Xue and Liang, "Relationships between IPR and Technology Catch-up," 349.

19 Eurostat, "Research and Development Expenditure as Percent of GDP," http://ec.europa.eu/eurostat/en/web/products-datasets/-/T2020_20.

20 Richard Suttmeier and Xiangkui Yao, "China's IP Transition: Rethinking Intellectual Property Rights in a Rising China," The National Bureau of Asian Research, NBR Special Report, no. 29, July 2011: 8.

21 State Intellectual Property Office of the People's Republic of China, *2014 White Paper on Intellectual Property Rights Protection in China*, http://eng lish.sipo.gov.cn/laws/whitepapers/201507/t20150722_1148206.html.

22 IP5 Offices, *Statistics Report 2013*, 19, http://www.fiveipoffices.org/statistics/statisticsreports/2013edition/chapter2.pdf.

23 "2015 Intellectual Property Rights Protection in China," *SIPO*, http://eng lish.sipo.gov.cn/laws/whitepapers/201607/P020160721403876149335.pdf.

24 Suttmeier and Yao, "China's IP Transition: Rethinking Intellectual Property Rights in a Rising China," 13; State Intellectual Property Office of the People's Republic of China, *2014 White Paper on Intellectual Property Rights Protection in China*.

25 "IV. Patent Application and Examination," *2015 SIPO Annual Report*, http://english.sipo.gov.cn/laws/annualreports/2015/201606/P020160603402726016621.pdf

26 Tony Chen, "Western Ways, Good and Bad," *Financial Times Asia*, 21 July 2004.

27 Suttmeier and Yao, "China's IP Transition: Rethinking Intellectual Property Rights in a Rising China," 13.

28 World Intellectual Property Organization, *PCT—The International Patent System Yearly Review: Developments and Performance in 2010* (Geneva, 2010), 12–13; also see World Intellectual Property Organization Infographic, *Who Filed the Most PCT Patents in 2014?*

29 See World Intellectual Property Organization Infographic, *Who Filed the Most PCT Patents in 2014?*

30 Drahos, "The US, China and the G-77 in an Era of Responsive Patentability," 10.

31 Xue and Liang, "Relationships between IPR and Technology Catch-up," 348.

32 Xue and Liang, "Relationships between IPR and Technology Catch-up," 348.

33 Michael Jacobs and Xinzhu Zhang, "China's Approach to Compulsory Licensing of Intellectual Property under its Anti-monopoly Law," *Competition Policy International* (Autumn 2010): 181–215.

34 Wenqi Liu, "Establishing a Safeguard System for Intellectual Property Protection for Chinese Private Enterprises," *Journal of Intellectual Property Rights* 14 (May 2009): 226–235, 233.

35 Jeffrey Duncan, Michelle Sherwood, and Yuanlin Shen, "A Comparison Between the Judicial and Administrative Routes to Enforce Intellectual Property Rights in China," *The John Marshall Law School Review of Intellectual Property Law* 7 (2008): 536.

36 Account based on James McGregor, "China's Drive for 'Indigenous Innovation': A Web of Industrial Policies," Global Intellectual Property Center, Global Regulatory Cooperation Project, US Chamber of Commerce, 27.

37 James McGregor, "China's Drive for 'Indigenous Innovation': A Web of Industrial Policies," 26 and 28.
38 Suttmeier and Yao, "China's IP Transition: Rethinking Intellectual Property Rights in a Rising China," 13.
39 Chen, "Western Ways, Good and Bad," 1; Suttmeier and Yao, "China's IP Transition: Rethinking Intellectual Property Rights in a Rising China," 13.
40 China IPR, *Summarizing the SPC's 2015 White Paper*, 22 April 2016, http s://chinaipr.com/2016/04/22/summarizing-the-spcs-2015-white-paper/.
41 DEQI Intellectual Property Law Corporation, "Statistics of IP Cases of First Instance in Chinese Courts," 20 January 2015, www.lexology.com/library/detail.aspx?g=e947e076-add3-497d-9661-f54089868bb5.
42 Li-Wen Lin and Curtis Milhaupt, "We are the (National) Champions," The Center for Law and Economic Studies, Columbia University School of Law, Working paper no. 409 (November 2011).
43 US Chamber of Commerce, "China's Drive for 'Indigenous Innovation'—a Web of Industrial Policies" (July) 2010, www.uschamber.com/report/china%E2%80%99s-drive-indigenous-innovation-web-industrial-policies.
44 United States Trade Representative, "2015 Report to Congress on China's WTO Compliance," December 2015, 121–122, https://ustr.gov/sites/default/files/2015-Report-to-Congress-China-WTO-Compliance.pdf; The US–China Business Council, "Competition Policy and Enforcement in China," September 2014, www.uschina.org/sites/default/files/AML%202014%20Report%20FINAL_0.pdf; US Chamber of Commerce, "Competing Interests in China's Competition Law Enforcement: China's Anti-Monopoly Law Application and the Role of Industrial Policy," 9 September 2014, www.uschamber.com/report/competing-interests-chinas-competition-law-enforcement-chinas-anti-monopoly-law-application.
45 US Chamber of Commerce, "Competing Interests in China's Competition Law Enforcement: China's Anti-Monopoly Law Application and the Role of Industrial Policy," 75.
46 US Chamber of Commerce, "Competing Interests in China's Competition Law Enforcement: China's Anti-Monopoly Law Application and the Role of Industrial Policy," 76.
47 United States International Trade Commission, *China: Effects of Intellectual Property Infringement and Indigenous Innovation Policies on the US Economy* (2011).
48 US Chamber of Commerce, "China's Drive for 'Indigenous Innovation': A Web of Industrial Policies," 33.
49 Xue and Liang, "Relationships between IPR and Technology Catch-up," 350.
50 This section draws on 33 interviews, conducted between September 2011 and April 2012, cited by interview number to preserve anonymity: academics like Fan Gang, Liu Guoguang, Wu Jinglian, Yu Yongding, and Li Yang, central government staffers like Cheng Jingxue, Yuan Jian, and Zhao Quanzhou, and US-based experts like Lin Yifu, Zhu Min, Nigel Chalk, Bert Keidel, Olin Wethington, and David Loevinger.
51 Nicholas Lardy, *Foreign Trade and Economic Reform in China* (Cambridge, Mass.: Cambridge University Press, 1992), 24–27.
52 Interview 20; Barry Naughton, *The Chinese Economy: Transition and Growth* (Cambridge, Mass.: MIT Press, 2007), 389.

156   *Bruce Reynolds and Susan K. Sell*

53 Edward Steinfeld, *Playing Our Game: Why China's Economic Rise Doesn't Threaten the West* (New York: Oxford University Press, 2010), 17–18.
54 Steinfeld, *Playing Our Game: Why China's Economic Rise Doesn't Threaten the West*, 94.
55 "Signs of Success," *The Economist*, 11 December 1997.
56 Interviews 1, 2, 15, 20, 27, 32, 33.
57 Morris Goldstein and Nicholas Lardy, *The Future of China's Exchange Rate Policy* (Washington, DC: The Petersen Institute for International Economics, 2009).
58 For an authoritative study documenting the primacy of US imbalances, see Olivier Blanchard and Gian Maria Milesi-Ferretti, "Global Imbalances: In Midstream?," IMF Staff Position Note SPN/09–29 (22 December 2009).
59 Interview 32.
60 Interviews 2, 7, 14, 22, 29.
61 "China Won't Revalue Yuan Under Speculative, Political Pressure," *Xinhua Finance News*, 22 June 2005.
62 Logan Wright, *The Elusive Price of Stability: Ideas and Interests in the Reform of China's Exchange Rate Regime* (Washington, DC: George Washington University PhD Thesis, 2009), 221–225.
63 Interviews 1, 6, 15, 20, 23, 29, 32, 33.
64 Interview 19.
65 Personal communication from Albert Keidel.
66 Steinfeld, *Playing Our Game*, 110–111, documents active lobbying by manufacturers starting in July 2008.
67 Interview 12.
68 Ngaire Woods, "Global Governance after the Financial Crisis: A New Multilateralism or the Last Gasp of the Great Powers?" LSE/Wiley Online, 27 January 2010.
69 Hal Hill and Jayant Menon, "Asia's New Financial Safety Net: Is the Chiang Mai Initiative Designed Not to be Used?," *Voxeu*, 25 July 2012, http://voxeu.org/article/chiang-mai-initiative-designed-not-be-used.
70 Sarah Hsu, "China and the Trans-Pacific Partnership," *The Diplomat*, 14 October 2015, http://thediplomat.com/2015/10/china-and-the-trans-pacific-partnership/.
71 This is a rather "realist" view of Chinese motivations. One could imagine a Chinese meta-goal: strengthening global governance as a whole, in order to stabilize the world environment that enables rapid Chinese growth. We assume that this motive is at best a minor factor in explaining Chinese behavior within global governance.
72 Panel Report, China—Measures Affecting the Protection and Enforcement of Intellectual Property Rights, WT/DS362/R, 26 January 2009, adopted 20 March 2009, www.wto.org/english/tratop_e/dispu_e/cases_e/ds362_e.htm.
73 Peter Yu, "The US-China Dispute over TRIPS Enforcement," Drake University Law School, Occasional Papers in Intellectual Property Law, no. 5: 33.
74 Daniel Gervais, "International Decision: China—Measures Affecting the Protection and Enforcement of Intellectual Property Rights," *American Journal of International Law* 103 (2009): 549–555, 550–551.
75 Gervais, "International Decision: China—Measures Affecting the Protection and Enforcement of Intellectual Property Rights," 552.

76 Annex B, Submissions of China, B-7-8, www.wto.org/english/tratop_e/disp u_e/362r_b_e.doc.
77 Annex B, Submissions of China, B-8, www.wto.org/english/tratop_e/dispu_ e/362r_b_e.doc.
78 Yang, "Bringing the Question of Chinese IPR Enforcement to the WTO under TRIPS," 13.
79 Excerpt from China's intervention at the WTO TRIPS Council meeting, 26–27 October 2010, http://lists.keionline.org/pipermail/a2k_lists.keionline. org/2011-June/000554.html.
80 Emily Tan, "AIPPI—IP Bridge of the World," *China Intellectual Property, China Daily*, 11 September 2015, http://ipr.chinadaily.com.cn/2015-09/11/ content_21843344.htm.

7 China's involvement in global health governance

Progress and challenges

Yanzhong Huang

- **Impact on global health governance**
- **Impact on domestic health governance**
- **Opening the black box**
- **Conclusion**

The past three decades have seen profound changes in the biological and political worlds, which have fundamentally altered the landscape of global health governance (GHG). David Fidler, a professor at Indiana University Law School, defines global health governance as "the use of formal and informal institutions, rules, and processes by states, intergovernmental organizations, and non-state actors to deal with challenges to health that require cross-border collective action to address effectively."[1] Along with the rising number and variety of global health problems and the expansion of global health processes is the increase in quantity and diversity of global health players. Changes in the international systems have led to not only the rise of powerful non-state actors calling the shots in Geneva (e.g., the Gates Foundation), but also the growing participation of emerging powers. While these countries are traditionally players in GHG, the power shift has bestowed upon them new opportunities to more directly and deeply engage in global health governance than ever before.

Among the emerging powers, China has provided development assistance for health since the 1950s.[2] Also, due to the sheer size of its population, China has long been a major force to reckon with in global health. Yet conscious and direct engagement in GHG is a relatively recent development for China.[3] It was not until the late 1970s that China paid membership dues to the World Health Organization (WHO). The threat of the HIV/AIDS epidemic since the 1990s and the 2002–2003 Severe Acute Respiratory Syndrome (SARS) crisis provided further impetus for the country to engage in GHG. Since 2010, with its growing economic prowess, international pressure for China to shoulder more global health responsibilities has also risen.[4]

As China becomes more integrated into the outside world, one would expect China to play a much bigger role in GHG initiatives, institutions, and processes. Because of its population size and geo-economic importance, not only do China's shifting health policy priorities and its health system capacity building have global repercussions, but the form and substance of its health diplomacy might provide alternative approaches to GHG and also might affect the willingness and capacity of other countries to cope with global health challenges. Conversely, the dynamics of GHG, as reflected in the proliferation of various influential actors, growing normative pressures and discourses, and the availability of additional external resources and information channels are all expected to have a profound impact on China's domestic governance and health policies.

This chapter examines the effects of China's participation in GHG by addressing two interrelated questions. First, how has China's involvement had an impact on GHG? Second, to what extent has China's GHG involvement resulted in changes in its own domestic health governance? A comprehensive and in-depth understanding of the impact of China's involvement in GHG is needed in order to understand the effectiveness and dynamics of GHG, not only because China plays a critical role in the complex dynamics among health, development, and security, but also because the rise of China has raised tremendous expectations on its engagement in GHG. An improved understanding of the dynamics of China's GHG participation, in turn, helps increase China's capability to be a constructive partner in GHG. Ultimately, such insight would create a stronger foundation for international players to cooperate in addressing global health challenges.

In examining China's impact on GHG, this chapter looks at its effectiveness in promoting cooperation in health-related development, its contribution to global disease prevention and control, as well as its role in global health rule-making. An examination of the impact on domestic health governance is conducted by exploring the role of GHG in domestic health agenda-setting, policy formulation, and policy implementation.

Impact on global health governance

China as an aid donor

Beginning in the 1960s, driven by China's desire to expand its political influence in the developing world, China increased its foreign aid.

Chinese foreign aid reached an all-time high in the 1970s.[5] During the years between 1963 and 1982, 6,500 Chinese health workers joined medical teams and served a total of 70 million people in 42 countries, including 32 countries in Africa.[6] The content of Chinese health aid practice bore the firm imprimatur of the Maoist health system, which focused on equity, primary health care, community participation, and devolved decision-making.[7] This occurred at a time when it was increasingly evident that the Western-based medical model (which emphasized hospital-based treatment, curative care, and high-technology interventions) was becoming increasingly unaffordable to people in the developing world. In this respect, the export of the Chinese health-care model not only improved people's health status of the recipient countries, but also presented an alternative model of health-care provision in limited resource settings.[8]

Since the 1980s, there have been significant changes in the form and substance of China's health aid program. With the resumption of its seat in the United Nations (UN), China began to explore international development cooperation opportunities that combined its aid money with funding from the UN and other multilateral agencies.[9] Rather than focusing simply on the dispatch of medical teams, China diversified its forms of health aid to include infrastructure building and human resources development. Instead of treating foreign aid purely as a "political task" or providing only "one-way" free aid, as Xu Jiajun shows in her chapter in this volume, China since the mid-1990s has emphasized the economic aspects of foreign aid and used it to promote mutual benefits, trade, and market expansion. In order to expand its political influence and boost pharmaceutical exports in Africa, the government launched a broader charm offensive to construct health-care facilities and donate medicine to Africa. At the Sino-African Summit in November 2006, President Hu Jintao pledged US$37.5 million in grants to supply artemisinin-based drugs and to build 30 antimalarial centers in Africa. By the end of 2009, China had completed more than 100 hospitals and health-care centers and donated a tremendous amount of medical equipment and drug products.[10] More recently, China responded to the Ebola epidemic in Western Africa with unprecedented generosity. By late November 2014, China had offered $123 million worth of humanitarian aid to the global Ebola control efforts, China's largest ever response to an international humanitarian crisis.[11]

The contribution of China's health-related development assistance on GHG nevertheless should not be exaggerated. As the world's second-largest economy, with the largest holdings of foreign exchange reserves, China is still not considered an active donor to global health. Until recently, it made only a nominal contribution to the Global Fund to Fight AIDS, Tuberculosis, and Malaria. However, in the meantime, it had been aggressively seeking Global Fund grants, so much so that critics argued that China threatened to undermine the entire premise behind the Global Fund.[12]

Perhaps more importantly, since GHG is narrowly defined in terms of engaging critical stakeholders while bringing coherence to the global health initiatives and projects, it is necessary to examine the degree to which China's health aid aligns with international practice.[13] Unlike most Organisation for Economic Co-operation and Development (OECD) countries, Chinese health aid does not come attached with political strings (except in the case of Taiwan). Thus, China's aid programs run in direct competition to programs that emphasize governance, accountability, and human rights. Second, Chinese programs are not fully aligned to the needs of the recipient countries. In addressing the threat of infectious diseases, for example, less interest was given to tackling major health threats such as HIV/AIDS and tuberculosis (TB). Third, despite its growing interest in multilateralism, China still prefers to provide bilateral aid. The lack of transparency in its bilateral aid programs makes it next to impossible to gauge the full extent and nature of its health aid program. Fourth, while the United States and other OECD countries have moved away from tied aid, China's health aid was repackaged to promote the exports of its pharmaceuticals.[14] In Tanzania, for example, the Chinese government bought the anti-malarial drug Cotecxin from Beijing Holley-Cotec to make donations to local hospitals and clinics.[15] Finally, the lack of participation of Chinese civil society organizations (CSOs) in health aid further narrows the space of cooperation between China and other donors. Successful implementation of foreign aid projects often hinges upon the support of civil society groups. The United States President's Emergency Plan for AIDS Relief (PEPFAR), for instance, channels resources to nongovernmental organizations (NGOs) that propose and implement programs abroad.[16] Chinese citizens and NGOs began to participate in global health-related humanitarian aid in the mid-1980s, but so far they have played only a very limited role in global health aid. All this raised concerns about the coherence of health-related development assistance.

Contribution to global disease control

China's contribution to GHG goes beyond development assistance to a particular region. China is now a leading supplier of drugs and drug ingredients in the world. According to a 2007 General Accountability Office (GAO) report, China has the largest number of registered drug manufacturers exporting drugs to the United States. In 2008, China also accounted for 14 percent of the $31 billion market for active pharmaceutical ingredients (APIs).[17] China's push for exports has contributed to lower costs of some lifesaving drugs and vaccines for the world's poor and provides major new competition for big Western pharmaceutical companies. As noted by a senior official at the GAVI Alliance, China's entry into the vaccine market should be considered a potential "game changer."[18]

However, if there is an event that taught China the importance of seriously engaging GHG, it is the 2002–2003 SARS crisis. SARS highlighted China as a "weak link" in GHG.[19] It generated momentum for China to strengthen its disease surveillance and surge response capacities. It also created strong incentives for China to establish mechanisms to effectively communicate with the international community on public health issues. In 2004 China began to work with the Joint United Nations Programme on HIV/AIDS (UNAIDS) to issue joint reports on China's AIDS spread and control. In compliance with the revised International Health Regulations (IHR), the Chinese government has made significant progress in cooperating with WHO and the international scientific community in sharing data and information about disease outbreaks. China's willingness to share H5N1 virus samples was in sharp contrast to Indonesia, which used the idea of "viral sovereignty" to justify its refusal to cooperate with WHO in avian influenza sample sharing and disease reporting.[20] Efforts to narrow the internal health governance gap and improve transparency contributed to the WHO's Global Outbreak Alert and Response Network (GOARN), and strengthened its early-warning and surveillance activities.

In the wake of SARS, China has demonstrated an ability to orchestrate multilateral cooperation over international health at the global, regional, and even sub-regional levels.[21] At the global level, China has shown strong interest in working closely with major international organizations in disease prevention and control. In January 2006, China hosted an International Pledging Conference on Avian and Human Influenza. During this event, the international community pledged $1.9 billion for preventing and controlling avian flu, including $10 million from China. In June 2009, during the global fight against the H1N1 pandemic, China took the initiative of hosting the International Scientific Symposium on Influenza A (H1N1) Pandemic Response and Preparedness. Two years later, China organized the first meeting of health ministers from the BRICS (Brazil, Russia, India, China, and South Africa) countries, who pledged in the Beijing Declaration to explore the transfer of technologies to enable poor nations to produce cheap and effective lifesaving medicines for diseases such as HIV/AIDS, TB, and hepatitis. China has also been active in participating in regional health forums such as the Association of Southeast Asian Nations +3 (ASEAN+3) Summit. Through these venues, China proposed a series of important initiatives on the control of avian flu and the management of public health emergencies.

The new health diplomacy nevertheless has its limits. In responding to international public health emergencies, China's contribution is still marred by concerns of cover-ups and lack of transparency.[22] On 1 March 2013, for example, scientists in Shanghai had already identified a novel Influenza A virus (later confirmed to be H7N9), but the local media obeyed a request by health authorities and continued to deny there was anything unusual. In a manner reminiscent of the communication failure during the SARS outbreak, Shanghai health authorities did not inform China Center for Disease Control and Prevention (CDC) officials in Beijing about the new virus for nearly two weeks. During the 2009 H1N1 pandemic, China likely violated the IHR by instituting trade- and travel-restrictive measures not based on WHO recommendations or a legitimate public health justification.[23] The discrimination against Mexican citizens and the ban on pork products from North American countries also sent a signal to other countries that those complying with IHR and honestly reporting diseases in their territories would not be rewarded but instead punished by other countries.[24] The overreaction and the pursuit of short-term domestic political goals undercut trust and goodwill among states, potentially exacerbating the "stag hunt" dilemma in international disease prevention and control.[25]

There are also concerns about China's potential misuse of its influence in GHG, especially in the WHO. In recognition of the unprecedented authority and power of the WHO demonstrated during the SARS crisis, China has shown strong interest in using the international health agency as a central venue to engage in GHG. In 2006, China mobilized its entire diplomatic apparatus to lobby for the election of Margaret Chan as the WHO director-general. During the H1N1 outbreak the Chinese government cited the support of Chan and WHO to justify its aggressive response toward the outbreak, while simultaneously, Chan herself refused to criticize China for the very travel and trade restrictions that had contradicted her agency's advice.[26] China threw its support to Chan again when she was seeking reelection. In

January 2012, Chan was nominated by the WHO executive board to be the next WHO director-general. For the first time since the 1960s, there was only one candidate nominated for that position. Some speculated that the fear of fighting an unwinnable war with China was the primary reason for the absence of more candidates.[27]

China's role in shaping global health rules

China has also shown a willingness to cooperate with other players to set the rules and norms of GHG. Even with the largest state-owned tobacco monopoly in the world, China surprised many in negotiating the Framework Convention on Tobacco Control (FCTC). China supported important provisions, including one that gave public health precedence over free trade and another that allowed government bodies to sue tobacco companies in accordance with their domestic laws. China was considered the "least vigorous" opponent among the "big four" (China, Japan, Germany, and the United States). Equally important, China was directly involved in the revision of the IHR, one of the most radical changes to occur in the international governance of public health emergencies since the mid-nineteenth century.[28] Few would deny China's determination to defend the validity of sovereignty as an inviolable principle in governing international affairs. Keenly aware that introduction of the universality principle might be used by Taiwan to seek formal WHO membership, thereby undermining China's sovereignty and territorial integrity, China's chief negotiator made it clear that "health is a very important issue, but sovereignty and territorial integrity are more important to a sovereign state. China will firmly defend its sovereignty and territorial integrity at all cost." Playing China's sheer population size as a trump card, he further warned that "the future IHR has no universality without China's participation."[29] However, in the meantime, China has shown great flexibility in revising the IHR. It dropped its opposition to include the universal application when the chair of the draft committee substituted "all people" to "all countries" so that the new text reads: "The implementation of these Regulations shall be guided by the goal of their universal application for the protection of all people of the world from the international spread of disease" (Article 3.3). Similarly, China, a country that attaches utmost importance to social–political stability, showed flexibility in allowing the WHO to take into account sources of information provided by non-state actors in making decisions. Its negotiators indicated that it preferred the WHO to deal with such information and found it acceptable when the wording was changed to "sources other than notifications or consultations."[30]

Despite these stances, China's overall approach toward shaping GHG rules and norms remains narrow and limited. Unlike Brazil, which has shown leadership in global health rule-making over a wide range of issues, China was not an active participant in the discussions over universal access to HIV/AIDS medications or pharmaceutical intellectual property rights. Also, China's participation in GHG is not always positive. During the negotiations of the FCTC, China, along with Japan, Germany, and the United States, were the leading opponents of key provisions to minimize the treaty's effectiveness. With a representative of the tobacco industry included as a member of its delegation, China called for deletion of pictorial warning labels on tobacco packages from the proposed text and joined the United States against NGO access to the informal sessions.[31] In addition, while allowing WHO to interact with Taiwan, the implementation of the 2005 Memorandum of Understanding (MoU) China signed with the WHO Secretariat set out clear restrictive procedures on such contact. Among others, the invitation of Taiwanese health experts or dispatch of WHO experts to Taiwan should be justified from "both a technical and policy point of view" and must obtain the approval of the People's Republic of China Ministry of Health.[32]

Impact on domestic health governance

China is widely believed to be resistant to international intervention in what it defines as internal affairs because of its particular sensitivity on the issue of state sovereignty. Yet as Lieberthal and Oksenberg's study of China's energy sector and Economy's research on China's environmental protection efforts have suggested, outside forces can still intrude into the seemingly opaque and exclusive Chinese body politic to exert influence in its public policy process.[33]

Like other sectors, the impact of foreign forces on the health sector is not new. However, the scope, significance, and nature of that influence vary across time. The United States-led blockade and isolation of China in the early Cold War forced the latter to "lean toward one side" and prioritize health-related international cooperation with communist countries. In the late 1950s, China moved to abandon the Soviet development model in pursuit of an approach that emphasized mass mobilization and decentralization. With direct international exchange minimized, more indigenous policy experiments such as Cooperative Medical Services were popularized in China. In the 1960s, China's lack of significant interaction with the outside world not only sustained a clear demarcation between domestic and international health, but also reduced the need to respond to international demands and pressures over domestic health governance issues.

The frequency of intersection between domestic health policy and the outside world increased in the 1970s when China resumed its membership in the UN and the WHO. In December 1978, China signed a historic MoU with the WHO, paving the way for the WHO to designate 41 research institutes in China as WHO Cooperation Centers. In addition, China began to contribute to the United Nations Children's Fund (UNICEF) and use loans from the World Bank to improve medical education and rural health care. Meanwhile, China and the United States began to cooperate under the auspices of a 1979 Health Protocol. While much of this activity was carried out on a bilateral basis, the space of China's health governance has expanded tremendously. If in the Mao era China paid little heed to international influence in internal health policymaking, now it found itself a calculating actor vis-à-vis three sets of new policy actors: Western states and international governmental organizations (IGOs); an increasingly assertive international civil society; and multinational companies, including pharmaceutical firms.

Today, IGOs (e.g., UN, UNICEF, World Bank, WHO), non-state actors (e.g., Gates Foundation, Oxford Committee for Famine Relief—OXFAM), major pharmaceutical companies (e.g., Merck), and foreign government agencies (e.g., the US Centers for Disease Control and Prevention—CDC) all have offices, programs, or businesses in China. In engaging with these global health actors, China has become exposed not only to transnational networks, but also to new information channels and governance mechanisms that could affect China's domestic health governance structure and process. An analysis of this interaction shows that the international actors, processes, and institutions of global health do indeed shape the health policy agenda-setting, policy formulation, and implementation in China.

Global health governance and health agenda-setting

By investing in China's surveillance and laboratory capacity building and by providing formal and informal policy feedback, global health actors facilitate policy learning in China's health governance, which in turn has transformed an internally inspired nongovernmental systemic agenda into a governmental agenda in China. Moreover, global health processes, through bilateral and multilateral exchanges, international media coverage, and policy reports released by reputable international agencies, have been instrumental in reclassifying public health conditions in China into problems requiring policy response. In the meantime, this interaction has brought a new discourse on health-related issues to the fore. This is especially the case when a public health threat is reframed as a development or security challenge.

As a result, the Chinese government increasingly sets its health agenda-setting regime to mirror the organizational goals of global health actors and institutions. China's HIV/AIDS agenda-setting is a case in point. Until the mid-1990s, there was no serious attention to the rising HIV/AIDS problem at the national level.[34] Contradictory to the government's Pollyannaish attitude, the UN officials warned that unless effective measures were taken, China could have over 10 million HIV cases by 2010.[35] The UN warnings against the backdrop of the rapid spread of HIV/AIDS in China alarmed the Ministry of Health officials. In early May 1998, the Minister of Health presented an update on the HIV/AIDS situation to a State Council meeting, aiming to increase government awareness of HIV/AIDS.[36] From then on, HIV/AIDS began to draw attention from national leaders.

On 6 May 1998, in a move that was believed to be the first of its kind, Vice Premier Li Lanqing met in Beijing with Peter Piot, executive director of UNAIDS. In this process, UNAIDS and other international health actors became allies of the Ministry of Health in pushing for shifting the domestic policy agenda. In a rare move, a UN report entitled *HIV/AIDS: China's Titanic Peril* was released in June 2002. The report criticized the Chinese government on the grounds of its insufficient political commitment.[37] While Chinese officials rejected the report, it became clear by the end of 2002 that HIV/AIDS was not just a public health problem, but also one that has significant social, economic, political, and security implications, and therefore demanded the highest level of attention. In a speech at China's Zhejiang University in October, UN Secretary-General Kofi Annan defined AIDS as a problem relating to development and security, and called for "leadership at every level" to deal with the epidemic.[38] That same month, China announced plans to provide "comprehensive care and treatment" for HIV/AIDS victims in 100 counties hit particularly hard by the disease.[39]

Not all international engagements lead to positive change in the health-care agenda. Driven by their own interests or organizational objectives, international actors sometimes send signals that are used by the Chinese government to justify sustaining unproductive policies. Again, take China's HIV/AIDS control. Until the release of the 2002 UN report on China's HIV/AIDS, international pressure on China to effectively address HIV/AIDS remained low. The lack of understanding of the true HIV/AIDS situation in China led foreign health observers to endorse existing government measures. In 1991, a WHO official was reported as having expressed confidence in China's ability to curb the spread of HIV/AIDS on the grounds that China had an excellent county-town-village epidemic prevention system in the countryside.[40] Another WHO expert went so far as to call China "the first country to have policies and plans in place before an epidemic."[41] Such statements sent signals to the Chinese leadership that permitted them to justify inattention and inaction.

Global health governance and China's health policy formulation

Compared to the Mao era, when anti-intellectualism often led to marginalization of expert opinion in the policy process, the post-Mao state rebuilding has increased the importance of the consultative process in policymaking. Policy formulation is the development of effective and acceptable courses of action for addressing what has been placed on the policy agenda. The emphasis on expert opinion led to the establishment of various new policy research organs at different levels and the use of national surveys and case studies for more scientific decision-making. International exchanges between Chinese government officials, researchers, and international agencies (foreign governments, IGOs, and think tanks) have facilitated information flows within the government, thereby enhancing its ability in policy formulation. International actors can and do exert influence in a variety of ways: through official visits; conversations with government leaders; circulation of policy papers; and international conferences.

China's interaction with the US CDC and Food & Drug Administration (FDA) contributed to its establishment of similar agencies, the China CDC and the China FDA (CFDA). China's participation in GHG and exposure to dominant international health norms and institutions also provided the opportunity for China to familiarize itself with the most appropriate or legitimate means to pursue domestic health governance. International pressure, for example, played an important role in persuading China to tackle HIV/AIDS prevention and treatment in a pragmatic and transparent way. For a long time, the government deemphasized measures such as condom use and access to anti-retroviral drugs. Indeed, most health experts then agreed that it was impossible to try to control AIDS with special medicines and condoms.[42] In March 1994, Michael Merson, executive director of the WHO Global AIDS Program, publicly called for China to implement a nationwide sex education program and to encourage the use of condoms.[43] In response to his request, a State Council-approved policy report in September 1995 formally incorporated the idea of behavioral intervention for HIV-infected people and high-risk groups.[44] Later, with support from the Gates Foundation and other global health entities, China also began to emphasize the treatment of people living with HIV/AIDS in its strategies of HIV/AIDS prevention and control.

Transparency and timely information sharing is another important international norm China learned from its engagement in GHG. After the country's first application to the Global Fund was rejected (in part because of the government's closed attitude about the problem), health officials decided to talk more candidly about the disease. In September 2002, China raised its estimate of the number of Chinese infected with HIV/AIDS in an attempt to show some good-faith efforts on AIDS to help its application. Since 2004 China has worked with UNAIDS to issue joint reports on China's AIDS spread and control.

In addition to transforming the government's health governance agenda, international health actors and regimes have affected the choices available for decision-makers, while playing a critical role in affecting the timing of government action. To some extent, China's crisis-driven policy process highlights the importance of international forces.

Take SARS. Western news media began to report aggressively on SARS in China and the government's cover-up of the outbreak on 3 February 2003. On 15 March, the WHO issued its first global warning about SARS. While China's government-controlled media were prohibited from reporting on the warning, the news circulated via mobile phones, email, and the Internet. On 25 March, three days after the arrival of a team of WHO experts, the government acknowledged for the first time the spread of SARS outside Guangdong. The State Council held its first meeting to discuss the SARS problem two days after the *Wall Street Journal* published an editorial calling for other countries to suspend all travel links with China until it implemented a transparent public health campaign. The same day, the WHO issued the first travel advisory in its 55-year history, advising people not to visit Hong Kong and Guangdong, prompting Beijing to hold a news conference in which the Minister of Health promised that China was safe and SARS was under control. Enraged by the minister's false account, a retired surgeon at a military hospital sent an email to two TV stations, accusing the minister of lying. While neither station followed up on the email, *Time* magazine picked up the story and posted it on its website on 9 April, which triggered a political earthquake that led to the sacking of Beijing's mayor and the Minister of Health. As

Tan Yeling nicely summarized, "the Chinese government's change in position in April 2003 to admit the full extent of the SARS outbreak and to declare the situation a national emergency, would not have occurred without the actions, countervailing authority and pressure from the global scientific community and in particular the WHO."[45]

Compared with its reactive response to international pressure during SARS, since 2003 Beijing has actively sought international input in health policy formulation. In formulating its policy on the new round of health-care reform, the government invited nine policy organizations to submit proposals, including the WHO, World Bank, and McKinsey. Based on the input and feedback from both national and international experts, China formally released a new health-care reform plan in April 2009.

Despite the growing participation of international actors, their role in policy formulation is confined to the analytical phase, defined by John Kingdon as "the process of specifying alternatives that narrows the set of conceivable alternatives to the set that is seriously considered for governmental action."[46] International actors have a say in this process so long as their policy ideas are technical, fiscally feasible, and/ or congruent with the values of the domestic policy community. However, policy ideas must be authorized through a political process before being enacted, which is where decision-makers, not specialists, have their way. When a health issue is placed in the realm of realpolitik, however, it runs the risk of being "dependent on the logic of such politics— which is not based on science and not subject to public deliberation and peer review, but on the Machiavellian instincts of those in power."[47] The discrepancy between government openness and receptivity in alternative specification on the one hand and the autonomy of decision-makers in policy enactment on the other may explain why "good" international influence in one case may have negative effects on another. The lessons that Chinese government leaders drew from SARS had a powerful impact on their response toward the 2009 H1N1 outbreak.[48] Political leaders, however, were more interested in presenting an image that the government was acting differently in combating H1N1 and that it placed top priority on people's health and well-being. As a result, China was among the most aggressive among nations in responding to H1N1, only to find that most of the draconian measures were not necessary, or were even counterproductive.[49]

Global health governance and China's health policy implementation

Although various factors can affect policy implementation, state capacity is a key variable in connecting the wheel to the rudder. Building state capacity also means building effective partnerships and institutions internationally. Often purely local solutions to capacity building are unlikely to be successful and capacity needs to be imported from external sources, such as foreign aid.[50] GHG actors and processes can increase the government's financial capacity and strengthen the bureaucratic capacity through technical assistance, policy counseling, and personnel training.

The engagement of global health actors is particularly intense in China in the area of HIV/AIDS prevention and control. UNAIDS and the WHO play a major leadership and coordination role. With the blessing of national authorities, numerous governmental and non-governmental international initiatives also operate major programs in China. They provide funding directly to the government and forge partnerships with local government actors in health policy implementation.[51] While foreign governments work with Chinese partners at the national and provincial levels, numerous international charities, foundations, non-profits, and companies have programs and projects that focus on making a difference at the community level by "providing technical advice, education, and awareness programs; harm reduction interventions; health care worker training; media training; and peer group counseling programs; and by providing funds directly to local implementing agencies."[52] Such GHG actors include: the Clinton Foundation, which deviated from its standard practice of facilitating negotiations between drug suppliers and governments and focused instead on providing technical and in-kind assistance in China; Merck, which launched a five-year, $30 million partnership to combat HIV/AIDS comprehensively in the Liangshan prefecture of Sichuan province; Project HOPE, whose projects involved training health-care providers in local areas; the Gates Foundation, which funded various reproductive and rural health projects in China that have HIV-related components; and Bayer China, which forged a partnership with Tsinghua University aimed at strengthening news media and information dissemination on HIV/AIDS.[53]

Among those international partners, the Global Fund has been in a unique position to influence China's anti-HIV policy. In addition to being an important funding source, the Global Fund, through the country coordinating mechanism (CCM), helped promote the development of domestic health-related NGOs and community-based organizations (CBOs), as well as the holding of open, transparent, and thoroughly documented elections of their CCM NGO representative in April 2006. Through the election processes, awareness of the necessity and merits of public participation was greatly strengthened among civil society groups. For most of the NGOs that participated, the elections marked their first experience with self-organization.[54]

The active engagement of global health actors by no means guarantees the successful implementation of their initiatives or programs. Interference from entrenched domestic special interests may prevent China from honoring its international obligations by distorting the domestic policy/program design. In 2003, China signed the WHO's FCTC and pledged to ban smoking in workplaces and indoor public spaces by January 2011. However, due to the powerful influence of the tobacco industry in the drafting and enforcement of tobacco-related policies, the deadline passed without any major change. The Ministry of Health banned smoking in indoor public places in March 2011, but the ban was largely disregarded. Indeed, during 2006–2011, China's cigarette production rose by 17 percent, making China's anti-tobacco policies among the least effective in the world.[55]

GHG players also found it difficult to influence policy implementation because of the tensions in central–local relations. As Gill and others have observed:

> Even when funds are made available in poorer areas to combat HIV/AIDS, such as a major World Bank loan or a grant from the central government, there is no assurance that the resources will be spent efficiently by local government officials, and there is always the possibility that funds for one project will be diverted to fund a different program that lacks resources and is determined to be a higher priority.[56]

The frustration of international donors and NGOs also reflects the collision between the traditional state-centric approach and a new governance approach that incorporates other actors and accepts them as legitimate partners. In engaging international players, the Chinese government seems to be consistent in disallowing these players to dominate the domestic health projects and initiatives.

Opening the black box

In much of the discussion, this chapter examines China's participation in GHG as if the state is a unitary actor. Also, it stresses the critical importance of the issue of sovereignty, as indicated by China's focus on official, state-based institutions in engaging GHG. This state-centric approach, which we have seen in other areas of global governance discussed in this book, makes sense in an authoritarian state where effective civil society participation in domestic health policy or global health remains extremely low. While international engagement provides important sources of information and resources for disease prevention and control, it also threatens the Chinese state's historical monopoly regarding the control of public health information. Government officials at various levels often distrust these health-promoting CSOs, viewing them as organizations with political agendas that potentially threaten the Communist regime. This in turn leads to sustained suppression of genuine health-promoting NGOs and activists in China. NGO leaders are often harassed by police and security officials, with lucky ones (such as Gao Yaojie and Wan Yanhai) leaving the country and unlucky ones (Hu Jia) ending up in jail. In May 2011, news came out that the Global Fund had frozen grant payments to China worth hundreds of millions of dollars. The Fund's decision was "rooted in a collision between the fund's conviction that grassroots organizations must be intrinsically involved in the fight to control diseases like AIDS, and the Chinese government's growing suspicion of any civil-society groups that are not directly under its control."[57] Government bias against CSOs led to the inclusion of many government-organized NGOs (GONGOs) in the CCM, which receive the bulk of the Global Fund funding and resources. This not only resulted in inefficiency in fund use, but also hindered the rise of an independent and autonomous civil society. It is no surprise that China's NGOs lacked the skills and experience to engage the Global Fund as effectively as more seasoned NGOs in other countries. In the absence of effective participation of CSOs, China not only finds it difficult to comply with global health rules, but also faces implementation problems in coping with major health challenges.[58] Its shift from reactive response to overreaction in fighting H1N1 influenza is a case in point. The findings here are consistent with those of Hale and Roger (Chapter 11), who found environmental NGOs to be weak in China, and those of Bartley and Zhang (Chapter 10), who found private labor standards certification organizations to have a limited effect in China relative to official organizations.

It does not follow, however, that the state is a unitary rational actor in the policy process. Since the 1980s, as part of the post-Mao state rebuilding, the health policy process has no longer served as the barometer of top-level power jockeying and policy conflicts. Instead, it has been "normalized" and returned to the administrative "neutral" zone.[59] Despite the growing attention paid by the top political leaders to public health, health care, and health diplomacy, China's engagement in global health continues to be a backburner issue for the top leadership. This might explain why China still does not have a specialized development assistance agency similar to the United States Agency for International Development (USAID). Unlike the United States, China does not have foreign aid laws, so its existing foreign aid policies are based on ad hoc central ministerial documents and regulations, which are not subject to approval by the legislative branch.[60] Consequently, China's engagement in GHG mirrors the tensions among bureaucratic actors with different authorities, resources bases, and visions of participation in GHG.

While China's aid program is primarily managed by the Ministry of Commerce (MOFCOM), four central institutions are considered crucial in China's health-related development assistance: MOFCOM, the National Health and Family Planning Commission (NHFPC, formerly the Ministry of Health), the Ministry of Finance (MOF), and Ministry of Foreign Affairs (MOFA). In addition, the roles of provincial governments and state-owned enterprises are also important, especially in terms of the delivery of medical services.[61] When it comes to emergency humanitarian aid and disaster relief, MOFCOM is no longer the primary decision-maker. Instead, MOFCOM, the MOFA, MOF, and the People's Liberation Army (PLA) General Staff Department all play a role in the dispatch of medical teams overseas as part of the China International Search and Rescue (CISAR) team. In combating infectious diseases with global spread, even in the post-SARS era, coordination problems can still be identified between central and local governments, between the functional health system and non-health system, and between the NHFPC and other health-related bureaucratic actors (e.g., CFDA, Ministry of Agriculture).[62] Due to bureaucratic infighting, China was not even able to post a health attaché to its embassy in the United States, although the United States has one in China.[63]

The same problem can be identified in the negotiation and implementation of the FCTC. The representative from China Tobacco Monopoly Administration was strongly resistant to the Ministry of Health efforts to push for a legally binding international agreement on tobacco control.[64] With support from the National Development and Reform Commission (NDRC), whose representative was head of the Chinese delegation, and eventually the State Council, China approved the FCTC. However, when the Ministry of Industry and Information Technology replaced the NDRC as the lead agency in implementing the treaty in 2008, China became less cooperative in tobacco control.[65]

Interestingly, bureaucratic conflicts did not appear to be critical in the negotiation and implementation of the revised IHR in 2005, nor in the protocol amending the Agreement on Trade-Related Aspects of Intellectual Property Rights (TRIPS) in 2006. This was the case because the Ministry of Health as a weak ministry was dominated by other, more powerful bureaucratic actors. The IHR negotiations, for example, were prevailed over by the MOFA, whose chief negotiator attached stronger importance to state sovereignty than to global health. The TRIPS negotiation was led by MOFCOM, which worked closely with the Ministry of Health representative in pushing for provisions that balanced intellectual property protection with public health needs.[66] Unlike Brazil or India, the adoption of the Protocol Amending the TRIPS agreement was followed by the absence of invoking the provisions for seeking compulsory licensing for patented drugs in China. Meanwhile, Chinese pharmaceutical firms seemed to be content to produce generic drugs and export APIs and therefore did not have strong incentives to apply for compulsory licensing. This lack of interest from all the major actors accounts for the seemingly "unitary" state disincentive to encourage its drug manufacturers to make cheap copies of medicines still under patent protection. In other areas of GHG, because many international health norms and standards are soft laws, their constraints (and opportunities) are not strong enough to trigger active participation from critical stakeholders other than the NHFPC. In this regard, the pattern of China's participation in global governance is not characterized by active involvement of vested interests, as described by Tu Xinquan regarding state-owned enterprises and government procurement (Chapter 4).

Conclusion

A close examination of China's participation in GHG suggests two parallel and interrelated processes that seem to defy pessimistic logic. On the one hand, China's participation is making a difference in GHG processes and outcomes. Through its health-related foreign aid, it contributes to the health system capacity building in the developing world, especially Africa. Its rise as an exporter of pharmaceutical products also promises to be a game changer in the access to medicine and vaccines. Equally important, as its engagement becomes more substantial, it has shown strong interest and flexibility in global health agenda-setting and rule-making. On the other hand, despite the opaque and exclusive authoritarian structure in China, global health players, norms, and processes still have a significant role to play in the country's domestic health governance. Influential global health actors are often critical in moving "latent" public health issues to the governmental agenda. They can affect not only the timing of government action, but also the content of policy design. International actors can also affect policy implementation by influencing the financial and bureaucratic capacities in China. The country pursues a pragmatic approach which combines the utilitarian logic of reaping material benefits from participating in GHG, the realist objective of expanding its global power and influence, a neoliberal interest in pursuing absolute gains from international cooperation, and the constructivist attempt to become a responsible stakeholder in the system.

To be sure, China's engagement in GHG thus far is still narrow, limited, and not always constructive. As evidenced in its handling of the H1N1 outbreak in 2009, while China recognizes the importance of international cooperation in coping with global health challenges, realpolitik continues to drive its foreign policy behavior in international health cooperation. Approaching GHG in an individualistic and state-centric manner threatens to lead to further fragmentation of the global health regimes. However, as we have seen in trade and other regimes, the discrepancy between the neoliberal penchants of international cooperation and the realist-driven actual state response is not unique to China.[67] Similarly, the influence of GHG players, processes, and institutions on domestic health governance is limited and is not always positive. The global health community may send certain signals to the Chinese government, which may subsequently be used by China to justify the maintenance of ineffective policies. The influence of major global health players in Chinese domestic policy formulation is mainly confined to the analysis stage. When the discussions and pressure move from the scientific to the political area, decision-makers have more freedom to disregard international pressure or rules. Ultimately, foreign actors may have little influence in determining the outcomes of policy implementation at the local level. The constraints and limits of GHG on domestic health governance may be attributed to a state-centered governance approach, but they also reflect problematic state–society relations and the influence of entrenched domestic special interests.

These constraints and limits are not static as the domestic and international context for China's engagement is changing. In view of the growing international pressure for shouldering more global responsibilities, nationalist intellectuals and officials might still view the demands and pressures as part of an international conspiracy to thwart China's development.[68] However, more pragmatic officials strongly feel the need to expand China's participation in GHG. The NHFPC, for example, is following the Swiss example and drafting its own global health strategy.[69] As David Shambaugh observed, after 2009 China has actually stepped-up its contributions to various global governance activities in many areas, including public health, humanitarian assistance, and disaster relief.[70] True, little progress has been made on the domestic front in terms of state–society relations—indeed, the operation space for genuine NGOs has been shrinking since 2012. This has raised concerns about China's willingness to be receptive to international norms, pressures, and influence. However, President Xi Jinping has shown great interest in global governance. In January 2017, he expounded his vision of the world as a "community of common destiny" which transcends all kinds of differences in human society while seeking to reap the greatest possible benefits for all.[71] As China portrays itself as a champion for globalization and as its clout on the international stage increases, it is anticipated to play a much bigger role in GHG.

Notes

1 David Fidler, "From International Sanitary Conventions to Global Health Security: The New International Health Regulations," *Chinese Journal of International Law* 4, no. 2 (2005): 325–392. Pang provides a similar definition: "the formal and informal institutions, norms and processes that govern or directly influence health policy and outcomes worldwide." See Tikki Pang, Nils Daulaire, Gerald Keusch, Rose Leke, Peter Piot, Srinath Reddy, Andrzej Rys, and Nicole Szlezak, "The New Age of Global Health Governance Holds Promise," *Nature Medicine* 16 (November 2010): 1110–1181.

2 State Council Information Office, *White Paper on China's Foreign Aid*, April 2011.

3 Yanzhong Huang, "Pursuing Health as Foreign Policy: The Case of China," *Indiana Journal of Global Legal Studies* 17, no. 1 (Winter 2010): 105–146.

4 Jack C. Chow, "China's Billion-Dollar Aid Appetite," *Foreign Policy*, 19 July 2010.

5 Hongxi Yang and Kaiming Chen, "Zhongguo duiwai yuanzhu: chengjiu, jiaoxun he liangxing fazhan" (China's Foreign Aid: Achievements, Lessons and Healthy Development), *Guoji zhanwang (World Outlook)* no. 1 (2010): 49–50.

6 Huang, "Pursuing Health as Foreign Policy," 105–146.

7 Wang Ningjun, "Chinese Foreign Health Aid (1963–2003): A Case of Jiangsu Province," MA Thesis, Central China Normal University, May 2009.

8 Kelley Lee, *The World Health Organization (WHO)* (London: Routledge, 2009).

9 Deborah Brautigam, *The Dragon's Gift: The Real Story of China in Africa* (Oxford: Oxford University Press, 2009).

10 State Council Information Office, *White Paper on China's Foreign Aid.*
11 Zhongguo Wang, 3 November 2014. www.mofcom.gov.cn/article/zt_abl/column02/201411/20141100783564.shtml.
12 Chow, "China's Billion-Dollar Aid Appetite."
13 WHO, "WHO Reform for a Healthy Future: An Overview," 20 July 2011, www.who.int/dg/reform/en_who_reform_overview.pdf.
14 Brautigam, *The Dragon's Gift.*
15 Wang Ningjun, "Chinese Foreign Health Aid," 35.
16 Nora Y. Ng and Jennifer Prah Ruger, "Global Health Governance at a Crossroads," *Global Health Governance* 3, no. 2 (June 2011), www.ghgj.org.
17 Laurie Garrett and Yanzhong Huang, "CFR Symposium Backgrounder on Food and Drugs: Can Safety Be Ensured in a Time of Increased Globalization?" Council on Foreign Relations, 31 January 2011, www.cfr.org/pharmaceuticals-and-vaccines/cfr-symposium-backgrounder-food-drugs-can-safety-ensured-time-increased-globalization/p23968.
18 Gillian Wong "China Prepares for Big Entry into Vaccine Market," *Associated Press*, 29 November 2011.
19 Stewart Patrick, *Weak Links: Fragile States, Global Threats, and International Security* (Oxford: Oxford University Press, 2011).
20 Richard Holbrooke and Laurie Garrett, "Sovereignty That Risks Global Health," *Washington Post*, 8 August 2008.
21 Huang, "Pursuing Health as Foreign Policy."
22 Yanzhong Huang and Christopher J. Smith, "China's Response to Pandemics: From Inaction to Overreaction," *Eurasian Geography and Economics* 51, no. 2 (March–April 2010): 162–183; Yanzhong Huang, "Red Flags in China's Disease Control," *East Asia Forum*, 18 February 2014, www.eastasiaforum.org/2014/02/18/red-flags-in-chinas-disease-control/.
23 Huang, "Pursuing Health as Foreign Policy."
24 According to the Mexican Ministry of Foreign Affairs, China was the only country where Mexicans had been confined against their will. "Mexico Hits at China's Quarantine Policy," *Financial Times*, 5 May 2009.
25 Bei Tang, "Jizhi sheji yu guoji weisheng hezuo zhong de kunjin" (Regime Design and the Ddilemma in International Health Cooperation), *Ouzhou yanjiu (European Studies)*, no. 3 (2009): 107–118.
26 Huang, "Pursuing Health as Foreign Policy."
27 Author's interview with a senior WHO official, 20 February 2012.
28 Fidler, "From International Sanitary Conventions to Global Health Security," 325–392.
29 Ambassador Sha Zukang's statement, 12 November 2004, www.china-un.ch/chn/gjhyfy/hy2004/t172226.htm.
30 Interview with a senior Swiss health official, 20 February 2012.
31 H. M. Mamundu and S. A. Glantz, "Civil Society and the Negotiation of the Framework Convention on Tobacco Control," *Global Public Health* 4, no. 2 (2009): 150–168.
32 World Health Organization, "Implementation of the Memorandum of Understanding Between the WHO Secretariat and China," 12 July 2005.
33 Kenneth Lieberthal and Michel Oksenberg, *Policy Making in China: Leaders, Structures and Processes* (Princeton, N.J.: Princeton University Press, 1988); Elizabeth Economy, *The River Runs Black: The Environmental Challenge to China's Future* (Ithaca, NY: Cornell University Press, 2004).

Public policy refers to what governments do as they transact with civil society, the economy, and states within a global state system. See Ira Katznelson, "Policy History: Origins," in *International Encyclopedia of the Social & Behavioral Sciences*, ed. Neil J. Smelser and Paul B. Baltes (Amsterdam: Elsevier, 2001), 11541.

34 Yanzhong Huang, "The Politics of HIV/AIDS in China,"*Asian Perspective* 30, no. 1 (Spring 2006): 95–105.

35 "China Could Face 10 Million AIDS Cases by 2010, UN Warns," *Asia Pulse*, 12 January 1998.

36 "China Could Face 10 Million AIDS Cases by 2010, UN Warns," *Asia Pulse*.

37 *HIV/AIDS: China's Titanic Peril—2001 Update of the AIDS Situation and Needs Assessment Report*, The UN Theme Group on HIV/AIDS in China (2002).

38 Huang, "The Politics of China's HIV/AIDS."

39 Feng Zhang, "Nation Vows to Contain AIDS." *China Daily*, 16 October 2002.

40 "China Sets Up to Fight AIDS," *Xinhua News Agency*, 22 July 1991.

41 Charles Hutzler, "Blood Problems, Poverty Point to AIDS Outbreak in China," *Associated Press*, 5 November 1995.

42 "Healthy Behavior Key to AIDS Eradication," *Xinhua News Agency*, 9 November 1990.

43 "WHO Warns China it Faces AIDS Epidemic," *United Press International*, 9 March 1994.

44 "Changes in China's AIDS Prevention and Control Policy Over the Past 19 Years," *Xinjingbao*, 30 March 2004.

45 Tan Yeling, "China's Role in the World: A Perspective through Global Health Governance," Centre on Asia and Globalization, Working Paper no. 006 (June 2009).

46 John W. Kingdon, *Agendas, Alternatives, and Public Policies* (London: Longman, 2011), 4.

47 Konrad Obemann, "Global Health and Foreign Policy," *The Lancet* 369, no. 9574 (May 2007): 1688.

48 Huang, "Pursuing Health as Foreign Policy," 105–146.

49 Huang, "Pursuing Health as Foreign Policy."

50 Andrew T. Smith, *Pretoria's Shadow: The HIV/AIDS Pandemic and National Security in South Africa* (Washington, DC: Chemical and Biological Arms Control Institute, 2002), 27.

51 Bates Gill and Drew Thompson, *Assessing HIV/AIDS Initiatives in China, A Report of the CSIS Task Force on HIV/AIDS* (Washington, DC: Center for Strategic and International Studies, 2006).

52 Gill and Thompson, *Assessing HIV/AIDS Initiatives in China*, p. 52.

53 Satoko Itoh and Susan Hubbard, *Doing Well by Doing Good: Innovative Corporate Responses to Communicable Diseases* (Tokyo: Japan Center for International Exchange, 2010), 77–82.

54 Jia Ping, *Democracy in Bud 2006/7 China CBO/NGO Representative Election* (Beijing: China Global Fund Watch Initiative, 2009).

55 Yanzhong Huang, "The Sick Man of Asia," *Foreign Affairs* 90, no. 6 (November/December 2011): 119–136.

56 Gill and Thompson, *Assessing HIV/AIDS Initiatives in China*, 8.

57 "AIDS Funds Frozen for China in Grant Dispute," *The New York Times*, 20 May 2011.
58 Civil society movements are "central to securing and ensuring adherence to a global health agreement." Lawrence A. Gostin et al., "The Joint Action and Learning Initiative: Towards a Global Agreement on National and Global Responsibilities for Health," *PLoS Medicine* 8, no. 5 (May 2011), e1001031.
59 Yanzhong Huang, *Governing Health in Contemporary China* (Abingdon: Routledge, forthcoming).
60 Huang, "The Sick Man of Asia."
61 Yanzhong Huang, "Domestic Politics and China's Health Aid to Africa," unpublished manuscript.
62 Huang, *Governing Health in Contemporary China*.
63 Interview with a senior Ministry of Health official, Beijing, 2 July 2010.
64 "Guojia Yancaozhuanmaiju Guanyuan Ceng Dama Weishengbu Guanyuan," ICEO-China Entrepreneurs Net, 8 June 2012, www.iceo.com.cn/shangye/37/2012/0608/250035.shtml.
65 "Zhongguoshi Kongyan Kunju," *Sciencenet.cn*, 15 May 2012, www.news.sciencenet.cn/htmlnews/2012/5/264102-1.shtm.
66 Yi Xiaozhun, "Speech at the International Symposium on TRIPS Agreement and Public Health," Ministry of Commerce, People's Republic of China, 7 July 2008.
67 In October 2009, the HHS secretary suggested that the United States would not donate the vaccine to poor countries until 150 million at-risk Americans had been inoculated against the H1N1 virus.
68 Interview with a Chinese scholar, Beijing, 6 April 2011.
69 Interview with a global health scholar, Geneva, 22 February 2012.
70 David Shambaugh, "Finding Common Ground," *China and US Focus Digest* 8 (October 2015): 9–11.
71 "Xi's World Vision: A Community of Common Destiny, a Shared Home for Humanity," *Xinhua*, 15 January 2017, www.ecns.cn/2017/01-15/241711.shtml.

8 Learning by doing

China's role in the global governance of food security

Katherine Morton[1]

- **Redesigning food security governance**
- **Can China feed itself and help to feed the world? Linking domestic concerns with international priorities**
- **Mutual benefits**
- **Conclusion**

On the 60th anniversary of the founding of the People's Republic of China (PRC), Vice Premier Hui Liangyu gave an address at the World Food Summit in Rome, in which he confidently announced that the Chinese people, who were once threatened by starvation, now lived in moderate prosperity. China had already met its targets for eradicating extreme poverty and hunger under the Millennium Development Goals (MDGs). In his words, China had achieved nothing short of a miracle, making "a great contribution to global food security, world peace and development."[2] Defining global responsibility in terms of national achievements is a recurrent theme in Chinese foreign policy discourse. As the world's most populous nation, it is difficult to refute the logic that China can best serve the world by first serving the needs of its people. An inward-looking global policy agenda, however, is difficult to sustain in the context of China's rising international status and expanding investments overseas. Addressing this new predicament is now a central feature of China's involvement in the global governance of food security. Is China likely to strengthen its participation in the broader effort to eliminate world hunger, or will an enduring commitment to national independence guide its approach?

To date, studies on China's engagement in collective efforts to ensure a reliable supply and fair distribution of food across the globe have been largely one-dimensional. Scholars and policy analysts alike have tended to focus upon the way in which food security concerns at the domestic level are likely to affect world food markets. The broader question of how China is contributing to the global effort to combat world hunger has been largely overlooked. While an emerging literature exists on Chinese aid, especially in relation to investment and aid projects in Africa, few studies have investigated China's contribution to international food aid.[3] Our understanding of Chinese participation in the international food regime is partial at best.

This chapter aims to address this issue by posing three fundamental questions: What is the relationship between China's domestic food concerns and its international priorities? How does the Chinese approach toward food security differ from that of traditional donors? And to what extent are Chinese values aligned with international norms and practices? A major challenge in assessing China's contribution to global food security is that both Chinese policy and the governing norms and institutions at the global level are in a state of flux. I would argue, however, that it is precisely within this evolving realm of global governance, unlike in trade where norms are more established, where Chinese involvement is more visible and arguably more likely to make a significant impact.

At a time of growing anxiety over China's rising power and influence in the world, geopolitical factors are influencing debates over its role in global governance. Concerns are growing that China may be seeking to undermine the current Western-dominated international order by pursuing its own agenda that is counter to pre-existing liberal norms and practices.[4] From a power-centric perspective, growing competition over food is just one more example of the struggle for supremacy in a world of scarcity. References to "food wars" and "food superpowers" have proliferated in both the Western and Chinese literature on global food security.[5] A major limitation with the realist worldview is that a monocausal explanation is inadequate for the purpose of assessing the complex motivations behind Chinese international behavior; it fails to engage with economic incentives, and ignores the potential for national and global interests to converge.

Alternative approaches that focus on international responsibility as the *sine qua non* of a rising power offer a more useful lens by highlighting both the cooperative and competitive elements of China's emerging influence within the international system. International responsibility generally refers to enhanced participation in addressing global concerns—stakeholder participation and burden sharing in the delivery of global public goods. This, in turn, entails greater involvement in the negotiation of international norms, both in relation to traditional norms vis-à-vis the right to autonomous political status, and evolving new norms such as the Responsibility to Protect, the non-use of military force to maintain border stability, and adherence to multilateral trade dispute mechanisms. While existing accounts of China's international responsibility reveal complex patterns of engagement that vary across issue areas, a consensus appears to be emerging that China is an important, albeit reluctant, stakeholder in global governance, intent on biding its time for the purpose of focusing attention upon its domestic priorities.[6] The concern emanating from liberal-oriented scholars is that China needs to be a stronger rather than a weaker player on the international stage.

I argue in this chapter that China's involvement in the global governance of food security reveals as much about the changing dynamics of domestic food security concerns as it does about China's international behavior. While some critics are eager to make a direct link between resource scarcity in China and high food prices on the international market, it is becoming more obvious over time that all states share responsibility for global food security regardless of domestic demand. Emerging powers such as China, India, and Brazil hold the potential to overturn the inertia within the current regime and bring about reforms that are more in keeping with today's world.

From this vantage point, China does need to be an active player in changing the rules of the game. The question is whether its current policies and practices are aligned with a reformist agenda that seeks to bring about collective benefits. Strong Chinese preferences for *food sovereignty*, *mutual benefits*, and *win–win cooperation* are at least partly aligned with evolving rules of international conduct. China does not stand in direct opposition to the international food regime. Rather it appears to be pursuing a pragmatic strategy of seeking to bring about substantial reforms from within. The challenge for the regime is that the Chinese government places a premium upon gaining experience before agreeing to a particular set of principles—learning by doing rather than learning by principle. Such an approach runs the risk of weakening the capacity of the regime to enforce legal constraints. As a strategic reformer, China is unlikely to sponsor binding commitments that restrict its scope for unilateral action.

This chapter begins with an overview of food security governance at the global level followed by a brief assessment of food security concerns within the Chinese domestic context. It then examines China's international engagement in relation to three key dimensions: the outsourcing of food production overseas; international food aid; and global policymaking. The chapter concludes with a broader analysis of how Chinese participation is likely to influence the rules and norms of international conduct.

Redesigning food security governance

Over the past four decades, the international food regime has evolved incrementally, driven by a constant struggle to balance the trade, humanitarian, and strategic interests of donors with the broader imperative of solving world hunger. Attempts to establish a mechanism for regulating international trade to deal with food surpluses have been constantly thwarted by exporter countries concerned about interference in trade relations; and efforts to set up international food reserves have been stymied by disagreements over the possible distorting effects of large-scale buffer stocks on price movements.

That said, the normative boundaries of the food aid regime have shifted considerably over the past half-century and more, especially in relation to decoupling food aid from surpluses and addressing the longer-term drivers of hunger and malnutrition. Rather than simply focusing upon short-term donor commitments aimed at directly feeding the world's hungry, new principles have surfaced that are more recipient-driven. Avoiding the disincentive effects of food aid upon agricultural development and recognizing the complex structural drivers of malnutrition are now key principles underpinning collective efforts to deal with hunger and chronic malnutrition.[7]

At the World Food Summit in 1996, food security was elevated onto the global policymaking agenda for the first time. Commonly understood as existing "when all people at all times have physical and economic access to sufficient, safe and nutritious food to meet their dietary needs and food preferences for an active and healthy life,"[8] food security is now a major priority across a diversity of international institutions. Yet, the legacy of food as a tool of foreign policy remains, leading to protracted debates over what constitutes responsible food aid in the context of rising food prices and widespread chronic hunger.

Stabilizing food markets

The global food crisis in 2007–2008 marked a watershed in the history of the world food system. Following three decades of relatively cheap food and reliance upon imports as a guarantee of national security, high and volatile food prices, combined with tight supplies, triggered major shortfalls leading to a crisis in world food markets.[9] The world food price index administered by the Food and Agriculture Organization (FAO) of the United Nations rose 45 percent in just nine months. This shock to international food markets had a regressive impact on the world's poor. Statistics provided by the Global Hunger Index revealed that the number of people facing chronic hunger surpassed a threshold of 1 billion in 2009.[10]

The first global food crisis of the twenty-first century was driven by multiple factors including rising energy prices and the consequent shift toward biofuel production, the global financial crisis and depreciation of the US dollar, "beggar-thy-neighbor" restrictions on exports, and natural disasters. As in the case of the global food crisis in the early 1970s, rising energy and food prices were closely interlinked. The rapid rise in biofuel production to reduce dependence on Arab oil stimulated financial speculation in grain markets which, in turn, led to a 30 percent increase in grain prices.[11]

At the Group of Eight (G8) Summit in 2009, leaders pledged US$22 billion over three years to support sustainable agricultural development (by 2012, 58 percent of this commitment had been disbursed). The food crisis also placed a spotlight on the need for reform of the FAO Committee on Food Security (CFS) established in 1974 following the World Food Conference. Now encompassing a wider group of stakeholders, the current vision is to develop a global strategic framework for food security and nutrition and to set new guidelines for international cooperation.

There is still a need to tackle major problems relating to international trade such as reducing competition between food and fuel, promoting open agricultural trade, and strengthening the regulation of food reserves in order to respond to emergencies. In these key areas, the Group of 20 (G20) has taken a leading role. Under the auspices of this informal grouping of finance ministers and central bank governors, concrete initiatives are underway to reinforce transparency in agricultural markets through the establishment of an agricultural market information system, to promote the exemption of export restrictions on emergency aid, and to create a regional pilot program for low-income and food-deficit countries in West Africa in collaboration with the Economic Community of West African States.[12]

It is within this evolving institutional context that China's role in responding to the global challenge of food security is so critically important. Now a major player in informal institutional settings such as the G20, BRICS (Brazil, Russia, India, China, and South Africa), and the Association of Southeast Asian Nations (ASEAN) together with Japan and South Korea, Chinese influence is more visible. As a prominent stakeholder in global governance, will China play a reforming role or is it more likely to act as a constraint upon collective action to safeguard its own interests? To address this question we must first explore the domestic motivations behind Chinese agricultural investments overseas and then proceed with an investigation of Chinese participation in international food aid and multilateral negotiations.

Can China feed itself and help to feed the world? Linking domestic concerns with international priorities

For many Chinese, the real economic miracle achieved over the past three decades of "opening and reform" is the fact that China has managed to feed 21 percent of the world's population on only 9 percent of the world's arable land. Critically important to political, social, and economic stability, self-sufficiency (*ziji zizu*) in food has been a central priority for Chinese officials and strategists for centuries. Dynasties have risen and fallen on the basis of their capacity to ensure sufficient food for a growing population. Above all, as a predominantly agrarian society, "the fear of a land in perpetual hunger" is deeply ingrained in the cultural mindset.[13]

To meet the national target of 95 percent self-sufficiency in grain consumption, China has the world's largest grain reserves (70 percent composed of wheat and rice) located at the central, provincial, and local levels.[14] According to official estimates, in 2007 grain storage capacity reached between 150 and 200 million tons, or roughly 30 to 40 percent of total grain production for that year (501,500,000 tons).[15] A State Council directive in 2014 announced an additional target of 50 billion kilograms (kg) (50 million tonnes) in grain storage to be met by 2015.[16] International emergency food aid is taken from China's largest grain reserves in Heilongjiang, Henan, and Shandong.[17]

Staying above the red line

At a superficial level, a national-level analysis of food productivity based upon agricultural production and trade statistics reveals that China is food secure. Between 1978 and 2010, per capita grain supply increased by 409 kg of grain per capita per annum.[18] The highest per capita production growth rates were in protein and fat-rich food groups, such as meat, dairy, oil, and fish (see Figure 8.1). In the first decade of the twenty-first century grain imports stabilized at around 5 percent of total grain supply.[19] However, imports have sometimes fluctuated, as in the case of large-scale purchases of wheat in 2004 to supplement dwindling stocks. More recently, China has enjoyed 11 consecutive years of bumper harvests of over 500 million tons of grain per year, largely on account of technological advances in high-yielding hybrid crop strains.[20] To maintain basic self-sufficiency, agricultural experts estimate that China will need to increase production capacity to a minimum of 580 million tons by 2020.[21]

Taking a longer-term perspective, China is increasingly food insecure. National indicators that measure the key sources of agricultural production—land, water, and labor—suggest that the task of sustaining self-sufficiency in the future faces enormous challenges. For planning purposes, 1.8 million *mu* (120 million hectares) of arable land represents the critical "red line" below which producing enough food to meet the demands of a rising population will not be possible.[22] China's per capita arable land constitutes only 40 percent of the world average, and more worryingly it is in a rapid state of decline. As a consequence of natural disasters, urbanization, severe ecological degradation, and environmental pollution, around two-thirds of available land in China is now classified as either barren or with low agricultural potential.[23] Water scarcity, made worse by the effects of climate change, further constrains China's capacity to increase agricultural productivity. Average per capita water resources in China are only 28 percent of the global average, and every year water supply to the agricultural sector falls short by roughly 20 million cubic meters.[24]

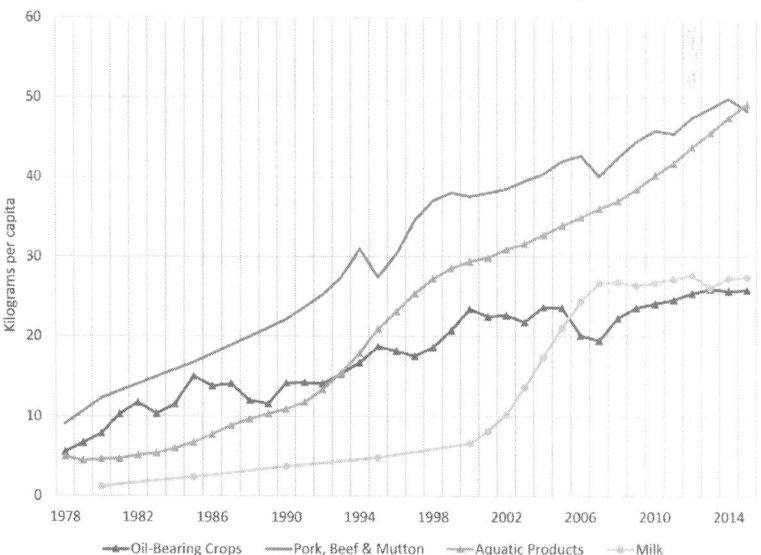

Figure 8.1 China's per capita production of major non-staple crops

Note: Oil-bearing crops refer to plants such as soybeans and coconuts whose seeds or fruits can be extracted to produce edible or industrial oils.

Source: *China Statistical Yearbook 2016* (Beijing: China Statistics Press, 2016), 412.

The so-called hollowing-out of the rural labor force is a third major concern in ensuring long-term food availability. Since the start of the Reform era, over half of China's rural labor force has migrated to urban areas in search of better employment. The rural labor force has aged more rapidly over time because the majority of migrant workers are young. Lower returns on traditional crops combined with the increasing costs of diesel fuel, chemical fertilizers, and pesticides, mean that smallholder Chinese farmers are increasingly turning to growing single crop rice or non-food cash crops. The more adventurous are seeking new opportunities to improve their livelihoods in distant lands.

Outsourcing the farm

In response to the multiple challenges of declining arable land, ecological degradation, climate change, and demographic and social changes in rural China, the government is pursuing a new strategy of outsourcing agricultural production overseas. Within the broader framework of the "going out" strategy, initiated in the late 1990s to promote the internationalization of Chinese state-owned enterprises, investing in agriculture alongside energy resources acts as a hedge against future increases in commodity prices. Agricultural investments have risen sharply in recent years, but we still have limited understanding of the nature and scope of the commercial activities involved.

Globally, statistics on Chinese agricultural investments overseas are notoriously unreliable. Unconfirmed business reports estimate that around 40 agribusinesses are now involved in farming overseas, pursuing different business models in accordance with local regulations. For example, in Venezuela and Zimbabwe, the state-owned Heilongjiang Beidahuang Nongken Group provides labor and machinery in exchange for 20 percent of the harvest, while it leases land for soybean cultivation in Argentina and Brazil.[25] Often, planned investments do not eventuate on account of regulatory restrictions. In an effort to protect valuable resources, land-rich countries are increasingly tightening supervision over foreign investment: Brazil has introduced new rules prohibiting foreign companies from owning more than 5,000 hectares of farmland, and both New Zealand and Australia are currently reviewing their procedures for approving land sales.

In the case of Africa, the new strategy of outsourcing the farm has reignited debates over China's perceived neo-colonial ambition with many critics suggesting that it is now "grabbing land" to produce food to ship home.[26] This accusation is refuted by the Ministry of Agriculture in Beijing on the grounds that such a scheme would be "ridiculously expensive" to implement. Indeed, evidence does not suggest that this is actually happening in practice. While Chinese corporations are producing food in neighboring countries for the domestic market, one example being the 400,000 hectare farm on the China–Russia border jointly owned by China's Huaxin Group and Russia's Armada software company, the situation is different on the African continent where commercial activities are aimed at producing food to meet local needs or to sell on the international market.[27] From a food security perspective, the logic underpinning the new strategy is more strategic. As one official from the Ministry of Agriculture aptly remarked, "if African states can grow more food themselves, they will be less reliant upon the international market, creating more space for China to import food."[28]

From recipient to stakeholder in global food aid

In 2005, China officially made the historic transition from food recipient to food donor, thus paving the way for its integration into the international food regime. For a brief period, following a donation of 577,000 tons of grain to the World Food Programme (WFP), China earned the prestigious title of the world's third-largest food donor. Four years later, it was also the first country to join the new strategic alliance for South–South Cooperation led by FAO, donating $30 million to a trust fund to support agricultural productivity in developing countries in accordance with the MDGs.

China's entry into the international food donor community was partly in response to international pressure. It was becoming more difficult to refuse requests from the WFP in light of the fact that many other developing countries, including India, Brazil, and South Africa, were already making sizable donations.[29] At the time, China was also enjoying a grain surplus. The upward trend in food availability meant that it did not face difficult trade-offs over domestic supply. Finally, the decline in agricultural investment from Western donors, especially in the wake of the global economic crisis, created a strategic opportunity for China to play a stronger role in global food security.

Conditioning food aid

While the importance of access, monitoring, and transparency are now widely recognized as core imperatives promoting the effective delivery of emergency food aid, new donors such as China, Russia, and India have yet to be socialized into evolving international practice. The

Chinese "no strings attached" approach is clearly at variance with the United Nations' "no access, no food" principle intended to enforce stricter government compliance over reaching those most in need. It also stands in stark contrast to the Food for Peace Act legislation in the United States that endorses the position that food should be used for the purpose of "encouraging the development of private enterprise and democratic participation."[30]

To date, China's emergency food aid has been heavily weighted toward North Korea. Between 2000 and 2010, China provided a cumulative total of 2,467,782 metric tons of food aid, 98 percent of which was directed to North Korea, only very small amounts were given to other countries before 2000—Zimbabwe, Mongolia, and Mozambique received the largest deliveries in the 1990s.[31] From a global perspective, China is now North Korea's top food donor, providing around 37 percent of total aid (2000–2010) compared with 23 percent from the United States. The decision by the United States to cut food aid to North Korea following its failed rocket launch in April 2012 means that China is now the sole major provider of official food aid, although trade in cheap food through unofficial channels across its 1,300-kilometer border now acts as a substitute to offset a tightening sanctions regime. Earlier progress made by the WFP in gaining access to all parts of the food distribution chain, including in remote areas, suggests that conditioning aid on a multilateral basis may still offer the best option for responding to chronic food insecurity.[32] However, China is unlikely to change its strong preference for bilateral aid to North Korea any time soon.

Beyond its neighborhood, China has started to operate more on a multilateral basis. It has agreed to a number of limited triangular purchases that allow for grain to be purchased in third countries. Chinese agencies are also working in partnership with the WFP, buying food locally and hiring local support to facilitate distribution. Such an approach has been used to provide food aid to Zimbabwe and Lesotho, and may well be expanded to different regions of the world.[33]

Mutual benefits

Chinese agricultural assistance is more widely dispersed across Asia, Africa, and Latin America. Over a ten-year period (2000–2010), the neighboring country of Nepal received the largest amount (4,198 metric tons) out of a cumulative total of 27,421 metric tons (see Figure 8.2). Administrative responsibility for implementing agricultural aid projects lies with the Ministry of Commerce in conjunction with the

Ministry of Agriculture and the Ministry of Foreign Affairs. The key stated aims of Chinese agricultural projects are threefold: to reduce poverty; to increase agricultural productivity (yield per hectare); and to build capacity over time.

The Chinese approach toward agricultural development assistance is firmly based upon the idea of mutual benefits. In official reports, a strong emphasis is placed upon exporting the value of the Chinese development experience. Highlighting the critical importance of agricultural reform in the early stages of China's "reform and opening," Chinese officials stress the longer-term benefits of increasing productivity growth in smallholder agriculture and meeting basic needs on the basis of limited foreign exchange.[34] Creating larger economies of scale to improve efficiencies in agricultural production and investing in complementary value-added industries related to agriculture are seen as critical components of a broader agricultural investment strategy.[35]

In the academic discourse, the value of Chinese agricultural assistance has been cast in even broader terms with references to legitimacy

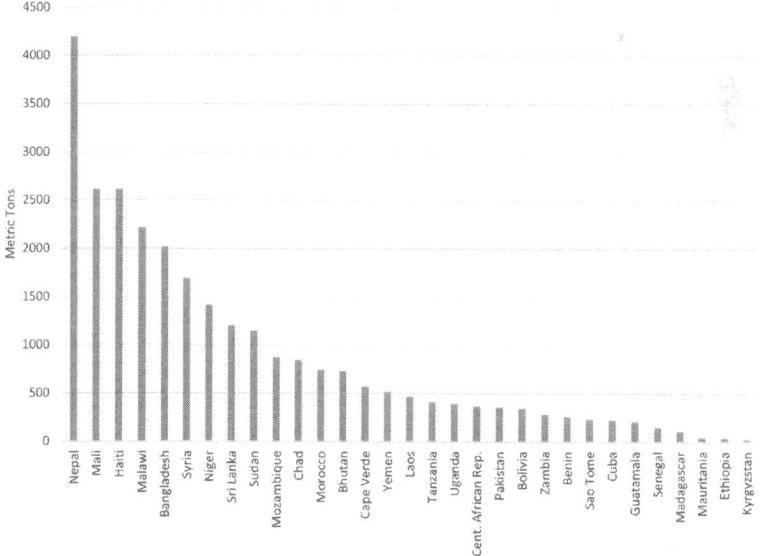

Figure 8.2 Chinese agricultural development assistance (2000–2010)

Note: Food aid deliveries are targeted to support agricultural, development, and nutritional projects. Grain can be sold on the open market, provided on a grant basis, or channeled through multilateral projects.

Source: Compiled by the author from the International Food Aid Information System (INTERFAIS), World Food Programme.

concerns and image maintenance. Wang Rui argues that China has a "right to speak" or "voice" (*huayuquan*) on matters relating to international food security because of its own miraculous achievement in feeding a huge population.[36] Chinese scholars have also noted the importance of countering the negative image of a neo-colonial power plundering African resources.[37] For Chinese investment and aid projects in Africa to work, it is deemed essential that the African people have greater trust in Chinese aid, Chinese companies, and Chinese products.[38]

The African showcase

Chinese agricultural assistance to Africa is seen as the showcase for demonstrating the value of the Chinese experience. In the words of former Chinese senior official Jia Qinglin in his address to the Eighteenth Session of the Assembly of African Union in January 2012, "we promote African development through China's development."[39] From the Chinese government perspective, cooperation between the two sides in the agricultural sector is seen to be highly complementary. Simply put, "China's agricultural development needs Africa's resources and markets, and the revitalization of African agriculture needs the experience and technology in China."[40]

China's involvement in agriculture in Africa dates back to the early 1960s, when a small delegation of agricultural specialists visited Mali to assist in the production of sugar cane and tea. As of 2009, China had completed 215 agricultural aid projects (168 projects related to farming, animal husbandry, and fisheries, and 47 projects related to water use and water conservation).[41] Aligned with the new China–Africa strategic partnership, support for agriculture has accelerated in recent years. At the Forum on China and African Cooperation Summit in November 2006, President Hu Jintao announced three key measures aimed at enhancing food security: establish 10 agro-technological demonstration centers (now increased to 23), dispatch 100 agricultural experts to African countries, and train 1,500 African agricultural technicians and experts in China.

The approach toward enhancing food security in Africa is technologically oriented toward increasing productivity. Technological transfer is taking place in relation to irrigation farming, seed technology, and agricultural mechanization. China controls the second-largest plant seed gene bank in the world and it is the largest producer of hybrid rice (produced by crossing two genetically different rice varieties, leading to a 30 percent increase in yield compared with inbred varieties). Famously invented by Yuan Longping in the early 1960s, hybrid rice now constitutes over 50 percent of China's total rice-growing area (15 million hectares).[42] It is in demand in African countries, as well as closer to home in countries such as Malaysia and Thailand that are increasingly reliant upon rice imports. Juncao (mushroom grass), invented by Lin Zhangxi at Fujian Agricultural University, is also being introduced to African countries to reduce deforestation by planting mushrooms on elephant grass.[43]

In the African context, as in other developing countries, China's overriding aid philosophy is one of self-reliance: "helping Africans to help themselves." The oft-cited Chinese saying, "giving someone a fish is not as good as giving someone a fishing rod" (*shou ren yiyu buru shou ren yiyu*) encapsulates one of the "Eight Principles of Chinese Economic Aid and Technical Assistance" announced in the 1960s.[44] In the contemporary global context, it also provides a useful analogy for highlighting the relationship between aid and investment. China has learned the lesson that development aid is a means and not simply an end in itself. Earlier Chinese agricultural projects failed on account of poor maintenance and the lack of recurrent funding.[45]

In a self-proclaimed attempt to depoliticize aid, the Chinese government responds to requests from recipient governments and then makes decisions over the allocation of funding on the basis of whether Chinese technology and know-how suits local conditions rather than on the basis of political preferences. The "One China" policy is the only exception to the rule, although this is now less of an issue given that only three African states (Burkina Faso, Saõ Tomé and Príncipe, and Swaziland) officially recognize Taiwan. In revealing preferences, Chinese officials do have a tendency to extol the virtues of authoritarian forms of governance. In the words of one official, "the fact that Eritrea is 70 percent self-sufficient in food production is a consequence of a strong single party state; it is much easier to work with strong governments such as Eritrea."[46]

Aid officials in Beijing now face a major problem of how to transfer projects to local partners upon completion. To date, Chinese agricultural aid has been exclusively conducted at the central government level. For very practical reasons, it is now recognized that "building relations with local partners" and cooperating with other donors are essential means of ensuring the sustainability of Chinese development aid.[47] The Tripartite Partnerships for Development in Africa between China, the United Kingdom, and Africa is a recent promising trend in this regard.

A second problem concerns how to leverage greater development benefits from Chinese commercial operations. Ironically, while the blurring of aid and commerce is generally seen as a major constraint on development effectiveness, for the Chinese government the problem is more that these two realms of investment remain overly distinct. In an effort to promote corporate social responsibility, government agencies such as the State-Owned Assets Supervision and Administration Commission (SASAC) are trying to encourage Chinese state-owned enterprises to invest some of their profits in agricultural assistance, as yet to no avail.[48]

Third, China's per capita grain consumption is only around 371 kg, slightly higher than the world average of 352 kg. The question asked by the Chinese public is why the government is sending food to Africa when its own people are still hungry. For the government, food aid to Africa requires public diplomacy targeting both domestic and international audiences. In this regard, China is little different from other bilateral donors, balancing domestic public interests with foreign policy objectives.

Global policymaking

It is within the global policymaking realm where Chinese influence over food security norms is likely to be most significant. China's strong preference for food sovereignty means that it has taken a major role in facilitating the regulation of food markets. For policymakers in Beijing, self-reliance remains the cornerstone of food security; relying on international markets is not seen to be a viable option.[49] At the height of the food crisis in 2008, low levels of import dependence meant that China was essentially shielded from the destabilizing effects of market fluctuations. In the words of the National Development and Reform Commission report on enhancing food security, "the world food market caught a cold, but China did not even sneeze."[50]

Firmly on the side of those advocating for the establishment of international reserves, China has supported the G20 initiative to create the regional pilot reserve program for West Africa referred to earlier. It is also involved in the Emergency Rice Reserve program as part of ASEAN+3. Given that two-thirds of the world's rice is produced in East Asia and intra-regional rice trade only makes up 5 to 6 percent of the world market, there exists a strong incentive for these countries to use rice as the test case for strengthening regional cooperation. Under the agreement, member states will stockpile 787,000 tons of rice with the highest donation (300,000 tons) from China, which currently holds around 42 percent of the world's rice reserves. Contributions to a \$4 million endowment fund are divided according to financial capacity with China, Japan, and South Korea contributing \$1 million each.[51]

At the World Food Summit in 2009, Vice Premier Hui Liangyu proposed the early establishment of a food security safeguard system encompassing early warning, emergency relief, macro-control, and regulatory functions.[52] The Chinese government has also promoted "guided development" of the biofuel sector based upon the principle of "not competing for land with food" and ensuring that "energy security [does] not come at a cost to food security."[53] It has increased donations to the FAO, the WFP, and the International Agricultural Consultative Group and now plays a stronger role in the FAO CFS. China was elected onto the 12-member bureau of the CFS for 2012–2013 and two Chinese experts, Professor Tang Huajun, vice-president of the Chinese Academy of Agricultural Sciences, and Professor Zurong Cai (Nanjing Normal University), serve on the High Level Panel of Experts established to inform the committee of emerging food trends.

To date, there is little evidence to suggest that China is playing an obstructive role within the FAO. Rather it seems to be taking a more strategic stance aimed at renegotiating the boundaries of reform. As a member of the drafting committee within the CFS, China supported the recently approved global guidelines on "responsible governance of tenure of land, fisheries, and forests in the context of national security."[54] The negotiations aimed at defining rights and responsibilities over commercial land acquisitions involved 96 states, UN agencies, private sector representatives, and nongovernmental organizations. China did support the overarching goal of safeguarding the rights of smallholder farmers. However, available reports reveal that the Chinese delegation did at times attempt to slow down the process and, along with South Africa and Egypt, China voted against the further endorsement of World Bank-supported principles for "Responsible Agricultural Investments that Respect Rights, Livelihoods, and Resources" on the grounds that a proper consultation process had not taken place.[55]

Changing the rules of the game: learning by doing

The above discussion has identified at least three key areas in which Chinese domestic food security concerns and international priorities converge. First, the traditional Chinese norm of self-sufficiency, once seen as being at odds with the market-oriented principles of economic development, now meshes more comfortably with the global policy agenda. In sharp contrast to its position taken at the World Food Conference in 1974 when it was the only country to express reservations over a resolution to establish a global food information and early-warning system, China is now a strong advocate of strengthening the global governance of food security.

Second, Chinese support for mutual benefits in relation to agricultural development assistance accords with global efforts to reduce the disincentive effects of aid interventions upon agricultural development. In many ways, China is reaping the rewards of being a latecomer in joining the donor community. Problems associated with Western-led official development assistance (ODA) to Africa in particular have been carefully studied. China has also gained useful experience as a recipient of ODA.[56] However, we still have limited knowledge of whether the Chinese approach is genuinely leading to positive outcomes for local beneficiaries.

Third, the Chinese principle of "different methods for different conditions" is in keeping with the current development philosophy at the international level that seeks to avoid a "one size fits all" donor mentality. Another principle of "Guidance, Step-By-Step," which means taking account of local conditions and implementing pilot programs, also reveals a preference for experimentation rather than the imposition of any particular model.[57] Contrary to the expectations of some commentators, the Chinese government is not intent upon exporting its development model uniformly to developing countries. Rather, the emphasis is more upon a careful consideration of what particular aspects of the Chinese experience may suit local conditions.[58]

In other ways, the Chinese approach toward enhancing food security at the global level is likely to lead to tensions amongst the donor community. Now at the vanguard of a reform-oriented agenda, it is by no means clear that China will take a leadership role in fostering a new compact between traditional and new donors within the international food regime. Two particular problems stand out. First, the principle of "mutual benefits" sets China apart from other traditional donors that are more intent upon meeting their international obligations. For China, international responsibility is still double-faced. In promoting agricultural cooperation, the basic principle of "putting ourselves first, seeking win–win cooperation," prevails over all other priorities. What this means in practice is that increasing agricultural efficiency overseas must not come at a cost to Chinese farmers' incomes and the protection of domestic industries.[59] Decoupling domestic interests from international aid may not be politically expedient in the short term, but it is difficult to see how China can truly become a stakeholder in global governance on the basis of a "China first" approach.

The second problem is that rhetorical support for the principle of non-interference in domestic affairs increasingly contradicts current Chinese practice. While some Chinese commentators have been quick to criticize the United States for linking its food aid with democracy promotion overseas, it is also the case that Chinese food aid is not devoid of politics; commercial and political interests intersect in ways that are difficult to disentangle. While the benefits of Chinese food aid can only be legitimately assessed on the part of the beneficiaries involved, the "non-interference" principle is proving increasingly problematic in contexts where the Chinese presence is exposed to local conflicts and instability.[60]

In the final analysis, China is in the process of changing the rules of the game. No longer on the sidelines, it is now a key player in negotiating the evolving norms of international conduct. In comparing China with other traditional donors a major difference lies in the fact that it places a premium upon the idea of gaining experience before endorsing a particular set of principles. In other words, the Chinese approach toward international cooperation is quintessentially pragmatic, based upon learning by doing rather than learning by principle. Strong Chinese preferences for food sovereignty, mutual benefits, and win–win cooperation present opportunities and challenges for the international food regime. Over time they may help to facilitate consent, especially between traditional and new donors, but it is difficult to see how such an approach can strengthen the global governance of food security in the absence of legally binding commitments.

Conclusion

In returning to the bigger question posed at the beginning of this chapter—whether China is likely to strengthen its participation in the broader effort to eliminate world hunger, or whether an enduring commitment to national independence guides its approach—it is fair to say that China is now an active participant in the international food regime, but current practice is still heavily weighted toward domestic concerns. It would be easy to conclude that the Chinese approach toward food security is contradictory, caught between the legacies of the past and the hopes for the future. Rather, I would argue that what we are currently witnessing is a broadening of the Chinese conception of self-interest.

Certainly, tensions exist over China's unyielding support for the principle of non-interference. In the future, the contradiction between investing in the resources of another state while proclaiming a politically neutral position over its future development trajectory will become more difficult to reconcile. On balance, however, humanity's visceral need for food may well prove to be the one global challenge that motivates responsible Chinese leadership.

Similar to the case of global health governance (Chapter 7), the findings in this chapter reveal that China is taking an active reformist stance within the international food regime. The difficulty in identifying the degree to which the Chinese government is likely to take a leadership role in bringing about substantial reforms lies in the fact that it seeks to strategically balance national and global interests. Just as domestic preferences are not a sufficient guide for describing China's international behavior, framing Chinese interests and values in terms of global responsibility can fail to capture some of the strategic factors underpinning its integration into the international system.

Interesting comparisons can be made between the Chinese approach toward international aid more broadly outlined in the analysis by Xu Jiajun (Chapter 9) and the issue-based regime on food security. In the case of the former, the normative parameters are already set and China is seeking to draw attention to its own distinctive style. This is having the unintended effect of increasing competition within the donor community. In the latter case, China plays a central role in the reform of the regime and its influence over the negotiation of norms is more direct. As a strategic reformer, the potential exists to significantly revise the rules of international conduct in ways that could bring about collective benefits. Much will depend upon whether China is willing to constrain its own behavior in accordance with international obligations.

Notes

1 I would like to thank the Indiana University Research Center for Chinese Politics & Business for supporting my fieldwork visit to Beijing in June 2012. I also owe a debt of gratitude to my research assistant Olivia Boyd.
2 Address by Hui Liangyu, Vice Premier of the State Council of the People's Republic of China, World Food Summit, Rome, 16 November 2009.
3 An important exception is Deborah A. Bräutigam and Tang Xiaoyang, "China's Engagement in African Agriculture: 'Down to the Countryside'," *The China Quarterly* 199 (2009): 687–706.
4 For diverse perspectives on the debate, see Robert Kagan, *The World America Made* (New York: Alfred A. Knopf, 2012); G. John Ikenberry, "The Future of the Liberal World Order: Internationalism After America," *Foreign Affairs* 90, no. 3 (2011): 56–68; and Trine Flockhart and Li Xing, "Riding the Tiger: China's Rise and the Liberal World Order," DIIS Policy Brief (Copenhagen: Danish Institute for International Studies, December 2010).
5 See Walden Bello, *The Food Wars* (London: Verso, 2009); and Tim Lang and Michael Heasman, *Food Wars: The Global Battle for Mouths, Minds, and Markets* (London: Earthscan, 2004).

6 Shaun Breslin, "China's Emerging Global Role: Dissatisfied Responsible Great Power," *Politics* 30, no. S1 (2010): 52–62; Katherine Morton, "China and the Future of International Norms," Strategic Policy Forum, Australian Strategic Policy Institute, 22 June 2011; and Gerald Chan, Pak K. Lee, and Lai-Ha Chan, *China Engages Global Governance: A New World Order in the Making?* (London: Routledge, 2012).

7 Raymond F. Hopkins, "Reform in the International Food Aid Regime: The Role of Consensual Knowledge," *International Organization* 46, no. 1 (1992): 225–264.

8 "Food Security," Policy Brief, UN Food and Agricultural Organization, Issue 2 (June 2006), p. 1.

9 Derek Headey and Shenggen Fan, *Reflections on the Global Food Crisis: How Did it Happen? How Has it Hurt? And How Can We Prevent a Next One?* IFPRI Research Monograph 165 (Washington, DC: International Food Policy Research Institute, 2010).

10 World Food Programme, "UN: World Hunger Reaches 1 Billion Mark," 22 June 2009, www.wfp.org/content/un-world-hunger-reaches-1-billion-mark.

11 Headey and Fan, *Reflections on the Global Food Crisis*, 30.

12 Food Security Portal, "G20," www.foodsecurityportal.org/category/category/g20.

13 I have borrowed this phrase from Professor Wen Tiejun, a leading agricultural expert, in Wen Tiejun, Lau Kinchi, Ceng Cunwang, He Huili, and Qiu Jiansheng, "Ecological Civilization, Indigenous Culture, and Rural Reconstruction in China," *Monthly Review* 63, no. 9 (February 2012): 29–35.

14 National Development and Reform Commission, *An Investigation Into China's Grain Situation 2009: Prospects and Policy Response* (Beijing: National Development and Reform Commission, 2009).

15 National Development and Reform Commission, *Enhancing China's Food Security*.

16 "China to Shore Up Grain Purchase, Storage," *Xinhua*, 26 June 2014.

17 Interview, Vice-Governor of Guangxi, Nanning, 6 June 2012.

18 National Bureau of Statistics, *Statistical Yearbook 2011* (Beijing: China Statistical Publishing, 2011).

19 Government of the People's Republic of China, *Outline of China's Medium- to Long-Term Food Security Plan (2008–2020)* (Zhongguo zhongchangqi liangshi anquan gangyao guihua (2008–2020)) (Beijing: Government of the People's Republic of China, 13 November 2008).

20 "Sustainability Concerns behind China's Bumper Harvest," *Xinhua*, 18 July 2014.

21 Quoted in Lan Xinzhen, "Agricultural Resolution," *Beijing Review* 1, 6 January 2011.

22 National Development and Reform Commission, *An Investigation Into China's Grain Situation 2009*.

23 Government of the People's Republic of China, *Outline of China's Medium- to Long-Term Food Security Plan (2008–2020)*.

24 Government of the People's Republic of China, *Outline of China's Medium- to Long-Term Food Security Plan (2008–2020)*.

25 "Agricultural Group Seeks Overseas Expansion," *China Daily*, 14 March 2011.

26 Here I am drawing upon Irna Hofman and Peter Ho's concept of "development outsourcing." See Irna Hofman and Peter Ho, "China's

200   Katherine Morton

'Development Outsourcing': A Critical Examination of Chinese Global 'Land Grabs' Discourse," *Journal of Peasant Studies* 39, no. 1 (2012): 1–48.

27 Cui Haipei, "Russia Land Lease Likely to Draw Foreign Investors," *China Daily*, 16 March 2012.

28 Interview, Foreign Economic Division of the Sino-African and South–South Cooperation, Ministry of Agriculture, Beijing, June 2012.

29 Shi Zhuanmin and Cao Guihua, "A Study of the New Strategy for Cooperation Between China and the United Nations World Food Programme" (Zhongguo yu lianheguo WFP xin yilun hezuo zhanlue yanjiu), *China Soft Science* 8 (2006): 84.

30 United States Government Food for Peace Act, Section 2, amended 22 May 2005, www.fas.usda.gov/excredits/foodaid/pl480/Food_for_Peace_Act. pdf.

31 Statistical data on Chinese food aid is compiled from the International Food Aid Information System (INTERFAIS), World Food Programme.

32 World Food Programme, "Korea, Democratic Reople's Republic (DPRK)," www.wfp.org/countries/korea-democratic-peoples-republic-dprk.

33 Interview, He Wenping, Institute of West Asian and African Studies, Chinese Academy of Social Sciences, Beijing, June 2012.

34 Interview, Foreign Economic Division of the Sino-African and South–South Cooperation, Ministry of Agriculture, Beijing, June 2012.

35 Shanghai City Agriculture Committee, "Short-Term Developments and Prospects in China-Africa Agricultural Cooperation" (Jin shiqi zhongfei nongye hezuo ji qianjin), 6 April 2012, www.shagri.gov.cn/wmfw/hwzc/ hygl/201204/t20120410_1315842.htm.

36 Wang Rui, "China Sends Timely Help for the Famine in Africa" (Zhongguo wei feishou songshang "jishiyu"), *China Agricultural Science* (September 2011): 46.

37 Shi Zhuanmin and Cao Guihua, "A Study of the New Strategy for Cooperation Between China and the United Nations WFP."

38 Xu Guobin, Wang Huisu, and Li Ronggang, "A Discussion of China and Sudan's Agricultural Cooperation Situation and Policy Responses" (Zhongguo yu sudan nongye hezuo xianzhuang yu duice taolun), *World Agriculture* 393 (January 2012): 83–85.

39 Jia Qinglin, Address to 18th Session of the Assembly of African Union, Addis Ababa, Ethiopia, 30 January 2012, www.focac.org/eng/zfgx/dfzc/ t899821.htm.

40 Shanghai City Agriculture Committee, "Short-Term Developments and Prospects in China-Africa Agricultural Cooperation."

41 Information Office of the State Council, The People's Republic of China, *China's Foreign Aid White Paper* (Beijing: State Council, April 2011), 7.

42 Edilberto D. Redoña, *Rice Biotechnology for Developing Countries in Asia* (Science City of Muñoz: Philippine Rice Research Institute, Philippines, 2011).

43 Tan Zhongyang and Hu Meidongxin, "Nations Learn How to Stay Fed," Fuzhou, Fujian, *China Daily*, 16 June 2012.

44 Information Office of the State Council, The People's Republic of China, *China's Foreign Aid White Paper*.

45 Interview, He Wenping.

46 Interview, Ministry of Agriculture.

47 Ministry of Agriculture, *Five-Year Plan for the Development of International Agricultural Cooperation (2011 to 2015)* (Nonye guoji hezuo fazhan "shierwu" guihua (2011–2015nian)) (Beijing: Department of International Cooperation, Ministry of Agriculture, 11 January 2012), www.moa.gov.cn/zwllm/zcfg/nybgz/201201/t20120111_2454566.htm.
48 Interviews, United Nations Representative Office Beijing, May 2011, and Ministry of Agriculture, June 2012.
49 National Development and Reform Commission, *Enhancing China's Food Security Must Be Built Upon Domestic Strategy* (Liangshi anquanxing qianghua lizu guonei zhanglue) (Beijing: National Development and Reform Commission, 2008).
50 National Development and Reform Commission, *Enhancing China's Food Security Must Be Built Upon Domestic Strategy.*
51 ASEAN, "AMAF Plus Three Countries Sign Agreement on Rice Reserve to Ensure Food Security," Jakarta, 7 October 2011, www.aseansec.org/26670.htm.
52 Address by Hui Liangyu, cited in Ministry of Foreign Affairs of the People's Republic of China, archives, www.fmprc.gov.cn/eng/wgdt/zyjh/t628178.htm.
53 Address by Hui Liangyu.
54 Report of the 38th Special Session of World Food Security (11 May 2012), www.fao.org/docrep/meeting/025/md958e.pdf.
55 Grain International, "It's Time to Outlaw Land Grabbing Not Make it Responsible," 17 April 2011, www.grain.org/article/entries/4227-it-s-time-to-outlaw-land-grabbing-not-to-make-it-responsible.
56 See Katherine Morton, "Epilogue: Can Lessons be Learned?" in Katherine Morton, *International Aid and China's Environment: Taming the Yellow Dragon* (London and New York: Routledge, 2005), 449–456.
57 Ministry of Agriculture, *Five-Year Plan for the Development of International Agricultural Cooperation (2011 to 2015).*
58 He Wenping, "The Balancing Act of China's Africa Policy," *China Security* 3, no. 3 (2007): 23–40.
59 Ministry of Agriculture, *Five-Year Plan for the Development of International Agricultural Cooperation (2011 to 2015).*
60 He Wenping, "China's Aid to Africa: Policy Evolution, Characteristics, and its Role," unpublished paper, 2010.

9 China's rise as development financer
Implications for international development cooperation

Xu Jiajun

- **Key landmarks in China's foreign assistance policies and practices**
- **China's foreign assistance philosophy**
- **The OECD-DAC aid regime**
- **A perspective on international development cooperation: which way to go?**
- **The DAC's "outreach strategy" to China on ODA**
- **Renegotiating export credit rules**
- **China-DAC Study Group**
- **The Asian Infrastructure Investment Bank**
- **Conclusion**

China's recent engagement with Africa and the launching of the Asian Infrastructure Investment Bank (AIIB) have sparked a heated debate about China's impact upon the international aid architecture. Some argue that China has undermined norms and rules established by traditional donors and should be socialized into the existing international aid regime.[1] Others maintain that as an "emerging donor," China has presented a "golden opportunity" for Africa and elsewhere, providing a "win–win" alternative through trade and investment to break the vicious circle of aid dependency.[2] Such polarized debates tend to create more heat than light, for both are based on unfair assumptions that, first, traditional donors are "morally superior" and "more effective" in achieving development outcomes, and second, that China has offered a new vision for aid effectiveness that has challenged traditional donors' development hegemony.[3]

This chapter aims to reframe the debate by exploring China's rise as a "development financer" rather than simply an "emerging donor." The exclusive focus by many on narrow official development assistance (ODA), which was established and defined by the Organisation for Economic Co-operation and Development's Development Assistance

Committee (OECD-DAC), fails to grasp the challenges and opportunities of China's practice of flexibly integrating diverse forms of development financing in its engagement with other developing countries. Looking back into history, this chapter argues that China's current practices in using official support to foster economic cooperation with developing countries are not new to DAC donors. China's arrival as a latecomer, against the backdrop of the international norm of de-linking aid from commercial flows, has created a space in which to explore how to better achieve synergies among different sources of development financing. This new prospect of mutual learning among different development financers comes with additional potential risks, including that a potential lack of coordination might lead to wasteful competition to the detriment of both development financers and recipients.

This chapter first examines key milestones of China's foreign assistance policies and practices to understand how they have been adapted to its own changing domestic situation and the international environment. Second, it explores the origin of prevailing DAC norms such as the definition of ODA, untied aid, and aid untying agreements in order to understand how the process of rule-making has been driven by DAC donors' coordinated efforts to promote burden sharing and to avoid competing amongst each other. The heart of the analysis draws on empirical cases (including that of the AIIB) to examine the likelihood of three possible scenarios of strategic interaction between China and traditional donors—no coordination, convergence, and mutual recognition and learning—in an effort to explore the implications of China's rise as a development financer within the broader sphere of international development cooperation.

Key landmarks in China's foreign assistance policies and practices

The notion of China as an "emerging donor" is misleading in the sense that both China's foreign assistance and its philosophy regarding foreign assistance date back to the early 1950s. This section examines how international and domestic political economy factors have influenced the evolution of China's foreign assistance policies and practices.

Evolution of China's foreign assistance policies

China's foreign assistance policies shifted in the late 1970s when China reframed its "Reform and Opening" policies from pursuing an idealistic "proletarian internationalism" to one of pragmatic "reciprocal benefits and mutual development." With the launch of the "socialist market economy" reforms in 1992, China's foreign assistance has progressively shifted towards greater commercial reciprocity. China's foreign assistance has gone through four stages.

In the first stage (1950–1977), China faced military threats, political isolation, and economic blockage from Western powers. To shape its international environment, China aligned itself with socialist countries and newly independent nations. Foreign assistance during this time was regarded as its own international obligation to help the so-called Third World fight against colonialism and achieve self-reliant development. Thus, from the very beginning of Chinese foreign assistance, Chinese leaders attempted to distinguish China's foreign assistance efforts from North–South foreign aid, and described Western "aid" as a tool of "colonialism"—the root cause of the backwardness of the global South. China's "assistance" to other developing countries in Africa, Latin America, and Asia was aimed to help these countries achieve national independence from colonial powers. In short, China's foreign assistance originated within the international political context of the Cold War and North–South confrontation, and was seen as starkly distinct from the mainstream aid discourse on "foreign aid" as a resource transfer from the rich to the poor that had an implicit undertone of compensation for past colonial exploitation. During this period, foreign assistance also helped China to achieve its foreign policy objective of gaining strong political support from Third World countries. China's quest for international recognition culminated in the resumption of its membership in the United Nations (UN) in 1971.

The second stage (1978–1991) is noted by the initiation of reforms designed to address the main drawbacks of the Chinese traditional foreign assistance system's derivation from the planned economy. During this time, economic viability was trumped by political considerations,[4] and centralized administrative management had failed to incentivize people to enhance efficiency.[5] A key goal was to establish China's "dual role" both as a recipient and a provider of foreign assistance, as articulated by Deng Xiaoping.[6] Accordingly, as a beneficiary of foreign aid, China proactively applied newly learned management skills and technologies to innovate its own foreign assistance programs, including setting up joint ventures in recipient countries and diversifying its mechanisms for providing economic assistance. From 1978 to 1991, China drew on its own development experience and determined that foreign aid could play a catalytic role in leveraging infrastructure financing, transferring management skills, and building institutions (such as an internationally competitive bidding system), thus helping to foster economic transformations.[7]

In the third stage (1992–2003), as domestic economic reforms took hold and China's role within the global economy expanded, China's foreign assistance policies were further reformed to meet new demands. In line with intensified domestic market reforms, the Chinese government began to encourage new market-oriented institutions to play a key role in mobilizing foreign assistance resources. In 1992, Deng Xiaoping confirmed publicly China's objective of establishing a socialist market economy, specifically through the planned use of economic reforms that would move the economy toward using market mechanisms as a more efficient means of allocating resources. In 1994, China established a set of three new policy banks: China Development Bank; China Export-Import Bank (Ex-Im Bank); and the Agricultural Development Bank of China. Concessional loans, funded from general budget resources, were introduced to use official finance systematically to leverage commercially oriented flows. This initial experiment led to a key policy decision at the Conference on Reforming Foreign Assistance in October 1995 to encourage the establishment of joint ventures between enterprises from both China and recipient countries to invest in projects with high economic returns. More broadly, foreign assistance was regarded as a toolkit for broader economic cooperation. For instance, China set up a Foreign Aid Fund for Joint Ventures and Cooperative Projects and issued low-interest loans via its new Ex-Im Bank.

This trend was strengthened with the official launch of the "Go Global" Strategy in 2000. Enterprises of all forms of ownership were encouraged to invest in overseas operations and expand their international business. This initiative was put into both the 10th Five-Year Plan (2001–2005) and 11th Five-Year Plan (2006–2010). Thus, foreign assistance was used during this time to mitigate risks and enhance competitiveness for Chinese domestic enterprises as they began to operate on the international market.

In the fourth stage (2004–present), China's foreign assistance policy has taken on new functions as a result of China emerging as a creditor country in an international monetary system still dominated by the United States.[8] Official reserves grew rapidly starting in 2000, and although they have fallen somewhat recently, still stand at approximately US$3 trillion. The Chinese government faces a huge challenge of transforming its massive official reserves into real assets and generating long-term income flows for the country.

This evolving international economic position has motivated China to intensify its strategic partnerships with African countries. The Forum on China-Africa Cooperation (FOCAC) was launched in 2000 and backed by annual top-level visits by Chinese leaders to Africa.[9] In 2006 China's African Policy was put in place.[10] China's economic assistance to Africa has progressively been integrated into the broader concept of "economic cooperation," including infrastructure, agricultural cooperation, investment, trade, and other types of financial cooperation. Since the early 1990s a new foreign economic policy toolkit has been put in place by the Chinese government. This toolkit uses foreign assistance to facilitate broader economic cooperation with developing countries in accordance with China's changing international economic situation and policy goals.

It is important to note that China's foreign assistance policy has a two-pronged approach made up of public and social services, and economic cooperation. The "social gift" aspect of China's foreign assistance has gone hand in hand with this new emphasis on economic cooperation. China has used grants in-kind gifts, and interest-free loans, administered by the Department for Foreign Assistance within the Ministry of Commerce, for projects that are meant to provide public goods or social services, such as hospitals, schools, public buildings, and technical assistance (see Figure 9.1).

In addition, while the main objective of this chapter is to describe China's bilateral foreign assistance, it is worth mentioning that China has also contributed to multilateral development institutions. In fact, since 2000, multilateral assistance has grown at a much faster rate than bilateral aid. The share of multilateral assistance as a percentage of total aid increased from 1.9 percent in 1997 to 3.4 percent in 2007 and, by at least one estimate, to 15 percent in 2013 (see Table 9.1).

China's foreign assistance philosophy

In 1964, Premier Zhou Enlai announced "The Chinese Government's Eight Principles for Economic Aid and Technical Assistance to Other Countries." These principles reflect the historic aid philosophy that has influenced China's modern aid practice. Here is a brief summary of those principles.

First, aid should lay the foundation for "self-reliant and independent" development. As Zhou said, "in providing aid to other countries, the purpose of the Chinese government is not to make recipient countries dependent on China but to help them embark step by step on the road to self-reliance and independent economic development."[11] China

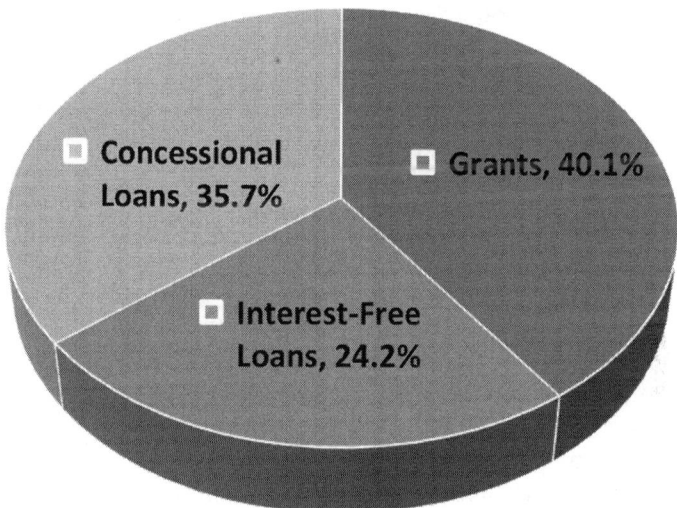

Figure 9.1 Composition of China's foreign aid expenditures (cumulative, year-end 2012)

Sources: China's Foreign Aid, White Paper (China Information Office of the State Council, People's Republic of China, 21 April 2011); and "China's Foreign Aid," Information Office of the State Council, The People's Republic of China, 10 July 2014.

Table 9.1 China's bilateral and multilateral assistance (US$, millions)

	1973	1987	1997	2007	2013
Bilateral assistance	2,787.7	375	420	1,103	6,035
Multilateral assistance	23	25	8	39	1,065
Total	2,790	400	428	1,142	7,100
Multilateral assistance share (%)	0.08%	6.25%	1.86%	3.41%	15.00%

Sources: The table is cited from Hou Xiong, "Principles and Practice of China's External Multilateral Assistance," Foreign Affairs Review 5 (2010): 57–58. The data on bilateral assistance in 1973 and 1987 are based on Zhang Yuhui's dissertation on China's External Assistance (2006). The data on bilateral assistance in 1997 and 2007 come from China Statistical Yearbook (1999, 2009). The data on multilateral assistance in 1973 are based on World Knowledge Yearbook. The data on multilateral assistance in 1987, 1997, and 2007 are based Xiong's (2010) estimation from the reports from international organizations. Data on 2013 are from Philippa Brant, "China's Foreign Aid: New Facts and Figures," The Interpreter, 8 July 2014, www.lowyinstitute.org/the-interpreter/chinas-foreign-aid-new-facts-and-figures.

Note: Because China does not publish full statistics on its bilateral or multilateral assistance, these data are estimates and may not be comprehensive or consistent across time.

placed a premium on its national independence immediately after World War II, like many other developing and then newly independent countries. It decided to seek "foreign assistance" as a means of accelerating its own development, an experience that shaped China's later philosophy as an aid lender. Fundamentally, China regards country ownership as a precondition for a functioning bilateral aid relationship.

China's achievements in poverty reduction—mainly, by lifting millions of people out of poverty—have been internationally recognized. Foreign aid has played a very marginal role historically in terms of China's own gross domestic product (GDP), never accounting for more than 1 percent of China's GDP (see Figure 9.2). Nevertheless, China's own experience as an aid recipient contributed to the modernization and learning processes of its later role as aid lender in a catalytic way, confirming the Chinese leadership's firm belief that economic growth is the key engine of poverty reduction.

Another long-held tenet of Chinese aid philosophy is that mutual benefit and reciprocity are at the heart of development assistance. This is best described by another key principle explained by Zhou in 1964, that China "never regards such aid as a kind of unilateral alms but as something mutual." For China, development is a learning process: aid should not only encompass resource transfer but also technology

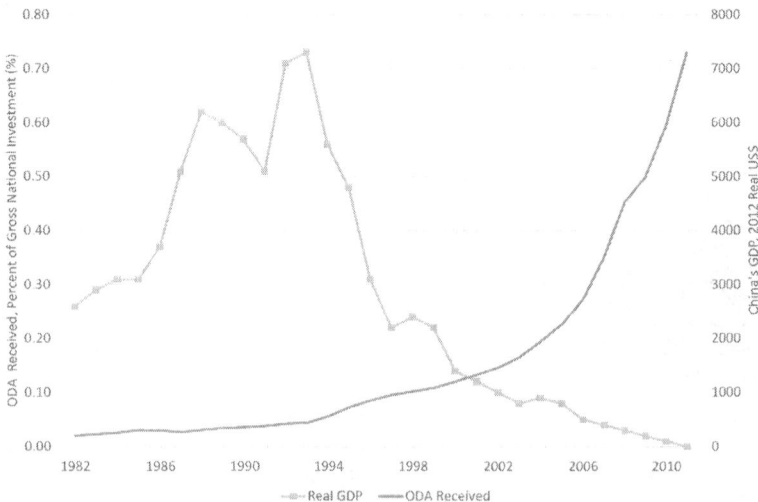

Figure 9.2 Comparison of China's GDP and net ODA received (1982–2011)
Source: "World Development Indicators," World Bank.

transfer and knowledge sharing with equal importance. Fundamentally, the developing relationship China has with its aid recipients is regarded as a two-way street in the effort to tackle development challenges.

Finally, the historic principles first outlined in 1964 dictate that aid should not be used to leverage policy reforms or to impose political conditions. From the perspective of the Chinese government, policy conditionality has negative connotations, recalling past experiences with inequitable treaties and extraterritorial concessions. China historically has been very skeptical about donor-led aid coordination. After China was founded in 1949, it was contained by Western powers and through this experience, China learned that aid from the Western world came with an inherent power asymmetry. Donor coordination could run the risk of developing into donor cartel. China took care to avoid such a cartel emerging among its own aid recipients.

The OECD-DAC aid regime

The norms and standards established by the OECD's DAC for concessional international assistance have been widely considered to constitute an international regime. It is important to put contemporary DAC standards into historical perspective in order to see how they emerged out of a specific international political economy and intensive international negotiations. This section limits its focus to DAC standards because the DAC is regarded as a norm-setting body for coordinated aid efforts among major official aid providers. It is important to recognize that DAC donors are far from a homogenous group. There are different aid philosophies and practices among and between European donors, the United States, and Japan. However, what categorizes them as a group is that they have established a concrete organizational platform to coordinate their aid policies by setting standards on what counts as "foreign development assistance" and how aid should be governed in relation to other official flows.

Defining ODA: how DAC donors "emerged"

The DAC of OECD was created in 1960 as an international club of aid-giving governments. The United States took the initiative to establish this donor club in order to exchange views, coordinate aid, and, most importantly, to exert mutual peer pressure to expand their aid programs.[12] In the context of the Cold War, economic aid served an important geopolitical objective of keeping the Soviet Union's influence at bay. In the late 1950s, the United States began to suffer a balance of payments deficit. Accordingly, the search for "a fairer share of the Western aid burden" became a main driver behind the creation of the DAC. The challenge faced by the United States was how to bring other Western countries, the "emerging donors" of the time, into the collective task of increasing the amount and the coherence of an overall Western aid effort in order to counterbalance the Soviet Communist influence.[13]

In order to achieve this primary burden-sharing objective, the United States initially put bilateral pressure on "laggards," especially Germany, to step-up their foreign aid efforts. However, other industrialized countries contended that they were already giving much more aid than assessed by Washington. The United States countered that the calculations of the Europeans were based on "a very wide, loose, an ultimately unacceptable concept of development aid."[14] Thus, in order to exert more pressure on these industrialized countries, the DAC became the forum to hammer out a much more rigid and confined standard definition of development assistance.

The rationale behind this new definition was that a common benchmark was necessary to measure "aid" efforts, construed as a "North–South transfer," on a comparable basis so that peer pressure could be effectively exercised on "free-riders"—namely Western industrialized countries failing to pay their due share in providing foreign aid while benefiting from a united military alliance (the North Atlantic Treaty Organization, or NATO), whose cost was largely shouldered by the United States.

To establish a common benchmark, DAC donors had gone through protracted negotiations to figure out how discounted a loan must be to meet the predetermined purpose of a North–South welfare transfer and how to calculate this "concessionality" or "grant element." To achieve consensus on these two key questions, DAC donors made compromises with each other to accommodate differences in domestic accounting methods and interest rates. A compromise was reached in the end that loans with a "grant element" of at least 25 percent calculated at a fixed 10 percent discount rate could be counted as "official development assistance."

Recently this standard definition has been called into question. When the fixed 10 percent discount rate was adopted in the 1972 Recommendation, it was a reasonable benchmark for assessing the opportunity cost to donors of making funds available for aid instead of investing them domestically. However, due to recent extended periods of extremely low long-term bond interest rates, the fixed 10 percent discount rate may qualify loans as ODA which may be more expensive than commercial loans. Although the fixed discount rate is outdated, it has been hard for DAC donors to change this deep-rooted standard definition, which is used to measure performance in meeting the UN target that rich countries should aim to spend 0.7 percent of their annual income on aid.

The primary focus on the "grant element" has helped to establish norms such as "the more concessional, the more development-oriented," and "grants are better than loans." The *1978 DAC Recommendation on Terms and Conditions of Aid* states that ODA to least developed countries (LDCs) "should essentially be in the form of grants, and as a minimum, the average grant element of all commitments from a given donor should either be at least 86 percent to each LDC over a period of three years, or at least 90 percent annually" as a group.[15]

This has exerted harmonization pressure on DAC donors, especially newcomers. For instance, before South Korea joined the DAC in 2009, a DAC Special Review recommended that South Korea should give more grants to the least industrialized countries in order to meet the above provision with which all other DAC donors currently comply.[16] The Republic of Korea's enthusiasm for loans can partly be explained by its own positive development experience as a recipient of aid loans and its deeply held belief that loans impose essential fiscal discipline on the recipient country and thus help them to build up creditworthiness on international capital markets and achieve self-reliant development. This development philosophy is also shared by Japan. In the context of the DAC's harmonization pressures, Japan's grant shares of its total aid disbursements increased from about 20 percent in 1978 to almost 60 percent in the 2000s. Yet Japan has often felt its views were marginalized by the harmonization pressures in the DAC, seeing itself cast as "a bad student" and shamed by "good performers" such as the United Kingdom and the Nordic countries. As of 2010, grants accounted for under 60 percent of Japanese ODA, compared to the DAC average of almost 90 percent.[17]

This emphasis on grants can be justified by the rationale of construing aid as North–South welfare transfer, which is consistent with the charity-based aid philosophy—aid as alms given by the rich to the poor. Indeed, the World Council of Churches played a key role in the idea and adoption of the UN aid target, which came to be cast in terms of the DAC definition of ODA. Thus, the benchmark for aid effort is the amount of net financial resource transfer. Intangible components of development effectiveness such as technology transfer and knowledge sharing are not captured. That many efforts with major development impact fall outside the tight definition of ODA is now being perceived as problematic, including by DAC donors. The DAC Chair has articulated this concern and the *Busan Partnership Document*, and re-articulated it at the Fourth High-Level Forum on Aid Effectiveness in December 2011, which makes reference to this wider concept of development impact.

De-linking aid from commercial flows: how an untied aid agreement was born

The untied aid principle has conventionally been justified on the grounds that aid should crowd out "selfish donor interests" and should not be used to promote trade.[18] Yet a closer examination of the rule-making process reveals that implementation of the principle has essentially derived from prolonged political negotiations among OECD countries to avoid destructive export promotion competition.

During the post-World War II period, government-supported export credit agencies became an active force in reconstruction. Although they played an indispensable role in mitigating risks and enhancing the competitiveness of domestic firms, the initial healthy competition among export credit agencies gradually led to "destructive competition"— aggressive softening of credit terms far below market rates to match those of their counterparts.[19] This escalation in race-to-the-bottom financing began to run out of control in the absence of a multilaterally agreed discipline, with spiraling public expenditure costs for exporting countries often used to subsidize ailing industries. Such crass competition could also do harm to poor importing countries in the long run, when financing terms became more decisive than just acquiring the best-quality and most appropriate goods and services at international market prices. Supply-driven capital goods could undermine local priorities, albeit that developing countries might benefit from "better than market terms" by playing off one export credit agency against another in the short run. Another danger was that poor countries might be tempted by "prestige projects" which could end up with poorly maintained capital assets and a growing external debt. Consequently, imprudent borrowing and lending contributed to the debt distress of developing countries in the 1970s and 1980s.[20]

To avoid the worst-case scenario of destructive competition, major developed countries sought to establish intergovernmental rules to regulate export credits. Yet negotiations turned out to be prolonged. While a Group on Export Credits and Credit Guarantees was established by the OECD in November 1963, *The Arrangement on Guidelines for Officially Supported Export Credits* (more commonly called the "Gentlemen's Agreement" or "Consensus") did not come into effect until April 1978.

A primary obstacle to introducing discipline was that its effectiveness depended on the voluntary compliance of all participant countries; no one wanted to have their own hands unilaterally tied when others were free to use official subsidies without constraints. Another difficulty was that a harmonized approach incurred different adjustment costs that implied winners and losers. However, coordination failure became more acute when the heightened competition over LDC export markets in the wake of the oil shock in the early 1970s escalated the level of export subsidies in many OECD countries. To avoid "beggar-thy-neighbor" policies, a "consensus" was reached to bring order, discipline, and transparency to the field of trade finance by laying out disciplines on maximum maturity, minimum down-payments, and minimum interest rates.[21]

However, this gentlemen's agreement did not resolve the question of how to separate officially supported export credits from ODA.[22] Participants had used "tied-aid credits" to effectively circumvent the discipline by linking aid financing granted by aid agencies with trade financing supported by export credit agencies, known as "mixed credits."[23] To level the playing field, under pressure from its domestic firms, the United States made a credible threat of escalation, compelling other OECD countries to negotiate the "Helsinki Disciplines" in 1991 in order to avoid prohibitively expensive subsidy competition.[24] This agreement prohibited tied and partially untied aid for "commercially viable projects" for richer developing countries.

In order to address this loophole, participant countries negotiated arduously to draw a line between "aid" and "export credits" along the spectrum of concessionality, ranging from pure grants to commercial loans in order to determine which credits should be subject to the jurisdiction of a "gentlemen's agreement." The rationale behind this benchmark was that tied aid credits with a larger grant element are more likely to be "aid motivated" since "aid" was considered as a North–South welfare transfer. On the contrary, tied aid credits with a relatively smaller grant element are more likely to be "competition motivated" for the purpose of donor self-interest.[25] Thus, the seemingly technical division between aid and export credits was deeply rooted in the underlying question, "what is foreign aid?" Even though in practice aid is still used as a subsidy to boost trade, in principle aid should be de-linked from trade promotion that serves donors' interests.

A practical political consideration behind this division was that export credits with a higher grant element would be "expensive enough" to prevent export credit agencies using them as a toolkit for trade subsidization. Accordingly, the gentlemen's agreement had progressively increased the grant element in order to expand the scope of the discipline on implicit trade finance in the form of "tied aid."

However, despite the above discipline, donor countries continued tied-aid practices for trade promotion to poorer countries to a point where it was not sustainable for both donors and recipients. In December 2000, the United Kingdom (UK) announced that it would unilaterally untie its aid, while also pressing vigorously for an OECD-wide agreement to untie financial aid to LDCs.[26] Before announcing this, the Department for International Development had consulted with the Department of Trade and Industry and the Confederation of British Industry. The rationale was that tied aid projects had become unsustainable in the UK. Commercially driven aid projects had promoted trade and exports, but had proven to carry risks of undermining development-based decision-making and in doing so, generating inappropriate projects and purchases and compromising the development needs of poor recipient countries. An illustrative case in point: in the 1970s, the UK ran a shipping subsidy fund at the time when British shipbuilding was becoming increasingly uncompetitive internationally. The UK had to offer extra subsidies to compensate for the prohibitive price of ships they provided to the Shipping Corporation of India. Thus, these ships were like "cathedrals in the desert," costly for both the donor and the recipient. Another motivation of the UK pushing for untying bilateral aid was that few domestic UK companies relied on aid to make profits. Most companies located in the UK were internationally competitive and could win contracts from foreign countries. If other donors untied their aid, these opportunities would increase. In addition, continuing scandals with UK tied aid projects—such as the case of the UK Pergau River project in Malaysia[27]—had encouraged nongovernmental organizations (NGOs) to push governments to untie aid.[28]

However, the United Kingdom's proposal was strongly opposed by France, where the government, industry, and parliament coalesced to defend tied aid. Many French companies depended on aid projects in former French African colonial possessions for profits. The national philosophy in France differed from Britain, too: as a champion of free-market principles, Britain opposed government intervention in industry whereas France defended the legitimacy of the role of government in industrial policy. This impasse was broken largely due to divergent interests within the French domestic bureaucracies. The French Treasury Ministry was in favor of reaching an agreement since the budget costs were high and the subsidized insurance guarantees amounted to unfunded contingent liabilities, while the Trade Ministry, with its goal to promote exports, opposed an aid untying agreement. After intensive negotiations, the DAC donors reached agreement in 2001 on a Recommendation on untying ODA to the LDCs, with the two exceptions of food aid and technical assistance. Food aid is an "off-limits subject" in the DAC—the United States has consistently opposed discussion of untying food aid due to political opposition in the Congress, although the US Administration and the US Agency for International Development (USAID) fully understand the costs of tied food aid from the perspective of economic efficiency and have made efforts to provide US food aid more flexibly. Japan opposed the untying of technical cooperation on the grounds that it is an intrinsic part of Japanese aid packages, and they believed that their consultants could not compete linguistically on the international market for consulting services.

In short, the 2001 Aid Untying Agreement has not only helped to bring further discipline to export credit markets but also contributed to mitigate drawbacks of tied aid practices. Informal incentives and established commercial channels can still ensure that domestic firms win contracts despite formal untying. The DAC continues to urge its members to ensure aid that is *de jure* untied should also be untied in practice.[29]

However, untied aid as "international best practice" continues to be questioned by some DAC donors. While the DAC Recommendation proposes that members untie aid "to the greatest extent possible"[30]— 100 percent of aid untying[31]—Japan and the United States maintain serious reservations about the scope of further untying.[32] A line of argument that can be heard in the ongoing debate runs as follows:

> Reports on progress with implementing the 2001 Recommendation focus on "how much" aid is untied but touch little on the developmental impact of untied aid projects; and, untied aid as a result becomes the dissemination of a "religion," with aid officials defending the untied aid principle like "missionaries" even though some untied aid projects may not serve a development purpose.[33]

An unintended consequence of the untied aid principle has been that by de-legitimizing the practice of using aid to promote trade and investment, DAC has neglected to focus on other official flows. In

2003, the DAC's Working Group on Financial Aspects of Development Assistance was abolished during a wider restructuring of the DAC machinery. The underlying rationale: aid untying is now in progress in the DAC, with annual reports on progress, thus the primary effort should focus on monitoring the indicators in the Recommendation to achieve the goal, which can be done by the DAC itself. Consequently, there is a "missing forum" in the DAC to assess the developmental aspects of other official flows as well as to coordinate among member states regarding other official flows. The call by the DAC chair in 2011 to bring "development-related financing" onto the DAC agenda and to extend statistical reporting bears witness that something has been missing from the DAC's policy and statistical coverage.

On the export financing front, another consequence of the untied aid principle was the banning of "tied aid credits" with a grant element of more than 35 percent for commercially viable projects. It was based on the assumption that private sector institutions and market processes would fill this financing gap to support infrastructure investment. This is one reason why OECD bilateral donors no longer finance power stations, telecoms, and industrial projects. However, the assumption of the existence of such well-functioning capital markets does not hold water in reality; risks in LDCs and other developing (and many developed) countries are still too high to attract unsupported private investors despite liberalization and reform during and since the 1990s. World Bank studies show that there is a huge "infrastructure deficit" in Africa estimated at $93 billion per year over the next decade. China's growing role as an infrastructure financer has helped fill this gap.[34] To meet these compelling development challenges, official support for the private sector can create benefits going well beyond "cheaper finance," including risk mitigation and market access facilitation, and also act as a catalyst for foreign direct investment. To address the neglected ODA support for infrastructure, the Infrastructure Consortium for Africa (ICA) was created to focus on scaling-up donor finance to meet Africa's infrastructure needs.

In short, while the Helsinki Disciplines and the 2001 DAC Recommendation on untying aid have helped avoid gross competition in export credit markets and reduced wasteful aid projects, the untied aid principle has taken on a life of its own, underlining a charity-based aid philosophy. This has led to counterproductive consequences of a neglected focus on how to promote synergies between official support and commercial flows to enhance productivity and the transformation of recipient countries. An article in the *Financial Times* reported that most of the world's infrastructure financing in the coming decades would be financed by the major Asian export-import banks and other official development banks,[35] with some facilitation by private investment banks, so that it now becomes inevitable to extend the mode of thinking and international cooperation on development financing.

A perspective on international development cooperation: which way to go?

A thorough understanding of the two traditions of development cooperation helps pave the way to analyzing how strategic interaction between China and DAC donors would unfold as China becomes a major player rather than a marginal "outsider." This section starts with an analytical framework to conceptualize three potential scenarios (see Figure 9.3), and then moves to empirical cases to test which way ahead is more likely.

The interaction between China and DAC donors is strategic in a sense that China's policy depends on how DAC donors respond to China's rise as a development financer and vice versa. This could lead to three outcomes: (scenario 1) compliance with existing DAC rules and standards; (scenario 2) no coordination/competition; or (scenario 3) mutual recognition and mutual learning.

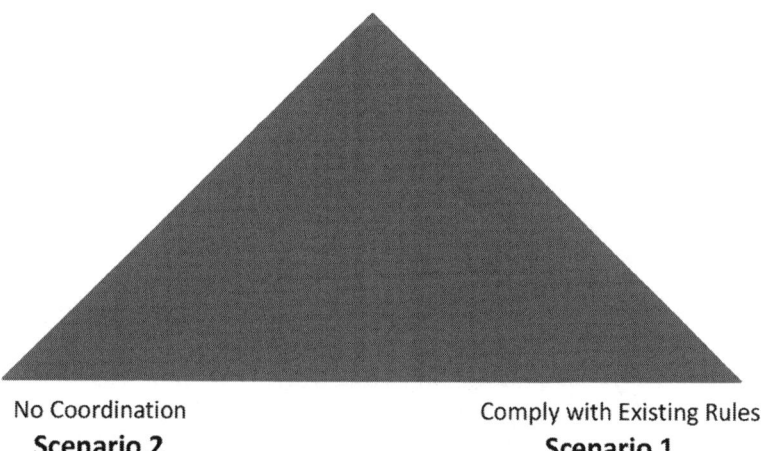

Scenario 3
Mutual Recognition and Mutual Learning/
Reshape Rules within Multilateral Framework

No Coordination   Comply with Existing Rules
Scenario 2   **Scenario 1**

Figure 9.3 Possible scenarios of strategic interaction between China and DAC donors

The first scenario would lead us to expect empirical evidence ranging from China's compliance with DAC's ODA reporting system to its membership in OECD-DAC. This would follow the path established by several "emerging donors" like Australia in 1971, New Zealand in 1973, Spain in 1991, and more recently South Korea in 2010. For many of these countries, joining the donor club has served as a recognition of their international status, and in the case of South Korea marked its full emergence as a developed country.

The second scenario would lead to the prospect that export credit agencies from both sides compete to provide cheaper finance by escalating subsidies without paying due attention to the development impacts of their activities. Within this scenario, one key question is if their trade finance has helped borrower countries to upgrade their participation in global value chains or if it has led to more commodity trade dependence. Another key question is if their official support for domestic firms has helped to upgrade the competitiveness of these companies or simply used taxpayers' money to accumulate unsustainable credit mountains (i.e., another developing country debt crisis).

The third scenario would go in the direction of coexistence of "diverse, differentiated, and dynamic" development philosophies and practices.[36] It is described as diverse because no single model can dictate best aid practice and rule out alternative development thinking and practice. It is differentiated in the sense that it adopts a diagnostic and experimental approach to figure out "what fits" rather than create a "one-size-fits-all" prescription. It is dynamic in that it promotes mutual learning to tackle common challenges rather than top-down, donor-driven aid coordination.

The DAC's "outreach strategy" to China on ODA

In response to the rising influence of China's foreign aid, OECD-DAC initially attempted to bring China into the "mainstream" donor club as an "emerging donor." In 2005 DAC adopted the Outreach Strategy—"Enhanced Engagement"—which "aim[ed] to bring partners closer to the OECD and what it stands for by engaging them closely in OECD processes while supporting their own reform processes through the adoption of OECD practices, policies, guidelines or instruments."[37]

Despite the efforts devoted by the DAC in this direction, two major obstacles stand in the way of materializing the "Outreach Strategy." First, seen through the eyes of China, "engagement" by DAC donors implies that non-DAC donors are expected to be "normalized" into mainstream "international best practice." Moreover, some African voices have been skeptical about these mainstream recipes and want China to stay outside the donor club so as to provide alternative options. Second, as an aid recipient, China itself avoided any donor-led aid coordination and is skeptical about arrangements that carry the risk of a donor cartel that puts pressure on a recipient government to act in accordance with the will of the donor community.[38]

After its initial attempt, the DAC Senior High-Level Meeting in April 2011 approved a new statement entitled "Welcome New Partnerships in Development Cooperation," which signaled a sea change in its attitude toward emerging donors. It first tries to distance the geo-political history of ODA and to seek common ground with emerging donors by stating that "ODA is not defined as a North-South transfer, but rather its criteria relate to the development purpose, concessionality, and the official nature of such flows of resources."[39] Most importantly, it shows a willingness to promote mutual learning by stating that, "[w]e welcome the contribution of all providers of development co-operation resources and expertise, and hope to forge new relationships with these new partners through open dialogue without preconditions."[40] In November 2011, the DAC agreed on a "Global Relations Strategy" embodying this new approach.

This change in DAC attitude paralleled China's proactive strategy to publish its first *White Paper on Foreign Aid* in April 2011. An important driver behind the formulation process was China's participation in the High-Level Forums on Aid Effectiveness in Paris (2005) and Accra (2008). In Beijing, Ministry of Commerce officials pushed to promote action to improve "aid effectiveness," recognizing the relevance of this effort as China's aid programs grew rapidly. The aid effectiveness theme is reflected explicitly in both the April 2011 *White Paper on Foreign Aid* and the September 2011 *White Paper on Peaceful Development*.[41]

Renegotiating export credit rules

From a historical perspective, export credits as a trade finance facility have played an instrumental role in providing protection to exporters and private investors against possible risks in foreign markets when domestic firms of developed countries went abroad to compete on an international market.

Yet as latecomers, developing countries lack sufficient governmental budget, expertise, and institutions to afford this crucial tool to promote their trade and investment. To fill this gap, the United Nations Conference on Trade and Development (UNCTAD) proposed as early as 1975 to establish an international Export Credit Guarantee Facility with financial support from developed countries to promote exports from developing countries. However, this proposal never materialized due to lack of support from rich countries. "To their mind export diversification should primarily be the responsibility of developing countries themselves."[42]

Like other poor developing countries, China aspired to diversify its trade and upgrade its industry in order to succeed in the international market, but there was "a missing instrument" in China's trade and investment finance during the early 1990s. China was eager to learn from advanced OECD countries on how to effectively use export credit rules to develop this "infant industry" and enhance the international competitiveness of its national enterprises. However, China's request at that time to participate in the OECD Export Credit Agency (ECA) informal discussion process as an observer was refused. So, China's Ex-Im Bank proceeded to learn by itself how to innovate financing instruments to support its domestic firms to seek business abroad.

Just over a decade later, China is now seen from the OECD perspective as "much too large and important in the global trade and trade finance picture to remain outside the multilateral system." Thus the OECD-ECA informal process has been quietly looking to bring China into the existing export credit regime, noting that China was missing the opportunity to participate in shaping existing and new disciplines and risking international friction. Lack of information on specific terms of Chinese export credits has fueled more fear, alongside the concern about China's Ex-Im Bank's practice of tying credits to the purchase of Chinese goods and services. Yet, as Bräutigam points out, it is misplaced to refer to this practice as "tied aid," for China was not part of the arduous rule-making process of deciding the dividing line between aid and export credits (a technical definition which appears arbitrary from the perspective of those outside political negotiation processes).[43] As Chinese firms have gained experience and become competitive, China's Ex-Im Bank has reduced the level of tying from 70 percent to 50 percent.[44]

China's competitiveness pressures on OECD countries have prompted the United States to boost its export credits substantially to enhance its commercial relationship with developing countries. For instance, in the case of Indonesia, the Export-Import Bank of the United States supported export credits that went hand in hand with the USAID Economic Growth Assistance Program.[45]

Will this lead to another round of coarse competition among export credit agencies? What does it mean for developing countries to have more alternative sources of financing? Some argue that "to the extent that creditors have in the past been a cartel, giving them bargaining power to extract concessions from clients, they may now lose that leverage on borrowing governments."[46] However, it should be noted that there is a real risk of a race to the bottom if these export credit agencies compete essentially to provide cheaper finance by aggressively matching each other's terms. Past experience has shown that a lack of necessary coordination among creditors can lead to worse-off situations for all, which could also impose a high cost on borrowers, in terms of development impact and unsustainable debt accumulation.

Then would China comply with the existing rules? The chance seems slim. In response to the "leveling the playing field" argument, China, like other latecomers, would argue that developed countries attempted to "kick away the ladder" on which they relied in the past to boost the competitiveness of their own companies. Given the fact that the Export-Import Bank of the United States was established in 1934 and celebrated its 75th anniversary in 2009, China could argue that imposing a uniform rule amounts to forcing a child to race against an Olympic athlete—the field is level, but the game is not fair. A counter-argument would be that China's Ex-Im Bank has grown up to be a mature adult within a very short period and should become part of the system of international rules.

Despite the signs of intensified competition, China and the United States have decided to renegotiate export credit rules under a multi-lateral framework. During Xi Jinping's visit to Washington in February 2012, China and the United States agreed to open talks on setting guidelines for export-credit financing. The two sides agreed to make "concrete progress towards a set of international guidelines on the provision of official export financing that, taking into account varying national interests and situations, are consistent with international best practices."[47]

China-DAC Study Group

A China-DAC Study Group was established in 2009, based on a mutual engagement between the DAC and China's Leading Group on Poverty Alleviation of the State Council. Any expectation that the Study Group could be a vehicle for bringing China into the DAC mainstream was confounded.

The Chinese counterpart—the International Poverty Reduction Center in China (IPRCC)—and the DAC participants reached agreement early on that "to succeed, it must be a two-way learning process." Moreover, given that the goal was to enhance development experience sharing with African countries, Africa should have a place at the table. It was jointly decided to work via five major events, mainly: development partnerships; agriculture; food security and rural development; infrastructure; and enabling the environment for enterprise development. Through this series of international conferences, the Study Group has involved over 500 participants from China, Africa, and the donor community. The final report provides conclusions summarized into three related parts: "what Africa can learn from China"; "what China can learn from DAC donors"; and "what DAC donors can learn from China."

The report signals three new directions. First, it emphasizes that development is a learning process and it is important to construct networks for adaptive learning and to upgrade participation in global value chains. Second, the state has an indispensable role in promoting economic growth. Thus, with these two orientations established, the report frames development cooperation in terms of the economic transformation process, going beyond aid effectiveness to a wider development effectiveness concept applied to Africa. In this vein, it draws attention to the knowledge transfer in South–South cooperation by "maintaining the recent momentum of support for agriculture and infrastructure development, working in relevant forums with emerging countries with special knowledge and expertise," and "examining how aid reporting can better capture the technical co-operation activities of emerging countries in terms of their impact, and not just their monetary cost." Third, the report recognizes the role of China's co-financing in building up Africa's own dynamics of development. Thus, it signals a new policy direction by "exploring how trade, investment and aid linkages and financing packages can mobilise additional actors and capital for economic transformation processes in Africa."[48]

In short, the China-DAC Study Group has transformed the one-way harmonization effort into a two-way learning process. In this partnership with China, the DAC has gone beyond its initial DAC-centric mindset and recognized that China has much to offer based on its development experience. Moreover, the Chinese participants have always emphasized that China's development paths have their own limitations and have created new development challenges, including regional disparities and environmental degradation. What works in the China context may not work well for African countries.

This still-evolving, two-way engagement is reflected in China's endorsement of the *Busan Partnership Document* agreed upon at the Fourth High-Level Forum on Aid Effectiveness in December 2011, with implementation on a voluntary basis for South–South partners, and in its observer status in the new Global Partnership on Effective Development Co-operation.

The Asian Infrastructure Investment Bank

The AIIB was first strategically put forward by Chinese President Xi Jinping and Premier Li Keqiang during their respective visits to Southeast Asian countries in October 2013. The primary motivation behind China's decision to initiate the AIIB was that China aspired to gain more influence in the field of international development but made little progress in the existing US-centric multilateral development banks. For instance, China decided to become a new donor in the World Bank's soft window—International Development Association (IDA)—in 2007, primarily because China sought to gain more influence upon the Bank's rule-making from within. IDA is financially dependent on donor governments, for its concessional financing (known as "soft loans") is far below market interest rates. To keep afloat, IDA has to be periodically replenished by donors. To hammer out IDA Replenishment Agreements, IDA deputies have to go through successive negotiation meetings, usually taking up a whole year to reach consensus on both how to finance IDA but also how to govern IDA. As a former IDA recipient, China was full of indignation that the IDA donor forum (the "IDA deputies"—representatives from donor governments at IDA replenishment negotiations) had grasped de facto decision-making power, surpassing the executive board in the formal governance procedures of the World Bank. Consequently, recipient countries had little voice at the IDA replenishment negotiation table where priorities and policies were set, but had to bear the direct consequences of donor-driven policy orientations (even if they were not the right recipes for how to cope with development challenges).[49] Yet so far China's direct policy influence through its participation in IDA replenishment negotiations has been limited, though it is stepping up efforts to shape the agenda. Hence, China has adopted a "two-leg" strategy by reforming the existing institutions and establishing new multilateral institutions. In other words, slow progress in gaining desired influence motivated China to exercise an "exit" option by creating a set of new institutions.

Establishing new multilateral institutions does not mean that China aims to subvert existing rules. As recorded in China's list of outcomes for President Xi's state visit to the United States in September 2015, China sought to ensure that any new development finance institutions it sponsors would be structured and managed professionally. China has also vowed to ensure that the AIIB is "lean, clean, and green."

Meanwhile, the launch by China of the AIIB has profoundly shaken up the world of development finance. The AIIB is a key instrument for creating a new economic and political geography in Eurasia and beyond. China's own roadmap for its Belt and Road Initiative (BRI) lays out the detailed geography, in terms of specific corridors of connectivity, both East–West and North–South, linking up the Asian, European, and African continents, with a branch also angled toward the South Pacific. Realizing this vision requires addressing the shortcomings of short-termism and excessive risk-averseness in existing multilateral development banks. China is the architect of a very significant enlargement of the international development financing system, with varying degrees of buy-in from traditional players.

Conclusion

This chapter explores the implications of China's rise as a development financer on international development cooperation. On the one hand, the rise of China has created a space for alternative development thinking and practices that may have been marginalized in the mainstream foreign aid regime. On the other hand, it has posed a challenge on how to better govern the linkage between aid, trade, and investment to avoid crass competition and distorted development efforts. Furthermore, China has not set out intentionally to challenge the existing norms, but its methodology and way of thinking create space to revisit the fundamental questions about what aid is, how aid helps to deliver development outcomes, and how aid is related to other financing instruments.

In comparison with other international regimes, China's rise as a development financer has posed a more fundamental question regarding the future of the US-led liberal international order.[50] At the heart of this international order are openness and rule-based systems. Yet this order has unresolved tensions and dilemmas due to power disparities among and within states which influence the shaping of rules and institutions, and the emergence of the rising powers. These tensions have become more acute as US dominance within the order is giving way to a more diffuse and shared system of authority and rule.[51]

This brings about the question of what will come next in this changing landscape of the hitherto US-led liberal hegemonic order. Will it be transformed into a more inclusive and concert-based system, or fall apart into chaotic and fragmented blocs? The answer hinges on how rising powers like China position themselves in relation to the existing international institutions. Their international behaviors are in turn shaped by how traditional powers react to the new clout of rising powers. Looking forward, a visible trend is that China and traditional powers are reshaping the rules and norms of international development through mutual recognition and mutual learning. In the case of ODA norms, China began to show willingness to learn how to improve its aid effectiveness when traditional donors shifted away from imposing compliance pressure on China. In the case of export credits, China and the United States are renegotiating export credit rules as China's trade finance has become an indispensable force. In the case of the China-DAC Study Group, China and DAC have engaged in two-way learning of development experiences, rather than a process of one-way harmonization. In the case of the AIIB, China has proactively taken leadership in establishing a "lean, clean, and green" multilateral development financing institution to address the drawbacks of the existing ones, while learning their good practices.

These strategic interactions are shaping the direction of the liberal institutional order. While it is too early to tell if the future will bring transformation or chaos, this chapter indicates that China as a "reform-minded stakeholder" has a high shared stake in operating within rule-based international institutions. Yet this does not necessarily mean that China's learning curve is a process of compliance as a passive rule-taker. Rather, China is learning how to reshape the rules.

Notes

1 Moises Naim, "Rogue Aid," *Foreign Policy*, 1 March 2007.
2 Dambisa Moyo, *Dead Aid: Why Aid is Not Working and How There is a Better Way for Africa* (London: Allen Lane, 2008).
3 Ngaire Woods, "China, Emerging Donors and the Silent Revolution in Development Assistance," *International Affairs* 84, no. 6 (2008): 1–18.
4 Zhou Hong, "China's Foreign Assistance and the 30th Anniversary of Reform and Opening-up Policy," *World Economy and Politics* 11 (2008): 35.
5 Shi Lin, *China's Contemporary International Economic Cooperation* (Beijing: CASS Press, 1989), 89.
6 Deng Xiaoping, *Selected Works of Deng Xiaoping, 2* (Beijing: People Press, 1993), 112.
7 World Bank, *China and World Bank: A Partnership for Innovation* (Washington, DC: The International Bank for Reconstruction and Development, 2007), 5–7.
8 Ronald I. McKinnon, *Exchange Rates under the East Asian Dollar Standard* (Cambridge, Mass.: MIT Press, 2005).
9 See Forum on China-Africa Cooperation website, www.focac.org/eng/.
10 Ministry of Foreign Affairs of People's Republic of China, *China's African Policy*, January 2006, www.fmprc.gov.cn/eng/zxxx/t230615.htm.

11 "Zhou Enlai Proposed Eight Principles of Foreign Aid," www.people.com. cn/GB/historic/0218/5805.html.
12 Carol Lancaster, *Foreign Aid: Diplomacy, Development, Domestic Politics* (Chicago, Ill. and London: University of Chicago Press, 2007), 70.
13 Gerardo Bracho, "The Origins of the Development Assistance Group (and the OECD): The Western Emerging Donors and the Aid Burden Sharing Agenda," *OECD Symposium on the DAC's 50th birthday*, 15 December 2011: 1.
14 Bracho, "The Origins of the Development Assistance Group," 8.
15 DAC, "DAC Recommendation on Terms and Conditions of Aid," 1978, www.oecd.org/dac/aidstatistics/31426776.pdf.
16 DAC, "DAC Special Review of the Republic of Korea's Development Co-operation," 8 August 2008.
17 OECD-DAC Aid Statistics, www.oecd.org/dac/aidstatistics.
18 Academic research has shown that while motivations of giving aid are mixed, partly driven by humanitarian concerns, aid has been used to serve donor interests. See David Halloran Lumsdaine, *Moral Vision in International Politics: The Foreign Aid Regime, 1949–1989* (Princeton, N.J.: Princeton University Press, 1993); Alfred Maizels and Machiko K. Nissanke, "Motivations for Aid to Developing Countries," *World Development* 12, no. 9 (1984): 879–900; Thomas Andersen, Henrik Hansen, and Thomas Markussen, "US Politics and World Bank IDA-Lending," *Journal of Development Studies* 42, no. 5 (July 2006): 772–794.
19 John Ray, "The OECD 'Consensus' on Export Credits," *The World Economy* 9 (September 1986): 295–310, 296.
20 Øygunn Brynildsen, *Exporting Goods or Exporting Debts? Export Credit Agencies and the Roots of Developing Country Debt* (Brussels: Eurodad, 2012).
21 Ray, "The OECD 'Consensus' on Export Credits," 304.
22 Ray, "The OECD 'Consensus' on Export Credits," 304.
23 Andrew Moravcsik, "Disciplining Trade Finance: The OECD Export Credit Arrangement," *International Organization* 43, no. 1 (1989): 173–205, 182.
24 Steven Hall, "Managing Tied Aid Competition: Domestic Politics, Credible Threats, and the Helsinki Disciplines," *Review of International Political Economy* 18, no. 5 (2011): 646–672.
25 Ray, "The OECD 'Consensus' on Export Credits," 307.
26 The UK "decided to untie all UK development assistance from 1 April 2001." See *UK Government White Paper on International Development*, December 2000: 323.
27 The case of the UK's Pergau River project in Malaysia was a scandal of a "bad" aid project because it used cheap finance to distort what aid projects would best serve development, see World Development Movement, "Tied Aid and Development: Pergau Dam," www.wdm.org.uk/past-campaign/tied-aid-and-development-pergau-dam.
28 Action Aid, "In Whose Benefit? The Case for Untying Aid," April 1998.
29 OECD, "Welcome New Partnerships in Development Co-operation," DCD/DAC (2011) 10/REV1 (2011): 3.
30 OECD, "DAC Recommendation on Untying Official Development Assistance," DCD/DAC (2001) 12/FINAL (2001): 3.
31 OECD, "The Accra High Level Forum (HLF3) and the Accra Agenda for Action," 2008, www.oecd.org/fr/cad/efficacitedelaide/theaccrahighlevelforum hlf3andtheaccraagendaforaction.htm.

32 OECD, "Implementing the 2001 DAC Recommendation on Untying Aid: 2010 Review," DCD-DAC (2010) 16-REV2 (2010): 6–7.

33 "Implementing the 2001 DAC Recommendation on Untying ODA to the LDCs: 2005 Progress Report," Organization for Economic Cooperation and Development, 2005, www.oecd.org/dac/35029066.pdf, p. 10.

34 Vivien Foster and Cecilia Briceño-Garmendia, eds, *Africa's Infrastructure: A Time for Transformation* (Washington, DC: World Bank), 65; Vivien Foster et al., *Building Bridges: China's Growing Role as Infrastructure Financier for Sub-Saharan Africa* (Washington, DC: The International Bank for Reconstruction and Development, 2009).

35 Henny Sender, "Finance: The Path to Power," *Financial Times*, 20 August 2012.

36 Homi Kharas, Koji Makino, and Woojin Jung, eds, *Catalyzing Development: A New Vision for Aid* (Washington, DC: Brookings Press, 2012), 4.

37 OECD, "The DAC Outreach Strategy," DCD-DAC (2005) 18-REV1.

38 Nilima Gulrajani, Sarah Mulley, and Ngaire Woods, "Who Needs More Coordination? The United Nations and Development Assistance," *Journal of International Law & International Relations* 2, no. 1 (2005): 27–39, 35.

39 "Welcoming New Partnerships in International Development Co-operation," OECD Development Assistance Committee Statement - 6 April 2011, www.oecd.org/dac/47652500.pdf.

40 "Welcoming New Partnerships in International Development Co-operation," OECD Development Assistance Committee Statement - 6 April 2011, www.oecd.org/dac/47652500.pdf.

41 China's Information Office of the State Council, "China's Foreign Aid," 21 April 2011; China's Information Office of the State Council, "China's Peaceful Development," 6 September 2011.

42 UNCTAD Secretariat, "Enhancing South-South Trade and Investment Finance," 11 October 2005, 2.

43 Deborah Bräutigam, *The Dragon's Gift: The Real Story of China in Africa* (Oxford: Oxford University Press, 2009), 153.

44 Bräutigam, *The Dragon's Gift*, 174.

45 USAID website, "Fact Sheet: Economic and Trade Cooperation with Indonesia," http://indonesia.usaid.gov.

46 Todd Moss and Sarah Rose, "China Ex-Im Bank and Africa: New Lending, New Challenges," *Center for Global Development Notes*, November 2006.

47 Reuters, *U.S., China Agree to Negotiate Export Credit Deal*, 14 February 2012, www.reuters.com/article/2012/02/14/us-usa-china-exportcredits-idUSTR E81D1YV20120214.

48 China-DAC Study Group, *Economic Transformation and Poverty Reduction: How it Happened in China, Helping it Happen in Africa* (Beijing: China Financial and Economic Press, 2011).

49 Jiajun Xu, *Beyond US Hegemony in International Development: The Contest for Influence at the World Bank* (Cambridge: Cambridge University Press, 2016).

50 John Ikenberry, *Liberal Leviathan: The Origins, Crisis, and Transformation of the American World Order* (Princeton, N.J. and Oxford: Princeton University Press, 2011).

51 Ikenberry, *Liberal Leviathan*, 280–283.

10 China and global labor standards
Making sense of factory certification

Tim Bartley and Lu Zhang[1]

- **The contested terrain of labor standards in China**
- **Opening the black box: portraits of certified factories**
- **Comparing certified and uncertified firms**
- **Conclusion**

The globalization of production has spurred important debates about transnational business and labor rights. Fearing that competitive global production systems would degrade labor conditions, labor rights activists have often called for the globalization of labor standards.[2] Attempts in the 1990s to add a "social clause" to the General Agreement on Tariffs and Trade (GATT) and to incorporate labor standards into the World Trade Organization (WTO) failed, leading activists to look for other ways of enforcing labor standards. The traditional international regime for labor rights and standards, based on conventions of the International Labour Organization (ILO), is symbolically important but lacks enforcement power. Yet a different sort of labor regime has emerged as firms and nongovernmental organizations (NGOs) have developed private labor standards for global supply chains. In response to anti-sweatshop activism in North America and Europe, large retailers and brands in the apparel, footwear, consumer electronics, and food industries have developed codes of conduct for their suppliers, have sent auditors to assess compliance, and have sometimes encouraged suppliers to get certified as having decent labor conditions. Groups like the Fair Labor Association (FLA), Ethical Trading Initiative (ETI), and the Business Social Compliance Initiative (BSCI) have arisen to oversee factory auditing, and organizations like Social Accountability International (SAI), the Worldwide Responsible Accredited Production (WRAP) program, and the International Council of Toy Industries (ICTI) have developed certification programs. By 2014, over 3,300 facilities worldwide were certified to the

SA8000 standard developed by SAI and approximately 1,700 were certified to the WRAP standard developed by the American Apparel and Footwear Association.

The notion of third-party certification has proven especially intriguing to scholars, in part because it has become a prominent form of "private regulation" across a number of different industries and issues, from labor to environmental sustainability to fair-trade.[3] Certification can in some situations improve firms' market positions or help them respond to activist pressure. Yet evidence is mounting that even credible, third-party certification programs rarely live up to their image and that factory auditing often fails to generate compliance.[4] Serious questions remain about what exactly global standards and certification are and are not capable of doing, their effectiveness in different industries and nations, and their role in broader fields of global governance.

China looms large over all of these questions, given its huge role in global production and its growing impact on global governance. Over the past three decades China has experienced explosive economic growth, surging exports, and massive foreign investment, becoming "the world's factory." In the process, "made in China" has become synonymous in the minds of many with sweatshop conditions and the repression of labor rights. Yet China has also become the epicenter of attempts to improve factory conditions through voluntary standards, auditing, and certification. The rapid growth of Chinese exports in apparel, footwear, toys, and consumer electronics, especially after China's entry into the WTO in 2001, drew a great deal of attention to issues like forced labor, appalling working conditions, the harsh militaristic style of managers in export-oriented factories, and the exploitation and marginalization of migrant workers. By the early 2000s, most large US and European brands and retailers were engaging in some type of factory auditing in China, whether done by their own compliance staff or by external auditors. Some firms were also calling for suppliers to be certified by WRAP or to the more stringent standards of SA8000. Certification expanded rapidly in China, as did the broader discourse of corporate social responsibility (CSR). Domestic industry and government actors soon developed their own program, the China Social Compliance 9000 for Textile and Apparel Industry (CSC9000T) standard.[5]

In this chapter, we examine the dynamics and effects of factory certification in Chinese export-oriented consumer products industries. We address several questions. How have initiatives originating outside China—most notably, the SA8000 standard—been shaped by the Chinese context and potential competition from domestically driven standards (like CSC9000T)? What are the circumstances in which factories get certified and to what extent does being certified reliably indicate compliance with standards? To what extent are there clear differences between certified and non-certified factories? Although there is a great deal of discussion of CSR in China, many of these basic questions have remained unanswered. Our attempt to answer them contributes both to the discussion of private forms of global governance and to the questions about China and global governance that are central to this volume.

To answer these questions, we draw on approximately 50 interviews with various players involved with private labor standards in China—auditors, factory managers, compliance staff for international brands, migrant labor NGOs, and workers—conducted in 2010 and 2011, mainly in Guangdong Province, Shanghai, and Beijing. In addition, we analyze new data from a survey of managers in manufacturing firms in Guangdong Province. In general, we find that factory certification's role in shaping labor conditions in China is quite circumscribed. In the worst cases, factories have been certified despite falling well below the purported standards. Even in the best cases, where certification does seem to mark above-average factories, there are severe limits on what certification can achieve.

In what follows, we first examine the terrain in which certification has operated in China, then look more closely at certified factories, particular challenges in the certification process, and the extent of differences between certified and non-certified factories. We conclude by discussing the links between certification and the evolution of labor rights and regulation in China, as well as the ways in which our domain of labor standards contributes to the broader analysis of China and global governance.

The contested terrain of labor standards in China

It is widely held that with the mobilization of China's millions of cheap and disciplined workers who have no independent trade unions and right to strike, a "race to the bottom" has been unleashed, producing an endless downward spiral in labor standards and labor rights around the world.[6] Clearly, the labor situation in China has posed great challenges for international labor advocates. Yet in recent years, China has witnessed a rising tide of labor unrest with the mass movement of capital into China and the deepening of marketization and commodification of labor. According to official Chinese government figures, "mass incidents" increased rapidly from 8,709 incidents in 1993 to 87,000 incidents in 2005, among which about one-third were labor-related.[7] The number of labor disputes also increased dramatically during this period, from 48,121 in 1996 to 350,182 in 2007.[8] Faced with mounting labor unrest, the Chinese central government passed three new labor laws in 2007, in an attempt to stabilize labor relations and pacify disgruntled workers. In 2008, one year after the implementation of the new labor laws, 1.2 million workers filed over 693,465 labor dispute cases with Chinese authorities, a 98 percent increase from 2007.[9] The new labor laws are said to have raised awareness of rights among Chinese workers who are now more willing to stand up and defend their rights through a formal legal system.[10] Against the backdrop of Beijing's attempt to change from an export-led development model based on cheap labor to a more balanced one based on domestic consumption (and thereby higher wages), Chinese workers' rising resistances coupled with their growing bargaining power, derived from a labor shortage and changing demographics, have led to ongoing changes in the balance of power between labor and capital at the workplace.[11] Clearly, labor relations in China have become quite contentious.

The terrain of international labor standards has at times also been quite contentious. The SA8000 standard played a particularly important and provocative role in introducing labor-oriented CSR to China. This program was founded in 1997 by the Council on Economic Priorities, a New York-based non-profit organization focused on socially responsible investing and shopping.[12] SA8000 quickly became so central to the discourse on CSR in China as to lead to the Certification and Accreditation Administration of China (CNCA), which is charged with approving certification bodies, to seek to clarify that "SA8000 certification is not the same thing as CSR."[13]

There are several reasons why SA8000 made such a splash—symbolically at least—in China. First, it mimicked the style of standards issued by the International Organization for Standardization (ISO), such as ISO 9000 and ISO 14001, which had become a de facto requirement for many Chinese exporters. Second, the SA8000 standard generated more controversy than the codes of conduct of individual companies or programs like WRAP or the FLA because it sought to address the problem of freedom of association in China. Most other codes of conduct endorsed freedom of association but were silent on the question of how this could be implemented in China or other countries where freedom of association is legally restricted. SA8000 called for "parallel means" of worker representation (such as worker committees) where trade unions could not be independent. While this provision earned SA8000 a modicum of credibility among international labor advocates, it also fed into a reaction from Chinese industry and government officials, who framed SA8000 as an illegitimate foreign intrusion. As one labor scholar put it, "before 2005, the government was very defensive about SA8000 ... [and] saw it as [a] trade protection measure."[14] The *People's Daily* warned that "voluntary standards could become a trade barrier that consumes the profits of Chinese exporters and denies them their biggest advantage in foreign trade, inexpensive labour."[15]

In this context, domestic actors developed their own set of voluntary labor standards. At the request of China-, Taiwan-, and Hong Kong-based companies, the Chinese National Apparel and Textile Council (CNTAC) introduced its CSC9000T standard in 2005.[16] This was a clear attempt to appropriate the discourse of international standards, as well as to tailor them to the realities of Chinese manufacturing. The CSC9000T standard focused on management systems more than out-right performance, on domestic labor law more than international norms, and on gradual improvement more than pass–fail compliance. The initiative's 2006 annual report included an astute analysis of the limitations of existing auditing and certification models, noting the drift toward falsification, the problem of individual auditors' skill and integrity, and the contradictions between brands' compliance and sourcing practices.[17] Yet CSC9000T also reinforced the role of the All-China Federation of Trade Unions (ACFTU) as a legitimate mode of worker representation and treated the use of formal labor contracts as more of a goal than a requirement.[18] Although the program does not certify compliance, it did include procedures for internal and external evaluation of factories, and by the end of 2007, some auditing firms had been named as evaluators and nine apparel manufacturers had been designated as CSC9000T implementers.[19]

While many observers initially viewed CSC9000T as an industry- and state-sponsored threat to international standards initiatives, CNTAC very quickly began to collaborate with international buyers, building especially on personal connections between CNTAC and the European brands in the BSCI.[20] In 2008, CNTAC and BSCI agreed to explore "compatibility between two systems and thus lay foundation for further cooperation and mutual recognition."[21] Though CNTAC and SAI had little communication, they became indirectly linked by virtue of their shared ties with BSCI, since BSCI and SAI had already come to an agreement whereby BSCI members would use SAI-accredited auditors.[22] Recently, some observers have begun to suggest a three-step process for factories, starting with the CSC9000T program, then moving to BSCI-endorsed auditing, and finishing with SA8000 certification.[23]

Several factors seem to have kept CSC9000T from becoming a strong domestic competitor to international standards like SA8000. International buyers remained more interested in their own systems than in CSC9000T.[24] In addition, state actions that might have privileged domestic over international standards were not forthcoming. The CNCA has not explicitly endorsed SA8000, but importantly, neither has it weighed in against SA8000 as it has in some other international standards projects. CNCA announced in 2004 that SA8000 certifications would require its approval,[25] but it did not explicitly promote the Chinese standard or restrict other labor standards from operating in China.[26] Overall, SAI has gotten what participants described as a "yellow light" from CNCA—not outright approval but not interference either.[27]

Some observers continue to describe SA8000 as "illegal" in China, citing the lack of explicit government endorsement and the vexing issue of worker representation. One vocal critic complains that SA8000 is not a truly international organization—just a US group—that invokes vague international norms (e.g., ILO conventions, Universal Declaration of Human Rights), and treats Taiwan as a separate country.[28] In slightly more measured terms, one specialist noted that "SA8000 asks you to do things in China that are against the law, which gives factories a reason not to do anything."[29]

Although tensions remain between international norms and domestic cultures of production, since approximately 2005, the Chinese government has sought to incorporate CSR as a pillar of the "harmonious society."[30] Indeed, the Chinese Communist Party (CCP) has promoted CSR standards and reporting for private and state-owned companies alike, and has embraced some (though not all) international CSR standards.

Opening the black box: portraits of certified factories

The number of SA8000-certified facilities in China grew from just 28 in early 2001 to over 600 in mid-2014. Yet many observers suspect that the growth of certification in China has been largely due to lax auditing, and sometimes to outright fraud. As one factory owner put it, "I believe among every 10 certified factories, nine are fake."[31] By all accounts, Chinese factories can rarely, if ever, meet the standards for maximum hours of work prescribed by Chinese labor law—no more than 44 hours per week and no more than 36 hours per month of overtime—which is required by both SA8000 and WRAP. In one SA8000-certified factory in Guangzhou, employees reported working for approximately 11.5 hours per day on Monday through Saturday, plus at least eight hours on most Sundays, amounting to as much as 77 hours per week.[32] Such factories may have achieved certification either by falsifying records or by having the certification audit done during low-production seasons. Several SA8000-certified factories have been found, on later inspection, to have serious problems with workplace safety and child labor.[33] Speaking about certification programs in general, a compliance official for an international brand suggested that "some factories are getting certified by just hiring a consultant to get them certified," and that some brands tell factories "if you're certified, we won't bother you with audits."[34]

It is clear that essentially no factories can fully meet the letter of the standards—whether these are the basic standards of ICTI and WRAP or the more challenging standards of SA8000. However, it is less clear what does happen in factories that are certified. What leads managers to seek certification, and what kinds of changes do they make in order to get certified? How much variation is there among factories certified to the same set of standards? In the next section, we address these issues by examining profiles of some certified factories. Admittedly, these may not represent all certified factories or reveal the full implications of certification, but they do help us begin to open what has been heretofore largely a black box to the research community.

Comparing SA800-certified factories

If the SA8000 standard truly serves as a "high bar" that reliably differentiates the very best factories from the rest, then we should expect certified factories to be fairly similar in their performance, at least on the key criteria for certification. Instead, we find evidence of substantial variation among SA8000-certified factories. In one especially egregious case, a factory in Shandong Province, making candles and candle-holders for Tchibo, was certified despite what were later revealed to be horrendous health and safety practices. The dark factory, lacking in fresh air and rife with fire risks, had workers making candles by hand over a primitive gasoline bottle stove and workers were not supplied with protective equipment.[35] Even in factories with less dire conditions, it is clear that certification does not necessarily mean real standardization of practices. For instance, although worker committees have been promoted by SA8000, we could find little evidence of sustained, empowered worker committees in any Chinese factories. The one documented case of an active, empowered worker committee was in a factory that has since lost its orders from the brand that had promoted SA8000, as well as its visionary manager who had supported the worker elections.[36] This case led observers to doubt that there could be any semblance of a committee left. In fact, many certified factories lack even a rudimentary committee. Auditors do little to check whether there is a well-functioning committee, instead simply asking factory managers if a worker representative exists. "Auditors don't really understand the purpose of the committee," admitted one certification representative.[37]

A brief comparison of two garment factories in Guangzhou suggests that there can be substantial variation among SA8000-certified factories. This information is based on interviews with several workers, conducted by Chinese research assistants outside the factories. Though it provides only a partial view of each factory, this information is sufficient to identify at least one key difference—working hours.

PK Garment produces sport shorts and pants for export for Billabong and several other brands.[38] Given Billabong's promotion of SA8000 as part of its compliance program, it is likely that the brand directed the factory to get certified. The research assistants found three workers to interview, who reported working 11 to 12 hours per day, six days a week, with one Sunday off per month and shorter hours on most other Sundays. A 70+-hour work week like this is certainly not uncommon in Chinese factories, but it contravenes both Chinese labor law and SA8000's limit of 60 hours per week (though with exceptions under rare circumstances). The workers reported earning RMB 1,500–2,200 per month at PK.

Similar wage rates—RMB 2,000–2,400 per month—were reported by workers at KC Garment Manufacturing, a Hong Kong-owned factory that produces pants for Nike and Seven Wolves, a Chinese brand. Here, however, employees reported working approximately 11 hours per day, five days per week, and just four hours per day on Saturdays. There is reportedly no work on Sundays. This 59-hour work week, and especially the lack of work on Sundays, marks KC as unusual in Chinese export-oriented industries. In both factories, workers had at least a vague awareness of SA8000 certification, though in neither case did workers demonstrate knowledge of the content and implications of the standards.

The reason for the difference between these two factories is not clear, but we suspect it reflects some combination of factors that have been identified in previous research. First, it is possible that workers at KC are misrepresenting their hours of work, perhaps consistent with coaching by management. As many researchers and journalists have discovered, such coaching is rampant, and workers often go along with the charade for fear of reprisals from management, the loss of orders, or preferences for large amounts of overtime compensation. By some accounts, certification raises the likelihood of lying to auditors (and potentially to researchers as well), since the revocation of an all-or-nothing judgment, such as a certificate, could have major consequences for the firm. Despite this, we suspect that there are real differences in working hours across the factories that could be accounted for by other factors.

It is clear that not only do some brands impose more scrutiny than others on their suppliers, but some brands are more likely to enter into relationships with suppliers that allow for some small but useful degree of trust, cooperation, and joint problem-solving.[39] In addition, scholars have found that differences in the organization of work can sometimes allow productivity gains that allow for somewhat shorter work hours.[40] Though Nike has not relinquished the sourcing practices that give rise to cut-throat competition and exploitative labor relations, the company is known for its attempts to build relationships with key suppliers and to push for innovations that can increase productivity. Our comparison suggests that something above and beyond factory certification may be necessary to support decent conditions in labor-intensive industries. Whether or not certified factories are better on average than non-certified factories, it is clear that certification is not a sufficient condition for compliance.

High-tech electronics: certification as a competitive advantage

A portrait of another SA8000-certified factory illustrates how some firms may seek to use labor standards certification to solidify a competitive advantage. While most firms appear to get certified in response to a specific demand from a buyer, a different path has been taken by at least a handful of Chinese firms—and may become more prominent in a context of labor shortages and movement up the value chain. The following information is based on a factory visit and interviews with company management by the authors in July 2011.[41]

High-Tech Electronics was founded in 2006 as a Sino-Korean high-tech joint venture and became a wholly Chinese private high-tech company in 2007. The company is currently China's number one mobile television terminal resolution provider and has the largest market share of any manufacturer. Because it held a monopoly until very recently, its profit margin was 15 to 20 percent in 2010 and reportedly even higher when there was less competition.

High-Tech got SA8000 certification in 2009. According to a top manager, the company aimed high from the very beginning and viewed the process of getting certified as a process of self-improvement and becoming a sector leader. It was also viewed as good publicity for a company supplying to well-known multinationals, although most of its customers were not themselves engaged with SA8000. The certification process took roughly one year and involved cooperation between the human resources (HR) and production quality control departments, plus several audits by Bureau Veritas (BV), an SAI-accredited auditor that the company chose for being inexpensive, with audits over three years coming to a total cost of about RMB 60,000–70,000.[42]

The company had about 110 production workers when we visited it. Brief observation in the factory revealed that most production workers were females in their early twenties. Although the repetitive simple assembly work did not require high skills, it required care and dexterity, typically seen as befitting young female workers. In fact, the HR manager told us explicitly that the company preferred 21- to 22-year-old female workers with some working experience in electronics. Most were from less developed provinces outside Shanghai, such as Anhui, Sichuan, Jiangsu, and Hubei, with at least a middle school education. About 40 percent had high school or technical vocation school education. Some workers had worked at the company since it was founded in 2007, but annual labor turnover was around 20 percent. Beginning in 2010, formal employees could sign three-year labor contracts with the company, and they were eligible for unfixed labor contracts after two renewals of the three-year labor contracts according to the new Labor Contract Law. However, most production workers were agency workers from a labor dispatch agency located in a suburb of Shanghai. These workers signed labor contracts with the labor agency and they were not formal employees of High-Tech. Although agency workers were paid by High-Tech directly, their social security premiums were handled by the labor agency based on the Shanghai suburb standard, which was much lower than the Shanghai city standard.

The HR department at High-Tech had four full-time staff. The company union was chaired by one of its vice presidents. The current worker representative was a regular production worker from Sichuan who was elected by workers. According to the interviewed managers, the worker representative had complained several times about meal quality on behalf of workers.

Regular working hours were eight hours from 8:00 am to 5:00 pm, with an hour for lunch and short breaks in the morning and in the afternoon. Workshops were clean with air-conditioners, though they were not on when we visited in July. Production was organized by assembly lines with a relatively low automation level. According to the interviewed managers, the company was still in the process of building new workshops and adding new lines which could advance the organization of production.

Average wages were about RMB 2,200–2,500 per month, which was considered more than the local average. According to the HR manager, labor costs accounted for less than 15 percent of the company's total production costs. There was no difficulty in recruiting workers because of the company's good working conditions and reputation for treating workers fairly. The managers also told us that many workers wanted more overtime, but because SA8000 set a limit, workers were actually unhappy about having less overtime and thus smaller paychecks. As the vice president of the company commented, "the SA8000 and other international certification programs should consider China's own unique conditions."[43]

Overall, the information we gathered about High-Tech suggests a factory where workers are receiving somewhat higher wages and working fewer hours than is typical. It is also a company that proactively embraced certification. On the other hand, it appears that the company's labor contracting practices conflict with SA8000's requirement that "the company shall not use labor-only contracting arrangements, consecutive short-term contracts, and/or false apprenticeship schemes to avoid fulfilling its obligations to personnel under applicable laws pertaining to labor and social security legislation and regulations."

Excellent Umbrella: certification to meet customers' demands

Labor standards certification is, of course, not limited to SA8000. For factories producing for some US brands and retailers, WRAP certification has become common. For those in the toy industry, certification to the ICTI's Caring, Awareness, Responsible, Ethical (CARE) program is quite common. While these standards are in some ways less rigorous than those of SA8000, they may in some circumstances help to support improvement in labor conditions in factories, as suggested by the example of Excellent Umbrella. The information is based on a factory visit and interviews with the factory owner by one of the co-authors in June 2011 in Dongguan, Guangdong Province. The co-author was also allowed to walk around the factory workshops and talk with workers without any management presence.

Excellent Umbrella is a Taiwanese-owned company founded in 1993, which exports mainly to the United States, Europe, South Korea, and Japan. It is a supplier to Walmart, Target, Disney, and several other companies. In addition to being certified by ISO 9001, the factory has been certified to the ICTI CARE standard, which calls for decent conditions and systems for continuous improvement in labor management. It was first certified by the ICTI standard in 2006 and re-certified in 2011. Ms. Wang, the factory owner, claimed that certification is necessary to receive orders from customers like Disney and Walmart. In addition to certification, the factory is subject to scrutiny from Walmart's auditors and the Société Générale de Surveillance (SGS) auditors hired by Disney.

Observation in the factory and brief interviews with workers revealed working hours of approximately 10 hours per day, six days per week. Wages are based on piece-rates, with a base rate of RMB 1,100 per month (the local minimum wage) and an average earning around RMB 2,200 per month. The workshops appeared clean and had electric fans on, but there were no air-conditioners and the space felt hot. The level of automation was low, with most work being done by hand.

Ms. Wang was frank that her company engaged in some "make-up" for auditors, such as having workers memorize prepared answers for auditors. On the other hand, she asserted that the certification and auditing process had some positive effects, especially on workplace safety and workers' dormitory conditions. For instance, Excellent Umbrella had added a new fire-alarm system, installed extra fans in the workshops, refurbished factory toilets, and reduced the number of workers living in each dorm room from 12 to eight in the process of preparing for auditing and getting certified. Ms. Wang considered those requirements easy to meet and good for the factory as well. Meanwhile, Ms. Wang mentioned that after studying the prepared materials to deal with auditors, workers had become more aware of their rights and asked for better working conditions and overtime pay. She summarized the impact of certification and auditing: "it becomes real if a company fakes a long time." This case exemplifies how relatively small but meaningful changes might come about through certification. It also suggests a process by which superficial actions to satisfy auditors could gradually accumulate into substantive change in conditions and the operation of a factory.

Comparing certified and uncertified firms

While certified factories routinely fail to meet the letter of the standards to which they are certified, this does not necessarily undermine the meaning of labor standards certification. If certified factories are systematically better than other similar factories, even if neither has perfect conditions, then this might be considered a virtue of certification. Indeed, our interviews reported above reveal what many researchers and practitioners have suspected, mainly that despite serious problems, certified factories are on average better than non-certified factories. One labor standards consultant noted that, "companies that get certified at least have an awareness." They are at least more likely to "know that fire extinguishers should be there; others may never think about it."[44] The leader of a migrant worker NGO argued that all factories have a long way to go to reach the high standards of decency and compliance with Chinese labor law, but nevertheless suggested that "comparatively speaking, if a factory had certification, protection of workers would be better."[45] A brand compliance official who criticized certification recognized that "certification puts you in a different level because you've gone through it. But we would still want to check it [rather than trusting the certification]."[46]

However, is it true that certified factories are better on average than others—and if so, in what ways are they better? This important question has not really been tackled by researchers, largely due to the difficulty of getting information on comparable certified and non-certified factories. In this section, we report results from our analysis of new data from a survey of managers in manufacturing firms in Guangdong, led by scholars at the Guanghua School of Management at Peking University.

The research focused on five major manufacturing centers (Shenzhen, Dongguan, Zhongshan, Huizhou, and Foshan), and companies in apparel, textiles, footwear, electronic products, electrical equipment, paper products and printing, and plastics.[47] The sampling strategy was designed to over-sample SA8000 factories, using the public list of SA8000-certified factories as of June 2010. Other firms were selected through business directories and personal contacts, with an attempt to include a variation of relevant types of firms across cities and industries. In total, approximately 26 percent of the firms in the sample are SA8000 certified. The certified firms in the sample most commonly produce electronics/appliances (36 percent), footwear/sporting equipment (17 percent), and apparel/accessories (14 percent). Since the sampling technique deliberately over-sampled certified factories, these are not meaningful as an estimate of the prevalence of certification across or within industries, all of which would be far lower, but it does allow us to identify differences between certified and uncertified firms.[48]

Our analysis considers some ways in which certified factories might provide a different working environment from non-certified factories. First, we consider managers' attitudes toward HR management. The survey asked managers to rate the importance of the HR office in their company.[49] Though this does not measure exactly how HR procedures are used, it does tap into an important aspect of managers' perceptions. Given SA8000's emphasis on management systems and formal personnel policies, we would expect certified factories to attach greater importance to HR management. As a second measure, we consider whether the factory has a medical clinic (which 43 percent of the sampled firms do). One might expect certified factories to be more likely to have a clinic for several reasons. First, CSR initiatives like SA8000 can be seen as a way of encouraging firms to take on welfare functions (some of which were once provided by the *danwei*) to which migrant workers lack access in contemporary China. Second, though SA8000 does not require a health clinic, it does emphasize occupational health and safety structures and stipulates that, "in the event of a work related injury, the company shall provide first aid and assist the worker in obtaining follow-up medical treatment." In sum, these two measures allow us to assess whether SA8000 certification is linked with more formalized structures for the employment and care of workers. In both analyses, we control for several other factors that might be expected to shape the outcome—namely, firm size, export orientation, foreign ownership, profits, and cash flow (as rated by the surveyed managers), and industry. We also control for other forms of scrutiny or pressure for standards, namely being visited by a government labor inspector in the previous year and having a majority of the factory's production going to buyers who demand labor standards through a code of conduct or similar policy.

As shown in Table 10.1, we find that managers in firms that are SA8000 certified do indeed attach greater importance to the HR office/department than managers in uncertified firms. Being visited recently by local labor inspectors also increases the importance that managers attach to HR management, which most likely reflects the role of the Labor Contract Law in promoting HR systems.[50] On the other hand, factories that simply have most of their production going to clients who demand labor standards (i.e., have codes of conduct) do not attach greater importance than others to HR. Neither are export orientation, ownership, or industry linked to the perceived importance of HR.

When it comes to the likelihood of having a medical clinic for workers, we find no discernible difference between certified and uncertified factories. Clinics are more likely in factories producing footwear or sports equipment and in factories where most clients demand labor standards. There is a suggestive effect of firm size on the existence of a clinic, but it does not reach conventional levels of statistical significance.

Table 10.1 Regression analyses of HR and health infrastructure on SA8000 certification and other selected variables

	Importance of HR department (OLS)	Health clinic (logistic regression)
SA8000 certified	0.333*	−0.545
	(2.03)	(−0.87)
Government inspected in 2009	0.304*	−0.229
	(2.21)	(−0.43)
Majority of production under codes of conduct	−0.122	1.298*
	(−0.78)	(2.08)
Log # employees	0.0916	0.376
	(1.40)	(1.39)
Majority exported	0.0751	−0.391
	(0.46)	(−0.62)
Foreign-owned	0.0991	−0.209
	(0.59)	(−0.33)
Profit	0.140	−0.302
	(1.16)	(−0.66)
Cash flow	−0.0919	0.694
	(−0.57)	(1.11)
Industry: apparel/accessories	−0.155	0.993
	(−0.73)	(1.10)
Industry: electronics/appliances	0.0164	0.0885
	(0.10)	(0.16)
Industry: footwear/sports equipment	−0.0659	2.615*
	(−0.28)	(2.13)
Constant	3.211***	−4.154*
	(6.11)	(−2.03)
N	88	89

Source: Authors' calculations based on the survey data described in the text.

Notes: "Other" industry omitted from calculations. $^+p < 0.10$, $^*p < 0.05$, $^{**}p < 0.01$, $^{***}p < 0.001$ 2-tailed tests, t-statistics in parentheses.

Overall, these findings paint a mixed picture of the meaning of SA8000 within factories. This type of certification seems to support at least a discursive emphasis on HR management. Certification does not appear to matter for the existence of a medical clinic, though other types of CSR standards do appear to be linked to the existence of a clinic. In supplemental models, we have also examined some possible business benefits of certification. Notably, SA8000 is not associated with the perceived ease by management of recruiting workers. Neither do SA8000 factories appear to be different from others in terms of their long-term partners, stability in orders, or growth in clients or orders. These results—while not definitive, due to data limitations—raise important questions about the direct benefits of certification for both workers and firms. At the very least, they remind us that there is enough variation among certified firms that strong patterns in outcomes are hard to find.

Conclusion

CSR, global governance, and the evolution of labor regimes in China

For scholars of labor, private regulation, and global governance, the case of China illustrates challenges of enforcing labor rights privately via supply chain standards. The space for independent labor activism is heavily constrained, and the culture of factory management in China has evolved around assumptions of strong managers and docile workers. It is not surprising that the direct effects of factory certification have been quite circumscribed. Certification is not a reliable marker of decent labor conditions, and when production demands clash with the requirements of labor standards, the former nearly always win out. Although private labor standards have failed to transform labor conditions in China, our study does suggest that they have played a role in catalyzing discussion of CSR, in the maturing of HR management, and in the discussion of worker representation and communication with management (through committees, for instance). At times, private labor standards have also been one vehicle through which migrant workers have learned about what they are entitled to, but all of these processes have been far more constrained than often claimed.

The weaknesses of certification and related forms of private labor regulation are certainly not unique to China. Factory auditing has often failed to spur compliance or widespread improvement and attempts to certify decent factories often generate false positives.[51] On the other hand, there is some evidence of higher rates of non-compliance in audited factories in East Asia than in other regions.[52] When it comes to certification, our fieldwork suggests that problems with the quality and integrity of the auditing process, while not uncommon elsewhere, may be especially severe in China. Audit fraud in Chinese factories has been widely documented, admitted by trade associations, and was discussed openly by many of the people we interviewed.[53] The large number of factories being audited and China's seemingly unparalleled culture of long working hours in labor-intensive industries may be responsible for the large amount of documented audit fraud in the country.[54] Our fieldwork also indicates that oversight from those with an interest in maintaining the integrity of labor standards has been lacking in China. For instance, SAI, which developed the SA8000 standard, has worked closely with companies, local NGOs, and government agencies in several Central American countries, but local partners in China have expressed concern that SAI and its accreditation body, Social Accountability Accreditation Services, "have not really been thinking about the challenges here."[55] A new SAI project in China may help to improve quality control in factory certification, though the challenges of transforming Chinese labor conditions through voluntary labor standards remain substantial.

For scholars of China's participation in global governance, the case of labor has some interesting features. While the Chinese government has not been active in engaging with global labor standards systems, it has not been passive when it comes to domestic labor conditions and their implications for control and social stability. Furthermore, historically, Beijing's approach to labor issues has had an indirect but profound influence on global governance of labor. For instance, attempts by international labor advocates to link labor rights with trade were dealt one partial defeat when China's most favored nation status with the United States was de-linked from human rights concerns in 1994. The subsequent decision by the WTO to avoid involvement in labor rights issues was a second major defeat. Though opposition to a "social clause" in the GATT/WTO came from a number of developing countries, it is notable that the contradiction between internationally defined "core labor rights," especially freedom of association, and domestic labor practice is especially stark in the case of China. The failure of these and other attempts to get intergovernmental global governance of labor is one of the reasons for the rise of the private labor standards that this chapter has examined.[56] Indirectly, the Chinese government's position on labor has influenced global governance, if only by helping to divert it from one arena to another.

The experience of global labor standards in China should not be dismissed but rather should be viewed as part of a dynamic process. The more important question is not "are private standards effective?," but rather "what role do private standards play in dynamic and multifaceted political economy of labor?" Our research shows that it is possible for private labor standards to productively connect with other forms of labor advocacy and that the interplay of international norms and domestic governance can spur new experiments and coalitions for social change. However, more important forces in driving social change are workers' collective action (whether organized or unorganized) and government enforcement of labor laws and regulations (often in response to the former). As the 2010 autoworker strikes in China suggested, disruptive wildcat strikes can result in significant gains for workers (e.g., rising wages, improved working conditions, greater responsiveness of unions to workers on the workshop floor) and amplified social effects that catalyze the transformation of work and industrial relations.[57]

Certainly, as Kennedy's introduction to this book points out, Beijing's priority in the reform era has been skewed heavily toward supporting rapid economic growth and those interests that most directly help achieve this goal (i.e., managers and capitalists) over social and environmental developments such as labor standards. However, it is also important to recognize the centrality of maintaining social stability as the CCP's fundamental political logic. The Party's pursuit of economic growth is not the goal but a means through which to strengthen regime legitimacy and to maintain its monopoly of political power. Indeed, there have been clear signs of the Chinese central government's reorientation in its development strategy since the mid-2000s, when the accumulated social and environmental ills raised the alarm regarding the sustainability of a single-minded, unbalanced economic growth model and the regime legitimacy based on this growth model.

Especially in the wake of the 2008 global financial crisis, the Chinese government explicitly stated that the primary task of China's economic structure adjustment is to shift from an export-led growth model based on cheap labor to a more balanced and sustainable one based on "expanding domestic demand," and thereby higher wages for Chinese people. By the end of 2010, almost every province and municipality in China had increased its monthly minimum wage by an average of 23 percent.[58] The policy shift, coupled with China's changing demographics, growing bargaining power, and the increasing consciousness of the young generation of Chinese workers, has signaled ongoing major changes in the balance of power between labor and capital at the workplace. While it remains to be seen where and how these developments will evolve, it seems clear that "bottom-up pressures from workers and concerns about social unrest from ruling groups" that have propelled improvement in labor standards elsewhere throughout the twentieth century are also important forces at play in China's evolving domestic labor regime and its engagement with global governance of labor standards.[59]

Notes

1 We thank the Indiana University Research Center for Chinese Politics & Business and their Initiative on China and Global Governance for partial funding for this project. Some of the research was also funded by the American Sociological Association's Fund for the Advancement of the Discipline and the Summer Research Award and Grant-in-Aid for Research of Temple University.

2 Anita Chan and Robert J. S. Ross, "Racing to the Bottom: Industrial Trade Without a Social Clause," *Third World Quarterly* 24, no. 6 (2003): 1011–1028.

3 Tim Bartley, "Certification as a Mode of Social Regulation," in *Handbook on the Politics of Regulation*, ed. David Levi-Faur (Northampton, Mass.: Edward Elgar, 2011), 441–452; Benjamin Cashore, Graeme Auld, and Deanna Newsom, *Governing Through Markets: Forest Certification and the Emergence of Non-state Authority* (New Haven, Conn.: Yale University Press, 2004); David Vogel, "Private Global Business Regulation," *Annual Review of Political Science* 11 (2008): 261–282.

4 Gay Seidman, *Beyond the Boycott: Labor Rights, Human Rights and Transnational Activism* (New York, NY: Russell Sage Foundation/ASA Rose Series, 2007); Richard Locke, Matthew Amengual, and Akshay Mangla, "Virtue out of Necessity?: Compliance, Commitment and the Improvement of Labor Conditions in Global Supply Chains," *Politics & Society* 37, no. 3 (2009): 319–351.

5 CSC9000T (China Social Compliance 9000 for Textile & Apparel Industry) is a Social Responsibility Management System based on China's laws and regulations, international conventions and standards, and China's particular situations.

6 The sole official union in China—the ACFTU—is subordinate to the Party-state and is widely considered to be either unable or unwilling to defend workers' interests in the market economy.

7 The Chinese government stopped publicizing such numbers in 2005. However, various sources have pointed to continuing rapid increase in the number of "mass incidents" throughout China. Yu Jiangrong, "Riots and Governance Crisis in China" [Zhongguo de saoluan shijian yu guanzhi weiji], Speech at the University of California, Berkeley, 30 October 2007.

8 National Bureau of Statistics (NBS) and Ministry of Human Resources and Social Security (MOHRSS), *China Labour Statistical Yearbook* (Beijing: China Statistics Press, 2010).

9 NBS and MOHRSS, *China Labour Statistical Yearbook*.

10 "Chinese Government Says Labor Disputes Doubled in 2008," *China Labour Bulletin*, 11 May 2009, www.china-labour.org.hk/en/node/100461.

11 One good illustration of these changes is the success of the 2010 auto-workers' strikes in winning employers' concessions, which quickly produced a ripple effect with a wave of strikes across sectors and regions pushing a rapid trend toward wage increases in China.

12 As the anti-sweatshop movement in the United States gained steam, this organization brought together several groups of brands with codes of conduct and eventually joined with some—like Toys 'R' Us, Avon, Otto-Versand, and the global certification firm Société Générale de Surveillance (SGS)—to create the SA8000 standard and a system for certifying factories.

13 "SA8000 Renzheng muqian buyi guangfan tuixing," *Worker's Daily*, 12 October 2004.

14 Interview, Beijing, 9 December 2010.

15 "SA8000 Requires Positive Attitude," *People's Daily*, 6 July 2004.

16 Interview with compliance program representative, Beijing, 15 July 2011.

17 Similar arguments have been made by scholars critical of private regulation. See Locke et al., "Virtue Out of Necessity?"; Ngai-Ling Sum and Ngai Pun, "Globalization and Paradoxes of Ethical Transnational Production: Code of Conduct in a Chinese Workplace," *Competition and Change* 9, no. 2 (2005): 181–200.

18 China National Textile and Apparel Council, *Annual Report 2006* (CSC9000T).

19 China National Textile and Apparel Council, *Annual Report 2007* (CSC9000T).

20 Interview with NGO representative, Hong Kong, May 2007.

21 China National Textile and Apparel Council, *Annual Report 2009* (CSC9000T).

22 Interview with program representative, Beijing, July 2011.

23 Interview with certification representative, Beijing, December 2010.

24 Interview with factory managers, Guangzhou, November 2010.

25 Pacific Institute, "International NGO Network on ISO," *INNI Online Update* no. 9 (2005), https://web.archive.org/web/20061007121030/http://inni.pacinst.org/inni/inni_online_update_9.htm.

26 Interview with labor standards consultant, Beijing, July 2011.

27 Interview with certification representative, Beijing, December 2010.

28 Interview with CSR researcher, December 2010.

29 Interview with certification official, January 2011.

30 Li-Wen Lin, "Corporate Social Responsibility in China: Window Dressing or Structural Change?" *Berkeley Journal of International Law* 28, no. 1 (2010): 64–100.

31 Interview, Dongguan, June 2011.

32 Interviews with workers, Guangzhou, November–December 2010.

33 Interview with certification representative, Shenzhen, November 2010.

34 Interview, Shanghai, July 2011.

35 Interview with certification representative, Shenzhen, December 2010.

36 Yan Huang, "Labor Solidarity in Contract Manufacturing: The Staff Committee Experiment in Xinda Company as an Example," *Chinese Journal of Sociology* 28, no. 4 (2008): 20–33; and "From Words to Action: A Business Case for Implementing Workplace Standards," Center for International Private Enterprise, and Social Accountability International (2009), www.cipe.org/publications/papers/pdf/SAI.pdf.

248 *Tim Bartley and Lu Zhang*

37 Interview with certification representative, Shenzhen, November 2010.
38 For this and other factories where interviews were conducted, we are using pseudonyms for factory names.
39 Stephen J. Frenkel and Duncan Scott, "Compliance, Collaboration, and Codes of Labor Practice: The Adidas Connection," *California Management Review* 45, no. 1 (2002): 29–49; and Locke et al., "Virtue out of Necessity?"
40 Richard Locke, Thomas Kochan, Monica Romis, and Fei Qin, "Beyond Corporate Codes of Conduct: Work Organization and Labour Standards at Nike's Suppliers," *International Labour Review* 146, no. 1–2 (2007): 21–40.
41 We were introduced to the company by the local government as an international research team studying the impact of SA8000 in China. The company's vice president, the human resources (HR) manager, and the production quality control manager met with us and provided the information. The interviews were conducted in Chinese and were recorded and translated into English. We also visited the company workshops accompanied by management.
42 According to China Labour Watch, BV has also been much maligned for the quality of its audits, probably more than any other auditor in China. China Labor Watch, "Corrupt Audits Damage Worker Rights: A Case Analysis of Corruption in Bureau Veritas Factory Audits" (2009), www.chinalaborwatch.org.
43 Interviews, Shanghai, July 2011.
44 Interview, Beijing, July 2011.
45 Interview, Guangzhou, December 2010.
46 Interview, Shanghai, July 2010.
47 The original research also included some non-manufacturing firms, but these are excluded from our analysis.
48 Assessing whether certification in and of itself caused any observed differences would require additional inquiry and is beyond the scope of this chapter.
49 We take the mean of their responses on a scale from 1 (does not matter) to 5 (very important).
50 Interview with a labor standards consultant, Beijing, July 2011.
51 Locke et al., "Virtue out of Necessity?"; Locke et al., "Beyond Corporate Codes of Conduct"; and Seidman, *Beyond the Boycott: Labor Rights, Human Rights and Transnational Activism.*
52 Locke et al., "Virtue out of Necessity?"
53 China Labor Watch, "Corrupt Audits Damage Worker Rights: A Case Analysis of Corruption in Bureau Veritas Factory Audits"; International Council of Toy Industries CARE Foundation, "Joint Declaration on Integrity Issues in Toy Industry Audits," 2010, www.icti-care.org/uploadfileMgnt/0_2013912174354.pdf.
54 Anita Chan and Hong-zen Wang, "The Impact of the State on Workers' Conditions—Comparing Taiwanese Factories in China and Vietnam," *Pacific Affairs* 77, no. 4 (Winter 2004/2005): 629–646.
55 Interview with certification representative, Shenzhen, November 2010.
56 Tim Bartley, "Institutional Emergence in an Era of Globalization: The Rise of Transnational Private Regulation of Labor and Environmental Conditions," *American Journal of Sociology* 113, no. 2 (2007): 297–351.

57 Lu Zhang, *Inside China's Automobile Factories: The Politics of Labor and Worker Resistance* (New York: Cambridge University Press, 2015).
58 *China Labor Bulletin*, "Chinese Government Says Labor Disputes Doubled in 2008."
59 On the parallel, see Global Labor Strategy, "Why China Matters: Labor Rights in the Era of Globalization" (2008), http://laborstrategies.blogs.com/global_labor_strategies/files/why_china_matters_gls_report.pdf.

11 Domestic politics and Chinese participation in transnational climate governance

Thomas Hale and Charles Roger

- **Trends in Chinese participation in TCG**
- **Transnational governance and domestic political factors—revised expectations**
- **Conclusion**

The efforts of China's central government to reduce greenhouse gas emissions are far more ambitious than those of other countries at a similar level of development, as well as those of, for example, the United States federal government.[1] However, they are also insufficient to stem the steep increase in greenhouse gases emitted by Chinese industry and Chinese consumers. China is the world's largest emitter of greenhouse gases, accounting for roughly a quarter of the world's total. Even on a per capita basis it now rivals the European Union (EU) and could overtake the United States by the end of the decade.[2]

Climate change is, of course, the archetype of a global commons problem. However, China's approach to the issue has been largely driven by domestic factors. Despite a relatively high level of ambition at the national level, China has been reluctant to commit itself to a multilateral treaty establishing specific, verifiable, and binding emissions reductions targets. Its opposition to such targets, a minimum requirement for the developed countries, and particularly the United States, is commonly cited as the key blockage to efforts to negotiate a successor to the Kyoto Protocol.[3]

In this chapter we focus on Chinese participation in an area of the global climate regime outside multilateral negotiations.[4] While such talks have failed to deliver substantive reductions in emissions, and seem unlikely to do so in the near term, a host of projects and initiatives have arisen at the regional, national, and sub-national levels, and in the private and non-profit sectors, filling some of the so-called "governance gap." Examples include reductions at the municipal level, voluntary reductions from firms, and various methodologies for pricing and trading carbon credits. Many of these actions link across borders to form transnational governance, which we understand as "the processes and institutions, formal and informal, whereby rules are created, compliance is elicited, and goods are provided in the pursuit of collective goals" when the actors involved are sub- and non-state actors from different countries.[5]

In the face of continuing multilateral gridlock, some observers have suggested that transnational climate governance (TCG) might hold some promise for mitigating the worst consequences of climate change.[6] Ultimately, however, whether these non-multilateral actions are able to provide a meaningful complement, or even alternative, to a "global deal" depends on whether or not they come to include a sizable number of Chinese actors. Given China's vast—and rising—share of global emissions, no system of TCG that fails to include a substantial portion of Chinese actors can hope to mitigate climate change on a significant scale. Yet, our understanding of Chinese actors' engagement with TCG remains limited, both empirically and theoretically.

On the empirical front, we have little understanding of the prevalence of TCG initiatives within China. Existing studies have examined Chinese involvement with individual TCG schemes, but offer no comprehensive picture of the scale, scope, and robustness of Chinese participation.[7] At present, it is unclear what kinds of TCG initiatives Chinese actors participate in and which actors have been involved. Without answers to these questions, however, our ability to gauge the prospects of TCG within China, and more generally, remains limited.

On the theoretical front, we have little understanding of the factors that shape Chinese participation in TCG. Much of the existing literature on transnational governance has been developed within the context of Western liberal democracies and in economies in which the state plays a less direct role in the economy than in emerging economies like China.[8] Relatively less attention has been given to the politics of transnational governance in other types of states, leaving unanswered the question of how variation in domestic political institutions and state–society relations conditions actors' engagement with transnational governance. Given that domestic political institutions are widely thought to shape participation in global governance generally, this lacuna must be filled if we are to explain adequately existing patterns in transnational climate governance.[9] China presents a crucial case in which to explore these dynamics.

Our chapter attempts to make progress on both fronts. Empirically, the chapter offers the first comprehensive study of China's participation in TCG. In recent years, scholars of transnational governance have pieced together a fuller picture of TCG at the global level, developing databases of TCG initiatives that document the types of initiatives that exist and the different actors involved, as well as other data on issues and various institutional features.[10] For this chapter, we have adapted our own database to examine Chinese actors' engagement in TCG.[11]

Working inductively from these findings, we then tease out the assumptions that existing approaches to TCG make regarding domestic political conditions and we consider how these might vary systematically. Several studies have demonstrated that features of domestic contexts help to explain why some transnational schemes (corporate certification schemes and public–private partnerships) become widely adopted in certain states but not others.[12] Building on and complementing these efforts, we seek to state in more general terms how the emergence and spread of transnational governance can be affected by domestic conditions. Accounting for the context of "fragmented authoritarianism" in which Chinese actors find themselves is, we argue, essential for explaining the extent and character of their participation in different types of initiatives.

Trends in Chinese participation in TCG

Globally, TCG is a recent phenomenon. It emerged rather haltingly in the 1990s, when a few schemes became active around the time of the 1992 Earth Summit, such as Energie Cities (created in 1990) and the E8 (created in 1992). More schemes began to appear around the time of the 1997 Kyoto Protocol. TCG then "took-off."[13] This trend can be clearly seen in Figure 11.1, which is based on a database of 75 TCG initiatives that we have compiled and which confirms the findings of others.[14] Between 1990 and 2000, the number of TCG schemes in the database grew from two to 12 schemes, and then to 75 by 2010.

A large majority of those initiatives (53, or 77 percent) are active in countries in the developing world, and many involve Chinese participants. We find that just under half of all the initiatives in our database (33 in total, or roughly 44 percent) are active in China to some extent. Further, the number of initiatives active in China has grown quite significantly in a short period of time. As Figure 11.1 shows, the first initiative in China appeared in 1999 and the number steadily grew from 2002 onward.

The initiatives in our dataset engage a broad range of activities, including information sharing and networking (IN), standards and commitments (SC), financing-related activities (F); and operational

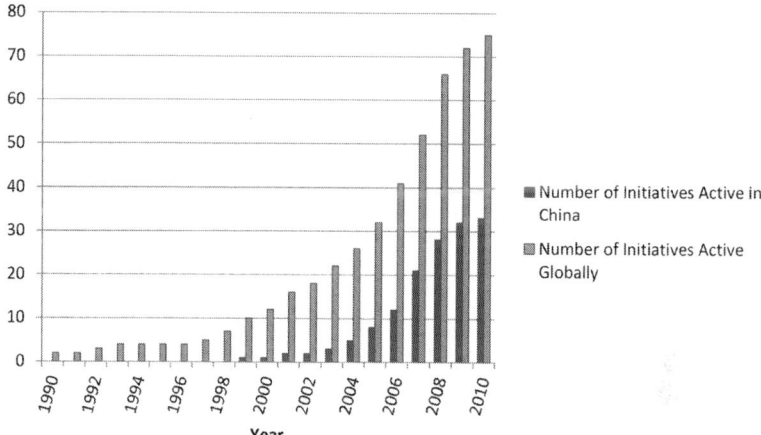

Figure 11.1 Cumulative number of initiatives in China vs. globally (1990–2010)
Source: Database developed by the authors. For details, see "Coding the Transnational Climate Governance Database," http://link.springer.com/article/10.1007/s11558-013-9174-0.

activities (O) (see Figure 11.2).[15] SC schemes are those primarily involved in coding and implementing specific rules intended to reduce emissions by specifying, certifying, and monitoring global best practices. IN schemes are those designed to build capacity by sharing knowledge, experiences, and information, or which record emissions and commitments. O activities are those that perform governance services or provide collective goods, such as facilitating markets, supporting research and development, or helping to initiate other transnational partnerships. Finally, F initiatives are a specific class of operational schemes that help to facilitate, direct, and provide funding to climate change-related projects and programs.

All of these kinds of TCG schemes are active in China to some extent. SC schemes are dominant overall (46 percent of the total in 2010). They are followed in order of importance by IN, O, and F schemes, with shares of 28, 16, and 10 percent, respectively. IN schemes were the first to appear in China, with the earliest becoming active in 2001. The first financing scheme (the World Bank's Prototype Carbon Fund—PCF) only appeared in 2005, when the first PCF-funded projects in China started, five years after the first financing initiative appears in our global dataset. The number of SC schemes grew four-fold in 2007, quite late in our global dataset, and well after the initial increase in the total Chinese growth rate in 2004.

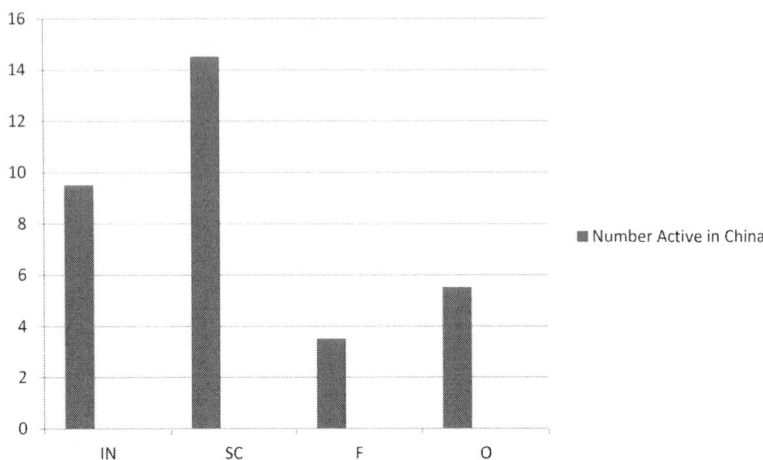

Figure 11.2 Initiatives active in China by initiative type

Source: Kenneth Abbott, "The Transnational Regime Complex for Climate Change," *Environment and Planning C: Government and Policy* 30, no. 4 (2012): 571–590.

The emerging pattern of schemes (Figure 11.3) shows that 2007 stands out as a unique year in the China dataset. This year saw not only the single largest increase in the number of SC schemes, but also the largest increase in the number of IN schemes. Similarly, 2006 saw the largest single increase in the number of O schemes. Together, these events suggest that the three-year period from 2005–2007 was a crucial one for the growth of TCG in China, beginning with the first financing initiative and ending with the largest year of growth in SC schemes. Since then the growth rate has tapered off in China and the rest of the world as well, although this is likely to be a statistical artifact.

One of the most interesting trends to emerge from our analysis is the difference between China and the rest of the world in terms of the kinds of actors "targeted" by TCG schemes (see Figure 11.4). In our global database businesses are the largest category of target participant, followed by local governments, carbon market participants, governmental/ sub-national governmental units, and consumers, respectively. In China, on the other hand, there is a noticeable decrease in the share of businesses and local governments. Carbon market participants, by contrast, comprise a much larger share of the total in China relative to the global database—jumping from third to first place—as do governmental/ sub-national governmental units.

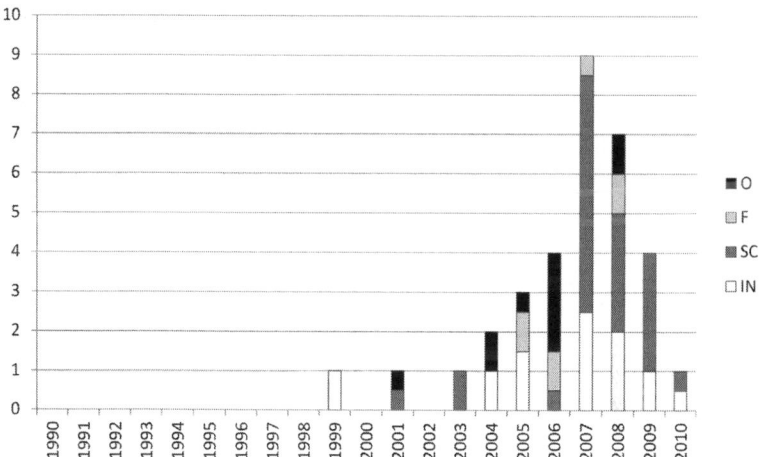

Figure 11.3 Kinds of initiatives active in China by date first active (1990–2010)

Source: Database developed by the authors. For details, see "Coding the Transnational Climate Governance Database," http://link.springer.com/article/ 10.1007/s11558-013-9174-0.

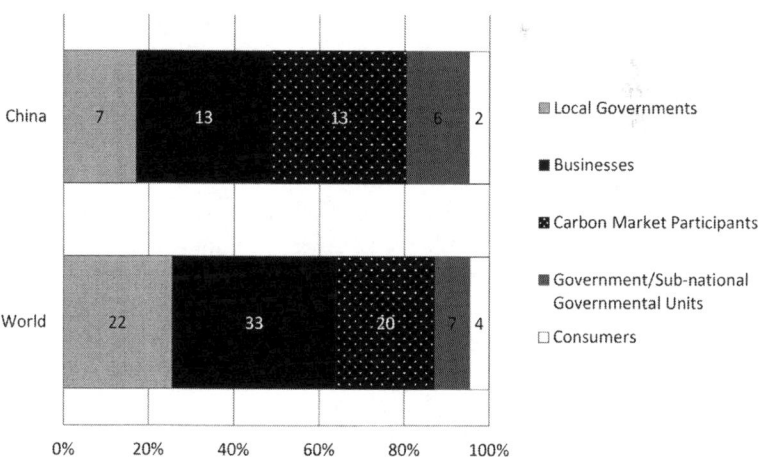

Figure 11.4 Participants targeted by Transnational Climate Governance (TCG) schemes in China vs. globally

Source: Database developed by the authors. For details, see "Coding the Transnational Climate Governance Database," http://link.springer.com/article/ 10.1007/s11558-013-9174-0.

Participation in TCG has therefore grown rapidly in China, as Chinese actors participate in a large number of TCG schemes. However, when we peek below the surface of this pattern Chinese participation generally remains shallow and uneven. Carbon markets are by far the most successful area. Voluntary and compliance carbon markets have expanded significantly since 2005. The credits traded on the European Emissions Trading Scheme were worth some US$120 billion in 2010 and primary credits generated through the United Nations Framework Convention on Climate Change's (UNFCCC) Clean Development Mechanism (CDM) were worth around $1.5 billion. Voluntary carbon offset markets, though they had been strongly affected by the 2008–2009 economic downturn, came in at $1.2 billion. In each of these markets China occupies a dominant position. By the end of 2014, China was the largest source of certified emissions credits for the CDM, accounting for 60 percent of the total Certified Emission Reductions (CERs) issued, and 49 percent of all projects registered.[16] China was also a significant source of the CDM credits used under the EU Emissions Trading System (EU-ETS) (since EU-ETS began accepting CDM-certified credits, although the EU has since restricted eligible CDM credits to those from least developed countries). China is less dominant in voluntary carbon offset markets yet still plays a major role, and there is evidence of a nascent voluntary market emerging in China as well, largely growing in response to the new pilot emissions trading schemes that have appeared and the National Development and Reform Commission's (NDRC) evolving policies on carbon offsetting.[17]

Carbon offset standards have grown in step as an essential dimension of such markets. In the case of compliance markets, the adoption of voluntary carbon standards such as the Gold Standard generally has a positive effect upon the price of carbon credits. Gold Standard-certified carbon credits are sold at a premium of 5 to 25 percent over basic compliance credits, dependent upon project type, location, and characteristics of the sale.[18] In the case of voluntary carbon markets, offset standards and auditors play an even more important constitutive role by providing credible information to buyers about the quality of voluntary offsets and by establishing procedures for quantifying and, ultimately, pricing the emissions saved. Different carbon offset standards also allow buyers to purchase credits with additional "co-benefits," which can also favorably affect their price. As China has become more involved in each of these markets as a producer of both compliance and voluntary emissions credits, it has turned into a major adopter of carbon offset standards. In 2012, around 27 percent of the voluntary carbon offset projects certified by the Verified Carbon Standard and 16 percent of those certified by the Gold Standard—two of the most prominent offset standards—were located in China (see Figure 11.5). China ranked as the second most significant user of both standards, behind only India and Turkey. Its participation in this important area of TCG is therefore significant.

By contrast, transnational municipal networks and transnational corporate governance schemes, which are both central facets of TCG globally, have encountered major challenges in China. Consider first the role of local governments. Transnational municipal networks are a major area of TCG worldwide, and, as our database shows, 17 percent of the TCG initiatives active in China in 2012 target local governments as participants.[19] However, this figure was much lower than the world average. The experience of ICLEI (Local Governments for Sustainability, previously International Council for Local Environmental Initiatives), the oldest sustainability network of local governments, is exemplary. Its Cities for Climate Protection program has had considerable success over the years, particularly in Australia and the United States.[20] It has made numerous inroads across the developing world as well. However, while it is nominally active in China, ICLEI recorded only one Chinese member (Shenyang) in 2012, a rate of participation far below many other large developing countries.[21] In

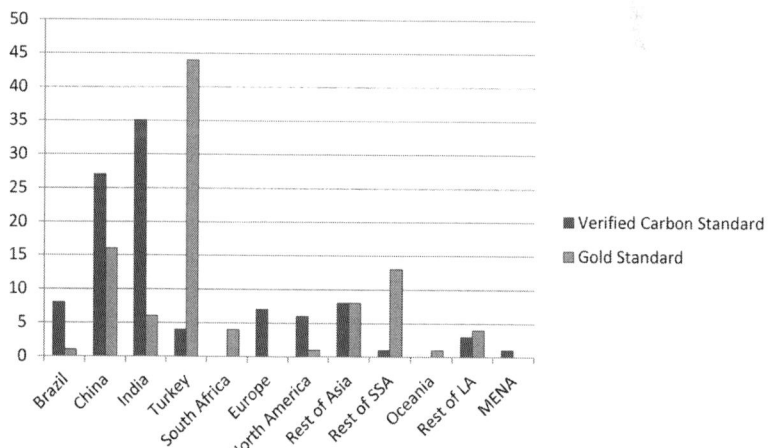

Figure 11.5 Locations of projects using voluntary offset standards, share of total in 2012

Source: Database developed by the authors. For details, see "Coding the Transnational Climate Governance Database," http://link.springer.com/article/10.1007/s11558-013-9174-0.

comparison, there were 20 members in Brazil and 36 in India. Also, while ICLEI had numerous regional offices throughout Asia, there were none for China. Local officials in China had little incentive to join networks like ICLEI because their benefits may have been mismatched with local priorities. Involvement in networks that focus on reducing emissions may not have helped to bolster the position and resources of officials vis-à-vis other groups within the government and civic body that are more concerned with pressing local environmental issues. Other municipal networks with a strong emphasis on air pollution, such as the World Bank's Clean Air Initiative, appeared relatively more successful in China than those focusing exclusively on climate change.

Transnational initiatives focusing on corporate actors—such as the UN Global Compact, Caring for Climate, the (now defunct) Carbon Neutral Network, the Carbon Disclosure Project (CDP), and the Global Reporting Initiative (GRI)—encountered similar difficulties in China. Globally, businesses are the main kind of actor targeted by TCG schemes, but in China, there were fewer schemes targeting businesses and their results are mixed at best. In terms of uptake, the GRI may have been the most successful of the corporate reporting initiatives in China. By 2012, Chinese firms had submitted 278 corporate social responsibility (CSR) reports since the GRI's engagement in China first began in 2007. However, the quality of reporting was highly uneven in China, with only 29 reports above an "A" application level; only 42 have been certified by GRI or a third party. What is more, these raw figures actually overstate the real number of corporations involved, since many of the same firms submitted reports in different years. The majority of the reports that received higher application levels also came from the same small group of firms, largely in the service sector. All these figures are much lower than the world average.[22]

The CDP has also faced challenges in China. In 2011, only 11 of 100 Chinese companies invited to participate opted to answer the CDP's annual questionnaire, far below response levels elsewhere.[23] Those that did were mainly from the banking industry. Trading and distribution companies, and firms from the hotel, restaurant, leisure, metals and mining, financial, construction, chemical, airline, and manufacturing industries uniformly did not respond. The distribution of participants in a recent CDP questionnaire and in the GRI toward service sector firms and away from sectors such as construction, mining, and chemicals is a trend plaguing other carbon reporting initiatives active in China. One effort to develop a common energy and emissions reporting framework specifically for China—the Energy and

Climate Registry—which is based upon the Climate Registry and Greenhouse Gas Protocol, found it difficult to attract participants in heavy industry. Only five Chinese companies were recruited in nearly three years of operation, and they were largely unwilling to publicly disclose their involvement.[24]

The problems confronted by the developers of the Energy and Climate Registry, a voluntary reporting system that companies and cities can use to track and reduce their emissions, are symptomatic of transnational corporate governance schemes in China. Its developers have found that most are unwilling to take part mainly due to concerns about having to divulge sensitive technical data about production processes and business practices that may give an edge to competitors, especially when the reporting scheme originated from outside China and was not directly supported by key ministries in the Chinese government.[25] Many companies also reported that they were waiting to see what rules would be made mandatory by the government before agreeing to voluntary disclosure.[26] A more general issue was that Chinese businesses often see little value in addressing environmental issues. Except for a few leaders, such as Lenovo and Haier, "beyond compliance" environmental protection has been seen as too burdensome and the value of CSR has not been widely appreciated. In the absence of external pressures or price incentives, such as those driving the adoption of carbon offset standards, Chinese businesses have not been actively involved in TCG.

Finally, Chinese actors have mainly participated in TCG schemes as followers rather than leaders. As of 2012, Chinese actors had been involved in the initiation of only four schemes (the Asia-Pacific Partnership on Clean Development and Climate—APP, Climate Savers, EcoPartnerships, and Methane to Markets). The vast majority of TCG schemes active in China were therefore foreign in origin. In all cases except one (Climate Savers, which included Lenovo as an initiating member), the initiating actor was the Chinese central government.

This last point demonstrates a key finding of our study: China's domestic political structures appear fundamentally to condition the scope and nature of sub- and non-state actors' participation in TCG. Local government officials and private corporations in China are reluctant to join initiatives without knowing how such actions will fit with existing or anticipated governmental regulations. There is little willingness to take initiative without government approval, and other more common drivers of participation are rather limited in their effects, particularly given the government's restrictions on civil society activities. The area in which Chinese participation in TCG is most robust—carbon markets—is, not coincidentally, an officially sanctioned program that is actively orchestrated by the NDRC and its provincial branches.[27] NDRC officials have also been eager to develop expertise in carbon trading to support China's experiments with city- and province-level emissions trading schemes. In sum, while transnational governance is usually seen as a "bottom-up" phenomenon, in China it often takes a government-led form.

Transnational governance and domestic political factors—revised expectations

Domestic politics clearly affect participation in transnational governance.[28] Bartley, a contributor to this volume, has shown how the nature of property rights and government dependence on industry affected the implementation of corporate certification schemes for forestry and apparel in Indonesia, strongly reducing the efficacy of transnational governance in these sectors.[29] The legacy of industrial policy, likewise, impacted the implementation of the Forest Stewardship Council and Responsible Care in Brazil and Argentina.[30] Pro-environmental ministries have also been shown to encourage greater participation in transnational governance, showing that bureaucratic politics can play a role as well.[31]

There are also some studies suggesting that similar dynamics operate in China. Certification schemes such as ISO 14001, an environmental management system standard, have been the most thoroughly explored.[32] Most existing work has focused on firms, which have been seen as under-participating in such voluntary programs.[33] Two chief factors are emphasized to explain low participation: the weakness of civil society under China's authoritarian system and the lack of internalized environmental values within Chinese firms, their primary customers, and investors. Yet there are reasons to think that, while true, these arguments are too simple.

First is the "weak civil society" argument. In their examination of the participation of Pacific Rim companies in three transnational governance initiatives (the United Nations Global Compact, the Free Burma Campaign, and ISO 14001), Drezner and Lu conjecture that closed regimes, in which civil society is less influential, will see less firm participation in voluntary programs, since adoption of standards often depends on local advocacy.[34] This is certainly logical, and the available evidence suggests it is often true. However, the Chinese authoritarian system's chilling effect on civil society and transnational governance is not absolute, especially not in the realm of environmental politics. The

Beijing-based Friends of Nature, founded in 1994, is widely considered China's first environmental nongovernmental organization (NGO). By 2004, the State Environmental Protection Agency estimated that some 2,000 NGOs existed. Today the figure is more than twice as large again.[35] There is no doubt that the last 15 years have seen the emergence of a significant Chinese environmental movement.[36]

Chinese environmental NGOs often prefer subtle tactics—including research, information sharing, public education, behind-the-scenes lobbying, and lawsuits—over more aggressive campaigning.[37] Moreover, foreign environmental groups are highly active in Chinese politics, and have formed deep organizational and operational partnerships with local NGOs. As a result, Chinese environmental politics have been relatively dynamic, even if they have been ultimately bounded by the closed nature of the political system. We should therefore expect domestic and foreign civil society groups to be engaged in the kind of lobbying, corporate outreach, and local-level activism that has been seen as a driver of transnational governance elsewhere. Indeed, TCG may be a particularly attractive strategy for NGOs precisely because of the constraints on more confrontational approaches.

The next issue is the "environmental values" question. Scholars frequently contend that Chinese corporations have internalized few environmental or "green" values, and face no pressure from domestic customers (who are not willing to spend more for greener products) or investors (who are often state-run banks), but this argument discounts some important nuances. Survey data consistently show that environmental issues are important for much of the Chinese public, especially in urban areas, although it is true that this has yet to translate into a significant willingness to engage in consumer activism. Although socially responsible investment is minimal, some transnational governance programs, such as ISO 14001, are widespread in China.[38] This participation has, so far, largely been driven by the need for Chinese firms to market to foreign companies that demand higher environmental standards (the "California effect") and by the diffusion of standards from foreign firms to their Chinese subsidiaries.[39] Without these incentives, Chinese companies are seen as unlikely to join voluntary regulatory programs.[40]

A weak civil society and limited market demand may account for the low participation of Chinese actors in TCG, but it does not sufficiently explain the patterns of Chinese participation that we do observe. Moreover, since the arguments are directed mainly at TCG involving firms, they may not apply to other forms of TCG, such as transgovernmental networks or carbon markets. Explaining uneven patterns of

Chinese participation in different forms of transnational governance therefore requires attention to other aspects of Chinese domestic politics and state–society relations.

We argue that it is most useful to view transnational climate politics in China through the prism of "fragmented authoritarianism," which sees politics under the nominally centralized and authoritarian Chinese state as more pluralist than official institutions and popular perceptions suggest. The original concept was largely limited to explaining intra-bureaucratic conflicts.[41] More recently, however, Mertha has proposed that an ever-wider group of actors within China, including the media and NGOs, now possesses unprecedented access to the policymaking process, as do commercial interests.[42] Indeed, existing work on the domestic politics of climate change in China paints a picture of Chinese politics at their most pluralist.

Consider the intra-governmental divisions: different units of the bureaucracy possess distinct policy goals, which inevitably come into conflict. The functional differentiation of China's ministries and sub-ministerial agencies make them accountable to different stakeholders, engender differing worldviews, and make an individual bureaucrat's success and chances for promotion linked to different—at times, incompatible—policy outcomes. China's national climate policies are an excellent demonstration of this phenomenon. Climate change was initially considered a scientific issue and responsibility for it was first given to the politically weak China Meteorological Administration (CMA), an administrative unit under the State Council. However, as the issue emerged on the international agenda, the Ministry of Foreign Affairs (MOFA) began to take a dominant role in outlining climate policy. Though nominally under control of a committee representing four units of the bureaucracy, the MOFA easily dominated the other more scientific bodies. However, as the issue became more connected to China's domestic political priorities at the end of the 1990s and early 2000s, several reorganizations occurred, the effect of which was to increase vastly the political salience of climate policy and put it under the control of the NDRC, the bureaucratic entity with broad responsibility for economic governance and the single most influential agency in domestic policymaking. The MOFA, Ministry of Environmental Protection, CMA, and the Ministry of Science and Technology all act as vice-chairs of the inter-ministerial coordinating body, each bringing distinctive priorities. The result is an institutionalized set of competing interests over Chinese climate policy, with economic development interests holding the dominant position.[43] The result of this bargaining is a unified policy position that is generally accepted across the central government, even if it does not reflect a consensus position.[44]

The second major axis of contestation within the Chinese state is between the central government, the provinces, and local authorities. Because implementation must ultimately occur at the local level and Beijing possesses only limited resources to monitor and enforce implementation, provinces and more local authorities possess significant de facto power to veto centrally determined policies. Again, this dynamic is particularly pronounced in the environmental realm.[45]

In addition, actors outside the government have been increasingly vociferous, as discussed above. Fragmentation within the Chinese state creates greater "space" for contestation outside it. A non-state interest group with no allies inside the state is unlikely to be seen as a legitimate actor in Chinese politics, but once an interest group can align with components of the Chinese state, that group's standing is considerably enhanced. The political space for contestation inside government and without is thus particularly large for issues like climate change, where the interests of dominant groups are split. These opportunities apply to foreign groups as well, which is how foreign NGOs can serve as a major impetus behind Chinese climate policy. Scientific epistemic communities, Schroeder argues, played a key role in this process, transmitting both knowledge about climate change and norms regarding how China might respond to Chinese colleagues in government-backed research institutes and in the relevant ministries. These officials and ministries then become the leading advocates for pro-climate policies within the Chinese government. While international NGOs have been part of this process, they have relied less on the "naming and shaming" tactics common in other areas (such as human rights), and opted instead for informal lobbying and positive incentives such as awards.[46] Linkages between foreign NGOs, local NGOs, and pro-climate officials in the national government can be quite close, creating effective transnational networks for climate advocacy.[47] At the same time, Zhang Haibin argues that the role of foreign NGOs is often overstated, with analysts mistaking access to policymakers for influence over them.[48]

We argue that a fragmented authoritarianism perspective suggests a series of modifications to the usual pathways through which TCG is created that have been identified by scholars. The fragmented nature of climate politics in China creates possibilities for TCG even as it conditions the form of TCG we should expect. Most theories of transnational governance ascribe to sub- and non-state actors a significant degree of political agency. Two assumptions lie at the core of this view. First, it assumes that sub- and non-state actors have independent preferences over policy. Yet when sub-national governments or bureaucratic actors are mere extensions of or are heavily influenced by a national government, they cannot be understood to hold meaningfully independent preferences. We should therefore expect less transnational governance in centrally controlled polities, in polities where market actors are dominated by the state, and in polities with weak civil societies. Second, the bottom-up mechanism assumes that sub- and non-state actors seek to realize their preferences through political activity outside lobbying the national government (such as by "naming and shaming" polluting corporations to improve their behavior, creating certification schemes, and taking unilateral action at the local level). This strategy requires capacity in terms of material resources and expertise to engage in political contestation, a political context in which such actions are accepted as legitimate with guaranteed rights to organize and exercise voice, and constitutional or de facto authority over local policy choices. All else being equal, we should therefore expect more engagement in transnational governance when sub- and non-state actors are relatively autonomous and when they possess and are able to use political resources with which to pursue their objectives.

In China, then, two important modifications to the bottom-up mechanisms may be required. First, a fragmented authoritarianism perspective suggests that we may need to re-think the nature of the actors who engage in bottom-up climate politics. The existing literature sees private firms, NGOs, and ambitious local governments as the primary creators of TCG. However, in a political system like China's, in which many meaningful policy contests are resolved within the state-party apparatus, we can expect significant agency to lie with governmental actors, especially those at the national level. Even when private interests instigate TCG, they are likely to desire governmental support to increase their legitimacy, meaning that partnered governance arrangements will be relatively more common than purely private ones. Second, when the firms with the most capacity to affect climate change are state-owned, we should also expect intra-state bargaining, not private–private bargaining, to determine when actors are likely to participate in TCG initiatives. While the literature has shown that private companies linked to export markets and foreign direct investment have been quick to adopt transnational governance, we should not immediately expect similar behavior from electricity utilities, construction firms, or the like. Naming and shaming will have little impact on state monopolies. Voluntary corporate programs will therefore likely receive little participation from Chinese actors.

This is why Chinese TCG is driven more strongly by government orchestration.[49] In this case, the capacities of sub- and non-state actors to affect governance can be thought of as a tool the state would like to employ, but one it cannot simply order these actors to deploy. Again, there is a core assumption of political agency. However, there is also an assumption that the state lacks absolute authority to order the changes it seeks (or, more plausibly, lacks the legitimacy or political capital to attempt such "command and control" strategies) and must therefore rely on a gentler strategy. As we have discussed elsewhere, orchestration offers a potentially powerful mechanism for ministries and local governments when they cannot realize their goals through the normal national policymaking process.[50] We should therefore expect the more environmentally oriented parts of the Chinese bureaucracy to attempt to bring sub- and non-state actors into TCG via this mechanism.

In sum, then, we would expect the autonomy, capacity, and social context of actors—key components of the mechanisms through which TCG is created—to be strongly conditioned by the nature of the state. Prima facie, these considerations might lead us to expect China's centralized, authoritarian government and the large role the state plays in the economy to significantly curtail Chinese sub- and non-state actors' engagement in TCG. In fact, we argue that domestic conditions in China are in some ways more favorable to TCG than may be expected, and that participation in TCG can even be quite strong when goals of TCG initiatives align with those of components of the state.

Conclusion

Chinese actors are important players in TCG. The nature of Chinese actors' participation, however, differs in some respects from conventional theoretical expectations. At the aggregate level, the composition of schemes active in China differs from global patterns. In China, entrepreneurial programs are less common, local governments have participated less in TCG than their counterparts, the central government has participated to a greater extent in TCG than elsewhere, and, largely as a result, carbon markets have been more important in China than elsewhere.

These differences derive from the domestic political context in which Chinese sub- and non-state actors operate. Though the centralized, authoritarian political system and state-led economy dampen the agency of many potential TCG creators and actors, the relative pluralism that characterizes Chinese climate politics also increases the possibility and utility of TCG as a strategy. It is often the incentives and opportunity structures the state creates that open up as a result of its fragmented nature, which determines the shape of TCG participation. As we have seen, TCG initiatives focusing on local governments have faced considerable challenges. Local officials have so far had little incentive to join networks like ICLEI, which over their 20 years of operation have acquired thousands of members elsewhere throughout the world. Corporate reporting initiatives, which have been an important form of governance in the domain of climate change, have been relatively less successful in China with strategic industries and when initiatives threaten to disclose sensitive information. Yet, where the TCG initiatives complement activities engaged in by the state, as with various carbon market initiatives, participation can be quite considerable.

These findings cast doubt on the hopes of TCG's more enthusiastic supporters that measures like corporate codes of conduct or city-level programs will have a large impact on China's growing emissions. Some of the kinds of initiatives that have been most common in the field of TCG, and highly effective in more liberal political contexts, face significant challenges without support from key players within the Chinese government. A major part of the problem is that the goals of some TCG schemes may have been mismatched with local priorities. Greater effort may therefore be needed in the future in order to create new schemes and adapt existing ones to make them more acceptable within the Chinese context, and to emphasize their local co-benefits. However, shifts within the Chinese state itself on the issue of climate change may also augur well for some initiatives, especially those that focus on municipalities. As we noted above, changes in local officials' incentives as a result of the growing importance of local emissions and energy efficiency targets may widen the scope for such schemes in the future. The carbon trading schemes currently being developed are also likely to raise further the incentives for participation. Thus, while the domestic context in China has so far had, on balance, a dampening effect upon Chinese involvement in TCG, changes in this context—and the goals of the state, in particular—may make TCG more important in the future.

Notes

1 Thomas Hale and Charles Roger, "Orchestration and Transnational Climate Governance," *Review of International Organizations* 9, no. 1 (2014): 59–82.

2 PBL Netherlands Environmental Assessment Agency, Institute for Environment and Sustainability (IES) of the European Commission's Joint Research Centre (JRC), "Trends in Global CO2 Emissions: 2013 Report," http://edgar.jrc.ec.europa.eu/news_docs/pbl-2013-trends-in-global-co2-emissions-2013-report-1148.pdf.

3 Björn Conrad, "Bureaucratic Land Rush: China's Administrative Battles in the Arena of Climate Change Policy," *Harvard Asia Quarterly* 12, no. 1 (2010): 52–64; David Held, Charles Roger, and Eva-Maria Nag, "Editors' Introduction: Climate Governance in the Developing World," in *Climate Governance in the Developing World*, ed. David Held, Charles Roger, and Eva-Maria Nag (Cambridge: Polity Press, 2013), 1–28.

4 Note that this chapter was largely written in 2012, well before many important subsequent developments associated with Chinese domestic climate policymaking and the new international context that has been created by the Paris Agreement. Much research in the field, including our own, has also subsequently extended and superseded the theoretical claims that are made here.

5 Karin Backstrand, "Accountability of Networked Climate Governance: The Rise of Transnational Climate Partnerships," Amsterdam Conference on Earth System Governance (2007); Philipp Pattberg and Johannes Stripple, "Beyond the Public and Private Divide: Remapping Transnational Climate Governance in the 21st Century," *International Environmental Agreements: Politics, Law and Economics* 8, no. 4 (2008): 367–388; Noah Toly, "Transnational Municipal Networks and Climate Politics: From Global Governance to Global Politics," *Globalizations* 5, no. 3 (2008): 341–356; Liliana Andonova et al., "Transnational Climate Governance," *Global Environmental Politics* 9, no. 2 (2009): 52–73; Harriet Bulkeley, Liliana B. Andonova, Michele M. Betsill, Daniel Compagnon, Thomas Hale, Matthew J. Hoffmann, Peter Newell, Matthew Paterson, Charles Roger, and Stacy D. VanDeveer, *Transnational Climate Change Governance* (Cambridge: Cambridge University Press, 2014); Hale and Roger, "Orchestration and Transnational Climate Governance"; and Thomas Hale and David Held, *Handbook of Transnational Governance: Institutions and Innovations* (Cambridge: Polity, 2011), 12, 15.

6 Global Governance Fund Climate Change Working Group, *Beyond a Global Deal: A UN+ Approach to Climate Governance*, April 2011; Thomas Hale, "A Climate Coalition of the Willing," *The Washington Quarterly* 34, no. 1 (2011): 89–101.

7 Zhang Zhongxiang, "The World Bank's Prototype Carbon Fund and China," *East-West Center Working Papers, Environmental Change, Vulnerability and Governance Series* 60 (2004); Gørild Heggelund and Inga Fritzen Buan, "China in the Asia–Pacific Partnership: Consequences for UN Climate Change Mitigation Efforts," *International Environmental Agreements* 9, no. 3 (2009): 301–317.

8 Indeed, most transnational governance, in the climate realm and beyond, originates in North America and Europe. Perhaps for this reason, Chinese scholars have yet to widely embrace the topic of transnational governance. Chinese language scholarship on the subject is small compared to other International Relations topics, and existing literature often seems to conflate global governance with transnational governance.

9 Helen Milner, *Interests, Institutions, and Information* (Princeton, N.J.: Princeton University Press, 1997).

10 Bulkeley et al., *Transnational Climate Change Governance*; Mathew Hoffmann, *Climate Governance at the Crossroads: Experimenting with a Global Response after Kyoto* (Oxford: Oxford University Press, 2011); and Hale and Roger, "Orchestration and Transnational Climate Governance."

11 For a more detailed discussion of our database, see Charles Roger, Thomas Hale, and Liliana Andonova, "The Comparative Politics of Transnational Climate Governance," *International Interactions* 43, no. 1 (2017), 1–25; and Liliana Andonova, Thomas Hale, and Charles Roger, "National Policy and Transnational Governance of Climate Change: Substitutes or Complements?" *International Studies Quarterly* (forthcoming).

12 Ralph Espach, *Private Environmental Regimes in Developing Countries: Globally Sown, Locally Grown* (New York: Palgrave Macmillan, 2009); Tim Bartley, "Transnational Private Regulation in Practice: The Limits of Forest and Labor Standards Certification in Indonesia," *Business and Politics* 12, no. 3 (2010): 1–34; and Liliana Andonova, "Boomerangs to Partnerships? Explaining State Participation in Transnational Partnerships for Sustainability," *Comparative Political Studies* 47, no. 3 (2014): 481–515.

13 Hoffmann, *Climate Governance at the Crossroads.*

14 Despite our best efforts to conduct a comprehensive search, the database is only indicative. It captures only a part of the total universe of TCG initiatives. Successful TCG schemes are likely to be overrepresented in the sample, since they are likely to last longer and attract more attention. Initiatives involving less prominent actors, or actors on the periphery of central climate governance networks, are likely to be underrepresented. This will possibly lead to a bias in the sample toward initiatives created by actors in the global North. Finally, the sample will likely be biased toward initiatives that have been studied and cited before in academic literature, resulting in some degree of path dependence in the selection of cases. Nevertheless, we can be fairly confident that the database selects the cases of transnational governance that weigh most heavily on the politics of climate change even if the actual number of schemes is much larger.

15 Kenneth Abbott, "The Transnational Regime Complex for Climate Change," *Environment and Planning C: Government and Policy* 30, no. 4 (2012): 571–590.

16 United Nations Framework Convention on Climate Change Clean Development Mechanism (CDM) Project Activities Page, "Distribution of CERs Issued by Host Party," http://cdm.unfccc.int/Statistics/Public/files/201409/cers_iss_byHost.pdf; United Nations Framework Convention on Climate Change Clean Development Mechanism (CDM) Project Activities Page, "Distribution of Registered Projects by Host Party," http://cdm.unfccc.int/Statistics/Public/files/201409/proj_reg_byHost.pdf.

17 For example, China Beijing Environmental Exchange (CBEEX) held a sale in June 2011 for 210,000 tons of carbon to an "honor roll" of customers including Baidu, Air China, Merchants Bank, and China Everbright Bank. Though largely symbolic (the amount of credits was equivalent to 0.002 percent of China's emission that year), the sale represented an important step toward testing and building a domestic carbon market.

18 Anja Kollmuss, Helge Zink, and Clifford Polycarp, *Making Sense of the Voluntary Carbon Market: A Comparison of Carbon Offset Standards* (Germany: World Wildlife Fund, 2008).
19 Michele Betsill and Harriet Bulkeley, "Cities and the Multilevel Governance of Climate Change," *Global Governance* 12, no. 2 (2006): 141–159.
20 Betsill and Bulkeley, "Cities and the Multilevel Governance of Climate Change."
21 The City of Shenyang is one of the largest industrial centers in China and has been greatly affected by local and regional air pollution. As a result, it has been at the forefront of municipal efforts to improve air quality in China, for instance, by administering a levy on boilers that effectively serves as a local carbon tax. In attempting to tackle local air pollution, city officials have found that such measures can also serve to mitigate carbon emissions. See ICLEI, Local Government Implementation of Climate Protection: Case Studies (1997), www.iclei.org/index.php?id=1476.
22 Global Reporting Initiative 2010, *Global Sustainability Reporting Statistics*, www.globalreporting.org/resourcelibrary/GRI-Reporting-Stats-2010.pdf.
23 Carbon Disclosure Project 2011a, *Carbon Disclosure Project, Report 2011, China 100 Executive Summary*, www.cdproject.net/CDPResults/CDP-2011-Chi na-Report-Exec-Summary.pdf; *CDP Cities 2011—Global Report on C40 Cities*, http://c40citieslive.squarespace.com/storage/CDP%20Cities%202011 %20Global%20Report.pdf; and Eun-Hee Kim and Thomas Lyon, "Carbon Disclosure Project," in *Handbook of Transnational Governance: Institutions and Innovations*, ed. Thomas Hale and David Held (Malden, Mass.: Polity Press, 2011), 212–218.
24 Interview with Project Officer, Energy and Climate Registry, Beijing, October 2011.
25 Interview with Innovation Center for Energy and Transport, Beijing, October 2011.
26 Interview with Energy and Climate Registry, Beijing, October 2011.
27 Miriam Schroeder, "The Construction of China's Climate Politics: Transnational NGOs and the Spiral Model of International Relations," *Cambridge Review of International Affairs* 21, no. 4 (2008): 505–525.
28 A study by Prakash and Potoski shows that domestic institutions affect the impact of transnational governance, showing that more stringent domestic environmental laws increased the effectiveness of ISO 14001 on corporate behavior. Aseem Prakash and Matthew Potoski, "Global Private Regimes, Domestic Public Law: ISO 14001 and Pollution Reduction," *Comparative Political Studies* 47, no. 3 (2014): 369–394.
29 Bartley, "Transnational Private Regulation in Practice: The Limits of Forest and Labor Standards Certification in Indonesia."
30 Espach, *Private Environmental Regimes in Developing Countries: Globally Sown, Locally Grown.*
31 Andonova, "Boomerangs to Partnerships?"
32 Petra Christmann and Glen Taylor, "Globalization and the Environment: Determinants of Firm Self-regulation in China," *Journal of International Business Studies* 3, no. 32 (2001): 439–458; Petra Christmann and Glen Taylor, "Firm Self-Regulation through International Certifiable Standards: Determinants of Symbolic versus Substantive Implementation," First Annual

270   *Thomas Hale and Charles Roger*

Conference on Institutional Mechanisms for Industry Self-Regulation, Dartmouth University, New Hampshire (2005).

33 For an overview of this literature see David Graham and Ngaire Woods, "Making Corporate Self-Regulation Effective in Developing Countries," *World Development* 34, no. 5 (2006): 868–883; and Simone Pulver, "Introduction: Developing-Country Firms as Agents of Environmental Sustainability." *Studies in International Comparative Development* 42 (2007): 191–207.

34 Daniel Drezner and Mimi Lu, "How Universal are Club Standards? Emerging Markets and Volunteerism," in *Voluntary Programs: A Club Theory Perspective*, ed. Matthew Potoski and Aseem Prakesh (Cambridge, Mass.: MIT Press, 2009), 181–206. On the Russian case, see Andonova, "Boomerangs to Partnerships?"

35 Guobin Yang, "Environmental NGOs and Institutional Dynamics in China," *The China Quarterly* 181 (2005): 46–66.

36 Jonathan Schwartz, "Environmental NGOs in China: Roles and Limits," *Pacific Affairs* 77, no. 1 (2004): 28–49; Phillip Stalley and Dongning Yang, "An Emerging Environmental Movement in China?" *The China Quarterly* 186 (2006): 333–356.

37 Schwartz, "Environmental NGOs in China: Roles and Limits"; Yang, "Environmental NGOs and Institutional Dynamics in China"; Stalley and Yang, "An Emerging Environmental Movement in China?"; and Shui-Yan Tang and Xueyong Zhan, "Civic Environmental NGOs, Civil Society, and Democratisation in China," *Journal of Development Studies* 44, no. 3 (2008): 425–448.

38 Changxing Di, "ISO 14001: The Severe Challenge for China," in *Growing Pains: Environmental Management in Developing Countries*, ed. Walter Wehrmeyer and Yacob Mulugetta (Sheffield: Greenleaf, 1999), 106–116.

39 David Vogel, *Trading Up: Consumer and Environmental Regulation in a Global Economy* (Cambridge, Mass.: Harvard University Press, 1995); Petra Christmann and Glen Taylor, "Globalization and the Environment: Determinants of Firm Self-regulation in China," *Journal of International Business Studies* 3, no. 32 (2001): 439–458; and Christmann and Taylor, "Firm Self-Regulation through International Certifiable Standards: Determinants of Symbolic versus Substantive Implementation"; Pulver, "Introduction: Developing-Country Firms as Agents of Environmental Sustainability?"

40 Shu Yi Chu and Heike Schroeder, "Private Governance of Climate Change in Hong Kong: An Analysis of Drivers and Barriers to Corporate Action," *Asian Studies Review* 34 (2010): 287–308; Lin-Wen Lin, "Corporate Social Responsibility in China: Window Dressing or Structural Change," *Berkeley Journal of International Law* 28, no. 1 (2010): 64–100.

41 Kenneth Lieberthal and Michel Oksenberg, *Policy Making in China: Leaders, Structures, and Processes* (Princeton, N.J.: Princeton University Press, 1988).

42 Andrew Mertha, "Fragmented Authoritarianism 2.0: Political Pluralization in the Chinese Policy Process," *China Quarterly* 200 (2009): 995–1012; Ka Zeng, *China Foreign Trade Policy: The New Constituencies* (New York: Routledge, 2007); and Scott Kennedy, *The Business of Lobbying in China* (Cambridge, Mass.: Harvard University Press, 2005).

43 Conrad, "Bureaucratic Land Rush: China's Administrative Battles in the Arena of Climate Change Policy"; and Hongyuan Yu, "Global Governance against Global Warming and China's Response," *Chinese Public Affairs Quarterly* 2, no. 4 (2010): 296–313; and David Held, Charles Roger, and Eva-Maria Nag, "A Green Revolution: China's Governance of Energy and Climate Change," in *Climate Governance in the Developing World*, ed. David Held, Charles Roger, and Eva-Maria Nag (Cambridge: Polity Press, 2013), 29–52.

44 Yu interprets this policy coordination as evidence against a fragmented authoritarian model, because the final policy is broadly accepted by the relevant actors, at least at the central level. Here we use the concept somewhat differently, more as a measure of the degree of interest divergence and open contestation present in intra-bureaucratic wrangling. Yu's empirical findings are consistent with this interpretation. Yu, "Global Governance against Global Warming and China's Response."

45 Elizabeth Economy, *The River Runs Black: The Environmental Challenge to China's Future* (Ithaca, NY: Cornell University Press, 2004); Benjamin van Rooij, "Implementation of Chinese Environmental Law: Regular Enforcement and Political Campaigns," *Development and Change* 37, no. 1 (2006): 57–74; and Gregory Fuller, "Economic Warlords: How de Facto Federalism Inhibits China's Compliance with International Trade Law and Jeopardizes Global Environmental Initiatives," *Tennessee Law Review* 75 (2007): 545–576. Kostka and Hobbs have traced the implementation of climate and energy efficiency policies mandated by the 11th Five-Year Plan in Shanxi province. They show how the provincial leaders, eager to achieve stringent energy-saving goals in order to please Beijing, bundled unpopular climate change policies together with generous incentives for local interest groups (such as favorable land-use allocations) to "log-roll"—the authors make explicit the analogy to pluralist political dynamics—interest groups into supporting climate policies. See Genia Kostka and William Hobbs, "Local Energy Efficiency Policy Implementation in China: Bridging the Gap between National Priorities and Local Interests," *The China Quarterly* 211 (2012): 765–785.

46 Schroeder, "The Construction of China's Climate Politics: Transnational NGOs and the Spiral Model of International Relations."

47 In this way, climate advocacy has organized along similar lines as business lobbying. See Scott Kennedy, "Transnational Political Alliances: An Exploration with Evidence from China," *Business and Society* 46, no. 2 (2007): 174–200.

48 Interview with Zhang Haibin, School of International Studies, Peking University, Beijing, October 2011.

49 Kenneth W. Abbott and Duncan Snidal, "Strengthening International Regulation through Transnational Governance: Overcoming the Orchestration Deficit," *Vanderbilt Journal of Transnational Law* 42 (2009): 501–578; Hale and Roger, "Orchestration and Transnational Climate Governance."

50 Hale and Roger, "Orchestration and Transnational Climate Governance."

Index

Page numbers in **bold** refer to tables

1997–1998 Asian financial crisis 73, 75, 143; China 27, 66, 68, 143, 145; ER and China 143, 145, 150; G20: 114; international monetary system 117

2008–2009 financial crisis 185; China 4, 5, 53, 56, 57, 58, 99, 245; developing country 115, 116; food security 184–5, 194; G8: 114, 125, 127; G20: 114–15, 120, 126, 127; global economic governance 4–5; international financial regulation 120, 151; international monetary system 117, 123; RMB 123; 'theory of Chinese responsibility'/ 'China threat theory' 57

Abe, Shinzo 84
ACFTU (All-China Federation of Trade Unions) 232, 246n6
ACTA (Anti-Counterfeiting Trade Agreement) 150
Africa: 2006 Forum on China and African Cooperation Summit 192; Economic Community of West African States 185; food security and China 185, 188–9, 192–4; foreign aid and China 202, 206, 222; GHG and China 160, 175; Tripartite Partnerships for Development in Africa 193; West Africa 185, 194
African Union 192

Agricultural Development Bank of China 205
agriculture 25, 33, 44; agricultural export subsidy 28; agricultural investment 188; FTA, China's strategy 70; FTA, Japan's strategy 74, 75, 76, 79, 80, 81; liberalization 75, 76; SSM 33; tariff 28, 33; *see also* food security and China
AIIB (Asian Infrastructure Investment Bank) 12, 147; China 3, 10, 61, 126, 151, 202, 223–4; Chinese motivations 223; 'lean, clean, and green' multilateral development financing institution 223, 225
AIPPI (International Association for the Protection of Intellectual Property) 150
AmCham (American Chamber of Commerce in China) 93
Annan, Kofi 167
anti-dumping: China 50, 58; Datong, Oak Hill Group/Bluestar 47–8; NME 71; Shenzhen, antidumping warning system 47; WTO 7; WTO and Chinese industry 47–8, 49, 50, 58
Antkiewicz, Agata 69–70
APEC (Asia-Pacific Economic Cooperation) 5, 83
API (active pharmaceutical ingredient) 162, 175

APP (Asian Pacific Partnership on Clean Development and Climate) 259
Argentina 188, 260
Art, Robert 110–11
ASEAN (Association of Southeast Asian Nations) 185; ASEAN+3: 74, 81, 83, 194; ASEAN+6: 74, 82–3; CAFTA 70, 80; FTA, China's strategy 66, **67**, 69, 70–1, 80; FTA, Japan's strategy 73, 81, 82–3; Japan–ASEAN Comprehensive Economic Partnership 74; leadership role in East Asia 82
Asia-Pacific regional integration 65–6, 81–4; China-led regional integration 83; EAC 81–2; RCEP 82, 84; renminbi Trade Settlement Scheme 124; TPP 82, 83–4; trilateral China/Japan/South Korea FTA 81, 83, 84; US 82
Australia 74, 257; FTA, China's strategy 66, **67**, 68, 72, 80
automobile industry 54–5, 70, 137

Bartley, Tim 12, 173, 228–49, 260
Bayer China 171
Bergsten, Fred 31–2, 33, 34, 35, 123
bilateral agreement 2; bilateral aid 161, 206, **207**; rivalry between multilateral and bilateral rule-making 75; WTO and Chinese industry 10, 54; *see also* BIT; FTA
BIT (bilateral investment treaty): DSM 85; FTA/BIT/WTO comparison 85; FTA, Japan's strategy 73, 74, 75–9, 87n38
Bräutigam, Deborah A. 220
Brazil 165, 260
Breslin, Shaun 27, 35
Bretton Woods system 117, 119, 122
BRI (Belt and Road Initiative) 3, 61, 224
BRICS (Brazil, Russia, India, China, South Africa) 147, 152, 163, 185; New Development Bank 126, 147
Bruderle, Rainer 131n49

BSCI (Business Social Compliance Initiative) 228, 232
bureaucratic politics 10, 13, 260, 262, 271n44; GHG and China 11–12, 174–5

CAFTA (China-ASEAN FTA) 70–1, 80
capitalism: global capitalism 4, 37; state capitalism 55
Carbon Neutral Network 258
Caring for Climate 258
Carlyle Group 53–4
CASS (Chinese Academy of Social Sciences) 104
CBO (community-based organization) 171
CCM (country coordinating mechanism) 171
CCP (Chinese Communist Party) 19, 25, 59–60; CSR 233; IPR 136
CDC (Center for Disease Control and Prevention, China/US) 163, 166, 168
CDP (Carbon Disclosure Project) 258
CEPEA (Comprehensive Economic Partnership in East Asia) 82
CFDA (China Food & Drug Administration) 168, 174
Chan, Margaret 163–4
Chen Deming 58, 95
Cheng, Shuaihua: *From Rule Takers to Rule Makers* xvii
Chile 66, **67**, 68, 69, 71–2, 73
China: 1978 Reform 4, 24; 1989 Tiananmen Square demonstrations 25, 137; 'China threat' 57, 68, 83; developed country status 28; developing country status 27–8, 36, 72; economic growth 36, 68, 148, 229, 245; emergent leadership 2–3, 5, 116; industrialization 25; isolation 24; a major power 57; market-economy reform 24–6, 36, 55, 205; 'One China' policy 193; open-door policy 45, 68, 135; open-door policy and WTO accession 45, 68, 98; peaceful development 68; pluralism 52, 126,

262, 271n45; responsible
stakeholder/power 6, 14, 43, 44–5,
56, 58; the world's second largest
economy 72, 120, 127, 160; the
world's second largest importer 50;
the world's second largest trading
nation 53; *see also* China as
authoritarian state; state
China Association of Foreign-Invested
Enterprises 48
China as authoritarian state 6, 9,
103–104, 173, 175, 193; fragmented authoritarianism 252,
262–4, 266, 271n44; TCG and
China 260–1, 264
China Development Bank 205
China International Chamber of
Commerce 57
Chu Zhaogen 58
CISAR (China International Search
and Rescue) 174
civil society: weak civil society 13,
259–61; *see also* CSO; NGO
climate change 250; 1997 Kyoto
Protocol 250, 252; governance gap
250; multilateral gridlock 251; *see
also* climate change and China;
TCG
climate change and China, 12–13,
188, 250, 262–3; climate advocacy
263, 271n47; CMA 262;
greenhouse gas emissions 93, 250,
251, 253, 256, 258, 259, 260, 266,
269n21; implementation of climate
and energy efficiency policies 263,
271n45; lobbying 261, 263, 264,
271n47; Ministry of Environmental
Protection 262; MOFA 262;
MOST 262; NDRC 262; NGO
263; water scarcity 187; *see also*
climate change; TCG and China
Climate Savers 259
Clinton, Bill 28
Clinton Foundation 171
CMI (Chiang Mai Initiative) 147, 151
CNCA (Certification and Accreditation
Administration of China) 231, 233
CNTAC (Chinese National Apparel
and Textile Council) 232
Cold War 165, 204, 209

Communist Revolution (1949) 26–7
competition 60; export credits 221;
foreign aid/DAC 12, 203, 212, 213,
216; FTA, Japan's strategy 73, 74,
75; MNC 52; technology
competition 93
consumption: balancing export-led
growth model with domestic demand
245; domestic consumption 25, 26,
132, 141
Copelovitch, Mark 23
Cotton Four 33
countervailing 7, 50, 58, 170
CPPCC (China People's Political
Consultative Conference) 57
CSC9000T (China Social
Compliance 9000 for Textile and
Apparel Industry) 229, 232–3;
ACFTU 232; CNTAC 232;
definition 246n5; limitations 233;
see also factory certification
CSO (civil society organization) 161,
173, 180n58; *see also* civil society;
NGO
CSR (corporate social responsibility)
229, 230, 231; CCP 233; factory
certification and labor standards
231, 241, 243; TCG and China
258, 259
culture 54, 60
currency *see* dollar; ER; international
monetary system; RMB

DAC (Development Assistance
Committee, OECD): 1978 *DAC
Recommendation on Terms and
Conditions of Aid* 211; 2001 Aid
Untying Agreement 215, 216; 2005
DAC Outreach Strategy 218; 2011
'Global Relations Strategy' 219;
2011 Welcome New Partnerships
in Development Cooperation' 219;
aid regime 203, 209; *Busan
Partnership Document* 212, 222;
competition and conflict 12, 203,
212, 213, 216; DAC donors
209–12; development assistance
210; food aid 215; France 214–15;
'Gentlemen's Agreement' 213;
Helsinki Disciplines 213, 216;

Japan 211, 215; ODA 210–12; origins 209–10; South Korea 211; tied aid 12, 161, 213, 214; UK 214; UN aid target 211; untied aid 203, 212–17; US 209–10, 213, 215; *see also* DAC donors/China interaction; foreign aid; foreign aid and China; OECD

DAC donors/China interaction 203, 217–18, *217*, 225; AIIB 223–4, 225; China-DAC Study Group 221–3, 225; compliance with existing DAC rules 203, 217, 218–19, 225; DAC's 'outreach strategy' to China on ODA 218–19, 225; mutual recognition and learning 203, 217, 218, 225; no coordination/competition 203, 217, 218, 219–21; renegotiating export credit rules 219–21, 225; *see also* export credits; foreign aid and China

DDA (Doha Development Agenda) 32, 105; 2001 Doha Ministerial Conference 34; 2008 mini-ministerial meeting 32, 33; China 4, 6, 10, 29, 31–3, 34–5, 36, 59; China's assertiveness 18, 34; deadlock 6, 10, 33, 36–7, 59; FTA 10; G4: 32; G6: 32; G7: 32; India 10, 33, 59; RAMs 34–5, 36; SSM 33–4; US 32, 33; *see also* WTO, Ministerial Conferences

De Gaulle, Charles 117

democracy 196–7; liberal democracy 6, 251

Deng Xiaoping 5, 145, 204, 205; 1978 'Reform and Opening' 135; 1992 Southern Tour 25, 137, 142

developed country: China as developed country 28; DDA 59; FTA 72, 80

development financer 12, 203, 217, 224

developing country 68; 2008–2009 financial crisis 115, 116; China as developing country 27–8, 36, 72; DDA 35, 59; export credits 219–20, 221; FTA, China's strategy 69, 72; G20: 115–16, 119,

125–6; GATT 21; TCG 252, 257; WTO 29, 31, 33

dollar: devaluation 146, 185; 'dollar system' 117, 122, 123, 127, 131n49; ER 134; ER and China 141–2; future of 114, 121–3, 127; nominal RMB/US$ exchange rate 141–2, *142*; *see also* ER and China; international monetary system

DRC (Development Research Center) 104

Drezner, Daniel 260

DSM (Dispute Settlement Mechanism) 85, 91; China 31, 49–50, 60, 149; China, losing WTO cases 54, 55, 56, 58; FTA/BIT 85; IPR and China 11, 133, 152; protectionism 58

e-commerce 7

EAC (East Asian Community) 74, 81–2

EAS (East Asia Summit) 82

EC (European Community) 137–8

The Economist 135, 143–4

EcoPartnerships 259

emerging powers 6, 8, 128, 158, 183

EPA (economic partnership agreement): EPA ratio 75, 87n32; FTA, Japan's strategy 73, 75–9

ER (exchange rate) 7, 9, 132; ambiguous rules 11, 13, 133; flexible ER with minimal government intervention 134; goal 150; IP/ER governance regime differences 133, 134; OECD countries 134; US dollar 134; *see also* ER and China; ERM; international monetary system; RMB

ER and China 11, 132, 141–8; 1978–1994: 142–3, 150; 1995–2005: 143–5; 1997–1998 Asian financial crisis 143, 145, 150; 2005–2010: 145–6; 2010–2015: 146–8; assertive and effective behavior 132, 133, 150–1, 152, 153; China as reformist 133, 153; 'currency manipulation' 132, 144; domestic interest 143–4, 151; four causal factors for Chinese changed behavior 132, 151–2; nominal RMB/US$ exchange rate 141–2, *142*; US dollar 141–2; *see also* ERM; international monetary system; RMB

ERM (exchange rate mechanism) 135, 143, 145, 150; China, dual-track ERM 142; IMF 133; IMF, Article IV 134; regulation benefits 134; *see also* ER; RMB

ETI (Ethical Trading Initiative) 228

EU (European Union) 68, 250; European Commission 100; FTA, Japan's strategy 84; GPA and China 92, 94, 100; WTO and China 10, 27, 30–1, 32, 35, 36–7

EU Chamber of Commerce in China 100

EU-ETS (EU Emissions Trading System) 256

Evenett, Simon 23

Ex-Im Bank (China Export-Import Bank) 205, 220, 221

Excellent Umbrella 238–9

export credits 212–13, 214; competition 221; developing country 219–20, 221; ECA 220; Export Credit Guarantee Facility 210–20; renegotiating export credit rules 219–21, 225; US 220, 221, 225; *see also* DAC donors/China interaction; foreign aid and China

exportation: agricultural export subsidy 28; balancing export-led growth model with domestic demand 245; China as the world's largest exporter 50, 72; Chinese pharmaceuticals 161–2, 175; export dependence 9, 25, 26; WTO's export controls on high-technology products 10, 51, 54–5, 61

factory certification 12, 228–49; certification/factory's working conditions relationship 12, 238, 239–40, 243; certification to meet customers' demands 238–9; China and global governance 230, 244–5,

246; CSR 231, 241, 243; differences between certified and non-certified factories 234, 236, 239–43; fraud and lax auditing 233–5, 239, 243–4, 248n42; growth of 233; HR management 240–1, *242*, 243; limited power of certification 12, 230, 243; medical clinic 241, *242*, 243; private forms of global governance 230, 243, 244–5; process and costs 237; state-centric approach 13, 173; third-party certification 229; wage rate 235, 238, 239, 245; worker committee/union 234–5, 237; working hours 233–4, 235–6, 238, 239, 244; *see also* CSC9000T; ICTI; labor rights; labor standards in China; SA8000 standard; SAI; WRAP

Fan, He: 'The United States, China and Global Governance ...' xvii

FAO (UN Food and Agriculture Organization) 184, 195; CFS 185, 195; South–South Cooperation 189

FCTC (Framework Convention on Tobacco Control) 164, 165, 172, 174

FDA (Food & Drug Administration) 168

FDI (foreign direct investment) 27, 28, 68, 73, 75, 138

Feng Huiyun 111

Fidler, David 158

Financial Stability Board 125

Financial Stability Forum 125

Financial Times 124–5, 216–17

Fitch Ratings Inc. 121

FLA (Fair Labor Association) 228, 231

FOCAC (Forum on China-Africa Cooperation) 206

food security: 1970s global food crisis 185; 1996 World Food Summit, Rome 184; 2007–2008 global food crisis 184–5, 194; 2009 World Food Summit, Rome 181, 194–5; food security governance 184–6; G20: 185, 194; hunger and malnutrition 184; *see also* food security and China

food security and China 9, 12, 13, 181–201; Africa 185, 188–9, 192–4; agricultural aid project 190–4, *191*, 196; agriculture 186–8; ambiguous/evolving norms 182; assessment 197; China as reformer 12, 13, 183, 195, 198; domestic demand of food 183, 186, 192, 194; food aid 12, 182, 183, 186, 189–90, 194, 195; food aid conditionality 12, 189–90, 193; food sovereignty 183, 194, 197; global governance of food security 181; global policy-making 12, 183, 194–5; learning by doing 12, 183, 195–7; mutual benefits 183, 190–7; non-adoption of international dominant norms 12, 190, 194; non-interference principle 196–7; North Korea 190; outsourcing production 12, 183, 188–9, 199n25; per capita production of major non-staple crops *187*; scholarship on 181–2; self-sufficiency 186–7, 193, 195; staying above the red line 186–8; win-win cooperation 183, 196, 197; *see also* food security

foreign aid 12; colonialism and 204, 214; motivations for giving aid 212, 226n18; Western aid norms, shortcomings 12, 13; *see also* DAC; foreign aid and China; ODA

foreign aid and China 9, 12, 160, 198, 202–27; 1995 Conference on Reforming Foreign Assistance 205; 2011 *White Paper on Foreign Aid* 219; 2011 *White Paper on Peaceful Development* 219; Africa 202, 206, 222; aid dependency 202; bilateral aid 161, 206, **207**; challenges to Western aid norms 12, 202, 224; China as 'development financier' 12, 14, 202, 203, 224; China as 'emerging donor' 202, 203, 218; China as recipient and provider of foreign aid 189, 196, 204, 208; China's philosophy/Eight

Principles of Foreign Aid 203, 206, 207–209; Chinese foreign aid laws, lack of 174; composition of China's foreign aid expenditures *207*; conditionality 209; economic cooperation 205, 206; evolution of China's foreign assistance policies 203–206; health-related foreign aid 159–61, 174, 175; learning by doing 204–205, 208; multilateral assistance 206, **207**; ODA *208*; 'social gift'/public and social services 206; tied/untied aid 12, 161, 220; *see also* DAC; DAC donors/China interaction; food security and China

foreign investment 53–4, 135–6, 188, 229; 1979 Law of Joint Ventures Using Chinese and Foreign Investment 135; protectionism 53

Fortune 500: 57

free trade 102, 164; benefits 58; free trade order 58; *see also* FTA

Friends of Nature 261

FSAP (Financial Sector Assessment Planning) 121

FTA (free trade agreement) 66, 105; Asia, overlapping trade regimes/noodle bowl 65; Asia-Pacific regional integration 65–6, 81–4; China/Japan comparison 10, 65, **67**, 79–81; Doha Round deadlock 10; DSM 85; FTA/BIT/WTO comparison 85; trilateral China/Japan/South Korea FTA 81, 83; US 78–9; *see also* FTA, China's strategy; FTA, Japan's strategy

FTA, China's strategy 10, 66–72, 84–5; agriculture 70; ASEAN 66, **67**, 69, 70–1, 80; Australia 66, **67**, 68, 72, 80; CAFTA 70–1, 80; Chile 66, **67**, 68, 69, 71–2; criticism 69, 72; developed country 72, 80; developing country 69, 72; liberalization 69–70, 72, 80, 83, 84; MOFCOM 72; multilateralism 66, 84–5; Pakistan 66, **67**, 71, 80; partners 66, 80–1; partners, selection criteria 69; policy implications 72, 81; policy shift from multilateralism to FTAs 66, 67–9; politicized FTA agreements 10, 69, 70–1, 79, 80, 81; pragmatic and flexible approach 65, 69, 71, 83; protectionism 66; resources-driven FTAs 68, 69, 71–2, 80; shallow, narrow, non-controversial agreements 10, 65, 69–70, 80; South Korea 66, **67**, 70, 80–1, 84; TPP 83; US market 66, 68; *see also* FTA

FTA, Japan's strategy 65, 72–9, 84–5; agriculture 74, 75, 76, 79, 80, 81; ASEAN 73, 74, 81, 82–3; BIT 73, 74, 75–9, 87n38; competition 73, 74, 75; comprehensive, bilateral FTAs with selective countries 65, 79, 80; developed country 80; double taxation treaty 79, 88n46; EPA 73, 75–9; EPA ratio 75, 87n32; EU 84; IPR 78; liberalization 72, 75–6, 79; lobbying 73, 74, 75; MAI 73, 75; Mexico 73, 74, 78, 80; moderate legalization on rules covered by the WTO 78–9; multilateralism 66, 72, 84–5; partners 73; partners, selection criteria 74, 75, 79, 80, 81; policy implications 79; policy shift from multilateralism to FTAs 73–5; protectionism 66; relatively aggressive investment liberalization and investment protection 76–8; social security agreement 79, 88n47; South Korea 77; Thailand 76; TPP 73, 79, 83; TRIMs 77; US 66, 74, 75, 83; WTO-plus 78; *see also* FTA; Japan

G4 (Group of 4) 32
G6 (Group of 6) 32
G7 (Group of 7) 32, 125
G8 (Group of 8) 113; 2003 Evian Summit 113, 129n17; 2008–2009 financial crisis 114, 125, 127; 2009 Summit 185; G8+5 dialogue 113, 118
G9 (Group of 9) 113
G10 (Group of 10) 113

G20 (Group of 20) 114; 1997–1998 Asian financial crisis 114; 2008 Washington Summit 114–15; 2008–2009 financial crisis 114–15, 120, 126, 127; 2009 London Summit 115, 116, 120–1, 125; 2009 Pittsburgh Summit 125, 147; 2010 Seoul Summit 124; 2010 Toronto Summit 121; 2011 Cannes Summit 124; 2012 Los Cabos, Mexico, Summit 125; 2016 Hangzhou Summit 116, 125; assessment 124–6; developing country 115–16, 119, 125–6; distribution of power 126; effectiveness 126; food security 185, 194; 'G20 Blueprint on Innovative Growth' 116; global economic governance 114, 124–6; legitimacy 126; US 114; *see also* G20 and China

G20 and China 10–11, 31, 59, 114, 125, 126, 128, 185; 2016 process 2–3, 5, 116; China as reform-minded status quo state 10–11, 112–13, 127; China as reformer 13, 127; Chinese emergent leadership 2–3, 5, 116; developing country 115–16, 125; food security 194; international financial institutions, reform of 114, 115, 118–20; international financial regulation 114, 115, 120–1, 127; international financial system, reform of 115; international monetary system, reform of 114, 115, 117–18; protectionism 116; *see also* IMF; international monetary system; RMB; status quo power; World Bank

G33 (Group of 33) 59
GAO (General Accountability Office) 162
Gao Yaojie 173
Gates Foundation 158, 166, 169, 171
GATS (General Agreement on Trade in Services) 91
GATT (General Agreement on Tariffs and Trade) 21; 1995 transition from GATT to WTO 27; accession 22–4; aims 21;

Article XXIV.8: 69; asymmetries in economic opportunity 22; China's accession 24, 26, 27; China's withdrawal 26–7; first mover advantages 22, 23; free trade order 58; GPA 91, 96; Japan 22; liberalization 21–2; Republic of China 4; rules 22, 23; Tokyo Round 23; Uruguay Round 23; WTO 21, 35; *see also* WTO
GAVI Alliance (Global Alliance for Vaccines and Immunization) 162
GCC (Gulf Cooperation Council) 66, **67**, 72
GGO (global governance organization) 132, 133, 135, 148
GHG (global health governance) 158; definition 158, 161, 177n1; OECD countries 161; *see also the entries below for* GHG
GHG and China 11–12; assessment 11, 175–6, 177, 198; bureaucratic politics 11–12, 174–5; CSO 161, 173, 180n58; Ebola epidemic 160; GONGO 173; IGO 166, 168; IHR 162, 163, 164, 174–5; lobbying 163; NGO 12, 161, 165, 173; sovereignty and state authority 11–12, 164, 165, 172; state-centric approach 13, 172–3, 176; *see also the entries below for* GHG; Global Fund to Fight AIDS, Tuberculosis and Malaria; health-related issues; HIV/AIDS; Influenza A; NHFPC; SARS; WHO and China
GHG, impact on China's domestic health governance 159, 165–72, 175–6; health agenda setting 166–8; health policy formulation 168–70; health policy implementation 170–2; shortcomings 172, 176; *see also* GHG and China; WHO and China
GHG, impact of Chinese involvement on 11, 159–65, 175; 2006 International Pledging Conference on Avian and Human Influenza 162; 2009 International Scientific Symposium on Influenza A 162; Africa 160, 175; BRICS 163;

China as aid donor 159–61, 174, 175; contribution to global disease control 161–4; exports of Chinese pharmaceuticals 161–2, 175; FCTC 164, 165, 172, 174; Maoist health system 160; shaping global health rules 164–5, 175; shortcomings 161, 163, 165; *see also* GHG and China; WHO and China
Gini coefficient 26
global economic governance 2, 9, 110, 127; 2008–2009 financial crisis 4–5; China 4, 5, 116, 125, 126, 151; G20: 114, 124–6; global trade governance 9, 147; international economic organizations 4, 118, 119; *see also* international financial institutions; international financial regulation; international monetary system
Global Fund to Fight AIDS, Tuberculosis and Malaria 161, 169, 171–2, 173
global governance 1–2; ambiguous rules 11, 13, 133, 182; clear rules 7, 11, 13–14, 133, 134; definition 1; food security governance 184–6; global governance architecture, gaps in 2, 7; non-state participants 12; UN 113; *see also* global economic governance; global governance and China; transnational governance
global governance and China: China as challenger of current global governance regimes 3, 13–14; China as reformer of current global governance regimes 3, 13–14, 148, 153, 156n71; China's socialization into the global community 3, 5; Chinese behavior 3, 7–8, 9, 13; Chinese behavior, compliance approach 3, 5–6, 13; Chinese convergence toward international standards 14; Chinese international responsibility 182–3, 196; encouraging alternative standards and rules of behavior 14; evolving Chinese participation in

global governance 4–6; factory certification and labor standards 230, 244–5, 246; global responsibility in terms of national achievements 181; 'live and let live' approach of mutual recognition' 14; normatively ambiguous global governance system, perspective shift 6–8; WTO accession 58–9, 61; Xi Jinping 177; *see also* GHG and China; global governance; status quo power
Global Hunger Index 184–5
globalization 2, 56, 177; economic globalization 2, 5, 58, 135; globalization of labor standards 228
GOARN (Global Outbreak Alert and Response Network) 162
GONGO (government-organized nongovernmental organization) 173
GPA (Agreement on Government Procurement) 89; accession negotiation 89; definition of government procurement 96–7; goals 90, 107n3; Japan 78, 100; non-discrimination 90, 91; Uruguay Round 96; WTO/GPA accession link 90, 107n5; *see also the entries below for* GPA
GPA and China 10, 89–109; academic and public involvement in GPA negotiations 105–106, 107; accession negotiations 94–6, 98; benefits and costs of accession 99–101, 105; China's reluctance to join the GPA 91; Chinese government procurement system 90–2, 96–8, 99, 101, 105, 106; corruption 90, 99, 105–106, 109n39; disputes over government procurement 92–4; EU 92, 94, 100; institutional and organizational constraints in negotiations 101–103, 106–107; key elements of China's GPA accession negotiations 96–8; lack of political momentum and will 98–101, 103, 106; major reform of the government and state sector

99; MOF 93, 100, 101–103, 105, 107; NDRC 93, 102; public tendering 90, 96, 97, 106, 109n39; SOE 10, 91–2, 96, 97; US 92, 94, 100; Working Party Report 91; WTO/GPA accession differences 89, 94, 98, 99, 101–103, 106, 107; WTO/GPA accession link 90–1, 94; *see also* GPA; GPA and China, documents and law
GPA and China, documents and law: 1998 *Interim Regulations on Government Procurement* 90; 1999 Tendering Law 90, 92, 97, 102; 2004 *Opinions on Implementation of Government Procurement of Energy-efficient Products* 93; 2006 *National Guideline on the Medium- and Long-Term Program for Science and Technology Development* 93; 2006 *Trial Measures for the Administration of the Accreditation of National Indigenous Innovation Products* 93; 2013 *The Decision on Major Issues Concerning Comprehensively Deepening Reforms* 99; CPC/*Centralized Procurement Catalogue* 97; PPT/*Prescribed Procurement Thresholds* 97; *see also* GPL
GPL (Government Procurement Law) 90, 92, 96–7, 100
Graham, Lindsey 145
Great Depression 58, 114
GRI (Global Reporting Initiative) 258
Gu Yongjiang 51

Hale, Thomas 12–13, 173, 250–71
He Yafei 118
health-related issues: CISAR 174; foreign aid 159–61, 174, 175; Ministry of Health 97, 167, 172, 174, 175; MOF 174; MOFA 174; MOFCOM 174; NHFPC 174; PLA 174; *see also* GHG and China; WHO and China
High-Tech Electronics 236–8
historical institutionalism 20
HIV/AIDS (human immunodeficiency virus/acquired immunodeficiency

syndrome) 161, 165; 2002 *HIV/ AIDS: China's Titanic Peril* 167; China 158, 162, 167–9, 171; WHO 171; *see also* GHG and China; UNAIDS

Ho, Peter 199n25

Hobbs, William 271n45

Hofman, Irna 199n25

Hong Kong 66, **67**, 69, 169, 232, 235; RMB 124

Hu Jia 173

Hu Jintao 5, 98, 122, 129n17, 146, 160; 2006 Forum on China and African Cooperation Summit 192; G20: 114–15

Hu Xiaolian 120–1

Huang, Yanzhong 11, 158–80

Huang, Yasheng 25

Huawei 53, 139, 140–1

Hui Liangyu 181, 194–5

ICA (Infrastructure Consortium for Africa) 216

ICLEI (Local Governments for Sustainability/International Council for Local Environmental Initiatives) 257, 266; Cities for Climate Protection program 257; Shenyang 257–8, 269n21

ICTI (International Council of Toy Industries) 228, 234; CARE 238–9; *see also* factory certification

ICTSD (International Center for Trade & Sustainable Development) xvii

IDA (International Development Association) 223

IGO (international governmental organization) 166, 168

IHR (International Health Regulations) 162, 163, 164, 174–5

ILO (International Labour Organization) 228, 233

IMF (International Monetary Fund) 1; 1997–1998 Asian financial crisis 117; China 4, 5, 117, 126, 146, 147; Chinese greater representation 11, 120; ERM 133, 134; international monetary system 119, 124; reform of 114, 118–20,

146–7; RMB and SDR 11, 124, 133, 146, 148, 151; SDR 118; voting power 120, 126, 146–7; *see also* international monetary system

India 57, 113, 152; 'ASEAN plus six' 74; DDA 10, 33, 59; SSM 33

Indonesia 162, 220, 260

inequality 25, 26; Gini coefficient 26; rural/urban population inequality 25, 26; World Bank 26; WTO accession 36

Influenza A: H1N1: 162, 163, 170, 173, 176, 180n67; H7N9: 163; US 180n67; *see also* GHG and China

innovation: 2006 *Trial Measures for the Administration of the Accreditation of National Indigenous Innovation Products* 93; 'G20 Blueprint on Innovative Growth' 116; indigenous innovation 53, 93, 136, 137, 138, 140, 141; Indigenous Innovation Product Accreditation System 93; WTO, restrain to China's innovation growth 55; *see also* IPR and China; technology

International Business News 58

international financial institutions 151; reform of 114, 115, 118–20; *see also* G20 and China; global economic governance; IMF; World Bank

international financial regulation 11, 114, 115, 120–1, 127; 2008–2009 financial crisis 120, 151; *see also* G20 and China; global economic governance

international institution 21, 224–5; accession of new members 22, 28; institutional development 24; interests of dominant powers 21, 22, 32; rules and procedures that preserve institutional advantages 22; WTO as international institution 28, 29, 32, 34, 35, 37; *see also* WTO and China

international monetary system: 1997–1998 Asian financial crisis 117; 2008–2009 financial crisis 117, 123; China 11, 117, 127, 151; dollar, future of 114, 121–3, 127;

'dollar system' 117, 122, 123, 127, 131n49; IMF 119, 124; reform of 11, 114, 115, 117–18, 122, 127; supra-sovereign international currency 118, 126, 151; tripolarity (US dollar/euro/renminbi) 123; US 205; *see also* ER; G20 and China; RMB

Internet 3, 53, 54, 169

IP (intellectual property): definition 134; IP/ER governance regime differences 133, 134; TPP 152–3; US 135; *see also* IPR; IPR and China; TRIPS; WIPO

IPR (intellectual property rights) 7; benefits and costs 134; Japan 78; OECD countries 134; *see also* IP; IPR and China

IPR and China 9, 11, 13, 72, 135–41, 153; 1978–1991: 135–7; 1992–2001: 135, 137–8; 2001–2015: 135, 138–41; anti-monopoly policies 135, 138, 139, 140–1; China, assertive and effective behavior 132, 133, 135, 148–50, 151, 152, 153; Chinese growth strategy 11, 132, 141, 151–2; clear, explicit rules 11, 133, 134; domestic interest 11, 133, 136–7, 151; four causal factors for Chinese changed behavior 132, 151–2; indigenous innovation 136, 137, 138, 140, 141; invention patent 136, 137, 138, 139; litigation 139–41, 149, 152; OECD countries 136, 137, 138, 140, 152; policy space 135, 152; R&D 136, 138, 140; SIPO 139, 140; technology and innovation 11, 136, 137, 138, 139, 141, 152; US/China tensions 11, 132, 135, 136, 137, 141, 149, 152; WTO Copyright enforcement case 149, 152; WTO's DSM 11, 133, 152; *see also* IP; IPR; IPR and China, documents and law; technology; WIPO

IPR and China, documents and law: 1992 MoU on IP 137; 2008 Anti-Monopoly Law 140; 2008 National Intellectual Property Strategy 138; 2010 National Patent Development Strategy 138–9; 2014 Action Plan on Further Implementing National Intellectual Property Strategy 139; Beijing Treaty on Audiovisual Performances 150; patent law 136, 137, 138, 141; *see also* IPR and China

IPRCC (International Poverty Reduction Center in China) 221

ISO (International Organization for Standardization) 231; China 4, 5, 261; ISO 9001: 238; ISO 14001: 260, 261, 269n28

ITO (International Trade Organization) 21

ITU (International Telecommunications Union) 4, 5

IWEP (Institute of World Economics and Politics) xvii

Japan 75, 143, 185; China/Japan tensions 82, 84, 128; DAC 211, 215; GATT 22; GPA 78, 100; METI 74; MITI 74; MOFA 79; TPP 73, 79, 82, 83, 84; US/Japan military alliance 83; WTO 85; *see also* FTA, Japan's strategy

JCCT (Joint Committee on Commerce and Trade) 94

Jia Qinglin 192

Jiang Zemin 52, 98, 143

Johnston, Alastair Iain 111

Keidanren (Japan Business Federation) 73–4

Kennedy, Scott 1–17, 50, 245; *From Rule Takers to Rule Makers* xvii; 'The United States, China and Global Governance: A New Agenda for a New Era' xvii

Keohane, Robert 22

Kingdon, John 170

Koizumi, Junichiro 74, 81–2

Kostka, Genia 271n45

labor rights 53, 230, 243, 244; anti-sweatshop activism 228, 247n12; globalization of labor standards 228; ILO 228; migrant worker 229;

NGO 228; *see also* factory certification; labor standards in China

labor standards in China 229, 230–3, 240, 243–6; child labor 234; labor disputes 230–1; labor unrest 230, 231, 245; strike 230, 245, 246–7n11; trade union 230, 231; working time 233; *see also* factory certification

Lamy, Pascal 50, 58, 72

Layne, Christopher 111

LDC (least developed country) 128, 211, 213, 215, 216

Lenovo (Legend) 136, 259

Li Keqiang 99, 223

Li Lanqing 167

Liang, Wei 10, 18, 65–88

liberalization: agriculture 75, 76; FTA, China's strategy 69–70, 72, 80, 83, 84; FTA, Japan's strategy 72, 75–6, 79; GATT 21–2; TPP 83; WTO 85; WTO and China 27, 29, 31, 34, 36–7

Lieberthal, Kenneth 165

Lim, Chin Leng 18

Lin Zhangxi 193

Liu Mingkang 151

Liu Zhijun 106

lobbying 13, 163; climate change and China 261, 263, 264, 271n47; Japan 73, 74, 75

Long Yongtu 58, 70, 104

Lu, Mimi 260

Ma Hao 150

MAI (Multilateral Agreement on Investment) 73, 75

Mao Zedong 24, 111, 166, 168; Maoist health system 160

market economy 246; 1992 socialist market economy reforms 204, 205; China, market-economy reform 24–6, 36, 55, 205; 'market economy' status 71

McKinsey 170

MDGs (Millennium Development Goals) 116, 181

Mearsheimer, John 110

Medeiros, Evan 111, 121–2

media 106, 169–70; Internet-based new media 53; WTO 53–4, 57, 59, 60

Merck 166, 171

Merson, Michael 168–9

Mertha, Andrew 262

Methane to Markets 259

Mexico 73, 74, 78, 80, 163, 178n24

MFN (most favored nation) 7, 85, 87n37, 91; China's status 101, 244

Ministry of Agriculture 174, 188, 189, 190–1

MNC (multinational corporation) 9, 53, 61; Chinese MNCs 64n39; competition 52

MOF (Ministry of Finance): GPA 93, 100, 101–103, 105, 107; health-related aid 174

MOFA (Ministry of Foreign Affairs) 113, 118, 127, 175, 262; health-related aid 174

MOFCOM (Ministry of Commerce) 43, 45, 55–6, 101; anti-dumping 47–8; DSM 49; health-related aid 174; WTO Affairs Division 46; *see also* MOFTEC

MOFTEC (Ministry of Foreign Trade and Economic Cooperation) 46, 47, 51, 54–5, 102, 103, 104; DSM 49; *The Knowledge of China's WTO Accession Reader* 43; Treaty and Law Division 49; WTO accession 43, 102, 103, 104; WTO Affairs Division 46; *see also* MOFCOM

Moody's Investors Service 121

Morton, Katherine 12, 181–201

MOST (Ministry of Science and Technology) 93, 262

MoU (memorandum of understanding) 72, 137, 165, 166

multilateralism: China 10, 66, 84–5, 152, 190; China, multilateral assistance 206, **207**; China, policy shift from multilateralism to FTAs 66, 67–9; Japan 66, 72, 84–5; Japan, policy shift from multi-lateralism to FTAs 73–5; rivalry between multilateral and bilateral rule-making 75; WTO and China 42, 52, 56, 57–8, 60, 61, 67

NAFTA (North American Free Trade Agreement) 73
Nakagawa, Junji 10, 65–88
NAMA (non-agricultural market access) 33–4
Narlikar, Amrita 18
Nath, Kamal 33
National Audit Office 96
National Science Foundation 136
nationalism 105, 145
NATO (North Atlantic Treaty Organization) 210
NDRC (National Development and Reform Commission) 93, 102, 174, 256, 260, 262
neoliberalism 176
NGO (nongovernmental organization) 1; Chinese environmental NGOs 12, 173, 261, 263; GHG and China 12, 161, 165, 173; Global Fund 171–2; harassed by police and security officials 173; labor rights 228; shrinking operation space for 177; untied aid 214; *see also* civil society; CSO
NHFPC (National Health and Family Planning Commission) 174, 175, 176–7
Nike 235, 236
NME (non-market economy) 71, 86n16

Oak Hill Group/Bluestar, Datong 45, 47–8
Obama, Barack 147
OBOR *see* BRI
ODA (official development assistance) 196, 203 210–12; China *208*; *see also* DAC
OECD (Organisation for Economic Co-operation and Development): ECA 220; ER 134; GHG 161; IPR 134; IPR and China 136, 137, 138, 140, 152; MAI 73; *see also* DAC
Ohls, David 23
Oksenberg, Michel 165
Ostry, Sylvia 22

OXFAM (Oxford Committee for Famine Relief) 166
Oxford Committee for Famine Relief 166

Pakistan 66, **67**, 71, 80
Pang, Tikki 177n1
Panitchpakdi, Supachai 30
PBOC (People's Bank of China) 114, 117, 120, 126, 148, 151
PCT (Patent Cooperation Treaty) 139
Pearson, Margaret 30
People's Daily 60, 116, 118, 232
PEPFAR (US President's Emergency Plan for AIDS Relief) 161
Piot, Peter 167
PLA (People's Liberation Army) 174
policy space 14, 54, 133, 135, 152
post-World War II order 3, 4, 6, 21; US-led global economic order 53, 56, 224
Potoski, Matthew 269n28
Prakash, Aseem 269n28
PRC (People's Republic of China) 4, 18, 24, 26, 31, 181; GATT 27; Ninth Five-Year Plan 68; reform 24
Primo Braga, Carlos 23
Project HOPE 171
protectionism: China 8, 66; domestic industry 7, 8, 53; DSM 58; foreign investment 53; G20 and China 116; global trade protectionism 58; Japan 66; rise of 56; US 53, 56; WTO 7; WTO and China 29, 42, 49, 50, 51, 57, 104

R&D (research and development) 136, 138, 140
RAM (recently acceded member) 29; China 29, 31, 34–5, 36; China's assertiveness and intransigence 34; DDA 34–5, 36; 'four Ls' 34; *see also* WTO and China
RCCPB (Research Center for Chinese Politics & Business, Indiana University) xvii–xviii
RCEP (Regional Comprehensive Economic Partnership) 66, **67**, 73,

147, 151; Asia-Pacific regional integration 82, 84

REACH (Registration, Evaluation, Authorization and Restriction of Chemicals) 46

realism 8, 110–11, 176, 182

Ren Xiao 10–11, 13, 110–31, 153

Republic of China 4

Reynolds, Bruce 11, 132–57

RMB (renminbi) 11, 122; 2008–2009 financial crisis 123; ambiguous ER rules 11, 13; appreciation 143, 144–5, 146; devaluation 25, 143–4; IMF's SDR 11, 124, 133, 146, 148, 151; internationalization of 3, 11, 114, 123–4, 127, 146; Trade Settlement Scheme 124; *see also* ER; ER and China; ERM; international monetary system

Roger, Charles 12–13, 173, 250–71

Rubin, Robert 143

rural area 25, 26, 188

Russia 27 128

S&ED (Strategic and Economic Dialogue) 151

SA8000 standard 228, 229, 231–2, 240–3; BV 237, 248n42; CNCA 231, 233; Council on Economic Priorities 231, 247n12; CSR 231, 241; fraud 233–4; growth of 233; high-tech electronics: certification as competitive advantage 236–8; 'illegal' in China 233; variation among SA8000-certified factories 234–6, 243; *see also* factory certification; SAI

SACU (Southern African Customs Union) 66, **67**

SAI (Social Accountability International) 228, 232–3, 237, 244; *see also* factory certification; SA8000 standard

Sany Heavy Industry 53–4

Sarkozy, Nicolas 124

SARS (Severe Acute Respiratory Syndrome) 158, 162, 163, 169–70, 174

SASAC (State-Owned Assets Supervision and Administration Commission) 194

savings 25, 26

Schroeder, Miriam 263

Schumer, Charles 145

Scott, James 9, 18–41, 111

Sell, Susan K. 11, 132–57

SEZ (special economic zone) 135

SGS (Société Générale de Surveillance) 239, 247n12

Shambaugh, David 110, 177

Shanghai 163, 237; as international financial center 123; New Development Bank 126, 147

Shi Guangsheng 49

Shingal, Anirudh 100

Singapore 147; FTA 66, **67**, 69, 73, 74, 76, 78, 80; RMB 124

Singh, Harsha V. 49–50, 56

SIPO (State Intellectual Property Office) 139, 140

SOE (state-owned enterprise) 188; domestic technology 55; GPA and China 10, 91–2, 96, 97; IPR and China 136; large investor in China 96, 108n21; reform 27, 52; 'state-advance, private recede' 55; WTO accession and 27, 52

Solís, Mireya 79

South Korea 66, **67**, 70, 80–1, 84, 185; DAC 211; trilateral China/Japan/South Korea FTA 81, 83, 84

South-South Cooperation 68, 222

SSIC (Social Survey Institute of China) 52

SSM (Special Safeguard Mechanism) 33–4; *see also* DDA

Standard & Poor's Financial Services 121

state: commitment to promoting industrial policy goals 13; factory certification, state-centric approach 13, 173; GHG and sovereignty 11–12, 164, 165, 172; GHG, state-centric approach 13, 172–3, 176; non-interference principle 196–7; interventionism 3, 55, 56; state as public service provider 45, 46–8, 60; state sector as the single largest investor in China 96, 108n21; TCG and China, state-centric approach 12–13, 259–60, 264–6; WTO, 'losing sovereignty' to Western developed countries 45; *see also* China; China as authoritarian state

status quo power 111–12; anti-status quo state 112, 128; changing the status quo 8, 14; China as reform-minded status quo state 10–11, 112–13, 127, 225; China as reformer 3, 8, 9, 13–14, 127, 133, 148, 152, 153, 156n71; China as reformer, and food security 12, 13, 183, 195, 198; China as revisionist 13–14, 111, 118, 128; China as revolutionary 9, 111; China as rigid status quo power 128; China as status quo power 9, 13, 111, 112, 127, 148, 153; problematic nature of 8; reform-minded status quo state 112, 127; reform/revision ambiguous distinction 13; rigid status quo state 112; status quo state 112, 127; *see also* G20 and China; global governance and China

Steinfeld, Edward 143
Stiglitz, Joseph 118
Sun Zhenyu 56, 95

Taiwan 161; 'One China' policy 193; UN 4; WHO 164, 165; WTO 30, 36
Tan Yeling 169–70
Tang Huajun 195
TB (tuberculosis) 161, 163
TCG (transnational climate governance) 251; 1992 Earth Summit 252; 1997 Kyoto Protocol 252; actors targeted by TCG schemes 254, *255*; developing country 252, 257; E8: 252; Energy Cities 252; origins 252; TCG schemes 252, *253*, 268n14; *see also* TCG and China; transnational governance
TCG and China 251–71; actors 254, *255*, 256, 264, 265; authoritarian

state 260–1, 264; carbon market 254, 256, 260, 265, 268n17; CDP 258; civil society, weakness of 13, 259–61; corporate actors 258, 259; CSR 258, 259; domestic political institutions/conditions 251, 252, 259–60, 262–5; Energy and Climate Registry 259; environmental values, lack of internalization 260, 261; fragmented authoritarianism 252, 262–4, 266, 271n44; Gold Standard 256, 257; GRI 258; ICLEI, Shenyang 257–8, 269n21; industry/business 12, 258–9, 264, 265, 266; ISO 14001: 260, 261, 269n28; local government 257, 259, 263, 265, 266, 271n45; municipal networks 257–8, 266; NDRC 256, 260; NGO 12, 261; participation 256, 259, 261, 265–6; patterns of TCG schemes 254, *255*, 261–2, 265; scholarship on 267n8; state-centric approach 12–13, 259–60, 264–6; TCG schemes 252, *253*, *254*, 259; Verified Carbon Standard 257; voluntary offset standards 256, *257*; *see also* climate change and China; TCG

technology: 2006 *National Guideline on the Medium- and Long-Term Program for Science and Technology Development* 93, 138, 140; 2011–2015 Twelfth Five-Year Plan 139; IPR and China 11, 136, 137, 138, 139, 141, 152; technology competition 93; technology transfer 61, 136, 141, 209, 211–12; WTO's export controls on high-technology products 10, 51, 54–5, 61; *see also* innovation
think tank 104, 168
Time magazine 169
The Times, London 118–19
TPP (Trans-Pacific Partnership) 72, 152–3; Article 30.5: 84; Asia-Pacific regional integration 82, 83–4; China 83, 153; IP 152–3; Japan 73, 79, 82, 83, 84; Obama, Barack 147;

trade liberalization 83; Trump,
Donald 2, 84; US 82, 83, 84, 147
transnational governance 251, 267n8;
definition 251; domestic politics,
impact on transnational
governance 260, 269n28;
sub-national and non-state actors
263–4; *see also* global governance;
TCG; TCG and China
Trepte, Peter 107n3
TRIMs (Trade-Related Investment
Measures) 28, 54, 77
TRIPS (Trade-Related Aspects of
Intellectual Property Rights) 78,
134, 175; China 138, 149, 150,
175; TRIPS-Plus 75, 150, 152–3;
US 150; *see also* IP; IPR
TRM (Transitional Review
Mechanism) 30–1; *see also* WTO
and China
Trump, Donald 2, 84

UK (United Kingdom) 28; DAC 214;
RMB 124; UK Pergau River
project, Malaysia 214, 226n27
UN (United Nations) 1; China 160,
166, 204; global governance 113;
Republic of China 4; Taiwan 4;
UN aid target 211
UN Global Compact 258, 260
UNAIDS (Joint UN Programme on
HIV/AIDS) 162, 167, 169, 171
UNCTAD (UN Conference on Trade
and Development) 219
UNFCCC (UN Framework
Convention on Climate Change) 2;
CDM 256
UNICEF (UN Children's Fund) 166
UNSC (UN Security Council) 128
urban area 25, 26
Uruguay Round 23, 54, 96
US (United States) 33, 250, 257;
Asia-Pacific regional integration
82; China/US clash 110–11; China/
US economic relations 37, 132;
DAC 209–10, 213, 215; DDA 32,
33; export credits 220, 221, 225;
FTA 78–9; FTA, China's strategy
66, 68; FTA, Japan's strategy 66,
74, 75, 83; G20: 114; GPA and

China 92, 94, 100; health-related
issues 180n67; international
monetary system 205; IP 135; IPR,
US/China tensions 11, 132, 135,
136, 137, 141, 149, 152; protectionism 53, 56; TPP 82, 83, 84,
147; TRIPS 150; US-led global
economic order 53, 56, 224; WTO
and China 27, 28, 30–1, 32, 33, 35;
WTO and China's accession 137–8;
WTO and Chinese industry 51, 57
USAID (US Agency for International
Development) 174, 215, 220
USTR (US Trade Representative) 32,
137, 150

Volcker, Paul 117

Wall Street Journal 169
Wan Jifei 57, 64n39
Wan Yanhai 173
Wang, Jiang Yu 18
Wang, Lei 23
Wang Ping 109n28
Wang Qishan 115–16, 118–19
Wang Rui 192
The Washington Post 122, 132
WEF (World Economic Forum) 1, 2,
3, 5
Wen Jiabao 95, 98–9, 146
Wen Tiejun 199n12
WFP (World Food Programme) 189,
190, 195
Whalley, John 69–70
WHO and China 4, 5, 158, 166, 168,
170; China's potential misuse of
influence on WHO 163–4; MoU
165, 166; SARS 169, 170; setting
global rules 11; Taiwan 164, 165;
see also GHG and China
Wilkinson, Rorden 9, 18–41, 111
Winham, Gilbert 32
WIPO (World Intellectual Property
Organization) 136, 139, 149, 150,
152
World Bank 104; China 4, 116, 117,
126, 166, 170, 223; Chinese greater
representation 11, 120; Clean Air
Initiative 258; inequality 26;
reform of 114, 118, 119–20;

'Responsible Agricultural
Investments...' 195; *see also* IDA
World Council of Churches 211
WRAP (Worldwide Responsible
Accredited Production) 228–9,
231, 233–4, 238; *see also* factory
certification
Wright, Logan 145
WTO (World Trade Organization) 1,
2; 1995 transition from GATT to
WTO 27; accession 22, 23–4; anti-
dumping/countervailing regime 7;
developing country 29, 31, 33; free
trade order 58; FTA/BIT/WTO
comparison 85; Green Room 4,
33; Japan 85; liberalization 85;
media 53–4, 57, 59, 60; membership
134; non-discrimination principle
43, 49, 91; power asymmetry 23;
protectionism 7; rules 23;
WTO-plus 23, 69, 72, 78; *see also
the entries below for* WTO; Doha
Round; GATT; GPA; international
institution
WTO and China 4, 5, 18–41, 59, 85;
adaptation and learning 9, 31, 35,
46; China's diplomacy 2001–2008:
29–31, 35; China's diplomacy post-
2008 31–5; China/US-EU tension
10, 27, 30–1, 32, 35, 36–7; Chinese
constructive role 10, 35; Chinese
intentions debate 18, 31, 35;
compliance with WTO rules 5,
30–1, 43, 93, 94, 95, 111; interests
of dominant powers 28;
liberalization 27, 29, 31, 34, 36–7;
multilateral trading system 42, 52,
56, 57–8, 60, 61, 67; noncompliance with WTO rules 6,
16n14; shift from a quiet to an
assertive member 10, 18, 29–31,
32–3, 35–6, 37; Taiwan 30, 36;
TRM 30–1; US 27, 28, 30–1, 32,
33, 35; WTO, impact on China
35–7, 42; WTO, impact on China's
domestic affairs 28, 29, 36–7, 52,
60; WTO, impact on China's
international relations 18–19, 20,
28–9; WTO, an international
institution 28, 29, 32, 34, 35, 37;

WTO, a key mediating variable 19,
37, 38n5; *see also* DDA; RAM;
WTO; WTO and China's accession;
WTO and Chinese industry
WTO and China's accession 24, 25,
26–9, 32, 34, 35, 66; 10th
anniversary of 52, 57, 59, 89;
academic and public involvement
104–105, 106; benefits 52–3, 57,
58–9, 61, 98, 104–105; China as
learner of WTO rules 43–4;
criticism 45, 52, 53, 54, 55, 61, 98;
debates on 52, 98; EC 137–8;
global governance and China 58–9,
61; high requirements for accession
9, 27–8, 30, 34, 36, 56, 61, 67, 69,
138; lack of clear rules governing
accession 28; NME 71, 86n16;
protracted process 27, 68; reasons
for 26, 67–8; reforms brought forth
by 24–6, 27, 45, 52, 57; skepticism
about WTO 46, 54, 55; state/
market/society relationship 45, 60;
US 137–8; WTO/GPA accession
differences 89, 94, 98, 99, 101–103,
106, 107; WTO/GPA accession
link 90–1, 94; *see also* WTO and
China; WTO and Chinese
industry
WTO and Chinese industry 10, 42–64;
anti-dumping 47–8, 49, 50, 58;
bilateral/regional agreement 10,
54; China's innovation and
competitiveness 53, 54–5; culture
54, 60; Datong, Oak Hill Group/
Bluestar 45, 47–8; early capacity
building: China as learner of WTO
rules 43–5; government-led defense
of Chinese interests 43, 45–8;
government-led industry 10, 42;
growing concerns about WTO
rules 52–6; harmonizing Chinese
laws with WTO rules 43; industry-
led defense of their interests 43,
49–51; interagency policy
coordination 55–6; learning and
using effectively WTO's rules 42;
learning to lead in WTO 56–60;
protectionism 29, 42, 49, 50, 51,
57, 104; public education

campaign 43, 44, 49, 104; Shenzhen WTO Affairs Center 45, 46–7, 48, 56; state intervention 55, 56; state as public service provider 45, 46–8, 60; state/market/society relationship 42, 48, 51, 59; trade friction 46–7, 49; trade remedy measures 45, 46, 49, 50, 51; US 51, 57; WTO Affairs Center 46–7, 48; WTO's constraints 10, 54–5; WTO's export controls on high-technology products 10, 51, 54–5, 61; *see also* DSM; WTO; WTO and China
WTO, Appellate Body 30, 59
WTO, Ministerial Conferences: 1999 Seattle Ministerial Conference 73; 2003 Cancún Ministerial Conference 31; 2005 Hong Kong Ministerial Conference 32, 59; 2005 Mini-ministerial Conference 59; 2013 Bali Ministerial Conference 36, 59; *see also* DDA
WTO Secretariat 30, 33, 44, 89
WTO staff 64n45; Chinese staff at WTO 59
WTO Trade Policy Review Mechanism 31, 47, 51
Wu Yi 94, 102

Xi Jinping 5, 132, 221; 2017 WEF, Davos 2, 5; AIIB 223; economic globalization 2; global governance 177
Xie Xuren 119
Xinquan, Tu 10, 89–109, 175
Xu Binjin 54–5
Xu Jiajun 12, 14, 160, 198, 202–27
Xu Kuangdi 57

Yi Xiaozhun 59
Yong, Wang 9, 10, 42–64, 111
Yu, Hongyuan 271n44
Yu Xiaosong 64n39
Yu Yongding 122–3
Yuan Longping 192–3

Zhang Gaoli 103
Zhang Haibin 263
Zhang, Lu 12, 173, 228–49
Zhang Xiangchen 46, 51
Zhang Yuejiao 30, 59
Zhao Hong 59
Zhou Enlai 206, 208
Zhou Xiaochuan 115, 117–18, 121–2, 151
Zhu Min 120
Zhu Rongji 27, 52, 70, 98, 145
Zoellick, Robert 6
Zurong Cai 195